D1606387

Augustine's Manichaean Dilemma, 1

Divinations: Rereading Late Ancient Religion

SERIES EDITORS
Daniel Boyarin, Virginia Burrus, Derek Krueger

A complete list of books in the series is available from the publisher.

Augustine's Manichaean Dilemma, 1

Conversion and Apostasy, 373–388 C.E.

Jason David BeDuhn

PENN

University of Pennsylvania Press

Philadelphia

Published by
University of Pennsylvania Press
Philadelphia, Pennsylvania 19104-4112

Printed in the United States of America on acid-free paper
10 9 8 7 6 5 4 3 2 1

Library of Congress Cataloging-in-Publication Data
BeDuhn, Jason.
  Augustine's Manichaean dilemma, 1 : conversion and apostasy, 373–388 C.E.
/ Jason David BeDuhn.
    p. cm. — (Divinations: rereading late ancient religion)
  ISBN 978-0-8122-4210-2 (alk. paper)
  Includes bibliographical references and index.
    1. Augustine, Saint, Bishop of Hippo. 2. Conversion—Christianity.
3. Manichaeism. 4. Apostasy—Christianity. I. Title.
BR65.A9 B395 2009
270.2092 B—dc22   2009018797

For Peter Brown

CONTENTS

CHAPTER NINE
A New Man?   244

Conclusion   286

Introduction

WHEN PEOPLE IN the Christian tradition, or even in the secular culture informed by the Christian heritage, bring up the subject of conversion, they think first of Augustine of Hippo. The concept of *conversio* owes its dissemination to his masterwork, the *Confessions*. Yet, despite the way in which the idea of a sudden, dramatic, complete transformation of self has been associated with this work, Augustine actually uses its pages to depict conversion as a lifelong process, a series of self-discoveries and self-departures within a restless journey seeking to find out (as Augustine conceived it) who one really is, or (as we might rather say) who one can be within the particular circumstances and resources of one's lifetime. His insight into the transilience of the self has a remarkably contemporary sound to it, echoed in a number of modern theories about self-forming processes. Augustine's story therefore provides us with an opportunity to explore the ways human beings make themselves by their choices and decisions with respect to the variety of identity options they encounter in their historical environment. His story is by no means everyone's story, but it is an informative one in the fluidity of selfhood it reveals. Before there was Augustine of Hippo, there was Augustine of Thagaste, of Carthage, of Rome, and of Milan; before there was Augustine the Catholic bishop and theologian, there was Augustine the Manichaean. The tale of these men is one of conversion, of apostasy, and of conversion again for a single historical individual, and for several selves.

Augustine made the first serious religious commitment of his life by joining the Manichaean community of Carthage as a young man, and he remained an adherent of the sect for more than a decade. I have outlined elsewhere the program of life that the Manichaean community promoted and sought to embody, together with the ideological rationales that served to contextualize and motivate that program.[1] As I have emphasized there, the nature of our sources on Manichaeism to a large extent forces us to work at a level of abstraction, making sense of Manichaeism as it presents itself, as a set of proposals and plans. We are missing much of what allows us to explore how other religions actually play out in practice, what they actually mean to their living adherents, how they are integrated into daily lives, how their ideals are modified by local conditions and expediencies—in short, the human reality of a lived religion.[2] Augustine provides a rather unique opportunity to study an actual individual Manichaean, albeit a failed one— that is, someone who attempted but ultimately gave up the Manichaean program and who, moreover, proceeded to offer critical comparisons and assessments of many aspects of his former Manichaean identity in light of his later Nicene Christian one.

So in Augustine we have the opportunity to see just how conversion and commitment to Manichaeism shaped the sort of person he became, how it turned his attention to certain aspects of experience, how it determined the kinds of inquiries he would bring to his existence, how it provided him with scripts and models of selfhood which he could perform amid the myriad exigencies of life. For more than a decade, Augustine subscribed to Manichaeism as defining a large part of who he was; he accepted subjection at its hands, and became one of the religion's points of articulation and embodiment, as a bargain with the clarity of purpose and stability of self it offered. This means that the Augustine who presented himself for conversion to Nicene Christianity in 386 C.E. was the product of a set of experiences and conditioning mediated and determined by Manichaeism that had largely supplanted the boy who had supposedly sucked Christianity from his mother's breast (*Conf* 3.4.8).

For this reason, a number of scholars over the years have emphasized the importance of understanding Manichaeism and Augustine's own experience of it, in order better to grasp what was at stake in his later articulations of Nicene Christianity. Among them, John O'Meara has stated:

> It is evident that one cannot hope to understand Augustine's mind
> or conversion without being well acquainted with the teaching of the
> Manichees. If, as Frend says, it is true that in becoming a Manichee

Augustine had not thought of renouncing Christianity, and if it is true, as was said of him in the fifth century, that Augustine could not free himself from Manicheism no more than an Ethiopian could change his skin or a leopard his spots, then it is important to know something about that African Church which approximated so closely to Christianity in its theory of the Paraclete, the eminent role it accorded to Christ, and its reverence for St. Paul, but which, for all that, was as different from true Christianity as the night is from the day.[3]

Likewise, Henry Chadwick has written that "some themes and assumptions of his Manichee decade succeeded in remaining with Augustine, even after his renunciation and sustained polemic in anti-Manichee treatises. . . . The attraction of Mani was never quite lost."[4] More recently, J. Kevin Coyle has contended that "to know Augustine, one must know Manichaeism. . . . Without Manichaeism, there would still have been Augustine, perhaps even Augustine the great theologian; but it would have been a different Augustine, with a different theology."[5] "More and more clearly," Johannes van Oort similarly maintains, "modern research has revealed the extent to which Augustine's life and works are linked to Manichaeism. His theology and philosophy would be difficult to understand without a basic knowledge of the 'Religion of Light,' its hymns and prayers, its ethical and dogmatic teaching, its mythology and theology."[6]

Yet such calls for closer attention to Augustine's Manichaean associations have largely gone unanswered in Augustinian studies. Scholars such as Coyle and van Oort have pioneered this area in recent decades; but the bulk of studies produced each year on Augustine still seem to consider his conversion a profound chasm, with Manichaeism left decisively on the other side—as if Augustine became an entirely new person on that day, or else rediscovered his true self by tossing away Manichaeism like an ill-fitting garment. In other words, the difficulty in taking Manichaeism into consideration in the study of Augustine is tied up with an unexamined perpetuation of models of conversion that we have reason to question.

Either assertions or denials of a significant place for Manichaeism in determining what Augustine represents historically must be grounded in a careful reconstruction of exactly what Manichaeism taught in Augustine's time and place, and precisely how Augustine understood or misunderstood it. As historians, we cannot assume that Augustine got it right, or that he represents it fairly, or that he is honest with us or even with himself about his debts to his former religion. It is our job to ferret out both his strategic distortions and his inadvertent misprisions of this relationship. While a tremendous revolution in the assessment of Augustine's testimony in light of Manichaean primary sources has taken place in recent decades within Manichaean studies, its results have been slow to reach those working in Augustinian studies. I hope that this book will accelerate that process, and in this way advance the ability of those studying Augustine to take fuller account of the role of Manichaeism in shaping the Augustinian legacy.

With Augustine we have an unusual convergence of textual persona and historical figure. Most people of his own time, and obviously everyone since, have known him primarily in his textual persona, and it is in that form that he has had his historical impact. This textual reduction of Augustine does not present the same problem here as it would to conventional biographical interests, because it is in precisely what we *can* know about Augustine that he really matters historically. This same concentration of our subject in textual utterance serves to delineate the particular aspect of self-performance I wish to pursue using Augustine as an example. Verbal self-performance marks a kind of commitment people make; it identifies the master discourse or self-concept to which they ostensibly are willing to be held by those whom they address. My interest lies in what it means to make such a commitment—and specifically a *religious* commitment—and how doing so subjects an individual to self-imposed and other-reinforced constraints on what one may henceforth do and say, that is, constraints on what a person may be as a person in the social setting of his or her life.

Conversion is a particularly dramatic kind of such social promise-making. It is one of the crucial passages that religions intensively script, providing models and language to help the convert shape an account of the past rejected self, the new embraced self, and the appropriate motivations that serve to justify and sustain the choice of one over the other. These scripts are appropriated by converts, and adapted to particular details in their lives and personalities, which in turn emerge into sharper definition in the process of being fit to such scripts, along with the new definitions of personhood and will they carry. In the case of a figure such as Augustine, the role of such constructions of conversion is accentuated by his public stature and the conditions under which he came to write of this momentous event in his life. "Augustine's account of his conversion in the *Confessions*," Paula Fredriksen reminds us, "is a theological reinterpretation of a past event, an attempt to render his past coherent to his present self. It is, in fact, a disguised description of where he stands in the present as much as an ostensible description of what occurred in the past."[7] In fact, when dealing with the singular moment of decision usually intended by references to "Augustine's conversion" (notably forgetting that other, earlier conversion to Manichaeism) we rely entirely on after-the-fact interpretation and rationalization of that event. Indeed, even the texts which start to emerge from Augustine around the time of his conversion to Nicene Christianity in 386–387 C.E. are public performances of self, not direct channels to his private motivations and intentions.

When we speak of "Augustine's conversions," therefore, we must be clear that these are textually embedded events, preserved for us precisely because they are pen-and-ink instead of flesh-and-blood. Any conjecture of what "actually" happened is speculative, based more or less on these texts. The more closely rooted such speculations are in a critical reading of these texts, and the more of the apparent incommensurables of these sources they find a way to coordinate, the better history they will be considered to be. But what, after all, is the significance of what "actually" happened? The private thoughts of an individual one sunny afternoon in a garden in Milan did not in themselves, after all, shape history. It was rather what this experience became fitted to as its explanatory narrative, how its affective significance was harnessed to a program, and most of all how the textual reformulation of the moment became an account to which the individual was committed, and by which he raised the significance of any number of other intellectual, moral, and political concerns—this was where history was made. Fredriksen again:

> What actually happened, what the convert actually thought or experienced at the time of his conversion, is thus not accessible to the historian. He must frame his questions differently, for he knows that he cannot know—any better, perhaps, than can the convert himself—what was perceived at the "moment of conversion." The historian works with the available evidence, the conversion narrative; and that narrative can reveal to him only the retrospective moment, and the retrospective self.[8]

That fact does not remove us as far from actual conversion as one might think, because, as Fredriksen hints and I will argue, actual conversion is the act of maintaining the converted self, the retrospective self committed to following through and sustaining a choice that may have been made for motives more or less inaccessible to the person's consciousness, let alone our historical gaze. Indeed, since consciousness itself, and the reasoning process with which it assesses its environment and itself, is changed by conversion, the convert becomes increasingly less able to reconstruct the motives that mattered at the time the choice was made. Rather, people become reflections of the narratives they repeat to themselves, and so the retrospective self is actually the self-making mechanism that keeps a momentary choice from slipping away into meaninglessness.

With Augustine, we are dealing with a series of these retrospective selves, these ongoing and unfolding commitments of self to a particular construct of identity and course of life. Despite his discussion of the stages in his intellectual development, and the steps and decisions in his thinking that trace a path from one way of looking at the world to another, Augustine offers us limited help in putting our finger on actual motives of his choices. He provides instead hindsight construals by which each of his acts of conversion is rationalized, and his prior frustration and error diagnosed. In fact, Augustine spills considerable ink in the months and years following his conversion to Nicene Christianity telling us in so many words that conversion and commitment do not and cannot come about on the basis of reason. He denies that we can properly understand the teachings of a religion from the outside, before its coordinated disciplines have purified and prepared our minds for a reasoning process in tune with the truth the religion offers. This necessity of leaping from one identity to another without the benefit of a continuity of premises and rules of reasoning gives conversion its special usefulness for exposing the transilient quality of selfhood in general.

When we hear Augustine speak of his conscious reasons for converting, therefore, we are already too late to catch the act of conversion itself. His discussion of the tenets of Manichaeism reports what he came to learn after deciding to join that sect on the basis of surface attractions we must somehow excavate from his later perspective. Everything he verbalizes about why Nicene Christianity is ultimately to be preferred to Manichaeism likewise belongs to post-conversion rationalizations that he articulates primarily in response to imagined objections to his choice. In both cases we see Augustine examining the implications of his conversion and applying his reason to understand—to explain to himself and to others—choices he has made for causes unarticulated at the level of reason. Yet if the causes are unarticulated, they cannot be introduced into the historical record; and if they remain absent from the historical record, it becomes impossible for us, as historians, to have anything on which to base a description or understanding or explanation of his conversions, other than speculative analogy from contemporary study of similar processes.

Only when the outcome of the hidden dynamics of intrapersonal forces yields conscious, discursive reflection does the individual have something to say that provides material for the historian to analyze. Because such discursive material is what we have available to us, we tend to think that we have in it a direct report of the causes of human behavior. This is a fundamental error. We are, in fact, merely examining and analyzing the articulated subset of effects in the individual's conscious thought of behavioral causes that may be largely hidden even from the individual him- or herself. Someone like Augustine provides through these articulations something closely akin to the historian's own analysis. He analyzes his own actions and seeks reasons for them. He certainly may have access to some information later investigators do not; that is his advantage, and gives later historians some prospect of finding in what he says some accurate recollection of actual thoughts-along-the-way that may have been factors alongside others in motivating his actions. At the same time, he may not recognize factors an outside observer can; that is his disadvantage, and the reason why Augustine's self-interpretation cannot be the last word, which he himself recognizes in the *Confessions* by repeatedly turning to God with his doubts about his ability to fully know himself. Yet his self-interpretation has the unique potential, in effect, to make itself true, because while it may not accurately reflect the actual or complete causes of his initial decisions, it becomes a template of selfhood against which his unfolding conduct is constantly measured. In other words, while the reasons he generates after the conversion are not necessarily the causes of the conversion, they become causes of maintaining the conversion—sustaining his commitment to the choice he made in converting.

All the information Augustine provides that historians have for so long discussed in terms of his conversion actually belongs, therefore, to a separate, distinct phase in his development that we might call *verification*, that is, the process of supplying discursive reasons for maintaining a choice of commitment or identification made originally for unarticulated, affective motives. We can see verification as a specific kind of that which we more generally refer to as rationalization, or providing post-hoc reasons for actions of all kinds. William Collinge has touched upon the particular circumstances to which

I am referring, in which Augustine found himself immediately following his conversion to Nicene Christianity.

> A religious belief is verified for a believer if, through believing and living in accordance with it, one is able to come to some understanding of what one believes, to find increased intelligibility in one's experience, and to achieve a pattern of individual and social life that is coherent and satisfying. It is falsified for a believer if it fails this test. This is not exactly a "public" criterion of verifiability, since one must be a believer in order to enact this test. But such a work as *De moribus* can serve as an armchair exercise in verification and falsification to the extent that it succeeds in showing that Catholic doctrine satisfied the demands of reason, can be lived by, and, when lived by, appeals to the reader, while Manichaean doctrine is logically incoherent and either impossible or undesirable to live by.[9]

We face a greater challenge in accessing even this verification stage of Augustine's conversion to Manichaeism, due to the fact that no document from this period survives. All the ways Augustine came to think about Manichaeism and apply it in his life have been obscured from our gaze by being overwritten from a later vantage point that seeks to undo those past choices in the verification of another option.

But even Augustine's conversion to Nicene Christianity involved a process of development in which later understandings of his faith displaced earlier ones, overwriting previous Augustines with successive ones. Augustine himself repeatedly admitted a course of development in his thought that he claimed could be traced on the pages of his compositions.[10] In keeping with this acknowledged self-development, the modern study of Augustine must heed the summons of James O'Donnell to a "vigorous effort of forgetting" in order "to see Augustine without his futures."[11] This requires the use of a rather sharply refracted version of Quentin Skinner's contextual method of interpretation, rigorously confining our reading of what Augustine means in a particular text to what he can mean at that particular point of his life, based on what he has been exposed to and the foundation he has established in previous thought-work.[12] In other words, we need to recognize how a person takes up and performs speech-acts from various available systems and traditions of convention, and gradually—through repetition, attention, coordination with other performances and practices—comes to perceive him- or herself as defined by those acts. This self-definition changes as the setting of the self changes, as it enters into new dialogues, passes through new experiences, gains access to new concepts and paradigms. And as each new permutation of the self emerges, it reconstrues its past in line with the current *telos* of its identity.

Anyone who takes up the subject of Augustine's conversion inevitably engages in a dialogue with the latter's own account of it in the *Confessions*. The reliability of what he says there is a notorious problem in Augustinian studies, particularly insofar as it diverges from material contemporaneous with the events it purports to describe. It is important to recognize that *both* his presentation of his thinking in the texts dating to the time of his conversion, *and* the representation of his thinking at that same time that he gives in the *Confessions*, are *equally constructed*, equally determined by the models, paradigms, tropes, conventions, and clichés available to him at the respective times of composition. The differences between the two accounts reflect the different rhetorical repertoires and respective larger ideological settings Augustine had available to him from which to work, and from which to construct himself. So we can set aside comparisons of the two sets of material that rely on relegating one to less reliability simply because Augustine was up to something in it. Augustine was always up to something, and that something always included formulating a performance of self that invoked familiar conventions and situated his identity within them.

But recognizing the situatedness of these two self-performances means accepting that Augustine the convert *could not* present his conversion at the time in the terms the Augustine of the *Confessions* could. He could not think the thoughts the later Augustine could, or construe his experiences within the frame through which the later Augustine could not help viewing them (see *Conf* 5.10.19, 5.11.21, 7.1.1–2). To the degree that performance of self *is* self—not only in the accidental way historians must accept, but more profoundly in how we experience and come to know ourselves—Augustine at the time of his conversion could only be the person presented to us in his selection of utterances and acts of the time; likewise, the Augustine portrayed in the *Confessions* could not possibly escape being to a large degree the retrospective image of who he had become by that later point in time, thrust back in time and interpolated into a past setting in place of the someone else he had been before.

No one would deny that Augustine underwent profound changes in the period covered in this study. Yet, from a certain set of modern historians and biographers of Augustine, there has been considerable resistance to the idea that such changes continued beyond his conversion to Nicene Christianity, and they have proposed in various forms that, in the words of Étienne Gilson, "Saint Augustine's central ideas were fixed from the moment of his conversion."[13] Because of who Augustine becomes sometime after his conversion, some want his conversion to be deeper, richer, and more proleptic than that of the average convert, and indeed more than it can possibly be given the conditions under which conversion occurs, our understanding of which has the benefit of a number of modern sociological studies involving living subjects. The results of these studies do not support the model of conversion as sudden, absolute, and complete that Augustine himself played a significant role in disseminating in Western thought, despite the inconsistency with which he maintained it. Instead, such research has brought to light the non-discursivity of both the causes and the act of conversion, the limitations on familiarity with a religion before one enters its ranks, and the selectivity of the convert's engagement with aspects of the religion that appeal to him or her.[14] One of my aims in this study, therefore, is to demonstrate that it is historically untenable to continue to imagine that Augustine knew and understood Nicene Christianity thoroughly at the time of his conversion, and therefore consciously held its every detail as an active belief determining the ends and means of his spiritual life.

In a more theoretical vein, I have approached my analysis of the specifics of Augustine's case within a loose framework of useful ways for conceptualizing and talking about the processes of self-formation and -reformation that seem to be involved. In the pages that follow, the reader will encounter occasional references to Foucault, Mead, Austin, Frankfurt, and Butler, among others. These significant voices of human self-examination have provided me with suggestive constructs with which to think about the content of the Augustinian corpus, rather than simply report it. While not embracing any one of these theorists dogmatically, I have found their differing perspectives complementary in proposing how different parts of the material interrelate within larger possibilities of significance.

Systems of human order—be they social, political, or religious—require certain kinds of acts of discipline and self-limitation in order to harness human individuals to the collective will such systems cultivate and prioritize. This is the sociocultural condition in which conversion occurs. Michel Foucault labored to dispel the myth of the preexistent individual who is socialized to such systems of order by constraint on his or her prior and inherent will. He argued that the person, the will, the soul itself is a product of these systems of order, which set about constituting selves appropriate to their purposes through various techniques of inculcating self-consciousness in human beings. They tell individuals who they are, where they come from, what is most essential about their identity, the purpose of their existence. That which we consider individuality is a manifestation of the varying degrees of *fit* between these programs of self-creation and the underlying genetic and experiential dispositions of human raw material. The human individual is neither a complete person constrained by social limits, nor a blank slate on which society can inscribe any selfhood it chooses without resistance. The individual plays an active role in embracing or rejecting, applying or resisting, adopting or transforming portions of the matrix of selfhood offered by the traditions within which he or she lives. We are, in effect, our own socializers, however consciously or unconsciously.

In studying "technologies of the self," Foucault sought to elucidate those systems of thought and practice "which permit individuals to effect by their own means or with the help of others a certain number of operations on their own bodies and souls, thoughts, conduct, and way of being, so as to transform themselves in order to attain a certain state of happiness, purity, wisdom, perfection, or immortality."[15] When we look back to the figure of Augustine, we find him explicitly declaring his project in his earliest writings to be one of seeking the attainment of exactly the things in Foucault's list: happiness, purity, wisdom, perfection, and immortality. These goals had priority for Augustine, at least initially, over any religious commitment. If he could have attained them without religion, he seems to indicate he would have done so. He chose first the Manichaean community, and then the Nicene Christian one, because he determined they had the possibility of supplying technologies of the self that would allow him to attain his goals. After more than ten years as a Manichaean, Augustine abandoned that tradition for Nicene Christianity. The story entailed in that change of direction involves a failed attempt to make himself a "Manichaean," and an ultimately successful one to become a "Catholic."

Judith Butler has in recent years continued certain lines of Foucault's inquiry into the formation of the subject through an individual's subordination to systems of power. She has explored what is entailed in the investment of such systems in individual subjects as the means of power's reproduction and historical persistence.

If conditions of power are to persist, they must be reiterated; the subject is precisely the site of such reiteration, a repetition that is never merely mechanical. As the appearance of power shifts from the condition of the subject to its effects, the conditions of power (prior and external) assume a present and futural form. . . . The reiteration of power not only temporalizes the conditions of subordination but shows these conditions to be, not static structures, but temporalized—active and productive.[16]

In this way, she enunciates a kind of vulnerability in social process, not only of the subject to sources of identity and meaning given by power, but also of power itself in its complete reliance on individual subjects to be the location of its articulation. In Butler's analysis, the subject is both "the *effect* of a prior power and . . . the *condition of possibility* for a radically conditioned form of agency" that permits systems to be reiterated across time.[17] For Butler, "subjection is a subordination that the subject brings on itself" without which power could not go from being a prior, external force to "the willed effect of the subject."[18] The term "conversion," I would suggest, refers precisely to this "subordination that the subject brings on itself" in order to constitute itself as a certain kind of subject, one that reproduces a religious system as its own willed effect on its own person.

Butler has seen the need to advance Foucault's earlier discussion of processes of self-formation and "technologies of the self" by more careful consideration of "the psychic life of power," that is, exactly how an originally external power becomes invested as a person's own sense of self.

In claiming that social norms are internalized, we have not yet explained what incorporation or, more generally, internalization is, what it means for a norm to become internalized or what happens to the norm in the process of internalization. . . . If forms of regulatory power are sustained in part through the formation of a subject, and if that formation takes place according to the requirements of power, specifically, as the incorporation of norms, then a theory of subject formation must give an account of this process of incorporation, and the notion of incorporation must be interrogated to ascertain the psychic topography it assumes.[19]

While Butler taps her own chosen resources to map that topography, I turn primarily to Mead, Austin, and Frankfurt, each of whom provides a particular way of thinking about what we are getting at when we speak of internalization.

George Herbert Mead is a foundational figure in the modern analysis of the self and its social and historical contingency. He attended to the social resources of the self, and to the role of language and its internalization in constructing identity and governing action. Like Foucault, Mead highlighted the active part individuals play in their own subjection, that is, how they adopt the attitude of others as a vantage point of self-scrutiny and self-limitation. He examined the connection between self-disclosure in social contexts and self-formation as an interiorization of those social contexts. In Mead's construct, the self observes itself in a constant process of unfolding, in speech and other self-characterizing acts. "We are continually following up our own address to other persons by an understanding of what we are saying," he observes, "and using that understanding in the direction of our continued speech. We are finding out what we are going to say, what we are going to do, by saying and doing, and in the process we are continually controlling the process itself."[20] Even the private act of writing a book—which in Augustine's method of dictation was not particularly private—"is still part of social intercourse in which one is addressing other persons and at the same time addressing one's self, and in which once controls the address to other persons by the response made to one's own [verbal] gesture," Mead notes. "That the person should be responding to himself is necessary to the self, and it is this sort of social conduct which provides behavior within which that self appears."[21]

Mead gets at self-reflexivity through his concept of the "I" and the "me": the "me" refers to the organized set of dispositions and responses incorporated from the available social context, including the burden of one's past conduct as a determinant of expectations of future conduct, while the "I" designates the emergent self in its moment-by-moment action on the basis and against the background of the prior self-organization of the "me." The "me" therefore represents a commitment of self, and calls for a certain kind of "I" in so far as one will meet the obligations made by previous actions of self-commitment.[22] The commitment of the "me" offers however much consistency and continuity is to be found in a person, by which we normally seek to identify and define the person as a self. But to embody consistently the commitment of the "me" requires self-scrutiny of each new act, and a responsiveness to oneself as a constantly emerging self-expression. In short, people learn about themselves and discover who they are, not by inherent self-knowledge, but through a constant process of self-observation and self-discovery—seeking, to the extent they are self-reflective, to find patterns of consistency and continuity that make them predictable to themselves as actors.

Religions offer scripts and models meant to guide that process of self-discovery, proposing exactly which sorts of self-phenomenon should be taken seriously as signs of the self, and which dismissed as adventitious or even invasive obscurations of true selfhood. They provide techniques designed to enable the "me" to constrain more effectively the "I," make the self more predictable, stable, and aligned with approved models of selfhood. In converting from one such system to another Augustine gained exposure to new terms and expressions that gave him material with which he could develop new insights into his own motivations, intentions, and meaning. "A person learns a new language and, as we say, gets a new soul," Mead explains. "He puts himself into the attitude of those that make use of that language. . . . He becomes in that sense a different individual."[23] Augustine learned new ways of expressing himself, new ideas *to think* as rote speech-acts, *before* he found ways *to think with* them, as operationalized parts of a system of dispositions that we call a self.

The degree to which such self-discovery and -negotiation takes place in engagement with language and discourse indicates the usefulness of approaching it in terms of the speech-act. With this concept and its elaboration, J. L. Austin has supplied researchers with more precise descriptive terminology for discussing how language functions as social action, and how a person positions him or herself as a participant in social interaction by employing conventions available in the language of a particular time and place.[24] As an author, Augustine did more than convey information. The texts he produced were acts, as surely as were his statements in public debate. He not only communicated ideas, but in the same breath identified himself with those ideas, avowed them, and promoted them as truth. His spoken and written statement thus had an illocutionary aspect, at different times presenting a different set of avowals or commitments to particular ideas. As his commitments changed, he repeatedly had to restate his analysis and opinion in order to reposition himself in the eyes of his audience; and in making new commitments, had to find ways to live up to them by rationalizing them and placing them in relation to previous commitments. With each set of illocutionary avowals, Augustine produced a perlocutionary impression of who he was, an apparent self made up of a body of speech. True to Austin's description of perlocutionary effects, as well as to Mead's understanding of self-formative processes, Augustine was part of the audience of his own speech acts; he had effects on himself. His invocation of certain conventions of speech in particular contexts triggered dispositions he had formed in himself, reinforcing his identification with the phrases as truths, his commitment to which constituted his character.

It is one of the working premises of this study that our practices work on us from the outside in. We perform speech-acts and other sorts of acts first of all by rote, by convention, by selective imitation of what we observe others do. We employ them as illocutions, as gestures that serve for social effects. By them we signal to others our membership in their group, our conformity to their rules and expectations. We thereby gain admittance to the particular social game in which we are interested, and develop facility in it. But all the while we are performing for others, we are performing for ourselves. No one is more exposed and constantly present to our performances than ourselves. We repeatedly experience ourselves performing acts, and even signal to ourselves in rehearsals and private practices where no one else is present. In this way we learn about ourselves, learn what we are willing and capable of doing, and come to connect those acts with the rewards and sanctions they elicit. In this way they take on meaning for us. Their conventionality yields to our own personal stamp upon them in our misprision, catechresis, syncretism, and idiosyncrasy. They take on the significance of their coordination within our personal system of thought and action, and in this organization of our meaningful acts we construct a self.

Yet acts of conversion and apostasy relate to more systematic processes of self-formation than those found in the ordinary social processes of everyday life. They involve deliberate performative avowals or disavowals of specific, organized sets of meaning. For thinking about and discussing such acts of comprehensive self-organization and re-organization, I have turned to Harry Frankfurt's analysis of the ordering of priorities and commitments that govern a person's responses to circumstances, and thus at any given time constitute the self. Frankfurt emphasizes that such self-organizing acts of volition have greater significance in defining a person's nature than the intellectual content of his or her mind.[25] As he points out, one cannot simply equate a person's total mental content with the person's identity. Some ideas in which we have no investment arise spontaneously within our minds or are introduced from external sources. Only when one identifies with a notion does it become an integral constituent part of the self.[26] In fact, Frankfurt considers the threshold of personhood to be reached only when an individual invests in and takes responsibility for a particular ordering of desires and impulses.[27]

Frankfurt hypothesizes that people tend to strive for the most efficient ordering of desires, one which minimizes conflict in decision-making and produces the condition of wholeheartedness. Each decision with respect to ordering desires is a step towards this goal, so that

> the person, in making a decision by which he identifies with a desire, *constitutes himself.* The pertinent desire is no longer in any way external to him. It is not a desire that he "has" merely as a subject in whose history it happens to occur, as a person may "have" an involuntary spasm that happens to occur in the history of his body. It comes to be a desire that is incorporated into him by virtue of the fact that he has it *by his own will.* This does not mean that it is through the exercise of the will that the desire originates; the desire may well preexist the decision made concerning it. But even if the person is not responsible for the fact that the desire *occurs,* there is an important sense in which he takes responsibility for the fact of having the desire—the fact that the desire is in the fullest sense his, that it constitutes what he really wants—when he identifies himself with it. Through his action in deciding, he is responsible for the fact that the desire has become his own in a way in which it was not unequivocally his own before.[28]

We can trace in Augustine's story a series of such self-constituting decisions, identifications of himself with one idea instead of and against another, prioritizing one sort of commitment over others. "It is these acts of ordering and of rejection—integration and separation—that create a self out of the raw materials of inner life," Frankfurt proposes.[29] Each decision shapes subsequent ones by creating a burden of coherence with the earlier decision—unless or until new attractions and commitments pressure earlier ones with which they are incoherent to yield. One does not always know the cost of a commitment when it is made, and may give it up in the face of growing awareness of undesirable consequences.[30] Such was Augustine's initial enthusiastic embrace of Manichaeism as the master discourse of the meaning of his life, or his equally impulsive venture of deriving that master discourse from a Platonically mediated Nicene Christianity.

I would scarcely claim to have forged a synthesis from these respective theoretical discussions of self-formation. I have only engaged them as partners in the specific task of finding significant correlations between the individual circumstantial utterances of Augustine. My interest lies in acts of conversion and apostasy as self-presentations, and therefore to some public degree self-commitments, promises of self-normativity and self-regulation. By presenting himself as a particular self, Augustine committed himself, and was consequently under some relative constraint, to act consistently with this presented self. Public commitment creates a self-normativizing feedback loop, bringing significant others into the apparatus of self-regulation through their gaze upon the subject, with its expectations of consistent selfhood. By processes described in various ways by the theorists just reviewed, Augustine came to be constituted as a particular pattern of "the relations to self," as Foucault characterizes it, "the forms in which one is called upon to take oneself as an object of knowledge and a field of action, so as to transform, correct, and purify oneself, and find salvation."[31]

By considering Augustine not simply biographically, but as a case of a self-making and remaking process that can be observed in others, I endorse not just the formulation and application of such theories in relation to his life, but also more generally a comparative approach to questions that arise about Augustine's changing self-performance. I do not shy away from using contemporary sociological studies of conversion and apostasy to contextualize aspects of Augustine's story. To the degree that comparative investigation of conversion and apostasy in different socio-cultural settings, and within distinct traditions of religious self-definition, reveals recurring patterns in the conditions and conduct of such self-reorientations, I think that we have tentatively delineated a type of human situation into which Augustine may be fit, without losing sight of the historically and discursively situated character of his individual case. I consider such sociological insights crucial to restore something largely lost from the historical record, namely, the unwritten circumstances of social engagement and expectation within which Augustine made his public gestures of commitment. I think Augustine's story can be helpfully informed by considering his situation in relation to others of the same type, just as I regard his story potentially to be more broadly informative, not just about the particular historical confrontation between Manichaeism and Nicene Christianity that most concerns us here, but about the process of transference of commitment from one system of identity to another within human cultures and societies generally.

I would like to suggest, therefore, that we think about how conversion works, both in Augustine's specific case and generally, by considering it in terms of an individual's self-commitment. An act of conversion entails an avowal, a deliberate declaration of intention to fulfill conventions of identification with a community and a tradition of self-construal and self-definition within a larger universe of meaning. The convert makes claims upon the religion with which he or she wishes to associate, and seeks recognition by and access to its institutional structures. By such acts, converts enter into situations of *answerability*, whereby they have expressed a promise to meet the expectations of the identity they have claimed. They form a power relation to themselves, arranging their various desires, priorities, and plans in conformity with what the community prescribes as an embodiment of its values and practices. The transformation of self that we tend to think of when we hear the word "conversion," therefore, actually follows upon the public gesture of conversion, and in fact cannot get started before this preliminary gesture is made. I would contend, further, that precisely this understanding of conversion as a gradual process following upon identification with a religious system is part of what Augustine sought to express by his dictum that "faith" must precede "understanding."

Augustine joined both the Manichaean and the Nicene Christian communities without being fully informed of all that was entailed in those commitments. These respective conversions behind him, he entered into a period of answerability and verification in which he undertook to define his identity within, first, the dualist cosmology and anthropology promoted by the Manichaean sect, and then the nondualist alternatives of emergent Nicene Christianity. The first failed and the second succeeded, in his own experience, in meeting criteria of verifiability he brought to bear, however consciously or unconsciously, including both lived effectiveness and—at least for someone like Augustine—coherence within paradigms of rationality to which he had been acculturated by his education and study of the philosophy of his age. He learned what he liked and what he wanted along a journey marked by a series of attempted self-constructions whereby he sought, by drawing on available repertoires of selfhood, to order his various desires into an organized, consistent self-performance.

Another character stalks the pages of this book, another example of an individual who entered into the bargain of subjection the Manichaean system offered: Faustus of Milevis. We know him only through his impact on Augustine. As leader of the African Manichaean community, he presented to Augustine a paradigm for a successful embodiment of Manichaean ideals that forced him to reconsider the aims of his own venture. Like Augustine, Faustus incorporated the Manichaean system in a partial and idiosyncratic way, changing the face of the very system he served as one of its points of articulation. He performed within sufficient terms of answerability to gain recognition as the regional normative authority of the sect; and yet in his individual resistances to complete conformity to its norms he created the particular conditions in which Augustine would decide whether to sustain or abandon his own experiment in Manichaean selfhood.

Both of these figures converted voluntarily to Manichaeism in a context where it remained an option of self-identification. Both found ways to construe themselves within the terms Manichaeism offered, even though they had been brought up as non-Manichaeans, socialized into a set of ideals, values, and concepts at serious odds with those found in the Manichaean community. Manichaeism represented a direct, countercultural challenge to the system of meaning into which both Faustus and Augustine had been socialized before they had any choice in the matter. To convert in such a context it to touch the third rail of social normativity, revealing the malleable foundations of truth and meaning, exposing the arbitrariness of the rules governing discourse, and undermining agreed-upon ideals of selfhood. The denial of this dangerous relativity motivates most of the polemical fury exchanged between religions, each seeking to reduce the other to the status of a subjected discourse. In monolithic cultures, rejection of the dominant paradigms of selfhood and one's authorized place within those paradigms amounts to a kind of dysfunction, consigning oneself to a marginal existence. But in pluralistic settings, rival paradigms vie for dominance, among which individuals can avail themselves of still viable options for aligning their identities. Augustine had choices to make about who he would be—how he would speak and think and act—because he had the luxury of living in a pluralistic time and place that was on the brink of disappearing. And we cannot ignore the fact that Augustine's ultimate choice of identity corresponded with the emerging dominant paradigm, and contributed to its elimination of its rivals.

The pluralistic religious environment in which Augustine's self-making occurred permitted him to try, and ultimately reject, one very visible self-identification before moving on to the one with which he is now unalterably associated. Even after that ultimate identification with Nicene Christianity, he underwent a number of less visible transformations in constant reference to Manichaean commitments he had left behind. J. Kevin Coyle has concluded, "a desire to prove himself non-Manichean is behind virtually everything he wrote, whether or not Manicheism was the explicitly identified adversary" and "one can say that Augustine's anti-Manichaean activity covers virtually his entire literary career."[32] Similarly, Paul More asserts of Augustine, "he never to the day of his death outlived the effects of this first surrender of his soul to a definite faith."[33] Thus, Augustine the convert was always inevitably also Augustine the apostate.

CHAPTER ONE

Becoming Manichaean

THE VERY TERM "conversion" carries with it certain implicit assumptions about a sharp and clear differentiation between identities and commitments from which and to which a person passes. The concept depends upon a boundary of exclusiveness that generally did not apply to the religious sphere in traditional Roman society. Philosophical schools provided the most common reference point, therefore, for talk of such a change of exclusive allegiance in Roman literate culture. So when Justin Martyr in the second century describes his quest for truth, his conversion to Christianity comes at the end of a string of previous identifications with such philosophical schools, and nothing in what he says suggests that Christianity belongs to a different category of social phenomena. It was the philosophical schools, after all, that proposed systematic ways of life, often coupled with specific apprehensions of the universe, whereas religion was a matter of cultic acts directed toward deities requiring no explicit theory. There had always been cultic initiations, of course, and some did develop into exclusive cultic associations around which people organized the conduct of their lives. Inscriptional evidence attests to non-Jews joining synagogue communities and adopting the rules of purity and ritual expected of members, and the literary record abounds with references to similar exclusive commitments to the lifestyle of the *Christiani*.

A common cultural repertoire shaped both the philosophical and non-philosophical sorts of calling, with initiations, master-pupil relationships, indoctrination, ceremony, distinctive dress and rules of conduct, and performative scripts for conveying partisan truths. This common culture of the called life thoroughly blurred a distinction between philosophy and religion that modern constructs may wish to impose, but only for those who wished to make such a commitment the center point of their lives. For most people, religion formed an ancillary technique in the service of secular goals, and philosophy remained the table-talk of would-be intellectuals. The Roman world was still far from being carved up into mutually exclusive religious segments at the time when Augustine was born into it. There could be no assumption that a person of Augustine's heritage and circumstances would be a "Christian," let alone a "Catholic," rather than a participant in some other religious subculture of the period, nor that he would be defined first and foremost by religious identity rather than philosophical allegiance, profession, political office, or property. All notions to the contrary are sheer anachronism. It bears emphasizing at the outset that, raised in a nominally "Christian" household, Augustine might well have continued throughout his life as only nominally so and largely identified in other terms. The construct of "conversion" presupposes a central place for either religious or philosophical commitment in his life which should not be taken as a given for him or anyone else living at his time.

To say that Augustine was raised a Catholic, then, as many biographies do, is to presume too much not only about Augustine personally but also about the state of Christianity at the time. Augustine grew to maturity in a diverse religious environment where, even among the Christians, local communities shifted from one communion to another based on the persuasions of individual bishops, new councils, and changing imperial favoritism. The Nicene "Catholic Church" that Augustine was eventually to join emerged in his own lifetime, and only solidified as an institution under the official recognition of the emperors Theodosius and Gratian in the last quarter of the fourth century.[1] Augustine would be baptized as a Christian of the Nicene school in the spring of 387, a mere seven years after that school gained the sanction of the Roman state as the "catholic" form of the faith. Back in Augustine's Africa, the Nicene party was definitely a colonial minority, present in the larger cities more closely tied to the central government, but practically absent from the smaller towns and countryside.[2] In the *Confessions*, Augustine never uses the term "Catholic" to characterize the faith of his childhood, and the word appears for the first time only when the setting shifts to Italy (*Conf* 5.10.20), where he perhaps first became aware of this new, imperially sanctioned designation for the Nicene faction of the larger Christian religion.

Nor should we make the mistake of thinking that most Christians paid any attention to the fine points of the Nicene versus non-Nicene debates. The dominant Christian force in Africa was the so-called Donatist party, whose relation to either side in those debates appears frustratingly ambiguous only because historians have allowed the ultimately victorious Nicene position to define for us what was really important to fourth-century Christians. On the contrary, the issues that divided Nicene from non-Nicene Christians were largely incomprehensible to the average Christian—or the average bishop, for that matter. Augustine was still just a priest in a relatively minor church when he was asked, due to his better education and rhetorical training, to explain the Nicene creed to the assembly of bishops who had decided to constitute themselves as the state-associated "Catholic" church in Africa. This hitherto rather amorphous body of non-Donatist churches would have been distinguished from the Donatists primarily by their comparatively liberal standards on readmittance of sinners to communion. Before Augustine and his associates launched an intense campaign to displace Donatist dominance in the 390s, it would be difficult to prove that the non-Donatist communion had any advantage on the Manichaeans in the competition for the hearts and minds of Africans.

The Seeker

Augustine's vivid image of sucking from his mother's breast the very same faith to which he would convert more than thirty years later is one of his more memorable rhetorical flourishes—and defiantly anachronistic. Augustine was born in the Numidian town of Thagaste in November 354 C.E., and was raised as a prospective, yet unbaptized, Christian of the local variety of his hometown. He faced two moments in his life when serious illness might have induced a quick baptism, once as a child and again when he was twenty-nine. The first time his mother refused to permit it, since the potentially damning indulgences of adolescence still lay ahead;[3] the second time Augustine was still sufficiently committed to Manichaeism to disdain the idea.

The defining element in Augustine's background was the Latin language, with all that came with it of traditional Roman culture and values. Augustine had the benefit of the well-established Latin education of the western empire, which he received in the predominantly pagan city of Madauros up to the age of sixteen. There he learned the works of Virgil, Cicero, Sallust, and Terence. It bears noting that all the literature Augustine studied shared a certain sanguine and conformist attitude toward the world and society. The universe was as it should be, this curriculum and its more philosophical penumbra emphasized, and one's task was to grasp this providential order and conform oneself to its unwavering dictates. For all of Augustine's originality, this dominant theme of his childhood education ultimately prevailed in his own vision of reality, undercutting his passing, youthful allegiance to a more revolutionary creed.

Augustine's evident ability inspired his father to scrape together the resources to further his education in the provincial metropolis, Carthage, the quintessential Big City of Africa. He arrived in 371 C.E., in his seventeenth year, to enter the ancient equivalent of college. The experience offered everything a small-town teenager could wish for. Away from parental scrutiny, he could indulge himself in carousing, drinking, sports, theater, and sex, along with occasionally attending classes and being exposed to new ideas and challenging intellectual questions. Although in his *Confessions* Augustine does his utmost to portray himself as a conscienceless, dissolute youth, his escapades—so far as we know them—were the sort of thing generally winked at under the mores of Roman society.[4] At least initially, he attended the public portion of the liturgy at the city's non-Donatist Christian basilica as a good place to meet girls (*Conf* 3.3.5).[5] Whatever one makes of Augustine's period of sexual exploration, it was relatively brief. He was still a teenager when he moved in with a woman to whom he claims to have been loyal for some fifteen years.[6]

Augustine's encounter with the ancient equivalent of college led to significant changes in his thinking, reorientation of his interests, and the energizing experience of maturing thought. The writings of Cicero loomed large in his education, and in his emerging identity. Of course, Cicero was a prominent literary and cultural touchstone of the age, admired by many of the key members of the new Christian intelligensia: Minucius Felix, Lactantius, Ambrose, Jerome, and—we must add—the Manichaean Faustus of Milevis. As Augustine tells it, the particular book that changed his life was Cicero's protreptic dialogue, the *Hortensius*.[7] Cicero's writing was full of the philosophical *koine* that still passed for "common wisdom" in Augustine's day. He incorporated into his works a valuation of the intellect over the senses, the mind over the body, as well as allusions to the heavenly origin and destiny of the soul, and to the pursuit of truth through cultivation of mental discipline. These platitudes and commonplaces could be adapted equally to either the Manichaean or Neoplatonic systems that later caught Augustine's fancy.

In hindsight, he claims that reading the *Hortensius* "changed my feelings and turned my prayers to you yourself, Lord" (*Ille vero liber mutavit affectum meum, et ad te ipsum, domine, mutavit preces meas, Conf* 3.4.7). Yet Cicero's work had little to say about God, focusing instead on the soul's divinity, its suffering in the world, and its ultimate reward in a blissful afterlife of perfection.[8] Cicero maintained that the soul must be prepared by the cultivation of virtue for the pursuit of knowledge that culminates in immortal transcendence.[9] Apparently following up this suggestion, and seeking such instruction in virtue, Augustine turned to the resources of his mother's faith. Taking up the Bible for the first time, he found it completely unappealing, "unworthy of comparison to the stately prose of Cicero" (*Conf* 3.5.9). He determined that he must seek elsewhere for a community of philosophers set upon the self-disciplined pursuit of ultimate truth. He found his answer, for a time, in Manichaeism.

When Augustine came to Manichaeism, therefore, he did so from a largely "unchurched" position. From all appearances, his own upbringing as a Christian catechumen had made little impression on him. Augustine's report of first venturing to read the Bible only in Carthage indicates that he was all but unfamiliar with the content of the Christian scriptures, despite being one of the more literate members of his society.[10] By the time he was eighteen, he had already outgrown the limited options of his childhood, and embraced a wider world of thought.[11] He had been exposed to intellectual culture in Madauros and Carthage, and had so avidly identified with it that one of his old pagan teachers would later write to him as a "seceder from my own faith" (*Ep* 16).[12] His interests extended into mathematics, astronomy, and physics. When he looked back at the traditions in which he had been brought up from the vantage point of his new philosophical interests, he found a "puerile superstition" which sought to frighten people away from all intellectual inquiry (*BV* 1.4; cf. *UC* 1.2). There is no reason to conclude that his primary identity was a "religious" one, that is, one defined by adherence to a cultic system.

The Manichaean Allure

Augustine's decade-long allegiance to Manichaeism is often treated with bewilderment by his expositors. How could such a man, the rhetoric goes, be attracted to "this strange sect,"[13] "this farrago of myth and taboo,"[14] be taken in by its "obvious follies and contradictions,"[15] be held by "a doctrine so tortuous, so equivocal, contaminated by fancies so grossly absurd,"[16] or "not reject an obviously flawed world-picture sooner than he did"?[17] Such comments reflect the success of Augustine's deliberate attempt later in life to drain all sympathetic understanding from his depiction of the Manichaeans and of his own earlier Manichaean self. As James O'Donnell has remarked, "it was violently contrary to Augustine's intentions at the time of writing *Confessions* to do full justice to the appeal the Manichees had for him."[18] Yet, in adding that, "He did not concede them the possession even of whatever virtues and strengths had held appeal for him," O'Donnell's characterization must be qualified by distinguishing Manichaeans from Manichaeism. We shall see that Augustine concedes many virtues, strengths, and good intentions to the Manichaeans as individuals, even while relentlessly disparaging the religious system that defined them. By the meager clues left to us by a writer who wished to concede as little as possible to Manichaeism, we must excavate an earlier Augustine from whose vantage point we can view African Manichaeism as a vital and successful religious option in late fourth-century Africa. It was this vantage point of the earlier Augustine that the Manichaean Secundinus claimed to know from these very same literary clues, when he wrote to Augustine later in life that "I knew you were one who loved lofty things, things that shunned the earth, that sought out heaven, that mortified the body, that set the soul alive" (*EpSec* 3).

A century before Augustine was born, the Christian movement existed as a complex set of related sects—some small and local, some stretched across the empire and beyond—displaying a wide spectrum of beliefs, practices, and organizations. Somewhere within this larger Christian spectrum stood Manichaeism. "In historical terms," Gedaliahu Stroumsa has observed, "one cannot see the conflict between Manichaeism and Christianity as a conflict between two independent religions . . . in the Roman Empire, at least, the Manichaeans considered themselves to be Christians, nay, *the* true Christians, while they condemned the Catholics for 'judaizing,' and hence for being unfaithful to the true doctrine of Christ. It would be surprising had not such a radical challenge left its imprint on the minds of those who successfully confronted it."[19]

Mani had begun to organize his sect around 240 C.E., drawing into it people from an assortment of religious communities beyond the eastern Roman frontier that traced their inspiration to Jesus of Nazareth. Declaring himself "the apostle of Jesus Christ," he created the "Church of the Holy," with both a centralized authority and an active mission program that gave his sect an organizational advantage over the generally weak networks that at that time held together the disparate Christian communities of the Roman Empire. By the end of the 260s, Manichaean missions had been established in Palmyra and Alexandria,[20] and by the 290s they had reached Carthage, where Augustine was to encounter them eighty years later.[21] Radiating out from a central authority led by a *primate* as successor to Mani (*MM* 8.11, 19.70; *Adim* 15.2), a hierarchical web of supervision (consisting in theory of twelve regional *maiores* [*Fort* 37] or teachers, seventy-two *episcopi* [*MM* 19.70; *Conf* 5.3.3],[22] and three-hundred-sixty *presbyteri* [*MM* 19.71–72; *Retr* 1.15.1][23]) provided a remarkably thin authority structure for the far-flung Manichaean missionary operation, spread already at the time of Augustine among a population of tens of millions of people across northern Africa, southern Europe, and large sections of Asia.

On 31 March 297 C.E., the Roman emperor Diocletian issued a rescript[24] to Julianus, proconsul of Africa province, in response to the latter's report of the presence in Carthage of a new foreign cult—the Manichaeans. Since it originated in Persia, with which Rome was in a state of war, there was some concern of subversion.[25] Diocletian was prone to agree with this concern, especially since his religious policy was reactionary against new and non-Roman religions in general. Moreover, in Diocletian's grand reconstruction of the Roman state, everyone needed to do his or her part, and the *otia maxima* of ascetic withdrawal that Manichaeism promoted ran contrary to his program.[26] He ordered Julianus to take all necessary steps to round up and execute the missionaries of this strange new faith.[27] Thus, the first Roman record of Manichaeism in North Africa—indeed in the Roman Empire as a whole—is a document of persecution.

The Manichaeans had arrived on fertile missionary ground. Roman Africa appears to have undergone a rapid "Christianization" in the closing decades of the third century, as Christians of many kinds, long present in small pockets in the cities, began to make serious inroads into the religious life of the general public. We have no way to ascertain the size that the North African Manichaean community had reached by Augustine's time. Although Augustine says it was small, and even that it wore that fact as a badge of honor (*SermDom* 2.24.78), it seems to have been present in most urban areas.[28] It could claim a significant component of wealthy and influential lay members, including such figures known to us through Augustine as Romanianus of Thagaste, Firmus of Hippo, and Mercurius of Caesarea (likewise, in Rome, Constantius).[29] Such individuals were in a position to protect the community from mob violence and the occasional government persecution; imperial legislation attests the use of rural estates as places of refuge. It attracted highly educated people (*MM* 19.71, 20.74), and its relative egalitarianism had appeal for women (Leo, *Sermon* 86.5).[30]

The Manichaeism that Augustine encountered was one of the major players in an environment of energetic religious debate in the last quarter of the fourth century, "a period of Christian intellectual history marked by a preoccupation with certain dualistically framed cosmological questions,"[31] involving the worth of the material world and the body, the degree of human freedom in the face of more powerful determining forces, and that primary problem of all monotheisms, evil. The artificial eclipse in the first half of the fourth century of such defining questions of religious identity by the rather arcane trinitarian debates had passed. Now controversy returned to issues affecting the entire ethos of religious life. The Manichaeans had staked out rather stable positions on those issues for a century; so, as they emerged into the full attention of their Christian rivals, we can track a corresponding rise in the anxiety of influence among those rivals. Augustine innocently walked right into the middle of that anxiety; he was the right man in the right place at the right time to become the flashpoint of concern on the part of the nascent "Catholic" community about taking possession of ground broken by Manichaeans before them without taking on the taint of Manichaeism itself. Manichaeism was never a major competitor in terms of raw numbers; yet it was perceived as a significant threat to its Christian rivals because of its coherence as a system of belief and practice, and its effectiveness as a highly organized community of faith.[32]

What specifically attracted people like Augustine to Manichaeism in late fourth-century North Africa? Because the earlier Augustine is partially obscured from our view by the overlayering of subsequent Augustines, we are at a disadvantage in trying fully to appreciate the attractions of Manichaeism for him. There are bound to be a number of elements of its appeal that have simply been bled out of the story, because they have been bled out of the "Catholic" Augustine. From the hindsight of his later faith, Augustine obscures his motivations for joining the Manichaean community behind an *apologia* for deviating from a course that would have led him to the Nicene fold sooner rather than later. He chooses to emphasize in the *Confessions* those aspects of Manichaeism that effectively challenged the rather rustic Christian faith to which he had been exposed as a child. Augustine explains the allure of Manichaeism for him by pointing out three areas where Manichaean views exposed problems with other forms of African Christianity: the problem of evil, the anthropomorphic view of God, and the violence and immorality of biblical heroes (*Conf* 3.7.12).[33]

We must be cautious, however, about assuming that all or any of these issues held concern for Augustine *prior* to his time with the Manichaeans. The discourse of identity he would learn as a Manichaean included a rhetorical repertoire of counterpoint, by which the system's tenets would be shown in their advantage over those of rival sects. A common trope of conversion rhetoric entails speaking of the "solutions" the adopted world view offers to "problems" the convert may or may not have actually had or considered before conversion, but which now are expressed as if a diagnosis of the convert's past condition of error. In effect, converts are provided with the rhetoric and imagery by which to construct a new past self coordinated to their new present self as a counterpoint.

Besides these specific contrasts that reach their full expression in the later hindsight of the *Confessions*, Augustine emphasizes—both in that narrative and in his earlier writings—his attraction to reason, the life of the mind, and the pursuit of truth. He acknowledges that the Manichaeans were the only ones talking about such things in Africa at the time. Augustine could see that the Manichaeans shared his wider interests in learning and the sciences, beyond the simple parables of Christian preaching. Augustine says that he was impressed by the Manichaean appeal to reason rather than blind faith (*UC* 1.2).[34] Such an attitude greatly attracted him in the aftermath of reading Cicero's *Hortensius*, with its compelling summons to the philosophical life, and its warning to withhold assent to anything unproven.[35]

> If, as was thought by ancient philosophers, and those much the
> greatest and most famous, we have souls that are eternal and akin to
> the divine, we must suppose that the more these devote themselves to
> their proper course, that is, to the cultivation of reason and the desire of
> investigation, and the less they mix and involve themselves in the errors
> and vices of mankind, so much the more easy do they find the ascent
> and return to heaven. (Cicero, *Hortensius*, Frag. 97 Müller)[36]

Augustine's entrance into the Manichaean community came very closely on the heels of reading this passage and other's like it in Cicero, and can be regarded as a direct consequence of the way it inspired him (*Conf* 3.7.12; DA 1.1).[37] "All my empty dreams suddenly lost their charm and my heart began to throb with a bewildering passion for the wisdom of eternal truth" (*Conf* 3.4.7).

As he scouted around Carthage for an embodiment of such a pursuit of truth, it was no accident that Augustine's interests fell upon the Manichaeans, with their appeal to "truth and truth alone,"[38] and their "numerous and huge books" (*libris multis et ingentibus*, *Conf* 3.6.10; cf. *Faust* 13.18). Manichaeism was an unusually literary religious community for the time, a feature that Mani had consciously set in place to distinguish his faith from others.[39] By contrast, the African Christianity known to Augustine could be characterized by contemporary pagan and Manichaean observers alike as little more than the worship of martyrs in place of the old gods (*Ep* 16; *Faust* 20.4). As C. P. Bammel has observed, "In the time of Augustine's youth Manichaeism was better equipped to answer philosophical objections to Christianity than was African Catholic Christianity."[40] It diverged from other Christianities in crucial areas where the common philosophical outlook of the age found difficulties with the more usual Christian line.

The Manichaeans invited open inquiry, which they contended would lead to a rational conviction of the truth of their teachings, in contrast to the demand for blind faith in the other forms of African Christianity.[41] Augustine's own frustrations with the latter made the Manichaean position compelling to him. "A certain childish superstition frightened me from the very act of inquiry" until "having become more courageous, I cast off that fog and persuaded myself that I should put my trust in men who teach rather than in those who order" (*BV* 1.4). Manichaeism offered Augustine liberation from fear and superstition and the prospect of a community of open-minded truth-seekers.[42] "For what else impelled me for nearly nine years," he would later write to a friend who remained a Manichaean, "to follow and listen to those men with care, except that they said that we were terrorized by superstition and that we were commanded to have faith before rational understanding, but that they urged no one to believe until the truth was fully discussed and proved" (*UC* 1.2).

Manichaeism seemed to hold out the confident assurance that truth was obtainable by means of rational inquiry, and that truth was the sect's business. It made "promises of knowledge and the disclosure of so-called secrets" (*GCM* 2.27.41), offering a complete system, with analysis and explanations of the order of the cosmos, the functions of nature, the complex inner states of the human, and all sorts of other things we would classify as natural science—"a veritable physics that had no equivalent in Catholicism," in the characterization of Jean de Menasce.[43] Other forms of African Christianity, maintaining the traditional distinction between religion as a system of practice and philosophy as a system of comprehending the cosmos, were devoid of positions on most of these subjects. Augustine would later defend the idea that such matters had nothing to do with religion, and people of the same faith were free to have differing opinions on them (*Conf* 5.3.5–5.5.8), while at the same time taking a leading role in furnishing his chosen religious system with a considerable body of dogma in these areas.

Augustine's youthful interests encompassed enthusiasm for knowledge of all kinds. From where he stood, Manichaeism in its North African setting looked more like a philosophical system than a religion—and that was an important part of its appeal. The Manichaeans generally adhered to inductive methods of reasoning fitted to the scientific epistemology of the time,[44] and congruent with the philosophical values of rationality espoused by Cicero.[45] Robert O'Connell notes how of a kind Cicero and Mani would have seemed to Augustine:

> the Manichees offered a version of the happy life remarkably in accord with the one Augustine claims to have found in Cicero. The Manichees insisted that our souls are other-worldly beings, both in origin and destiny. They trumpeted an ascetic ideal of purity, and notably of sexual purity. Finally, their depreciation (at least in principle) of earthly achievement, may well have resonated with what Testard describes as Cicero's austere ethical counsels.[46]

Augustine represents the Manichaean evidentiary and experiential argument for the dualistic explanation of evil as the most successful example of their adherence to reason over faith.[47] As their critic, he would contend that the supposed basis of Manichaeism in reason alone progressed no further than this fundamental conclusion, and that upon that one conclusion Manichaeans erected a baroque, unscientific fable. We should be cautious, however, about assuming that just because the Manichaeans gave priority to the problem of evil that it was this problem in particular that first attracted Augustine's serious attention.[48] We have no way of gauging Augustine's concern with evil prior to his Manichaean experience, and it may well be that it was this experience, with its decade-long inculcation of the concern, that made the problem of evil a permanent fixture of Augustine's thinking.[49] Biographers of Augustine are prone to depicting him as a sensitive youth deeply troubled by the problems of evil and sin. But we cannot be sure that this image of morbidity is anything other than an anachronistic projection of the later Augustine back into his own past, obscuring from view an earlier Augustine unconcerned, and then learning to be concerned, with the problem of evil.

Augustine famously declared his interest in only "God and the soul" (*Sol* 1.2.7), dismissing all else. Although this statement corresponds with his attraction to Platonic transcendentalism at the time he wrote it, it is in continuity as well with his attraction to the Manichaean dualistic outlook, by which God and soul constitute the consubstantial nature of the good. The Manichaeans had what appeared to be an exalted, philosophical view of God as a disembodied (although substantial) spirit, in sharp contrast to the crude anthropomorphism prevalent in popular Christian circles.[50] At one point, Augustine gives the impression that his pre-Manichaean philosophical reading had already led him to shun anthropomorphic views of God (*Conf* 7.1.1), and a reading of Cicero's *De natura deorum* would have sufficed to bring him to such a conviction. On this issue, Manichaeism may have provided the only palatable religious identity for Augustine at the time. His later attempts to portray the Manichaeans as crudely caricaturing popular theology notwithstanding, the evidence from the time demonstrates that Christians indeed were overwhelmingly inclined towards an anthropomorphic view of God. Roland Teske sums up the situation:

> What seems to have been the case is that the whole Western Church up
> until the time when Augustine came into contact with the Neoplatonic
> circle in the Church of Milan thought of God and the soul in
> materialistic terms. If whatever is real is bodily, as Tertullian and the
> prevalent Stoic materialism had held, then the fact that man is made in
> the image and likeness of God inevitably entails that God have the shape
> and form of the human body. And if the Church of Africa had no use
> for an intellectual understanding of the faith, if it rejoiced in the yoke
> of authority and terror of superstition and was largely content with the
> Old Latin Bible as its one book, it is easy to see why an educated young
> man like Augustine would be repelled by the Catholic Church into
> Manichaeism as a faith for the intellectuals.[51]

When Augustine later abandoned Manichaeism, it was not for a return to the anthropomorphic theology widely prevalent throughout the rest of the Christian world, but rather for an even more transcendental view of divinity offered by Platonism.

In the *Confessions*, Augustine claims that he was only interested in philosophies that contained the name of Christ, and that it was important to him that the Manichaeans made constant reference to God, Jesus Christ, and the "Paraclete" (*Conf* 3.6.10).[52] The Manichaeans actually held to a "higher" Christology than the other African Christians did, viewing Christ as pure soul, without a physical body that partook of the evil substance found in all ordinary humans.[53] We cannot be sure that such things really mattered to Augustine at the time. As part of his apology, of course, it was advantageous to say that in his misguidedness he had at least held fast to the name of Christ, however mistaken he had been about the legitimacy of the Manichaean claim to it. But which Christ: the sage, the prophet, the verbum of God, the prototypical martyr, or the supernatural being? His decade with the Manichaeans left mixed Christological results. On the one hand, his emergence from the Manichaean community entailed casting off any allegiance to their view of Christ as a divine "projection" of God, and instead regarding him within the philosophical paradigm of the great sage. On the other hand, well after his conversion he retained the Manichaean emphasis on Christ as personified wisdom and revealer, rather than as redeemer.[54] A remark of Augustine in *The Academics* appears to signify the continuation of an existing loyalty to Christ through a switch from Manichaeism to Platonism as the system by which Christ would be interpreted (*Acad* 3.20.43). But had this loyalty to Christ been a motivation to join the Manichaeans, or the outcome of a decade in their company?

Augustine had been schooled in the Roman virtues of self-discipline and restraint, and those who knew him as a young man described him as a sober individual, despite his own harsher self-judgment. Cicero's call to the detached life of philosophy in the *Hortensius* involved an austere ethic. The Manichaean emphasis on rationality and learning was similarly coupled with an ascetic ethical system couched in terms of self-cultivation rather than the crude thou-shalt-nots of other Christianities.[55]

In fact, nearly all of Augustine's other options among the Christian denominations of North Africa celebrated as heroes the patriarchs of the Old Testament, on whose morality the Manichaeans were unsparing in their criticism (primarily for polygamy, killing, and animal sacrifice). This was part of a larger Manichaean critique of the Old Testament as a crude and unwholesome book, something Augustine was in a mood to hear, fresh from his disappointing encounter with that text (*Conf* 3.5.9; 3.7.12–13). His disdain for it may at first have been only a reaction to its rude style and the unsophisticated character of its stories. But the Manichaeans transformed this into a moral critique of its teachings and characters. Augustine apparently accepted and agreed with these critiques without further concerning himself with biblical matters. Not only were biblical interests not a motive force in bringing him to the Manichaeans, but even after a decade with them he scarcely knew more of the Bible than a few stock catchphrases from the New Testament repeated in Manichaean instruction.[56]

His interest in the nobility of the virtuous person, on the other hand, connected with his education and formed a permanent part of this self-reflection. Gerald Bonner has offered the opinion that the chastity of the Manichaean Elect must have been admirable to someone so enthralled to his desires as Augustine felt himself to be.[57] Bonner argues, reasonably, that the role of the ascetic tales in Augustine's conversion as he gives it in the *Confessions* indicates that such things carried great spiritual weight with him. One might add to this evidence the fact that Augustine explicitly says that this was an appealing feature of Manichaeism to his associate Alypius (*Conf* 6.7.12).

But here again, caution is called for. Augustine's own account gives us little reason to think that he was attracted to continence or asceticism at the time he joined the Manichaean community. A decade as a Manichaean Auditor may have developed this interest in him with constant exposure to the valorization of ascetic disciplines. In this respect, Manichaeism offered the young Augustine a feature not pronounced in the other religious options of North Africa, to which the monastic movement had yet to come from Egypt and Syria.[58] In hindsight, Augustine characterizes Manichaean methods of cultivating ascetic conduct as ineffective, cancelled out by the religion's exalted view of the human soul as divine. As Peter Brown remarks, "The avoidance of 'confession' now struck Augustine as the hallmark of his Manichaean phase: 'it had pleased my pride to be free from a sense of guilt, and when I had done anything wrong not to *confess* that it was myself who had done it.'"[59] Although reflecting a fundamental misunderstanding about Manichaean teachings on moral responsibility,[60] the very idiosyncracy of Augustine's belief may tell us a great deal about what caught and held his interest in the sect, however mistaken he was that it taught what he preferred to believe.

Can we dig beneath the discursive identity of the textual Augustine to identify possible nonintellectual, affective, and practical appeals of Manichaeism? As Jean de Menasce has pointed out, Augustine's later anti-Manichaean work is all a matter of the head, a refutation of Manichaeism as a system of ideas. His own intellectualist tendencies find the fault here, despite any merits in Manichaean spirituality. What is missing from his account is what Manichaeism offered for his heart, in addition to what it provided for his head. Menasce wonders if Augustine's avoidance of this subject means that he sacrificed something affective about Manichaeism that he did not wish to discuss, trading Manichaean ethos and pathos for Catholic truth.[61] Or was he, after all, a man of deep thoughts but shallow feelings, except as a rhetorical performance such as we find in the *Confessions*? William O'Brien likewise has suggested that the Manichaean account of "God and the soul" brought together Augustine's two chief interests in a way that was powerful affectively, rather than intellectually.

> Someone searching for coherence in his own life, for assurance that an existence that bears the mark of death has meaning, would be drawn to the teachings of Mani as to a lodestone. The power of the myth to gather together in brilliant synthesis the movements of the heavens and the perturbations of the soul is a startling and thrilling thing to perceive.[62]

The Manichaean system becomes, in the later Augustine's hands, a desiccated and dissected corpse on which he performs an autopsy. All of its vitality as a lived system has been drained away. Augustine did not come to Manichaeism through a close reading of its texts or even a careful consideration of its full complement of teachings. He encountered a community of people who conducted their life in an appealing way.

The sect acted as a select association of the best and wisest (*UC* 16; *SermDom* 2.24.78)—making a virtue of their relatively small numbers in an historically proven recruitment tactic that appealed to Augustine's own evident elitism.[63] To Augustine, the Manichaeans probably seemed to offer something different from the superstition of the masses, the way that "lesser men" thought. As a Manichaean, he would be among the few privy to the secrets of the universe.[64] At the time he joined them, Manichaean separation from general society was voluntary and largely theoretical. They moved openly in society, viewing its spectacles with detachment while recalling their own spe-cial enlightened condition. When legal proscription came after some seventy years of liberty, it initially served only to heighten the atmosphere of initiation into secret mysteries[65] and to foster the bonds of a tight-knit community that Augustine highly valued.[66] As persecution persisted and intensified, however, it had a corrosive effect, particularly among lightly committed fellow-travelers such as Augustine.

Manichaeism may also have appealed to Augustine's artistic side. The Manichaean use of song in their religious services, practically unheard-of in the other Christian communities of the Latin west, could have exercised a powerful attraction on the man who would memorize and ponder the bibli-cal Psalms, as well as the novel compositions of Ambrose, and even write a treatise on music.[67] He refers on several occasions to having sung Manichaean hymns (*MM* 17.55; *Conf* 3.7.14, 10.33.49; *Faust* 13.18; *EnPs* 140.11). Primary Manichaean texts reveal a passionate liturgical life, and remind us of possible attractions that Augustine may have omitted or forgotten when recalling his entry into the sect.

The aspects of Manichaeism just reviewed all appear in one place or an-other in Augustine's own accounts of the sect's appeal. But we should take many of these as reasons more for his continued involvement than for his initial attraction. After all, Augustine says that he joined the sect "within a few days" (*facile ac diebus paucis*, *DA* 1) of reading the *Hortensius*. J. Kevin Coyle has remarked on Augustine's apparent habit of swift changes in direction in the face of new stimuli.[68] From initially positive impressions, Augustine was willing to give Manichaeism a try as a community of enlightened individu-als in pursuit of Truth. In the words of Leo Ferrari, "Augustine was inflamed with a strong desire for a *philosophia* whose nebulousness was matched only by his passionate dedication to it."[69] What he was expected to believe and do as a member of that community would only become clear to him after passing through the necessary initiation into the Manichaean community.

Initiation

We know nothing about Augustine's first contacts with Manichaeans in Carthage or how zealously he attached himself to them. There was more to his life than religion. He had a job as a teacher, a family life, a circle of friends, and his own avid intellectual pursuits. The ability of the Manichaean model of selfhood to impress itself upon him depended upon how large a place he gave Manichaeism in the overall scheme of his life. At the very least, he began in his nineteenth year (372–373 C.E.) to attend Manichaean meetings, listen to Manichaean instruction, read Manichaean literature, adopt the rules of conduct of an Auditor, and discuss Manichaean ideas with his friends, many of whom gravitated with Augustine towards association with the sect. Together they took the steps expected to enter into the ranks of the Manichaean community and gradually learned what Manichaeism was about and what was required of the person who wished to follow the Manichaean path to salvation.

Individuals interested in becoming members of the Manichaean community underwent a formal ritual of initiation that dramatized through performative acts and utterances the commitment to adhere to Manichaean teachings. Augustine makes no mention of such an experience, but his neglect of this subject should not surprise us. He had strong motivations to gloss over such details of his time as a Manichaean, and in general he showed little interest in religious ritual. Even his baptism into the Catholic Church, ostensibly the climax of the whole *Confessions*, receives just a single line in the work. Manichaeans rejected water baptism.[70] For them it was a vain washing of the outside of the body that could not possibly resolve the impurities which existed within the person. In its place, Manichaeans evidently performed a ritual sealing employing oil. We could not go far wrong in associating this ritual sealing with the moral construct of the "three seals" with which Augustine became well acquainted as a Manichaean.[71] The symbolism of "seals" of the mouth, hands, and breast implies an associated ritual enactment that formalized the Auditor's commitment. Presumably oil was daubed in the appropriate places on the body, accompanied by some invocations.

Augustine apparently found far more lasting meaning in the ritual act of first confession performed as part of the formal entrance into a Manichaean identity. The Manichaeans used this confession as the beginning of the self-reforming program the convert had entered, leading the individual through a lesson in how to articulate issues of identity and will in his or her personal experience. They conceptualized this confession as an act by which all the encumbrances of guilt accumulated by the individual in life up to that point were released. From this point forward, the adherent's new moral self would be formed through the confessional process, which henceforth formed a regular part of the adherent's practice. Through confession, a person rehearsed a discourse about the self offered by the religion, speaking aloud an account of personal experience that conformed it to the religion's approved terms of self-analysis.

Augustine's initiators sought in his own prior experiences proofs by which to demonstrate and inculcate their dualistic views of the nature of existence. Augustine probably was asked to search his memory for particular incidents in his life where evil seemed to leap out at him, or from him, as an inexplicable alien intrusion into his consciousness. His Manichaean mentors would have helped him to sift these events in order to show how evil revealed in them its true nature as a radical otherness. Augustine has preserved a remnant of this indoctrination process for us in the notorious "Pear Theft" reported in book 2 of the *Confessions*.

Our interest in the Pear Theft lies not in the event itself, which occurred when Augustine was around sixteen, nor in his recounting it when, in his forties, he wrote the *Confessions*, but rather in the traces discernible in the *Confessions* of a Manichaean interpretation of the event that has been written over by the later, post-Manichaean, Augustine. It has long been a source of astonishment that Augustine's ruminations on this seemingly trivial incident occupy half of book 2 of the *Confessions*, coming to some two thousand words.[72] Many modern commentators have taken it as a sign of either an extraordinarily sensitive conscience or a deep neurosis. Either might be a valid interpretation if we were indeed face to face with a flesh and blood Augustine wailing over such a petty misdeed more than twenty years after the fact. But instead we are confronted by a textual Augustine, one who writes deliberately, carefully, craftily, and soberly with specific purposes.[73] Augustine tends in his writings to go on at such great lengths when he is trying to solve an interpretive puzzle. The middle-aged Augustine of the *Confessions* is dealing not with a still raw guilt, but with an intellectual problem—a riddle previously solved by a Manichaean interpretation that is no longer acceptable to him. He tells us matter-of-factly that the sixteen-year-old Augustine had no compunction over the deed at all. As a man in his forties he is appalled, not by what he did specifically, but by the nature of evil revealed in the incident, which seems to contradict the understanding of evil accepted within the Nicene Christian community with which he now identifies. The layering of explanations for evil in the *Confessions* account exposes to us a *history of interpretation* of the incident in Augustine's life, that involves his learning to have what he apparently did not have at age sixteen—a moral reaction to his own conduct.

As Leo Ferrari has observed, the significance of the Pear Theft "becomes less puzzling in the light of . . . aspects of Manicheism" into which Augustine was indoctrinated and in light of which he would be led to understand his behavior as a human being.[74] Manichaeans believed that all living things shared a common life-force or soul possessing relative degrees of sentience.[75] Augustine reports that "I was gradually led to believe such nonsense as that a fig wept when it was plucked, and that the tree which bore it shed tears of mother's milk" (*Conf* 3.10.18). Such tales are found in the biography of Mani himself, where they are used to stress—as Augustine does in this passage—the key distinction between food being eaten by a worthy ascetic and being squandered on bestial people.[76] We probably have an earlier allusion, a decade before the *Confessions*, to this incident in Augustine's life being used by the Manichaeans to instruct him, when he refers in *The Morals of the Manichaeans* specifically to the imagined scenario of a *pear tree* lamenting the loss of its fruit if taken for an ordinary person rather than a Manichaean Elect (*MM* 17.58).[77] In the Pear Theft, the bestial squandering is highlighted by the literal pigs to whom Augustine and his fellow hooligans throw the pears.

It seems quite likely, therefore, that this rather trivial incident became greatly accentuated for Augustine in the confessional examination of his conscience that would have accompanied his early instruction in the Manichaean faith. Yet by the time Augustine came to write the *Confessions* such concerns as the sufferings of plant life or the appropriate recipient of alms scarcely mattered to him. They had heightened the meaningfulness of the incident at the time of its Manichaean interpretation, but are little more than narrative fossils in the *Confessions* account, where he turns his attention instead to the problem of how the theft belied a common explanation for bad actions that Augustine had learned from his readings in philosophy: namely, that they are motivated by something that the perpetrator experiences as a good (acquiring a needed or desired object, sensual gratification, expression of aroused emotion, etc.).[78] In fact, in his less profound moments of moralizing, Augustine works fairly comfortably in his writings with this same widely accepted model of the motivation to evil, so its denial in the initial probing of the incident in the *Confessions* offers a relic of a time when Augustine had found reason to call that model into question. Augustine states that the theft was, as far as he could tell, completely motiveless, and so revealed a mysterious perversity within him.[79] "I was gratuitously evil, and my evilness had no other cause than evilness itself" (*essem gratis malus et malitiae meae causa nulla esset nisi malitia, Conf* 2.4.9).[80]

This statement represents a perfect articulation of the dualist account of evil promoted in Manichaeism, one that Augustine tries later in his discussion to displace with the nondualist alternative of an *imitatio Adami*. The vividness of the incident and the amount of attention it receives suggest that it was an important part of Augustine's early moral reflections. The story is well-suited to be a Manichaean proof, and since converts to Manichaeism were asked to review their past lives only once, at their initial confession, this is the moment when a Manichaean reading of the Pear Theft is likely to have been formed.

Some probing Elect, acting in a role somewhat analogous to that of a modern psychoanalyst, ferreted out seemingly insignificant acts in Augustine's past as deeply meaningful within the framework of Manichaean understandings of the human dilemma.[81] Through the multilayered retelling twenty years later in the *Confessions*, we are just able to detect the effect to which the Manichaeans were able to use this episode to instruct the young Augustine.[82] This went well beyond the moralizing fables of weeping trees to an argument about the nature of evil and of the self. It was the apparent motivelessness of evil that the Manichaeans used as a proof against shallow philosophical explanations of evil as in some way a good for the perpetrator, such as the classic situation of the theft of bread by a starving man. Such situations were mere excuses for evil impulses that ultimately had no rhyme or reason, they argued. Evil cannot be accounted for simply as ignorance or misunderstanding of the good. Nor can it be explained as a good for someone else or some other part of an ultimately harmonious cosmos. It is an alien presence, an infecting disease, inexplicable as an act of will, wholly other to the reasoning mind. In its haphazard desire for things that may be in themselves good or beautiful (*Pulchra erant poma illa*: "Those pears were beautiful," *Conf* 2.6.12) it does not strive for its own betterment, but merely acts with blind acquisitiveness. At the heart of their construction of the self, the Manichaeans placed the recognition that evil impulses are *other*, that it is perfectly rational not to want to identify with some of the contents of one's own mind, or even the acts that might follow from them.

In writing over this earlier understanding of the forces at work in his bad conduct, the Augustine of the *Confessions* seeks to corral the deed within the self, by identifying a reasoning process, however misguided, by which what he did can be explained as an outcome of a desire originating with himself. His tentative treatment signals that he is not claiming to have recovered this reasoning process from his memory; he merely hypothesizes it as a motive unknown to himself at the time. The post-Manichaean Augustine is committed to owning the self even beyond the point where he can be aware of it. This choice is of the utmost significance for his entire mature system of thought. But, for the Manichaeans, Augustine's very lack of awareness of a motive for his misdeed was proof that such promptings come from outside the limits of the self. It was to this latter very different understanding of the limits of the self, and to the practices that promised to ameliorate its condition, that Augustine delivered himself as a convert sometime in 373 C.E.

CHAPTER TWO

Inhabitation

IN BEING ATTRACTED to Manichaeism, Augustine had been drawn to a system—a planned, promoted, coordinated set of practices and rationales for those practices. In contrast to the haphazard, largely unplanned, and evolving forces that shape human character and identity in the general social process, a formalized system such as an organized religion embodies a clearly articulated concept of human identity and action that is operationalized through programs of inculcation and reinforcement, supervised by experts with the authority bestowed upon them by the religion's adherents. Manichaeism had a repertoire of self-forming discourse and practice by which adherents discovered who they were within the ultimate terms the religion provided, and came to recognize the particular conduct by which they could obtain the goals proposed by the religion as meaningful responses to the human condition. The reorientation of the prior self toward the authoritative models of the Manichaean tradition occurred in the process of practice, in the midst of regimes of conduct—"moral," "dietetic," "disciplinary," "ritual"—offered as effective means within a particular apprehension of life's circumstances and purpose. As a "convert" to the faith, Augustine came with the prior conditioning of the self-forming forces of the broader society of Roman Africa. He had found available within that prior self the ability to desire something at least somewhat different for himself, and the willingness to reorder his priorities and goals; and so he put himself at the disposal—at least to some degree—of the self-reforming operations of the Manichaean sect.

Given the apparently impetuous circumstances in which Augustine

joined the Manichaean community, he seems to have acted under the immediate inspiration of Cicero's summons to a philosophical life that required
the cultivation of character and virtue as a prerequisite of ascertaining truth.
The Manichaeans projected the image of a tight-knit community of truth-
seekers, and Augustine evidently found both the object of their discourse
and the manner of their life to be in accord with his new interests. Conditioned by a culture that envisioned a single common truth approached by
many paths, as well as by the Manichaeans' own rationalist approach, he may
not have joined them primarily for prepackaged truths they could impart to
him, but rather for the company of like-minded souls encouraging each
other in the disciplined life that helped the mind reach for higher things.
Whether or not this is true, the first and most straightforward elements of
Manichaeism Augustine would have learned were the rules of community
life and expectations of personal conduct whose performance admitted one
to the company of the faithful. For that reason, we will consider first what
those expectations were, and the evidence we have for Augustine's fulfillment of them.

Any discussion of conversion must attend equally to this process of *inhabitation* into certain new ways of conducting oneself, alongside the more
commonly discussed indoctrination into certain new ways of thinking and
speaking. By inhabitation, I mean the instilling of a *habitus*,[1] a set of dispositions and orientations of conduct, by means of a system of promoted ritual
and non-ritual behaviors that through repetition and routinization invest the
convert's body with a distinctive visible self, identifiable as the product of engaging with a particular tradition of promoted conduct. In becoming a Manichaean Auditor, Augustine volunteered to become a subject through which
the Manichaean system articulated and perpetuated itself and its program;[2] he
agreed to be the subject of an apparatus of assessment informed by the goals
of this program, and to have his conduct measured according to his capacity
for achieving those goals.

Manichaean authorities sought to instill a particular *habitus* in adherents and make Manichaean selves of them, so that they would become efficient instruments of a salvational mission. Manichaean disciplinary regimens
limited and defined permissible performances of self, removing extraneous,
non-conforming conduct in order to qualify individuals as true selves according to Manichaean definitions of selfhood. They made Manichaean bodies,
corrected, perfected, and prepared as agents for specific performative func-

tions within the community. It can thus be said of the Manichaean program of inhabitation, as Talal Asad says of the later Christian monastic program in which ascetic discipline and liturgical practice formed a seamless whole, "Each thing to be done was not only to be done aptly in itself, but done in order to make the self approximate more and more to a predefined model of excellence. The things prescribed, including liturgical services, had a place in the overall scheme of training the Christian self."[3] Increasing mastery of this approved embodiment would advance the adherent to ever more significant roles within the overall operation of the work the Manichaean community organized itself to do in the world.

All these regimens and rituals were voluntary, chosen and accepted by individuals in a pluralistic environment where they had many other choices of self-development. Manichaeism reached its apogee of popularity in the Latin West in the same years as the other Christianities of the region began to display elements characteristic of Manichaeism, such as an ascetic ethic, the cult of the holy man rather than the martyr, hymnody, and confession. For all the ways in which Manichaeism could be looked upon as an alien intruder in Augustine's world, it made its home there effectively and left its permanent stamp upon it. The Manichaeans as Augustine encountered them were simply another of the many communities of spiritual practice available to someone such as Augustine looking to find a system of personal betterment, a support group of like-minded people, and a way of life by which he could make spiritual progress in the specific terms that had become meaningful to him. Whether Manichaeism could meet those preexisting terms, or "convert" Augustine to its own terms of spiritual progress, remained to be seen in the outcome of his time within the community.

But the choice of Manichaeism made a big difference in determining to what objects of scrutiny Augustine's attention would be drawn, and to what ethos of subjectivity he would be encouraged to conform. Augustine's decision to take up Manichaeism involved a commitment to enact the performances that constituted a Manichaean identity: to scrutinize his drives and desires, and rearrange them according to the paradigms given by the religion, harnessing and identifying with impressions and impulses compatible with those paradigms while regarding all other thoughts and feelings with suspicion and disassociation. In this way, the Manichaean system, as a "power that at first appears as external . . . assumes a psychic form that constitutes the subject's self identity" in a process that Judith Butler has analyzed theoretically and with application to more contemporary circumstances. "The form this power takes," she notes, "is relentlessly marked by a figure of turning, a turning back upon oneself or even a turning *on* oneself."[4] The subject is formed in this bifurcation of psychic and behavioral content, which occurred in Augustine's case through his performance as a Manichaean. Again citing Butler, "The performative is not merely an act used by a pregiven subject, but is one of the powerful and insidious ways in which subjects are called into social being . . . . In this sense, the performative is not only a ritual practice: it is one of the influential rituals by which subjects are formed and reformulated."[5] Potentially, Augustine could become entirely and only what Manichaeism proposed for him to become, reformulated into a new subject, if his identification with that future proved stronger than all of his other impulses and desires.

Discipline

Augustine and other Manichaean Auditors looked to the holy men and women called Elect for the principal example of ideal embodiment. Each Elect, living under vows of celibacy, poverty, and itineracy, formed the nucleus of a local cell of associated Auditors.[6] The Manichaean sect, in theory, operated as a highly organized network of such local cells, designed to maintain itself against the constant hostility of the forces of evil which made use of human political and social institutions to seek the community's destruction. The Elect often functioned as tutors to the children—both male and female—of their Auditor patrons.[7] Ideally, these children would be raised to be Elect; but at least they would receive a valuable education. In this way, the Manichaean Elect fit into the well-established social role of the philosopher-tutor, closely paralleling a similar adaptation to that role by ascetic tutors (such as Jerome) in other Christian communities in the late fourth century.

As an Auditor, Augustine was held to a less stringent code of discipline than the Elect, and was subject to less scrutiny. This is not to say that he was expected to be any the less a Manichaean. It is a fundamental misunderstanding of Manichaean polity to think of the Auditors on "the periphery" of the religion,[8] or to equate such a person with the status of a Christian catechumen.[9] The Auditor does not occupy some pre-initiated margin of the Manichaean community, but a position integral to the overall work of the religion.[10] Nevertheless, fewer forces of reinforcement operated on an Auditor's conduct. The

Elect exhorted, lectured, warned of both short-term and long-term consequences of entanglement in sin—but in the end had to rely on the Auditor's
own motivation and network of ties within the community to gain compliance with the religion's codes of conduct.[11] Augustine does not explicitly state
that he aspired to be an Elect, although the idea may be implicit in passages
where he talks of being unable to "make progress" in the religion.[12] It is at least
apparent that he expected further initiation into the "mysteries" of the faith
(*Conf* 5.3.3).[13] As long as he remained an Auditor he was expected to adhere to
the ethical precepts of the "Three Seals"; and, as Colin Starnes has insightfully
detected, this ethical paradigm appears to underlie Augustine's description of
his life as a Manichaean in the *Confessions* (*Conf* 4.2.2–3).[14]

The "Seal of the Mouth" governed both diet and speech, with the former
in particular being shaped by pantheistic notions of the omnipresence of the
divine in all living things taught by the Manichaeans. The Elect were notorious for their fasting, at a time when forms of Christian asceticism were more
focused on sexual continence. The rise of the Christian monastic movement,
which brought the novel addition of fasting to the existing practices of continence among specially dedicated members of the community, was greeted
with widespread suspicion of Manichaeism.[15] Some Elect went so far as to
eat only raw food, so as not to subject the divine element in it to the suffering of cooking and other preparations (*Faust* 6.4). Rules governing the diet
of Auditors were less stringent. The Manichaean bishop Faustus says that,
while "we require the priestly class to abstain from animal food," nonetheless
as an accommodation to less able individuals "we limit the prohibition to
the priesthood" (*Faust* 30.1),[16] and Augustine acknowledges learning of this
concession granted to him as an Auditor (*Faust* 30.5). Yet, despite his later rhetorical defense of meat-eating as a Nicene Christian, he apparently persisted
in the personal vegetarianism he had voluntarily adopted as a Manichaean
(Possidius, *Vita* 22.2). Manichaeism also prohibited all its adherents from the
consumption of wine, which is "the poisonous filth of the race of darkness"
(*Faust* 16.31)—allowing Augustine the later wry comment, "They acknowledge their God in the grape, but not in the cup" (*Faust* 20.13). Given the place
of wine in the Roman diet of Augustine's time, it was asking much of Auditors
that they adopt abstinence as the main dietetic gesture of faith. He reports
that the African Manichaean community allowed the consumption of vinegar
as well as *caroenum* (Greek *karoinon*; Italian *vino cotto*), that is, wine whose
alcohol content has been cooked away (*MM* 16.47). We have no information

on Augustine's conformity to this rule as a Manichaean; after his apostasy he held the general positive view of wine found in general society.

The "Seal of the Mouth" also enjoined using speech for good, which entailed truth-speaking and confession insofar as it did not abet evil, such as leading to someone's death. In his teaching of rhetoric, Augustine tells us, he sought to impart the tricks of the trade only to those who seemed to him motivated by good character (*Conf* 4.2.2). In hindsight, he criticizes the distinction he made as a Manichaean between using rhetoric to condemn the innocent, which he considered wrong and refused to practice, and using it to obtain the acquittal of the guilty, which in certain circumstances he considered justified according to his values at the time. In fact, his values are much the same in his study of *Lying*, penned circa 394–395 C.E., and so well after his conversion to Nicene Christianity, which supports defending the innocent by any means, including omission of facts, short of outright false statements.[17] This attitude—which he abandons by the time he writes *Against Lying*, circa 420 C.E.—reflects the Manichaean view of human solidarity, which gave no credit to human legal institutions and approved of dissimulation in defense of someone's life.

Manichaeism also embraced the sexual aspect of the ascetic ethic, enjoining celibacy for the Elect and restraint of sexual conduct for the Auditors as the "Seal of the Breast."[18] The Manichaean bishop Faustus cites Mt 19:12 in favor of "the youths of both sexes who have extirpated from their hearts the desire of marriage, and who in the Church act as eunuchs of the king's palace" (*Faust* 30.4). The Elect adhered to celibacy as part of the radical reformation of their bodily conduct necessary to their ritual function. Auditors did not face the same ritual requirements, and therefore could form sexual relationships if they wished. Faustus comments to a non-Manichaean Christian audience:

> To make virgins simply by exhortation, without forbidding to marry, is not peculiar to you. That is our principle too; and he must be not only a fool, but a madman, who thinks that a private law can forbid what the public law allows. As regards marriage, therefore, we too encourage virgins to remain as they are when they are willing to do so; we do not make them virgins against their will. For we know the force of will and of natural appetite when opposed by public law; much more when the law is only private, and every one is at liberty to disobey it. . . . [W]e too hold it equally foolish to prevent one who wishes, as it is criminal and impious to force one who has some reluctance. (*Faust* 30.4)

Accordingly, while not adopting the celibacy of the Elect, Augustine shifted in his sexual conduct from multiple affairs to monogamy (*Conf* 4.2.2). Although it has been common to attribute his monogamy during this period to inherent character traits in Augustine, one should not neglect the coincidence of this change in conduct with his exposure to the moral teachings of Manichaeism for an Auditor. Augustine insists that the woman concerned was, like his earlier *amores*, simply an object of his desire; the difference lay not in any overpowering love commitment, but in a conscious decision to remain monogamous. While his reasons go unstated in the *Confessions*, we can hardly disregard the expectations placed upon him by the Manichaean community to which he belonged. In hindsight, he can only criticize the limited reform effected by Manichaean values, which failed to instill in him a condemnation of sexual desire itself.

While permitting the Auditors sexual relationships, the Manichaean authorities discouraged reproduction, which Augustine later would come to regard as the sole legitimate purpose of intercourse.[19] But from the Manichaean vantage point, reproduction offered only a perpetuation of a world order in which the divine soul experienced affliction. Augustine refers to "the unrighteous law of the Manichaeans which, in order to prevent their God, whom they bewail as confined in all seeds, from suffering still closer confinement in the womb, requires married people not on any account to have children, their great desire being to liberate their God" (*Faust* 22.30).[20] Yet he concedes to the Manichaeans that they "allow many of your followers to retain their connection with you in spite of their refusal, or their inability, to obey you" in connection with the discouragement of reproduction (*Faust* 30.6). Augustine was not among these recalcitrant adherents, since he fully followed the Manichaean rule for Auditors on this matter.

Augustine's monogamous relationship was of the type sanctioned by Manichaean teachings on sexual conduct. The woman (Augustine never tells us her name) is variously referred to in modern scholarship as Augustine's "mistress" or "concubine," both terms carrying connotations for a modern audience that do not fit the options of spousal association in the Roman Empire of which Augustine made use.[21] The non-elite classes tended to opt for less formal domestic partnerships, or what we sometimes call "common-law marriages."[22] Augustine's relationship belongs to this latter, apparently quite common type.[23] She became pregnant and gave birth to a boy, whom the couple named Adeodatus,[24] prior to Augustine's conversion, upon which the couple adopted the birth control practices taught by the sect.[25] As Augustine tells us, this took the form of tracking a woman's menstrual cycle and engaging in sex only at times when impregnation was unlikely to occur (*Faust* 15.7; *MM* 18.65; *BC* 5.5). Augustine was also aware of, and may himself have practiced, *coitus interruptus* (*Faust* 22.30).[26]

We do not know whether his companion shared Augustine's Manichaean commitments. Augustinian scholars have usually supposed that she was and remained a "Catholic."[27] Henry Chadwick points to Augustine's remark (*Conf* 9.6.14) that their son Adeodatus was brought up in God's discipline (*in disciplina tua*) as suggesting that she raised the boy as a non-Manichaean Christian despite Augustine's allegiance to Manichaeism at the time.[28] This reading might be questioned, however, given that Augustine includes himself with the boy's mother as joint suppliers of this religious nurturance (*nutriebatur a nobis in disciplina tua*). By *disciplina*, therefore, he may mean no more than the strict moral upbringing common to Manichaeans and other Christians. The idea that Augustine consciously raised his son in the faith of his own mother at a time when he was in the schools and streets of Carthage deriding that very "superstition" stretches credulity. Similarly, Kim Power's argument, based on an assumed lack of opposition to the woman from Monnica,[29] overlooks both the latter's lack of influence over Augustine's life during his Carthage years and her immediate dismissal of the woman once she gained such influence after Augustine's conversion. The woman's vow as she was sent back to Africa "never to know a man again" (*Conf* 6.15.25; see Augustine's apparent reflections on the situation in *BC* 5.5), scarcely proves an intention to be baptized;[30] it could just as well signify plans to seek the shelter of the Manichaean community and perhaps even become an Electa. Or it could be nothing more than melodramatic hyperbole. It cannot be ignored that her reported vow of celibacy serves a dramatic purpose in the *Confessions* as yet another example of others giving up sex while Augustine cannot.[31] In reporting it, Augustine pointedly does not say that the vow was made "to You," that is, the God known through Nicene Christianity, nor does he remark on any efforts or prayers for his own conversion by this woman (as he does for his mother), nor does he speak in contrasting terms of her innocent piety beside his own heresy, as would be germane to his theme. It must be said, then, that there is nothing to suggest she was a Nicene Christian, and it was not necessary for her to be one to serve as a model of piety contrasted to Augustine's self-criticism in the *Confessions*, a role played just as well by the Manichaean Faustus and the religiously indifferent (if not atheist) Verecundus.

Regardless of the personal feelings and commitments of Augustine's companion, the couple apparently followed birth control faithfully—and successfully—for over a decade, even during their time in Italy, when most modern biographies regard Augustine as no longer a Manichaean. As we shall see, however, he maintained Manichaean practices for much of this time. Colin Starnes follows Pierre Courcelle in seeing an allusion to this commitment not to have more children in Augustine's reflections on the chance that a child might be born *contra votum*, "contrary to one's vow."[32] When he ceased to be a Manichaean, Augustine dismissed his companion, not for continence, but for marriage. A full marriage in Roman society was expressly contracted for the legal propagation of heirs, and that Augustine did not consider such a step while a Manichaean reflects his wholehearted commitment to the sect's disciplinary code regarding sex and reproduction against significant social pressure.[33]

Augustine also adopted the religion's abhorrence of violence to life, codified in the "Seal of the Hand." Manichaeans understood Christ's command to love our enemies in terms of the concept of mixture, by which even our enemies possess a quantity of good within them, for which reason "we should love our enemies now, because they have a part of the good" (*Faust* 19.24). Consequently, Manichaeans adhered to a strict pacifism.[34] Indeed, as a fragment (*frustum*) of God (*Conf* 4.16.31), one was expected to have empathy with all other portions of divinity spread throughout the world, and reverence for any of its manifestations.[35] Faustus, in addressing a non-Manichaean Christian, explains, "your religion resembles ours in attaching the same sacredness to the bread and wine that we do to everything," because all things are filled with the sacred presence of the "vulnerable Jesus" (*Faust* 20.2). Consequently, among the things taught by the Elect to the Auditor cells gathered around them, nonviolence had a high priority. Since the divine nature is invisibly present in all material reality (*Conf* 3.6.10), human interaction with the world must be conducted with the utmost self-consciousness (*Conf* 3.10.18). The Manichaeans went so far as to "maintain that the fruit suffers when it is pulled from the tree, when it is cut and scraped, and cooked, and eaten" (*Faust* 6.4).[36] Such concerns made agricultural practices problematic (*MM* 17), although absolution could be obtained for those who directed part of their harvest to the path of liberation through the Elect.[37]

Augustine's adherence to conduct reflecting this view of life is shown by his rejection of the offered services of a sorcerer on the grounds that his spells might involve killing "so much as a fly" (*Conf* 4.2.3). When he becomes an apostate from Manichaeism, this reverence of animal life disappears, and Augustine repeatedly insists that animals have been created for human use.[38] He came to ridicule Manichaean concerns about the cost of agriculture in the life of millions of worms and other insects, not to mention the pain experienced by plants at harvesting—ideas with which he was obviously well familiar as an Auditor. His later thinking follows the "common sense" view of the larger culture of his time regarding the inferiority of animals and their place as subservient to human needs, reinforced for non-Manichaean Christians by the account of creation in Genesis. Augustine's attitude in his Manichaean period stands out as an anomaly, therefore, doubtless reflecting his adherence to the Manichaean position contrary to the mores of the surrounding culture.

In general, however, the set of moral precepts Augustine followed as a Manichaean Auditor would not have radically distinguished him from other Christians in North Africa. For most of his career, Augustine acknowledged that in practice the Manichaeans lived within the limits of ordinary morality, although he suggested that this might be "only from a regard for the opinion of men, or from fear of human laws," or because certain good customs in their personal background make them adverse to crime, or, in a remarkable concession, because they live by the general principle (which Augustine dismisses as merely "natural") of "not doing to another what you would not have done to yourself" (*Faust* 15.7). As an apostate from Manichaeism, he objected primarily to Manichaean doctrine, not to the ascetic and devotional values that he largely shared with them even as a Nicene Christian.

Only in his initial years as an apostate, and in the very last years of his life, did Augustine venture to attack Manichaean conduct—and then only that of the Elect. Desperate to turn away trenchant criticism of the conduct of run-of-the-mill Nicene Christians that he, too, wished to reform with the zealotry of a new convert, he repeated several examples of hearsay and gossip about Elect malpractice in *The Morals of the Manichaeans*, only to be forced into publicly eating his words a few years later, when in his debate with the Manichaean Fortunatus he had to admit that he had no direct personal knowledge of any serious immorality among the Manichaeans (*Fort* 1–3). At the end of his career, equally desperate to shake off the Manichaean shadow that seemed never to leave him, he resorted to demonizing them by means of accusations obtained through intimidation and torture (*Haer* 46). The latter aspersions are hardly credible, while the former ones are relatively insignificant. Those anti-Manichaean writers who kept themselves above giving credence to the sort of wild accusations once directed at Christians generally—such as Ephrem Syrus—generally conceded that the significant differences between Manichaeism and the sort of Christianity they represented were more doctrinal than ethical.

> For their works are like our works as their fast is like our fast, but their faith is not like our faith. And, therefore, rather than being known by the fruit of their works they are distinguished by the fruit of their words. For their work is able to lead astray and appear as fine, for its bitterness is invisible; but their words cannot lead astray, for their blasphemies are evident. (Ephrem, *Fifth Discourse*, cxix)

Manichaean conduct distinguished itself not by the moral principles it espoused, but by the apparatus of inculcation employed to produce it, the techniques of forming the Manichaean as an ethical subject, including the practice—unique among the moral systems of late antiquity—of regular confession. Through confession, Manichaean teachers sought to cultivate in their followers a regime of self-scrutiny integral to the distinction and separation of the true self from the evil false self that dominated ordinary human beings. We have to do here with what Michel Foucault has termed the "determination of the ethical substance," by which he means "the way in which the individual has to constitute this or that part of himself as the prime material of his moral conduct."[39] The reader may have expected that treatment of Manichaean self-theory would be postponed to the following chapter on indoctrination; but the point I wish to make by raising the subject here is that this "theory" is the discursive ancillary of the practice that actually made Manichaeans on a regular, systematic basis regardless of their uptake of the religion's more theoretical elements. Indeed, we should consider whether the familiar distinction between theory and practice has much use when we are dealing with a practice of self-observation and self-determination in which "theory" merely provides the discursive tools by which to manipulate mental and emotional experience. For we find in Manichaean confessionary practice a concern that extends beyond management of external conduct into the inner drama of impulse and decision that precedes action.

Michel Foucault has queried these different degrees of moral engagement in the area of sexual morality in ways directly applicable to what we might consider the Manichaean interiorization of ethical focus.

Thus, one can relate the crucial aspects of the practice of fidelity to the strict observance of interdictions and obligations in the very acts one accomplishes. But one can also make the essence of fidelity consist in the mastery of desires, in the fervent combat one directs against them, in the strength with which one is able to resist temptations: what makes up the content of fidelity in this case is that vigilance and that struggle. In these conditions, the contradictory movements of the soul—much more than the carrying out of the acts themselves—will be the prime material of moral practice.[40]

As we saw with Augustine's initiatory self-examination, Manichaean leaders guided converts into what they regarded as insights into the inner workings of the individual from which self-contradictory behavior springs. The Manichaeans offered a program of discernment by which such self-contradiction resolved itself into "self" and "other," characterized respectively by good and bad impulses arising from within the individual formerly—and according to the Manichaeans erroneously—regarded as a single self. Coming to view one's impulses within this dualistic framework empowered personal resources of self-regulation through differential reactions to these two sorts of interior experience. Thus, among the various kinds of "ethical work" Foucault assays, all of which could be found among the Manichaeans as among most moral traditions of the age, confession worked "through a decipherment as painstaking, continuous, and detailed as possible, of the movements of desire in all its hidden forms."[41]

Such a regime closely resembled widespread philosophically-based practices of self examination, the so-called "care of the self" movement most closely identified with the Stoic tradition. The Stoic daily regimen entailed reviewing one's conduct and assessing it as good or bad, laboring as a kind of watchman of oneself, monitoring, sorting, and analyzing thoughts, words, and deeds. Michel Foucault captures the ethos of this practice:

The purpose of the examination is not therefore to discover one's own guilt . . . . If one "conceals nothing from oneself," if one "omits nothing," it is in order to commit to memory, so as to have present in one's mind, legitimate ends, but also rules of conduct that enable one to achieve these ends through the choice of appropriate means. The fault is not reactivated by the examination in order to determine a culpability or stimulate a feeling of remorse, but in order to strengthen, on the basis of the recapitulated and reconsidered verifications of a failure, the rational equipment that ensures a wise behavior.[42]

Similarly, the Manichaean practice aimed not primarily at establishing personal guilt—although remorse at one's failure to guard oneself sufficiently against being overwhelmed by evil impulses was elicited—but in identifying conduct alien to the inherent goodness of the self, from which one should strive to disassociate and be on guard against in the future. Regular confession cultivated vigilance rather than guilt—vigilance not against oneself but against another that entails a distinct mode of "ethical work" mentioned by Foucault, "in the form of a relentless combat whose vicissitudes—including momentary setbacks—can have meaning and value in themselves."[43] Other agonistic models of moral self-formation in the time of Augustine could be characterized in similar terms; but the dualistic construct of interior conflict offered by Manichaeism gave it a distinctive tenor that called into question conventional understandings of selfhood in late antiquity.

The interest I share with Foucault in this subject concerns how particular selves may be produced as products of rule systems such as the Manichaean disciplinary code, with its specific apparatus of inculcation and enforcement. In order to maintain his status as a member of the Manichaean community, Augustine had to perform regular self-scrutinizing acts of confession, and be subject to the assessment of his progress in the faith by his superiors in the community. By choosing to associate mostly with fellow Manichaeans, and to be constantly in their company, he also placed himself in the position of constant scrutiny by his peers, and the necessity of nearly constant visible performance of Manichaean conduct according to their expectations. It is in such ways that adherence to the ethical system of a particular community "commits an individual, not only to other actions always in conformity with values and rules, but to a certain mode of being, a mode of being characteristic of the ethical subject."[44] As a consequence, although individuals may "pass" by rote exterior performance of community rules and expectations without wholehearted commitment, we might imagine that such performance is accomplished more efficiently, and with less laborious self-consciousness, by internalizing the prompts to action as "beliefs," as it were, that one holds consistent with the regular expectations of one's conduct. Thus, the expectations of others may find a way to become one's self-expectations.

It is to such internalization of the prompts for conduct—which all moral systems intend, but may or may not inculcate successfully in those who visibly adhere to them—that Foucault wishes to restrict the term "moral" in its proper sense. He contends that moral action involves "a relationship with the self" that extends to a "self-formation as an ethical subject," which he sums up as:

> a process in which the individual delimits that part of himself that will form the object of his moral practice, defines his position relative to the precept he will follow, and decides on a certain mode of being that will serve as his moral goal. And this requires him to act upon himself, to monitor, test, improve, and transform himself. There is no specific moral action that does not refer to a unified moral conduct; no moral conduct that does not call for the forming of oneself as an ethical subject; and no forming of the ethical subject without "modes of subjectivation" and an "ascetics" or "practices of the self" that support them. Moral action is indissociable from these forms of self-activity, and they do not differ any less from one morality to another than do the systems of values, rules, and interdictions.[45]

Elaborating on this point of analysis, Judith Butler has connected it to treatments in Nietzsche and Freud of the genesis of "conscience" as the consolidation of a self-scrutiny and self-beratement.

> Conscience is the means by which a subject becomes an object for itself, reflecting on itself, establishing itself as reflective and reflexive. . . . In order to curb desire, one makes of oneself an object for reflection; in the course of producing one's own alterity, one becomes established as a reflexive being, one who can take oneself as an object. Reflexivity becomes the means by which desire is regularly transmuted into the circuit of self-reflection. The doubling-back of desire that culminates in reflexivity produces, however, another order of desire: the desire for that very circuit, for reflexivity and, ultimately, for subjection.[46]

It was precisely to analyze such reflexivity involved in self-formation that G. H. Mead employed the distinction between the "I" as the moment-by-moment novelty of action, and the "me" as the reference point of identity according to which each new act is assessed and adjusted.

Such "practices of the self" that form ethical subjects may be cultivated and enacted without particular self-reflection in monolithic societies, and a specific, culturally transmitted *habitus* may be developed in individuals as a set of prescriptions and prohibitions followed unreflectively as just the way things are done, as examined by Pierre Bourdieu. But Augustine's situation involves different conditions. In a pluralistic environment, he voluntarily committed himself to a countercultural system, whether he fully intended to or not. It is in such circumstances that self-formation takes on a more deliberate and self-conscious character, I would argue, and that isolated moral action refers to a unified moral conduct explicitly, rather than only implicitly. In other words, conversion in such circumstances potentially raises self-formation to a level of self-consciousness, a degree of self-manipulability, well beyond where such processes normally occur. And this would be all the more true in a system such as Manichaeism, where self-identification and self-formation stood at the very center of community focus. Augustine's "invention of the inner self"[47] or of the "introspective conscience,"[48] therefore, may have less to do with any inherent psychological peculiarity, interest, or genius on his part, and more to do with his conditioning by the heightened concern with self and interiority found in Manichaeism.

Ritual

As a Manichaean Auditor, Augustine had ritual expectations to meet as well. The disciplines whose observance authorized continued membership in the Manichaean community also served to qualify Augustine for ritual performance. This ritual performance, in turn, provided an extension of discipline as another means of habituating Augustine to distinctly Manichaean patterns of behavior. Certain regular patterns of ritual performance cultivated on a daily, weekly, or more extended periodic basis initially reminded Augustine of his commitment to the Manichaean religion, and over the course of a decade became an assumed pattern of action, a routinized self-expression as a Manichaean.

Daily prayer constituted the most basic of these routines. As manifestations of the divine, the sun and moon indicated the direction Manichaeans faced in offering their daily repertoire of prayers.[49] Manichaeans were taught to turn toward the sun in the day, and the moon at night, and "bow the knee" to them (*Faust* 14.11).[50] The rationale for these prescriptions involved regarding the two luminaries as a pure manifestation of the essence of God (*Faust* 21.4), "a particle of that light in which God dwells" (*GCM* 1.3.6), unpolluted with any mixture with evil (*Serm* 12.12; cf. *Conf* 3.6.10; *Faust* 9.2; 18.5.), and in this sense divine (*Serm* 12.11), and considered a manifestation of God's wisdom (*Faust* 5.11). Augustine later came to identify this attitude as a kind of paganism, a worshiping of creation rather than the creator (*Faust* 14.10),[51] even though acknowledging that he was taught that "you do not in a proper sense worship the sun," but rather believe that "he carries your prayers with him in his course round the heavens" (*Faust* 20.5)[52]—a key distinction attested as well by Alexander of Lycopolis,[53] Ephrem Syrus,[54] and even reported in Mani's own words:

> The other religious bodies blame us because we worship sun and moon, and represent them as an image; but they do not know their real natures. They do not know that the sun and moon are our path, the door whence we march forth into the world of our existence, as this has been declared by Jesus.[55]

Unfortunately, Augustine offers only a single, polemically distorted caricature of a Manichaean prayer, although we now have many examples of Manichaean prayers from Egypt and farther afield.[56] He further reports that Manichaeans swore oaths by the light, or by the name of Manichaeus or Mani, or by the Paraclete, whom they also understand to be Mani (*Faust* 19.22).

The Manichaeans adhered to the Christian tradition of religious assembly on Sunday (*Faust* 18.5). Hymn singing played a central role in such community gatherings, and was a major expression of Manichaean devotion at a time when song was absent from the services of most Christian religious communities in the western Roman Empire. Augustine makes frequent reference to singing hymns as an Auditor (*MM* 17.55; *Conf* 3.7.14, 10.33.49; *Faust* 13.18; *EnPs* 140.11), and could remember their lyric content by heart decades later (*Faust* 15.5). Such patterns of speech, inscribed on the memory, provided the repertoire of imagery and expression on which Augustine drew to conceptualize reality—something he himself recognized with frustration when he later sought to think in other terms to which he was starting to be exposed in Italy. In this way, ritual scripts serve to constitute the self who performs them, as pointed out by Wade Wheelock:

The actual utterances of the words of the liturgy, which will include
such very personal elements as expressions of attitudes and intentions,
causes one to take on the identity of a cultural ideal. The formalized role
is put into your mouth to speak and comes out as your own responsible
perception of and involvement in the situation. The first person of the
ritual text comes to life as the "I" or "We" of the participants who speak
the liturgy and who then proceed to fashion around themselves a whole
world out of language.[57]

The surviving examples of western Manichaean hymnody from the Coptic
Psalm-Book fit Wheelock's characterization perfectly, composed in such a way
as to put into the mouth of the performers expressions of identification with
actors in Manichaean mythic constructs, and of personally experienced confirmation of reality as Manichaeism characterized it. Augustine not only sang
such hymnic scripts, but also heard exposition of sacred texts at the weekly
congregations, as well as in smaller study groups (UC 9.22; CEF 5.6; *Conf*
4.8.13).

The Manichaeans maintained the custom—formerly widespread among
Christians, including the community in Thagaste to which Monnica belonged—of fasting on Sunday (*Ep* 36.12.27, 236.2; cf. Leo, *Epistle* 15.4, 135.5).
Augustine's later self-control in matters of diet certainly owed something to
the practice he received throughout his twenties in keeping such regular fasts.
The Elect alone fasted in connection with an additional religious assembly
on Monday (Leo, *Sermon* 29.5). The rest of the week, the Elect broke their
fast toward evening, in order to participate in a ritual meal. Auditors such as
Augustine brought food offerings to the Elect, who ritually consumed them.
Perhaps not all Auditors had daily contact with the Elect in this way, but only
as means and opportunity presented itself.

The offering of food constituted the central cultic act of most varieties
of religious practice throughout the Roman world. The shift from placing offerings on an altar before a representation of the presence of a god to placing
them before one or more holy persons for their consumption was a growing
trend at the time.[58] In one way or another, literally or metaphorically, the
stomachs of sacred persons took the place of altar-top fires. Manichaean belief
about the function and meaning of food ritual, however, stands dramatically
apart from that of other religious traditions. To the Manichaeans, food was
not sacred as a consequence of being offered to God, but because it actually

contained God, so to speak, in the particles of divinity it contained, in a kind of radical extension of eucharistic logic. "Particles of the supreme and true God were imprisoned in the fruit, unless released by means of the teeth and stomach of one of the holy Elect" (*Conf* 3.10.18).[59] As in the more familiar Christian eucharist, one offers God to God, the suffering God to the transcendent God. But the indwelling of God in the elements is not a temporary ritual achievement, as it is in the rival Christian liturgy of the time, but a constant state of nature, which the ritual participates in resolving. Because of the sacredness of food within the ritual economy of the Manichaean community, Manichaeans did not give food to beggars, but gave money instead (*Conf* 3.10.18; *Faust* 20.16).[60]

Despite a general disinterest in ritual evident throughout his career, Augustine evidently participated in the Manichaean ritual meal to the degree that he became thoroughly conversant with its form and theory (*Conf* 4.1.1). As a Manichaean, he tells God, "I thought that it [the food] was you" (*Conf* 3.6.10).[61] He was taught that "if one of the holy were to eat [the food] . . . he would digest it and breathe it out again as angels or even as particles of God . . . as he groaned in prayer" (*Conf* 3.10.18; cf. *MM* 17.55); and so through participation in this ritual he "sought to be purged of defilements by providing food for the so-called Elect or holy, in the hope that they would turn the food into angels and gods for us in the workshops of their bellies to be the agents of our liberation" (*Conf* 4.1.1).[62] With its place as the daily centerpiece of Manichaean life, the sights, sounds, acts, and ideology of the ritual meal permeated Manichaean identity. Augustine appears to play off the rhetoric of the ritual meal with a bit of self-conscious irony in the part of the *Confessions* where he relates his experiences as a Manichaean. The entire section is riddled with gustatory imagery and word-play. Augustine refers again and again to his hunger and thirst for God, and to the teachings "served up" by the Manichaeans as "dishes" that failed to satisfy. Although as an Auditor Augustine could not eat of the actual ritual offerings, he uses the setting of the meal as a rhetorical trope to refer to his "gulping down" of the Manichaean teachings, a famished man indifferent to the quality of what he was taking in.[63] In fact, Augustine uses the meal imagery so explicitly that his Donatist nemesis Petilian understood him to have actually been an Elect who participated in the ritual meals.

The daily meetings between Auditors bringing food to the Elect, as well as the weekly general Manichaean meetings, involved acts of confession and absolution that served an essential function in shaping the self-image of adherents. Auditors would kneel before the holy Elect and receive an absolution through the laying on of the Elect's hands.[64] Through confession, as already discussed, one applied dualistic analysis to one's own conduct, distinguishing "the light from the darkness" within oneself, and affirming and reinforcing identification with only the positive manifestations of self. Absolution was automatic upon personal recognition of the alienness of the committed sin to the true, good self, in sharp contrast to the rigorous programs of penance imposed within those Christian communities that did not expel people outright for post-baptismal sin. Augustine reports that, at least for him, the Manichaean system made it all too easy for him to avoid any sense of responsibility or compunction, and so did not achieve its intended effect of moral self-formation.[65]

The cycle of daily and weekly confessionary practice culminated once a year at "the feast you call the *Bēma*," which was held "with great pomp" in the month of March (*Faust* 18.5). On the model of such observances as the Jewish Yom Kippur, the Bema ceremony effected a purge of all sins from the preceding year and a recommitment to the Manichaean community and way of life in the shadow of the expected final judgment of one's ultimate destiny. A month-long Lenten fast and a series of vigils preceded the dramatic liturgy of the holy day, at which a seat on a raised platform stood symbolically vacant between the martyrdom of Mani and the imminent judgment of the world.[66] Augustine acknowledges participating in these observances (*CEF* 8.9).

Community

Augustine appears to have highly valued the sense of community provided by the tight-knit group of his fellow Manichaean Auditors (*Conf* 4.1.1; DA 11).[67] He describes in glowing terms the solidarity of companionship that helped him even in the face of the death of a close friend:

> talking and laughing together and kindly giving way to each other's wishes, reading elegantly written books[68] together, sharing jokes and delighting to honor one another, disagreeing occasionally but without rancor, as a person might disagree with himself, and lending piquancy by that rare disagreement to our much more frequent accord. We

would teach and learn from each other, sadly missing any who were absent and blithely welcoming them when they returned. Such signs of friendship sprang from the hearts of friends who loved and knew their love returned, signs to be read in smiles, words, glances and a thousand gracious gestures. (*Conf* 4.8.13)[69]

Augustine gives no such effusive description of companionship for any other time or company of his life.[70] Clearly, these fellow young men formed a circle of "significant others," to use George Mead's expression, whose views and attitudes would shape his own, and whose responses to his own words and actions would serve as a reference point for his own self-assessment. Within their common commitment, how they reacted to Augustine in his conformities to and deviations from that commitment constituted the primary reference point for how he came to see himself.

In the strong, positive sense of community conveyed by Augustine in his recollections of his time among the Manichaeans, we not only connect with one of the chief factors in conversion to and maintenance of a religious identity established in modern sociological studies, but also access the fundamental basis of self-formation according to the theory of George Mead. By identifying himself with superiors and peers within the Manichaean community, Augustine engaged with exemplars whose actions and attitudes provided the material for his own self-reflections. He entered into roles that he witnessed being modeled for him by specific others, gradually generalizing those observations into a set of tacit rules of conduct. Unlike general society, however, the sectarian setting provided an explicit articulation of many of those rules, making the conformation process more self-conscious and, at least potentially, more unambiguous and rapid.

In the terms provided by Mead's theory, Augustine would have formed a sense of self, a "me," that served as a point of reference and assessment for his impulses to action, built out of his experiences of how valued others around him had reacted to him in his past display of various actions and attitudes, and how he had felt as a consequence of those reactions. The convert actively works to form such a "me" as "an importation from the field of social objects into an amorphous, unorganized field of what we call inner experience. Through the organization of this object, the self, this material is itself organized and brought under the control of the individual in the form of so-called self-consciousness."[71] Mead gives this characterization not of the general socialization process of children, but of the at least partly deliberate reformation of self of an adult for whom a previous self has become problematic, reduced to an "amorphous, unorganized" condition due to uncertainties about goals and priorities. We must reckon with Augustine's complicity in and active facilitation of a process of inhabitation that he desired to be completed in his person. That is the situation of a convert. He and his companions worked together on each other, encouraging, reminding, exploring, discussing—and simply being in the room, in each other's sight as mutual witnesses to apt performance as Manichaeans.

Among his fellow Auditors were childhood friends from Thagaste such as Alypius, attracted by the ascetic lifestyle upheld by the Elect, and the other close, nameless friend who died while Augustine was teaching in Thagaste after completing his studies in Carthage. Other Manichaean comrades were found in Carthage. One of these was Nebridius. Although reportedly "sweet" and "amiable," he had a sharp mind and something of an iconoclastic attitude, over the years of their acquaintance pointing out to Augustine apparent flaws in the logic of Manichaeism, of astrology, and of Academic skepticism, even as the two avidly pursued interest in all three areas.[72]

These intellectually inclined young men formed a distinct group within the larger Manichaean community. Peter Brown has insightfully captured the complex relationship of Augustine and his circle with other African Manichaeans.

The Manichaeism of Augustine was the Manichaeism of a specific group, of the cultivated intelligentsia of the university of Carthage and of the small-town notables of Thagaste. . . . In the 370's, this Manichaeism of cultivated men seems to have come to the fore in Africa, with Augustine and his friends as its most active representatives. The men to whom Augustine will later write in order to undo the beliefs he had himself propagated, are a tribute to the success of this wing of the Manichaean movement. . . . This group, however, may have been somewhat peripheral to the movement as a whole. Other Manichees were far more doctrinaire. . . . When Augustine became a bishop they would openly challenge him on his own territory, as interpreters of S. Paul, rather than as exponents of a rationally-based "Wisdom." These men formed the hard core of African Manichaeism: they came to the fore as soon as renewed persecution (in 386) and the desertion of

Augustine and his impressive circle, had shaken the faith of the "Fellow Travellers."[73]

Their intellectual gifts, good education, and relative affluence no doubt helped them attain a certain status among the other Auditors. Augustine relates some anecdotes from his last years in the sect that appear to indicate that he was turned to by other Auditors for help in dealing with conflicts inside the community, perhaps as a kind of senior Auditor. But we should be cautious about overestimating the importance of Augustine's circle within African Manichaeism under the influence of his later prominence as a leader of Nicene Christianity. As one of thousands of Auditors in Africa, he indeed would have had the opportunity to meet some important people, such as the bishop Faustus, yet always remained somewhat removed from the circles of an Elect like Fortunatus.[74] We should also doubt the degree of initial impact attributed to Augustine's defection, even among the intellectual circle at the margins of African Manichaeism. While it is true that other Manichaeans would follow him into apostasy, many of his other former associates remained faithful, as his silence over the fate of specific figures to whom he made overtures, and the evident growing frustration of his later anti-Manichaean works, attest.

The Limits of Inhabitation

As a consequence of accommodating Manichaean precepts, therefore, Augustine was shaped in his conduct into a particular kind of person. He was faithful to the same woman throughout this period, zealously practiced birth control, applied ethical principles to his teaching, eschewed all forms of violence, and, even according to his opponents, was a quiet, well-behaved young man.[75] Even his studiousness found reinforcement in the sect's emphasis on reading and study. Moreover, we have from Augustine's pen repeated references to his active participation in Manichaean rites and religious observances beyond its moral code, including attending instructional and ritual meetings, singing hymns, listening to expositions of texts, performing his prayers, making confession, and receiving absolution. Through all of these behaviors, Augustine manifested to an outside observer a Manichaean self.

Yet in other respects he showed by his conduct the limits of his embodiment of Manichaean values. Since Manichaeans did not withdraw from general society into monasteries or closed communities, the sect had to contend with the persistence of the profane and the mundane in the lives of its members, particularly the Auditors. Augustine was not expected as an Auditor to disengage from the world to the same degree as the Elect. While the Elect were full-time religious professionals and virtuosi, Auditors had a life outside their Manichaean activities. Even as they devoted themselves to the daily ritual routine and world view of Manichaeism, therefore, Augustine and his friends continued to lead the life of young men about town, including attendance at sporting events and theatrical performances (*Conf* 4.1.1). Augustine reports that even the Elect were known to attend such public entertainments (*MM* 19.72); although elsewhere—tongue firmly planted in cheek—he uses the example of choosing the theater over a Manichaean meeting as something that might evoke a Manichaean analysis of the conflict of good and bad wills within us (*Conf* 8.10.23). He used his influence as a friend to dissuade Alypius from his obsession with violent sports during their time together in the Manichaean sect (*Conf* 6.7.11–12). As first a student and then a teacher of rhetoric, Augustine worked every day with content from the literature of his culture deeply at odds with Manichaean values. Augustine indulged his love of rhetorical performance, both in formal competitions and in informal public disputation. Manichaeism simply offered him another position from which to pose his challenge to the lesser men around him (*Conf* 3.12.21).

Augustine would later claim that his desire for sex and ambition for public honors persisted unabated by Manichaean teaching (*Conf* 8.6.13, 8.12.30), despite the earnest exhortation of the leaders of the sect (*UC* 1.3). Certainly, he continued in a sexual relationship and pursued career opportunities when they presented themselves, rather than adopting the more stringent dedication to religion of the Elect. At the same time, however, we must be aware that Augustine probably overdramatizes his enthrallment to precisely these two interests in order to portray himself in line with Cicero's characterization of the disturbed soul in *Tusculan Disputations*, where love of women (*mulierositas*) and desire for glory (*gloriae cupiditas*) are precisely the two examples offered (Cicero, *Tusc. disp.* 4.10.23–13.29). Likewise, Augustine's self-portrait of a tormented soul shattered by its moral failings and weaknesses owes not a little to Cicero's depiction of Alcibiades in the same work (Cicero, *Tusc. disp.* 3.32.77–78, 4.28.61).

With the themes and imagery of such rhetorically inspired constructs,

Augustine later depicted Manichaeism as too easy on its Auditors. It failed in his opinion to demand in strong enough terms a radical change of life that would constitute real moral progress. Augustine refers at one point to a favorite Manichaean expression for wholly mundane people: "Light has passed completely through him." Yet, he says to a Manichaean correspondent,

> I have no fear that you will think I was the dwelling-place of light
> when I was involved in the life of this world, nursing shadowy hopes
> of a beautiful wife, of the pomp of riches, of empty honors and other
> pernicious and deadly pleasures. All these things, as you know, I did not
> cease to desire and hope for when I was their zealous hearer. I do not
> attribute this to their teaching, for I confess that they carefully warned
> me to beware of these things. (*UC* 1.3)

In other words, a breakdown occurred between the sect's deployed methods of inculcating particular values and Augustine's motivations to take up those values voluntarily and completely. In the terms outlined by Harry Frankfurt, Augustine desired to become a Manichaean, but did not persistently will it.[76] His commitment to shape his life according to the Manichaean program remained only one of several conflicting desires and plans and failed to become one with which he wholeheartedly identified, as characterized by Harry Frankfurt in his analysis of such ambivalence of identity.

> All a decision does is to create an intention; it does not guarantee that
> the intention will be carried out. This is not simply because the person
> can always change his mind. Apart from inconstancy of that sort, it may
> be that energies tending towards action inconsistent with the intention
> remain untamed and undispersed, however decisively the person believes
> his mind has been made up. The conflict the decision was supposed
> to supersede may continue despite the person's conviction that he
> has resolved it. In that case the decision, no matter how apparently
> conscientious and sincere, is not wholehearted. Whether the person is
> aware of it or not, he has other intentions, intentions incompatible with
> the one the decision established and to which he is also committed.[77]

To the degree that we believe that Augustine truly wanted to reform his life according to Manichaean paradigms, his mixed success in this endeavor reflects tensions in his priorities that undermined the kind of self-consistency that Frankfurt terms "wholeheartedness."

> Here there is a lack of coherence or harmony between the person's higher-order volition or preference concerning which of his desires he wants to be most effective and the first-order desire that actually is the most effective in moving him when he acts. Since the desire that prevails is one on which he would prefer not to act, the outcome of the division within him is that he is unable to do what he really wants to do. His will is not under his control. It is not the will he wants, but one that is imposed on him by a force with which he does not identify and which is in that sense external to him.[78]

Hence what Augustine came to see as an inability to "make progress" in Manichaeism would have been construed within that tradition as the continuing dominance of external coercive forces of non-self. Frankfurt's analysis helps us to understand how this experience forms a typical obstacle to the formation of a coherent self. It has been commonplace to discuss such breakdowns in self-formation as a failure to "internalize" socially given values. Frankfurt sees internalization as a matter of identifying oneself with a generalized higher-order desire to heed particular lower-order desires, such as the desire to be chaste, or abstemious, or honest. The person prefers to see him- or herself as the sort of person who displays such characteristics. A system such as Manichaeism offers an entire template of such virtues, which the individual may see as corresponding more or less closely to the desired set of conducts. In this way, the system reproduces itself in the person who adopts the promoted set of dispositions to act, and who finds motivation in the attraction of such a self-template to adopt those features of the system additional to the person's original desires.[79] If the person remains resistant to some of those additional expectations of conduct, however much consciously or unconsciously, or if he or she finds attraction to features of another system as well, the person falls short of a wholehearted commitment to one system, and non-comforming desires continue to play a role in shaping what the person does.

Augustine's action in joining the Manichaean community indicates a higher-order desire to put himself in order, to make himself a more consistent, efficient person by actively selecting and prioritizing some of his wishes and plans over others. But in this self-organizing process, some parts of his thought and conduct drew his attention, others continued unscrutinized; some of his choices he made deliberately, others by default. Rather than do all this work completely on his own resources, he embraced Manichaeism as an existing system of self-organization. The relics we see of his many interests and evaluations have been fitted first to one and then another self-organizing system. The relative success or failure of each system for him depended on how well he understood it, how much of it he decided he liked, and how much he was motivated to give it his complete allegiance despite reservations about one aspect or another of a program that had been created by others without his particular issues and interests in mind. These same conditions and limitations of success held true as much after his departure from the Manichaean community as they did before. Since he adapted Nicene Christianity to his own evolving point of view in his well documented later life, we can justifiably posit the same basic idiosyncrasy in his earlier, less documented Manichaean period.

The transmitters of such systems as Manichaeism endeavor to reproduce themselves by eliciting conformity in converts such as Augustine through all the means at their disposal, creating a self-motivating and -regulating responsibility and answerability as a faculty within the individual members of the community. They undertake, in Friedrich Nietzsche's terms, the "task of breeding an animal with the right to make promises,"[80] with the capacity to be self-possessed. They seek to make the conduct of subscribers to their system predictable and "calculable" in the absence of external means of physical coercion or even social reinforcement—of which Manichaeism had practically none—indeed, to enable the continuation of the religion's methods and goals even in the face of such coercion and social pressure coming from non-Manichaean sources. "Man himself must first of all have become *calculable, regular, necessary*, even in his own image of himself, if he is to be able to stand security for *his own future*, which is what one who promises does!"[81] For a convert such as Augustine, who came to associate himself with the Manichaean program from a superficial acquaintance, such a full embodiment of the system necessitated the cultivation of a persistence of vision, which Nietzsche characterizes as "an active *desire* not to rid oneself, a desire for the continuance of something desired once, a real *memory of the will*: so that between the original 'I will,' 'I shall do this' and the actual discharge of the will, its *act*, a world of strange new things, circumstances, even acts of will may be interposed without breaking this long chain of will."[82] Through inculcating such a singleness of purpose, Manichaeism worked to reproduce itself in the form of a subject who freely and voluntarily wills and acts according to a paradigm of identity originally exterior and alien to him or her, an individual who in Michel Foucault's words "becomes the principle of his own subjection."[83] It potentially created an interior system of self-regulation to take the place of exterior authorities and observers—a Manichaean soul to inhabit (that is, sustain *inhabitation* toward an embedded *habitus*) Augustine.[84] Without at least some success in this endeavor, there would have been no perseverance in Augustine's initial impulse to be a Manichaean, and certainly not for a decade. As Judith Butler comments in her discussion of Nietzsche's genealogy of the conscience, "If we understand the soul to be the effect of imposing a form upon oneself, where the form is taken to be equivalent to the soul, then there can be no protracted will, no 'I' that stands for itself through time, without this self-imposition of form, this moral laboring on oneself."[85]

Yet since Manichaeism never totally dominated Augustine's set of identifications, no such singleness of purpose emerged in him. As members of a minority sect, the North African Manichaeans had to continue living in a larger society that did not share its values or beliefs. Only the Elect could effectively isolate themselves within an entirely Manichaean environment, relying on the Auditors to supply their livelihood, and engaging in continuous performance of religious obligations. Augustine moved back and forth between worlds, undercutting his absolute mastery of either situation. The "generalized other," as Mead terms it, constituted of his various significant social relationships, lacked the sort of univocality required of a total immersion in a particular value system. Moreover, by circulating through different social environments, he perpetuated self-consciousness of the persona he was performing, always aware that certain parts of his self were being engaged while others were suspended. For this reason, the organized system of his conduct could never become routinized and un-self-conscious, could never really embed itself as a *habitus*.

Despite the intentions and efforts of Manichaean leaders to reproduce the religion's template of selfhood in him, therefore, Augustine lived a disjointed life as someone who thought that he wanted to be a Manichaean. On the one hand, he made all the right gestures of commitment to the faith; on the other hand, he continued to be much the same person he had been before encountering Manichaeism.

We were alike deceivers and deceived in our various pursuits, both publicly through our so-called liberal ideas, and in private through our falsely-called religion. In one arrogant, in the other superstitious, and everywhere empty. On the one hand pursuing worthless popular glory, the applause of the theater and song-contests, ephemeral wreaths won in competition, the trashy spectacles, and intemperate lusts. On the other hand we sought to be purged of such filth by taking food to those called Elect and holy, so that they would turn the food into angels and gods for our liberation in the workshops of their bellies. (*Conf* 4.1.1)

We can see clearly in this characterization of Augustine's predicament the role played by the status of the Manichaean sect as a minority subgroup within the larger society, which over the course of his membership found it necessary to become increasingly clandestine in the face of the opposition of public institutions. Augustine spent much of his day performing as a non-Manichaean in public. That public life had rewards that he found himself unwilling to forego by adopting a more rigorous separation from it and more intensive commitment to being Manichaean. Perhaps because of the long view of moral and spiritual progress entailed in the Manichaean doctrine of reincarnation (a subject to which we will return), along with the readiness of forgiveness contained in Manichaean teachings on the cause of evil, Augustine appears never to have felt compelled by the religion—either in the implications of its teachings or in the means at its disposal to inculcate patterns of conduct—to make a radical break with his secular identity with its worldly engagements.

Colin Starnes has suggested that the imbalance of Augustine's very brief treatment of his relatively moral behavior due to Manichaean influence,[86] compared to his extensive discussion of how he considered his intellect to have been stunted during his Manichaean period,[87] indicates "that the external rites and practices of Manichaeism were far less important for him during these years than the practical consequences . . . of the logic he had adopted."[88] Although Augustine had compositional motives for this imbalance in the way he represented his time among the Manichaeans,[89] I believe that Starnes has correctly identified Augustine's priorities in this period of his life. "Religion" did not occupy the center of his identity. Participation in Manichaean ritual and disciplinary practices was simply the price he paid for association with a group of people with whom he wished to pursue primarily intellectual interests. Our next task, then, is to discern how and to what degree those interests were shaped by a decade of engaging them from within Manichaean discursive structures.

CHAPTER THREE

Indoctrination

GIVEN WHAT WE know of Augustine and his interests, Manichaeism was able to bring "religion"—that is, personal identification with a cultic community—into his life for the first time because of its engagement in the sort of philosophical and metaphysical discourse represented by his other studies. It offered perhaps the least cognitive dissonance with his intellectual pursuits of any cultic option in Africa. With this point of contact with his broader interests, it could serve as the overarching rubric and identity for his intellectual quest. Manichaean teachings nonetheless were integrated with the specific practices reviewed in the previous chapter, for which they served as rationales. By believing certain truths about the nature and condition of the universe and human beings within it, a person would be motivated to perform the prescribed disciplines and rituals that promised to produce desired results within that reality. Based on attitudes he displayed later in life, we may imagine with M. A. Vannier that, for Augustine, "The constraints of the sect constituted a transitory stage in the research of a rational explication of the world."[1] Taking his cue from Cicero, Augustine appears to have seen self-discipline primarily as a purification and training of the mind, which would then gain access to sublime truths unclouded by the body's passions. But Cicero was long dead, and highly organized philosophical schools appeared to be largely things of the past. The Manichaean system of such self-perfection would therefore have to serve in their stead, and in his immediate environment seemed to present a well organized and strongly committed operation.

Augustine therefore submitted himself to some degree to being defined in his speech and actions by his commitment to Manichaeism, without by any means perfectly embodying the values, views, and ideals of Manichaeism as the system was "supposed to be." In getting at the conversion process, we need to rid ourselves of two opposed and equally programmatic models of the human being. The first amounts to regarding people as passive receptacles into which faith is poured unaltered. The second views them as possessing essential selves that put on and take off public identities while remaining unified and intact. Neither model fits what we see in Augustine's or other cases of conversion. It would be presumptuous to assume that Augustine knew what he wanted for his life before he was exposed to various proposed identities and purposes put forward by such cultural entities as the Manichaean sect; just as it would be naive to consider him a *tabula rasa* on which Manichaeism could inscribe itself without resistance.

Augustine's indoctrination into the Manichaean world view had begun even before his initiation as an Auditor of the religion, in the various contacts he had with Manichaeans that first attracted him to the community. The initiation process included the confessional renarrativizing of his own past to provide personal, directly observed proofs that the universe possessed the characteristics Manichaeism attributed to it. Once initiated, Augustine attended Manichaean meetings and services, at which he received further instruction through didactic exposition of the religion's world view, moral exhortation, and hymn singing. His membership in the community brought opportunities for him to learn more about the religion from private conversation and reading. Through these means he acquired a rudimentary understanding of the faith's basic tenets and guidance in the way of life expected of those who wished to achieve the spiritual results the religion promised.[2]

Throughout the history of modern research into Manichaeism, the depth of Augustine's knowledge of it has been actively debated. We can sort this debate into four distinct questions. First, how much access did Augustine have, as a Manichaean layperson, or Auditor, to the full teachings and practices of the Manichaean sect? Despite his references to hearing exposition of Manichaean texts (*CEF* 5.6), as well as reading them for himself (*Conf* 4.8.13), some in the field have taken the position that he would have been denied access to inner teachings reserved for the Elect.[3] Augustine himself initially believed this to be the case, but by the time he left the sect, he had concluded that no such Manichaean esoterica existed. Auditors were taught fundamentally the same system as the Elect. Second, how avidly did he pursue his Manichaean studies and how comprehensive an understanding did he achieve? The amount of detail about Manichaeism Augustine was later able to marshal would seem to point to a fair level of competence in the system.[4] But J. Kevin Coyle has rightly cautioned that Augustine appears to have learned considerably more about Manichaeism *after* he left the sect, as part of his polemical research.[5] Moreover, the breadth of his nonreligious interests raises the question of just how much the minutiae of Manichaeism really mattered to him. Third, in what ways did the later Augustine deliberately distort what he knew of Manichaeism for polemical purposes? On several occasions he attempted to foist onto Manichaeans positions he regarded as logical consequences of their views, without regard for what they said themselves. Fourth, to what degree did Augustine misunderstand the lessons his Manichaean mentors tried to impart? This aspect of the issue has often been overlooked;[6] any discrepancies between his report and primary Manichaean material has usually been assumed to be deliberate distortion. But, as we shall see, Augustine probably misconstrued a couple of central concepts of the faith, a fact that may have contributed to his failure as a Manichaean. At times he seems to have read Manichaean teachings through popular ideas and themes of the broader culture to which they bore a surface resemblance. At other times, he may have been inattentive, received a poor exposition, or quite simply preferred to think of things in an unorthodox way.

In the first flush of enthusiasm, Augustine seems to have considered Manichaeism as a kind of master discourse to which everything else he learned fit as an ancillary discipline; "whatever I picked up by my own wits or by reading, I willingly ascribed to the effects of their teaching" (*DA* 11).[7] This was exactly the result Manichaean leaders hoped for in their open attitude to wider intellectual pursuits. Mani had confidently proposed that all the world's knowledge pointed inexorably to the truth revealed to him, or at least could be construed to do so, just as the water of all the world's rivers led to the sea, where it was assimilated to sea water.[8] From within the Manichaean *episteme*, the adherent's attention and manner of seeing would be directed along particular lines, so that all other knowledge and experience would be tinted by the explanatory matrix the religion offered.

Adherents of religious sects are often encouraged to engage actively in proselytization and disputation with outsiders as a means of reinforcing conversion and commitment, while potentially attracting new converts. Publicly performing a particular discourse involves putting oneself in the role of one's former and current preceptors, articulating teachings aloud, going over them again and again, explaining them, defending them—all in one's own hearing. It is noteworthy, therefore, that Augustine entered into such activity very soon after joining the Manichaean sect (*CEF* 3.3),[9] and recalls his performative repetition of Manichaean rhetorical arguments in a number of places.[10]

> I always used to win more arguments than was good for me. . . . And so, from their preaching, I gained an enthusiasm for religious controversy, and, from this, I daily grew to love the Manichaeans more. So it came about that, to a surprising extent, I came to approve of whatever they said, not because I knew any better, but because I wanted it to be true. (*DA* 11)

He remembered well the ease with which fault could be found with the naive faith and unreflective values of the garden variety African Christian, content with a simplistic notion of human free will,[11] and uncritically reverencing the problematic figures of the Old Testament.[12] For the new convert, winning such debates and winning others to the faith would serve as positive reinforcement of his own commitment, bringing others to see reality as he had accepted it. He would see that he had been right to place his faith in a belief system that proved persuasive to ever more converts. Participating in vocal performances in Manichaean meetings and public disputation, as well as rehearsing the religion's chief tenets and slogans to himself in private study, Augustine cultivated in himself a mind conformed to Manichaean ways of speaking about human experience. The more he spoke Manichaean phrases, and the more he constructed logical defenses of Manichaean positions alongside critiques of alternative views, the more his conscious mind—built upon the foundation of the language he was employing—took on a Manichaean cast. His ability to repeat these meaningful phrases and interpretations of reality years later, long after his departure from the faith, bears witness to his successful uptake of them during his time in the Manichaean community.

In this way, Augustine became a carrier of a particular apprehension and expression of reality, which we might do well to think of outside comfortable categories of "religious" versus other kinds of discourse. Indeed, Rebecca West has proposed that in Manichaeism the aesthetically inclined Augustine discovered "not so much a religion as a work of art," by which she means "the analysis of an experience, an expression of the consciousness of the universe at a particular moment,"[13] which Augustine learned derived from the spiritual insights of "Manichaeus, an apostle of Jesus Christ" (*CEF* 5.6; *Faust*

13.4)—otherwise known simply as Mani or Manes—who had lived in Persia about two hundred years after Christ and about one hundred years before Augustine himself (*Faust* 28.4; cf. *Nupt* 2.29.51). Augustine probably understood Mani within the culturally given category of the sage, the wise person such as Pythagoras to whom Nature unveils her secrets. Mani himself, however, interpreted his spiritual experiences within the tradition of theistic revelation, and specifically as fulfillment of Christ's promise of an advocate, a *paraklētos*, who would provide the definitive interpretation of Christ's teaching.

> The living Paraclete came down to me. He spoke with me. He unveiled to me the hidden mystery, the one that is hidden from the worlds and the generations, the mystery of the depths and the heights. He unveiled to me the mystery of the light and the darkness; the mystery of the calamity of conflict, and the war, and the great [. . .], the battle that the darkness spread about. Afterwards, he unveiled to me also how the light [. . .] the darkness, through their mingling this universe was set up [. . .]. He opened my eyes also to the way that the ships were constructed, to enable the gods of light to be in them, to purify the light from creation. Conversely the dregs and the effluent [. . .] to the abyss. The mystery of the fashioning of Adam, the first man. He also informed me about the mystery of the tree of knowledge, which Adam ate from; his eyes saw. Also the mystery of the apostles who were sent to the world, to enable them to choose the churches. The mystery of the Elect, with their commandments, the mystery of the catechumens their helpers, with their commandments; the mystery of the sinners with their deeds, and the punishing that lies hidden for them. This is how everything that has happened and that will happen was unveiled to me by the Paraclete, [. . .] everything the eye shall see, and the ear hear, and the thought think, and the [. . .]. I have understood by him everything. I have seen the totality through him. (*Keph* 1, 14.32–15.23)

Through such revelations, Mani had been able to discern the truths that lie buried in other forms of religion—including not only the several varieties of Christianity but also Zoroastrianism and Buddhism—as well as in the experiences of everyday life. His followers endeavored to demonstrate those truths to potential converts, and their arguments made on the basis of empirical observation and reason captured Augustine's interest, and his assent.

Theology and Metaphysics

In its cultic and devotional expression, Manichaeism shared a basic mono-theistic outlook with other Christianities; but it added to this a detailed and sophisticated metaphysics that explained exactly how God related to a world in which evil had a significant presence. Fundamental to everything Augustine was expected to understand and to do as a Manichaean was the dualistic nature of the universe. His Manichaean preceptors contended that the inherent polarities in human thinking reflected a dualistic reality (Titus of Bostra 2.13). They pointed to the evident evils of the world, both natural (earthquakes, plagues, famines; Titus of Bostra 2.24) and human-caused (war, misrule, social inequality, suffering of the innocent; Titus of Bostra 2.15, 2.22; cf. Ephrem, *Against Mani*, xciv). Dualism held a prominent place in the religious and philosophical life of late antiquity as an explanation for this apparent conflicted nature of existence, for example in a number of Pythagorean, Middle Platonic, and Gnostic schools of thought.[14] Indeed, the Christian polemicist Epiphanius contended that in its dualism Manichaeism "taught nothing less than the futile speculation of the Greeks" (Epiphanius, *Panarion* 66.14.3).[15] Like other dualists, the Manichaeans considered evil "natural," in the sense of an eternal (*Cont* 9), existent thing, a "race of darkness, which, you say, is produced from a principle of its own, and fights against the kingdom of God" (*Faust* 18.6). Humans experience the realm of darkness and its derivatives as evil because in our essential nature we derive from the realm of light, "the fruit of the divine root" (*Menoch* 172), of the same nature (*homoousios*) as God himself (Hegemonius, *Acta Archelai* 36.8–9; Jerome, *Contra Ioannem Hierosolymitanum* 21).

The principle of darkness or evil was identified (by "our theologian," says the African Manichaean bishop Faustus) with the Greek term *hylē*—literally "matter" (*Faust* 20.3, 21.1, 21.14; cf. Ephrem, *Fifth Discourse*, xcix)—which Augustine would have recognized as playing the same role of evil in many other dualisms of the time, especially among the Platonists and Pythagoreans. God's creation of the world out of an eternally coexisting matter occupied nearly the place of an orthodoxy among Middle Platonists. Ascribing all the negative qualities of the world to this recalcitrant raw material, they like the Manichaeans determined it to be entirely evil (*pantē kakon*) in its nature.[16]

But close scrutiny of the Manichaean system reveals that its dualism cannot be reduced to a simple division of reality into spirit versus matter as those terms are usually defined.[17] Manichaeism got caught in the middle of the rival dualistic paradigms of the age, and was faulted as unscientific by those who contended that matter per se is inert and qualityless. The Manichaeans agreed with Plato[18] and the bulk of the Pythagorean and Middle Platonic traditions in ascribing to matter a disorderly dynamism (*ataktos kinēsis*), lacking any purpose or reason (Titus of Bostra 1.18, Alexander of Lycopolis 2.4.24ff.; Epiphanius, *Panarion* 66.19.1).[19] While the "evil" of matter typically was explained in the philosophical discussions of the time as its disorderliness and recalcitrance to formative forces, in Manichaeism it had a more pronounced ethical and affective character, often defined simply as "that which hurts" (*quod nocet*).[20]

Manichaeism thus belonged to a trend of heightened sensibilities in late antiquity that gravitated around the question *unde malum*? James O'Donnell points out,

> The question itself . . . was less obvious to ancients than to moderns and bespeaks the concerns of late antique philosophy . . . rather than those of earlier times. It is insistence on the goodness of God that makes the question a pressing one—indeed, makes a hypostasized "Evil" emerge from the multitude of "evils" that beleaguer mortal life.[21]

The moral ambivalence of God as a *mysterium tremendum* had come to be modified by explanatory schemes that insulated him from direct responsibility for evil. Two alternative theodicies circulated among monotheists: the rebellion-and-fall theodicy and the absolute dualism theodicy. Since the early Christian traditions were metaphysically uncommitted and ambiguous, both of these theodicies found places in various elaborations of the Christian faith. By the time of the Constantinian peace of the early fourth century, the emergent Christian mainstream of the Roman West was largely committed to an extra-biblical mythology of the rebellion-and-fall kind, fixing the origin of evil within rebellious angels and their malign power over the world. Manichaeism arrived from the Persian East, meanwhile, with a synthesis that preserved the alternative thesis of an eternally coexistent evil that battles God for control of the world.

The dualistic solution to theodicy insists upon God's perfect goodness at the expense of his complete omnipotence. God produces only good things, and bad things exist and happen because there are limits on God's ability to prevent them. Augustine found dualism a compelling explanation for life's existential mysteries, and describes applying the Manichaean dualistic paradigm in his mental analysis of experience. He accepted that God was entirely good, and so in encountering any negative experience, "my soul . . . was unwilling to admit that anything that displeased it was truly yours. This was why it had strayed away into believing in a duality of substances" (*Conf* 7.14.20).

In referring to a duality of substances, Augustine introduces the third essential element of Manichaean metaphysics alongside its dualism and its theism, namely its materialism. Manichaean characterizations of the nature of God, the operation of the cosmos, and the inner working of the human person worked with the vocabulary and models of the dominant materialistic physics of its time. "In Manichaeism, then," N. Joseph Torchia observes, "Augustine merely found a . . . version of a materialistic strain of thought deeply embedded in natural science, philosophy, and popular culture."[22] All things were material substances of varying quantities and densities. The universe did not divide along the lines of spirit and matter, since spirit merely represented a less tangible modality of material reality. Augustine was taught by the Manichaeans to understand God to be "a corporeal mass" (*moles corporum*) and evil "a similar kind of substance, a hideous, deformed mass—either dense, when it is called 'earth,' or thin and subtle like an airy body, which they imagine as a kind of evil mind permeating that 'earth'" (*Conf* 5.10.19–20).[23] From such descriptions, Augustine says he "imagined that there were two antagonistic masses (*adverso sibi duas moles*), both of which were infinite, yet the evil more narrowly and the good more grandly," contiguous, distinct regions of unimaginable extent (*VR* 49.96; *MM* 9.14).[24] Augustine himself attests to his successful indoctrination into this account of reality when, in the *Confessions*, he repeatedly mentions being unable to think of God and evil in any other terms, even for some time after he had become disenchanted with Manichaeism for other reasons. It was only when he was exposed to a new discourse that he could supplant Manichaean ways of thinking in his own mind.

The Origins of the World

The Manichaeans conveyed their explanatory account of the origin of this unfortunate conjunction of two diametrically opposed realities within the terms of a mythological narrative. In certain respects, this resort to mythology put them out of step with the narrative trends of the age, and Gedaliahu and Sarah Stroumsa have suggested that, "Manichaeism represented the last significant outburst of mythological thought in the world of antiquity."[25] The generation of new myths by Gnostics and Manichaeans was criticized from an elite intellectual standpoint for which traditional myths could be interpreted as poetic expressions suitable to an earlier age. Later, in his anti-Manichaean polemics, Augustine tried to reciprocate for Manichaean criticism of the stories of the Old Testament by holding up some of the more baroque and dramatic imagery of Manichaean myth for ridicule. Yet mythological narrative fit quite well with popular modes of cultic discourse. The Manichaean tradition offered lavish descriptions of the two realms of existence in terms comparable to other Christian accounts of the wonders of heaven, the dreads of hell, and combat between their respective denizens.[26] With the close similarity of Manichaean mythic discourse to popular Christian ideas, Augustine's tactic would have appealed to only a small intellectual elite.

The Manichaean account of the origin, nature, and resolution of the problematic, mixed nature of the cosmos constituted a comprehensive mythic history of the universe, divided into three periods (*Faust* 13.6). In its overall pattern, the Manichaean *Heilsgeschichte* corresponded closely to a pattern widely shared among pagans and Christians: fall, fallen state, redemption. The Manichaean myth of a primordial attack of evil upon good and the consequent "fall" (more accurately, leap) of some of the inhabitants of heaven simply served the same role as the alternative Christian myth of the fall of angels and the temptation of Adam and Eve, or the Platonic myth (going back to Orphic and Empedoclean antecedents) of the fall of souls into material existence as a consequence of some vaguely defined error or sin.[27] In each of these communities, such narratives provided an explanatory backstory to the current unsatisfactory conditions of human existence.

Yet its dualistic premises gave the Manichaean backstory a distinctive set of emphases. Rather than a rebellion within God's own angelic ranks or a self-motivated descent into lower orders of being in the popular nondualist tales, the primordial catastrophe in the Manichaean account involved an assault on the divine realm of light by the wholly alien forces of evil.[28] On the same dualistic terms, God's good nature precluded meeting force with force, since good cannot share that or any other attribute characteristic of evil.[29] As with Christ's historical nonviolent response to the violence of his enemies, God's primordial response to the aggression of evil took the form of self-sacrifice, a preemptive surrender of part of his own substance that strategically deflected the incursion of evil and hobbled evil's power by diluting it with good.[30] Augustine had heard that "God did not seek to escape evil or to spare himself from harm, but that, on account of his natural goodness, he wished to bring order to the perverse and restless nature" of darkness (*MM* 12.25),[31] and, "having no other resource and finding no other means of resisting the enemy, under dire necessity, sent the good soul hither, a particle of his substance" (*VR* 9.16), "some portion or limb" (*quaedam portio et membrum*) of God, or an "offspring of his very substance" (*proles de ipsa substantia*; *Conf* 7.2.3). Consequently, "a part of God was mixed with the substance of evil in order to restrain it and to suppress furious outbreaks—these are your own words" (*MM* 15.36).[32] On this point also, Manichaeism took a position closely parallel to Middle Platonic dualistic accounts, in this case of an infusion of divine *nous* bringing some limited order to the formerly evil orderlessness of matter.[33]

Augustine reports doubts raised in his intellectual circles about the basic combat scenario of the Manichaean primordial myth. His friend Nebridius had first posed it, as Augustine relates the story to God in the *Confessions*.

> Those so-called powers of darkness, whom they always postulate as a horde deployed in opposition to you: what would they have done to you if you had refused to fight? If the reply is that they could have inflicted some injury on you, it would imply that you are subject to violation and therefore destructible. If, on the other hand, it is denied that they had power to injure you, there would have been no point in fighting. Yet the fighting is alleged to have been so intense that some portion of yourself . . . became mixed with hostile powers and with the natures of beings not created by you, and was by them so far corrupted and altered that its beatitude was changed to misery, and it could be rescued and purified only with help. (*Conf* 7.2.3)

That the very logic of the myth could be questioned in this way indicates that Augustine's associates were no circle of pious devotees. They retained grave reservations about some of the teachings of the religious community to which they belonged for a decade, and to that degree they undermined the Manichaean version of reality as their reality. Consequently, they inhabited an incomplete, fragmented cosmos.

Although Augustine later delighted in referring to this mythic event as a "defeat" of good by evil, Manichaeans actually understood it to be an effective act of strategy by which evil becomes permanently weakened in its ability to oppose the good (*Fort* 22). The sacrificed portion emanated by God "has been set out as bait, of its own free will, by the power on high, like a kid thrown into a pit to catch a beast of prey, which is excited and leaps down to get the kid, with the result that the beast itself is caught" (Epiphanius, *Panarion* 66.44.3), by God's providence (Alexander of Lycopolis 3.5.25–6.1).[34] "In the Manichaean legends, their God might be said to have been poison to the race of darkness; for he so injured their bodies, that from being strong, they became utterly feeble" (*Faust* 21.13). By permitting evil to assimilate a portion of the good, God permanently vitiates its independent will and power, leading inexorably to its final defeat and immobilization (Ephrem, *Fifth Discourse*, cxi).

The portion of himself that God voluntarily yields up to combat with evil constitutes the root of all life in the world, and of the conscious souls in which this life-force finds its fullest expression (Alexander of Lycopolis 3.5.21ff.).[35] This divine essence permeates the world (Titus of Bostra 2.60), and everything in it (*Faust* 3.6, cf. 20.11; 22.72).[36] The idea that the human soul, at least, has a divine origin was a commonplace of Greco-Roman thought. Many philosophical schools (among them Stoic, Pythagorean, and Platonic) held that a common life-force united all living beings, finding ever higher modes of expression culminating in the human conscious mind. Manichaeism shared with several of these theories the notion of an original reservoir of soul-substance, something akin to a world soul, from which all individual souls derive (Nemesius 2.18). In mythic terms, the Manichaeans described this original soul as "some wonderful First Man, who came down from the race of light to war with the race of darkness, armed with his waters against the waters of the enemy, and with his fire against their fire, and with his winds against their winds . . . armed against smoke with air, and against darkness with light" (*Faust* 2.3; cf. 24.2; *VR* 9). These "limbs, or clothing, or weapons" of the First Man were "mixed up with the race of darkness" and "became subject to confinement and pollution" (*Faust* 11.3; cf. 13.8, 20.17; *AC* 4).[37] Collectively, these five divine elements constitute the "vulnerable Jesus" (*Jesus patibilis*) crucified throughout the world (*Conf* 9.13.35; *Faust* 20.2), the "Son of Man" (i.e., collective child of the First Man) mentioned self-referentially by Christ (*Faust* 2.4). In other words, the Manichaeans transferred to a primordial event the same salvational sacrifice of God's "son" posited in mainstream Christian belief.

Manichaeism thus at one and the same time affirmed the divine nature of the human soul, and explained its far-from-divine condition in this world. Its "mixture" with evil takes its toll, resulting in suffering, moral erosion, and

loss of identity (Alexander of Lycopolis 3.6.3, 7.12.1f.). Similar ideas are entailed in all "fall" scenarios in the philosophical and religious traditions of
the age, some of which, like Manichaeism, stressed that the soul served some
necessary good task in its descent from its original divine quiescence. The
Manichaeans taught that everything has its place in the cosmos based on the
amount of goodness and light it contains (*Faust* 6.8; cf. Nemesius 2.18), which
is manifest in ways perceptible to human senses.[38] The divine material passes
from form to form in a process referred to as "transfusion" (*metaggismos*).[39]
"You consider it a crime to kill animals, because you think that the souls of
men pass into them, which is an idea found in the writings of some Gentile
philosophers . . . ; they dreaded slaughtering a relative in the animal, but you
dread the slaughter of your God, for you hold even the souls of animals to be
his limbs" (*Faust* 20.20; cf. Titus of Bostra 4.19).

While some dualistic systems considered the world itself to be the creation
and abode of evil, Manichaeans, like most Christians, followed the general
popular metaphysics of their day in attributing the world's form and order to
the creative act of a good God working with partially resistant material.[40] The
world forms an essential part of the plan of salvation in Manichaeism (*ME*
10.16). God extends his kingdom "beyond its old limits into the region of the
conquered foe," and constructs "new worlds in the region of darkness" (*Faust*
10.3), "making new worlds in a region belonging to another, to be the scene
of your imaginary triumph after your imaginary conquest" (*Faust* 15.7). Continuing in its mythic vein, the Manichaean tradition offered details of God's
world-construction closely akin to ancient Near Eastern mythic antecedents.
These made easy targets for ridicule from the vantage point of a Judaeo-
Christian cosmogony largely shorn of dramatic elements and *dramatis
personae*.[41] The Manichaeans taught that God emanated a series of unfolding
beings who not only met evil in the primordial combat, but took on key roles
in the construction and maintenance of the cosmos.[42] Ignoring the emanation-
ist theory behind these divine forms that integrated them into a fundamentally monotheistic outlook,[43] the later Augustine never misses an opportunity
to parade this appearance of polytheism in Manichaeism, or to find fault with
some of the details of the various episodes of conflict between these beings
and the forces of evil.[44] Nonetheless, they play essentially the role occupied by
angels in other Christian traditions, in various functions of combat with evil,
world construction, and world maintenance; various models for relating them
to the basic Trinitarian structure affirmed by Mani and his successors were in

circulation. These beings seem to have had little role in Manichaean worship beyond hymnic recitations of the events of primordial salvation history, however, and Augustine was not the only western observer to encounter a form of Manichaeism in which the more elaborate mythological elements did not receive nearly the attention they are given in most modern scholarship.[45]

In fact, a debate flared up in the late 1970s and early 1980s between François Decret and Michel Tardieu over the extent to which African Manichaeism represented a distinctively demythologized and "Christianized" form of the faith, in which Tardieu's reaction to such an idea led him into the historical difficulty of arguing for a more or less monolithic and static Manichaeism.[46] The question in its more nuanced form hinges in large part on whether the mythological details known from primary Manichaean sources from both Asia and Egypt were kept as living esoterica reserved for the Elect, or had become neglected fossils carried forward in the literature without significant application by either rank of believer.[47] In a comparison of Augustine's report of Manichaean myth with primary Manichaean sources from Egypt, John Maher has noted Augustine's apparent ignorance of several key members of the full Manichaean mythological pantheon, which suggests either a lack of concern in African Manichaeism with this elaborate theology or Augustine's own indifference to it as a Manichaean.[48] Augustine says explicitly that the Manichaeans he knew did not depict the elaborate pantheon of divine agents in art, nor offer any explanation of them (*Faust* 20.9).[49] All the graphic details of their appearance and actions Augustine relates apparently come from hymns, and did not form the subject of doctrinal exposition for Auditors such as Augustine.

Further details of the Manichaean myth were certainly not what Augustine was waiting for as the "mysteries" of the religion; on the contrary, having been exposed to this material as an Auditor, he expected that the Elect possessed symbolic, non-mythological interpretations of it, into which he hoped to be initiated. Surely, he thought, such dramatic accounts were symbolic, and the Elect held inner mysteries of interpretation that would pull away the veil of myth to reveal a rationalist account more "philosophical" than "religious" (*Conf* 5.3.3; cf. *BV* 1.4–5; *UC* 8.20).[50] Conditioned by the late antique interpretation of myth that pervaded his education and private reading, he considered religious discourse to be a set of parables or allegories into which the bare truth was rendered for mass consumption. After all, as the "theologian" of the Manichaean sect (*Faust* 20.3), Mani would be regarded first and foremost as a poet, not a philosopher; and even philosophers employed allegory. As an avid reader of things Pythagorean, Augustine would have found this cultural model of poetic exoteric truth and philosophical esoteric truth reinforced by the well known report about Pythagoras's methods of instruction, here in the version provided by Porphyry:

> The things he discussed with those who came to him he taught either explicitly or by parable, for he used two forms of teaching. And of those who came, some were called learners, others hearers. The learners were those who mastered the more detailed account of the science, worked out accurately; the hearers were those who heard only the summarized instructions from his works, without any more accurate explanation. (Porphyry, *Vita Pyth*. 36–37)[51]

Augustine passed a decade as a Manichaean awaiting such an exegesis, but it never came. His later decrial of their mythic literalism as a violation of cultural norms smacks of a rude awakening. When he reports an emphatic insistence among the Manichaeans he knew that Mani be taken literally, Augustine no doubt gives us the response to his own efforts to press the question when he belonged to their company.[52]

The upshot of the Manichaean account offered a cosmos "hard-wired" to operate in a liberating process, albeit constrained by the counteractive forces of evil (*MM* 15.36). The principle of dualism dictates that good cannot eradicate evil, but can only construct an existence that mitigates as much as possible the power of evil (*Conf* 13.30.45). The two sides of the battle are in theory evenly matched, but the providential strategy enacted by God from the very beginning gives good the decisive advantage. Thus, while giving evil its due in human experience, Manichaeism promoted a fundamentally optimistic vision of a universe filled with divine assistance and tending toward ultimate salvation for all living beings.

Human Nature and Salvation

In the teachings of the Manichaeans, humans come into existence within this world of conflict in a manner that makes them the focus of the efforts of both sides toward mastery. For the Manichaeans, humans were part of the animal kingdom, "creeping, walking, swimming, flying, each in its own kind," having use of the senses, and reproducing. "Indeed, the Manichaeans tell us of animals that could speak, and their speeches were heard and understood and approved of by all creatures, whether creeping things, or quadrupeds, or birds, or fish" (*Faust* 21.10). According to Manichaean myth, two bipedal animals, acting under the direction of evil, consumed creatures of all sorts, mated, and produced the first humans, bearing the familiar names of Adam and Eve.[53] Consequently, the human construct has a predisposition toward the evil it was designed to serve. "You say that all your limbs and your whole body were formed by the evil principle which you call *hylē*, and that part of this formative mind dwells in the body along with part of your God" (*Faust* 20.15).[54]

Humans contain higher concentrations of divine soul than other animals, but this goodness must coexist with even higher concentrations of evil (DA 1.1).[55] This mixture with "flesh" automatically defiles the good nature (*Conf* 5.10.20), corrupting it by constant contact with the dark side.[56] The divine substance retains its essential goodness, but is held hostage in a kind of delirium or slumber (*Conf* 7.2.3). Religion is the means by which this servitude is broken among humans, part of a larger work of salvation being wrought on the whole cosmos by emanations of God. Humans have the unique capacity for repentance, learning, and moral reform (*MM* 19.73), rooted in a responsive—and so at least in some degree free—will.[57]

The exposition of his own past conduct in dualistic terms at his initial confession stuck with Augustine as a powerful proof of the validity of Manichaean insight into the nature of evil, and he came to examine events around him from within the same Manichaean mental frame. To take one example, it often has been suggested that, when Augustine imagines his behavior as an infant in the *Confessions*, he is drawing in large part upon his observations of his own son Adeodatus, the only child with whom Augustine is likely to have had any extensive contact. Not previously remarked upon, however, is the degree to which these observations fit a Manichaean perspective on human nature, although penned more than a decade after he had abandoned that faith.[58] The passage seems to be constructed around the Manichaean ethical paradigm of the "Three Seals." He describes an infant *desiring* things that will harm him (seal of the breast), *crying out* for them (seal of the mouth), and *lashing out* violently at those who fail to respond to the desire (seal of the hand). Just these three actions, and no more, constitute Augustine's archetypal description of the inherent sinfulness of the human infant (*Conf* 1.7.11). He identifies emotions of desire, jealousy, and anger as signs of inherent iniquity, and asks God, if the newborn already bears such marks of sinfulness, where and when was one ever innocent (*Conf* 1.7.12). The Manichaean answer since abandoned, the author of the *Confessions* must admit that he does not know.[59] But as a Manichaean, he would have taken the behavior of his infant son as confirmation of evil inclinations rooted within all humanity, and requiring Manichaean disciplines to quell them.

The dualistic background to the human condition in the world—the doctrine of "mixture"—entails the view that human beings are not their own masters, that they contend relentlessly with contrary, disruptive forces in their personalities, and that they therefore cannot by their own resources of will achieve salvation. In part this condition is due to the variability of the constituents making up each human person, as light and darkness constantly recycle within the world. As Ephrem Syrus explains, "They say that there are bodies which are more evil than other bodies, and corporeal frames that are fouler than others, . . . such souls as chance upon perturbed bodies are more perturbed than others who happen to come to gentle bodies" (Ephrem, *Fifth Discourse*, cxviii). This was the fatalistic model of human experience that Manichaean leaders sought to cultivate within every Manichaean's self-reflection. According to this model, humans think and do evil things when the quantity of evil within them literally outweighs the good,[60] like one sumo wrestler pushing the other out of the circle of the human will. "Sin" refers to events wherein the good soul is compelled to participate in an evil act against its will (Titus of Bostra 1.29). The divine soul struggles to maintain its integrity in the face of evil's efforts to divide and conquer it. But it is doubly fragmented: first, the "soul" contained in each living thing is only a broken-off piece of the collective soul that entered into mixture with evil; and second, even this piece of "soul" has fractured into fragments that lack the coherence to control and direct the body or person in which they dwell. Even though the human being possesses more "soul" than any other living creature, it is congenitally fractured and morally incompetent. The forces of evil dominate the person, body and soul, with the particles of soul sunk in isolated torpor.[61]

This set of ideas bears a surface resemblance to common fatalistic notions widespread in the late antique world, in which the self is given voice as experiencing life as a helpless passenger, tossed and dragged about by forces beyond human control.[62] If Augustine failed to scratch beneath the surface, he might have reduced the more radical Manichaean teaching on the lack of coherent selfhood to this more familiar theme in the literature of his larger culture. It certainly sounds as if he did just that, based upon his conflation of Manichaeism with this more general fatalism in his earliest post-Manichaean writings. As a result, he appears to have formed a serious misunderstanding of the Manichaean view of personal responsibility. He tells us that, as a Manichaean,

> It seemed to me that it is not we who sin but some other nature (*nescio quam aliam . . . naturam*) within us that sins. My pride was gratified at being exculpated by this theory. When I had done something wrong it was pleasant to not confess that I had done it . . . . I liked to excuse myself and blame this unknown other thing that was within me but was not me (*nescio quid aliud quod mecum esset et ego non essem*). (*Conf* 5.10.18)[63]

Augustine's commitment to astrological fatalism, which taught that "the cause of sin is determined by the heavens and we cannot escape it," and that "man is guiltless" (*Conf* 4.3.4), accentuated fatalistic themes present in Manichaeism, producing an idiosyncratic moral theory that was ill suited to serve as a rationale for Manichaean confessional practice, undermining the latter's self-forming function.[64]

Contrary to Augustine's individually distorted perceptions, the Manichaean tradition has left a sizable body of texts that dwell at great length on the wrongdoing of the individual, the need for constant self-scrutiny and confession, the baring of the inner self to the healing of the physician Mani.[65] Although the soul remains in essence pure and good, its failure to resist the promptings of the evil nature with which it is mixed in the human body was considered moral failing by the Manichaeans.[66] The adherent had to take responsibility for that weakness of will, for that temporary unconsciousness of divine identity, in contrite acts of confession to the Elect. Augustine participated in the Manichaean practices of weekly confession, and annual absolution for confessed sins—remembered or forgotten—of the past year, without absorbing the sense of personal responsibility for sin that they were intended to entail. Perhaps Manichaeism absolved sins too easily for the moral point to get across to the average layperson. Perhaps the doctrine on sin had been reconstrued in its transmission to the North African scene in a way that made it more prone to the sort of reading Augustine gave it. Or perhaps the strength of Augustine's own ego filtered the teaching to his own level of comfort.[67] He may have seen the cyclic activity of confession as a demonstration of a lack of *progress*. When did the Manichaean practitioner advance to a sinless state? He held the opinion that "When you hear a man confessing, you know that he is not yet free" (*EnPs* 101(2).3). So why did the Elect, and those with long experience as Manichaeans, still confess as often and profusely as Augustine and the other novices? Why did Manichaeism not seem to *work* in its undertaking of completely reforming the self?

Moral and spiritual progress for a Manichaean entailed an immediate and clear mental differentiation of the self from invasive evils. One looked upon sin just as one recognized a fever, as not part of oneself, but indicative of something intruding into the body's condition. As one progressed, it became possible to recognize eruptions of evil more rapidly, and check their manifestation in overt action. One endeavored to open up an increasing space between impulse and action within which one could exercise the good will to turn evil back. Confession continued as a necessary reinforcement of this self-scrutiny. That an evil impulse could persist within oneself for more than a split second indicated that there was still room for improvement. For an Augustine who had not yet developed any significant appreciation of the complexity of the human interior, it all seemed a bit histrionic. With the buttoned-down mind expressed in his early writings, Augustine apparently could see only a simple either/or: either we have nothing to do with the sins committed by the actions of our bodies, or we have everything to do with them. As a Manichaean, he concluded that if the prompting to sin originates beyond the limits of the self, then the self is entirely unfree and innocent. He would just as readily accept the teaching of Ambrose, that since the prompting to sin originates within the self, the self is entirely free and guilty. Only as he continued his spiritual odyssey would he realize that neither answer fully accounted for the experience of sinning, and in seeking to articulate a more sophisticated account he would draw heavily on what he had since learned was the more nuanced view actually held among the Manichaeans.

Salvation in the Manichaean system, therefore, required an initial unilateral intervention by the transcendent forces of light—in short, grace. From Manichaeans in Syria, Ephrem heard that "The pollution of error is (too) great for them, unless sweet floods have come from their home a second time, and lessened the bitterness in which they were dwelling" (Ephrem, *Fifth Discourse*, cxviii), a "power whose nature cannot be overcome by the floods of evil" (Ephrem, *Fifth Discourse*, cii).[68] Augustine learned the same thing from

African Manichaeans, that the human soul had become "mixed with opposing powers" and "corrupted and altered to such an extent that its bliss was turned to misery and it could be rescued and purified only with help." Consequently, the soul had been "enslaved, defiled, and corrupted, and in need of aid from [God's] Word, which must necessarily be free and pure of contamination and corruption if it is to help" (*Conf* 7.2.3).[69] It is at this point of God's act of grace in redeeming humanity from its enslavement to evil that the Manichaeans speak of Jesus Christ, both as a particular historical prophet sent to awaken and save, and as the transcendent root of all such awakening interventions in human history.

> The divine nature is dead and Christ resuscitates it. It is sick and he heals it. It is forgetful and he brings it to remembrance. It is foolish and he teaches it. It is disturbed and he makes it whole again. It is conquered and captive and he sets it free. It is in poverty and need, and he aids it. It has lost feeling and he quickens it. It is blinded and he illumines it. It is in pain and he restores it. It is iniquitous and by his precepts he corrects it. It is dishonored and he cleanses it. It is at war and he promises it peace. It is unbridled and he imposes the restraint of law. It is deformed and he reforms it. It is perverse and he puts it right. (*NB* 41)

This statement, probably a direct quotation by Augustine of a Manichaean source, speaks of Christ in the role of revealer, awakener, and enlightener, just as he was known to the Manichaeans encountered by Alexander of Lycopolis in Egypt several generations earlier:

> Christ is an intellect (*nous*). When at some time he arrived from the place above, he liberated the greatest part of the above mentioned power, so that it could get on its way towards God. And finally, it was through his crucifixion that Christ provided us with the knowledge that the divine power too is fitted into, or rather crucified in, matter in a similar way. (Alexander of Lycopolis 4.7.14ff.)

Since Christ was a purely spiritual divine being,[70] and so could not be crucified in actuality,[71] his crucifixion served a didactic purpose as a dramatization of the soul's predicament (Alexander of Lycopolis 24.35.21–23). Augustine reports that he was given "as a reason for Christ's appearing to die, that he underwent in appearance all the experiences of humanity" (*Faust* 26.8). The historical Christ, then, is an epiphany of the "vulnerable Jesus" pervading all nature and ourselves (*Faust* 32.7), "crucified throughout the whole visible universe" (*EnPs* 140.12).[72]

Once awakened to its true identity and condition, by the transcendent Christ or one of his "apostles," the fragmented soul pulls together, undergoing a birth into selfhood, which the Manichaeans saw reflected in Paul's teachings on the New Man replacing the Old Man, transcending mundane divisions of gender, race, and class. "Man, then, is made by God not when from one he is divided into many, but when from many he becomes one," Augustine's Manichaean mentor Faustus declaims. "The division is in the first birth, or that of the body; union comes by the second, which is immaterial and divine" (*Faust* 24.1). Replacing the given Old Man with the spiritually attuned New Man constituted the Manichaean program of self-formation. Paul, as an apostle of Christ, describes himself repeatedly as the agent or assistant of this second birth (Gal 4:19; 1 Cor 4:15). Indeed, all of the "apostles"—the historical prophets and messengers of God—as well as the missionary Elect serve as instruments by which the divine call reaches human beings and transforms them.[73]

Starting with an epiphany of Christ himself—as the encapsulation of divine wisdom—to Adam,[74] God's revelatory agency operates on the souls throughout their gradual progress from one lifetime to the next. One after another, prophets have come to various parts of the world to call humans to awareness and to the path of liberation (*MM* 17; *Faust* 20.9).[75] These prophets included Zarathustra and the Buddha, as well as Jesus and Mani, and the Manichaeans were open to discovering other forebears as they explored the religious heritage of the world.[76] This distinctive universalism of the Manichaean message gave it the appearance of a liberal spiritual path open to all the wisdom of the world.

The effective call of God transmitted by the historical succession of prophets is personified as the "mind (*nous*) of light."

> [The Mind of] Light comes and finds the soul . . . . He loosens the
> mind [of the soul and releases] it from bone. He releases the thought
> [of the soul] from sinew . . . . He releases the insight of the soul from
> vein . . . . [He] loosens the counsel of the soul, and releases it from
> flesh . . . . He releases the consideration of the soul from skin . . . . This
> is how he shall release the limbs of the soul and make them free form

the five limbs of sin. . . . He shall set right the limbs of the soul,
form and purify them, and construct a New Man of them, a child of
righteousness. (*Keph* 38, 96.8–27)

Augustine would have been taught to understand his attraction to Manichaeism in terms of the intervention of the Mind of Light in his own thinking
process. From this initial step, Augustine could expect success in cultivating
certain tell-tale virtues similarly bestowed by the enabling gifts of the Mind
of Light.

[And] when [he] fashions and constructs and purifies the New Man,
then he brings forth five great living limbs out from the five great limbs.
And he places them in the limbs of the new man. He places his mind,
which is love, in the mind of the new man. Also the thought, which is
faith, he places [in] the thought [of the] new [man] whom he purifies.
His insight, which [is perfection, he places] in the insight of the new
man. His counsel, which [is] patience, he places in his counsel. Also
wisdom, which is his consideration, in the consideration of the new
man. (*Keph* 38, 96.27–97.4)[77]

The five liberated factors of soul, supported by the five "graces" bestowed
by the Mind of Light, together with the divine call and the answer by which
the individual soul indicates its awakening into consciousness, constitute the
"twelve limbs" of the formed and activated soul that is able for the first time
to direct the conduct of the human person toward liberational rather than
self-enslaving goals.

Even so, the elected person is not "at peace," as the later Augustine would
say. The still present forces of evil continue to "rebel" and attempt to regain
control over human thinking and behavior. The activated sense of identity
within the soul resists such eruptions of evil through the exercise of self-
discipline (*enkrateia*; *Keph* 98, 249, 16–21), assisted by the continuing presence of the Mind of Light and its gifts of virtue. Yet one remains vulnerable
to evil influences from within and without.[78] Evil's recurrent assaults can take
a person by surprise, and take advantage of lapses in diligence, leading to un-
controlled outbursts of sinful conduct. The Manichaeans regarded only such
lapses into evil conduct as personal "sin," properly speaking, since it is only
after the awakening and reunification of the fragmented soul that a person

becomes a responsible agent. The Manichaeans indoctrinated Augustine into a life's work of learning to discern one's true self from another voice within masquerading as one's soul, but in reality something totally alien to it (*Conf* 8.10.22–24). Thus the true, personal soul is an emergent, an amalgamation of divine elements that comes into coherence and self-consciousness only with Manichaean instruction and conditioning. Manichaeism thus inculcated in adherents such as Augustine a disciplined self-scrutiny, constantly assessing the raw material of impulses of thought and action against provided models of perfection, aiming at a perfect conformity of self to Manichaean paradigms. Such a perfectly conformed self was, the religion taught, the only vehicle for personal liberation out of the struggle of mixed existence.

This Manichaean teaching on relative human powerlessness in the face of evil and the necessity of divine grace to achieve liberation may have been seen by Augustine against the background of widespread fatalism prevalent in late antiquity, and effectively subsumed within it for him. The passivity with which he waited for something to happen to draw him out of his half-committed condition and enable him to "make progress" into the ranks of the Elect—or at least more evident spiritual progress—suggests that he heard this part of Manichaean teaching in such terms. To the degree that he gave it any serious attention, the Manichaean system of spiritual development fit in well enough with the general tenor of the late antique "care of the self" that it could be construed as a mere variation on the theme.

But Augustine would also have heard that, until one attains a state of stable personhood exemplified in the virtuous conduct of the Manichaean Elect, he or she is doomed to an ongoing cycle of reconfigured identity in one life after another. Rejecting popular belief in ghosts or lingering spirits of the dead,[79] as well as the idea of a hoped-for physical resurrection of the body, the Manichaeans professed an idea akin to metempsychosis.[80] Even Manichaean Auditors such as Augustine were not promised salvation at the end of their current life. If they made sufficient spiritual progress, they might hope to be reborn as people capable of accepting the full discipline of the life of the Elect (*Faust* 5.10). Otherwise, their still partially fragmented soul would fall apart and be distributed to multiple new embodiments, awaiting further divine aid in the cosmic struggle (Nemesius 2.18). Only the perfected selfhood of the Elect is capable of liberation.[81]

In the face of this denial of post-mortem immortality for the ordinary Manichaean believer, the death of a loved one provided a crucial moment for testing and reaffirming faith for Augustine. The death of his close friend and fellow Manichaean and its aftermath, retold in the *Confessions*, book 4, conveys a portrait of how Augustine's religious commitments both succeeded and failed in meeting this challenge (*Conf* 4.4.7–12.19). The length of his discussion of this event, comparable to that devoted to the Pear Incident, indicates once again a problem he finds the need to talk through at length.[82] For the problem lay in the fact that death poses a prime injustice in Manichaean thought, a purposeless violence perpetrated against an innocent being by the tragic mixture in this world of the living soul with elements of death that seek to overpower it. Such thoughts about death may stir anger and resentment and even a sense of mission in the one who entertains them, redoubling commitment to the great war of life against death; but they are not consoling thoughts. For Manichaeism, in the words of F. C. Burkitt, "there is no hope for a Man as such, for he is essentially a fortuitous conglomeration. The hope is that his Light-particles—roughly speaking very much what we mean by his 'better self'—may escape at death from the dark prison-house of the body."[83]

Accordingly, Augustine notes that, at the time of his friend's death, he "neither hoped that he would come back to life nor made my tears a plea that he should; I simply mourned and wept" (*Conf* 4.5.10). In other words, he adhered to the Manichaean rejection of a physical resurrection as the aimed-for future of the soul; rather, ascent of the soul now liberated from body was to be hoped for. But for the Auditor, there could be no immediate ascent. Instead, the soul was dissolved and "transfused" into disparate states and embodiments, there to continue its odyssey through the cosmos. The individual soul did not cohere, and there was no single state to be imagined for it. Thus, the dead person was literally gone, and there could be no fantasy of ever meeting him again. This understanding of death seems to be reflected in the devastating completeness of separation Augustine expresses in this part of his story. Manichaeism did not offer the immortality of the *individual* soul of all believers which was such a hallmark of the appeal of mainstream Christianity.[84] As he tells it in the *Confessions*, it was in his deep despair at the finality of his loss that Augustine began to recognize that he had not fully conformed his thinking to Manichaean views, and in that moment gained an inkling of the complexity of his own soul.[85]

> I had become a great enigma to myself, and I questioned my soul, demanding why it was sorrowful and why it so disquieted me, but it had no answer. If I bade it, "Trust in God," it rightly disobeyed me, for the

man it had held so dear and lost was more real and more lovable than the fantasy in which it was bidden to trust. (*Conf* 4.4.9)[86]

This internal dialogue captures the conflict of dispositions in a person as the dominant self-organization confronts experiences that appeal to supposedly suppressed or eliminated contrary desires, in this case for the personal immortality of Augustine's friend. He should not grieve, according to Manichaean understandings of the ephemeral character of the individual soul, and the religion's optimism about the destiny of all that constituted that soul. Yet he discovered that his grief was somehow more truly himself than the ideas meant to empower the domination and dispersal of such passions. Therefore this grief "rightly" disobeyed his will, from the hindsight of his later rejection of Manichaean teachings. The disobedient part of his soul that experienced grief was no less a part of him than his conscious will, contrary to Manichaean identification of such disobedient elements as alien to the self. While his ultimate judgment on this experience still lay in the future, he evidently could not bring himself at the time to consider this emotion an intrusion into his psychic life from an evil other. The emotional experience consequently called into question the entire Manichaean account of human nature. "Can it be that although you are everywhere present you have flung our wretchedness far away from you, abiding unmoved in yourself while we are tossed to and fro amid human trials? Surely not" (*Conf* 4.5.10). Here Augustine assays and rejects the idea that God has purposely sent souls into the turmoil of life and death, while he abides obscured and otiose in the realm of light, a characterization of the Manichaean primordial scenario he repeats in a number of places. While it fits his later vantage point as a critic of Manichaeism, it reflects as well the sort of resentment toward God typically expressed in the depth of personal loss.[87]

Yet Augustine successfully passed this challenge to his Manichaean identity. Through his grief he retained his Manichaean faith, and for nearly another decade. The seed of that continued commitment to Manichaeism is to be found in this very passage, where Augustine reports from his own thoughts a reaffirmation of the religion's conception of death. Augustine's thoughts of suicide were repelled by a contrary force.

Some kind of emotion opposed to this had sprung up in me, so that although my weariness with living was intense, so too was my fear of dying. I believe that the more I loved him, the more I hated death, which had taken him from me; I hated it as a hideous enemy, and feared it, and pictured it as ready to devour all human beings, since it had been able to make away with him. Yes, this was my state of mind: I remember it. (*Conf* 4.6.11)

So Augustine, in a typically Manichaean opposition of an *enthumēsis* of life battling against an *enthumēsis* of death within him,[88] drew upon what Manichaeism had to offer as a concept-based emotional repertoire with which to respond to death: a renewed antagonism to the alien nature of death, and a rekindled fervor to fight the good fight to defeat it utterly, not only for one's own sake, but for all living beings. "I felt that my soul and his had been but one soul in two bodies" (*Conf* 4.6.11)—for sure a familiar Roman expression for close friendship or love,[89] but at the same time an affirmation from a classically trained rhetorician of Manichaean notions of the unity of all souls which provides the foundation for sympathy for others in the struggle with death. The passage, which Augustine avers to be a vivid recollection of the actual stages of his thinking, shows Manichaean conditioning "kicking in" and effecting a recovery from a momentary disintegration of meaning. And so, "the fable did not die for me when any of my friends died" (*Conf* 4.8.13).

This rallying of himself for the cause led directly to his return to Carthage and reunion with the tight-knit Manichaean community there. In such company, he reconnected with the consolation that Manichaeism had to offer for death, the collective experience and purpose of the community of souls, through which one had a foretaste of their restoration to their original unity, "our minds were fused inseparably, out of many becoming one" (*Conf* 4.8.13). It is astonishing to see the later Augustine using such valorized rhetoric for the bonds of amity in the Manichaean community. Such language speaks volumes about the social dimension of his religious commitments, and the manner in which he sustained them through taking the perspectives of the significant others in his life as his own.

Manichaean ideology, therefore, required a long view of liberation that did not despair at the events of an individual lifetime, but looked forward to an ultimate dissolution of the temporary world of mixture where death was even a possibility. In the Mesopotamian heartland of Manichaeism, a dispute reportedly arose over whether all souls would be saved in the end, or not.[90] But by Augustine's account, western Manichaeism taught that some souls would be forever bound to evil, and there seems sufficient evidence to conclude that this was Mani's original teaching.[91] These lost souls are permanently affixed to the outside of the mass of darkness formed at the end of time (*Faust* 22.22).[92] Augustine skips over Manichaean accounts of the events at the end of the world, reflecting either his own disinclination to eschatology or his recognition that it did not differ substantially from Catholic beliefs. He makes only a vague allusion to "the fire in which the world will be burned up" (*Faust* 2.5; cf. Alexander of Lycopolis 5.8.1–4),[93] and jumps straight to the final state of things, when evil is confined to a single *massa* (Greek *bolos*), permanently disabled by webs of the remnant light souls driven into it.[94] Ironically, these binding elements remain with evil to fulfill their good function only because they have been so mingled and identified with evil that they have lost their ability to be extricated from it. "For Manichaeus, in his *Fundamental Epistle*, says that these souls deserved to be thus punished, because they allowed themselves to be led away from their original brightness, and became enemies of holy light" (*Faust* 21.16).[95]

With such teachings about the nature of the universe and the human being, Manichaean leaders endeavored to provide a total discursive environment within which converts could situate themselves, finding priorities, meaning, and purpose in their participation in the Manichaean cosmos. By living in a community of significant others who accepted reality in these terms and who repeated Manichaean teachings to each other in both formal and informal settings, adherents of the faith cultivated the dispositions needed to react to and interpret the world in accord with the religion's program. Increasing mastery of this apprehension of reality meant an ever more organized self, knowing what it was experiencing and how it should respond to it. Augustine would learn to like what Manichaeans liked, and dislike what they disliked; to feel about things what Manichaeans felt, and to pay attention to those aspects of personal experience that Manichaeans took to be significant. He would develop inclinations and propensities similar to those of other Manichaeans. He would acquire an ever greater capacity to perform Manichaean discourse, and receive the recognition that came with such expertise. In all these ways, Augustine would be enabled to establish a unified set of thoughts and attitudes that were aligned with those of people important to him, and that offered increasingly reliable determination of his reactions. Whatever stimuli, impulses, and desires that arose in his experience could be subordinated to Manichaean discourse and interpreted in light of it. Knowing the truth as Manichaeism presented it meant knowing his place and purpose in a meaningful universe.

Augustine expected further initiations into Manichaean "mysteries" as he made progress in the religion (*BV* 1.4).[96] The Manichaeans had an initiation ceremony reserved for the Elect that correlated certain ritual acts with the fundamental myth of the faith.[97] Yet Augustine seems to have imagined that further initiation would reveal philosophical truths hidden behind the myths, and reserved for the enlightened few. If he had persisted and progressed to entry into the order of the Elect, he probably would have been disappointed. As he later discovered, the African Manichaeans did not consider their myths symbolic parables for the masses, beneath which lay abstract truths of a philosophical nature. They understood the myths literally, with no room for allegorical interpretation. Both the elite of the Elect and the masses of the Auditors learned the same basic account of salvation history, with perhaps only nuances of difference in the emphases of the account. Progress in Manichaeism entailed not access to hidden doctrines, but development in self-discipline, in the solidification of a Manichaean self habituated to ways of behaving, speaking, and thinking that the Manichaeans considered the perfection of our humanity according to its inherent divinity.

A Personal Synthesis

Augustine joined the Manichaean community of Carthage as a support group of like-minded individuals within which he could pursue his own individual quest for truth. His enthusiasm for Manichaeism—the genuine enthusiasm of a new convert—was tempered with the distraction of his broader interests. Manichaeism was only one commitment among many, a single part of his complex identity as a young man of intellectual inclinations with a set of roles as student, teacher, rhetorical performer, family man, and friend. He says that he delighted in Cicero's exhortation "not to study one particular sect, but to love and seek and pursue and hold fast and strongly embrace wisdom itself, wherever found" (*Conf* 3.4.8). He read widely (among other things, Aristotle, some Pythagorean works, Cicero, Seneca, Varro, as well as various scientific and philosophical handbooks and digests), indeed "all the books of those sciences which they call the liberal arts, as many as I could cast my eyes upon" (*Conf* 4.16.30), and frankly states that Manichaeism was far from the sole source of his ideas at the time.[98]

It is essential that we understand this context of ideological and social pluralism in the young Augustine's life, as well as his personal decision to remain fully engaged in it, because it presented certain high hurdles to his achievement of an identity completely unified and committed around the Manichaean faith. A minority discourse endures a disadvantage relative to the dominant discourse of the larger society, with its claim on the "common sense" that persuades or compels by its appeal to public opinion, *ex consensu gentium*. Manichaeism attracted Augustine because he found correlations between its teachings and his own predisposed thinking, shaped by prior experience and conditioning. He continued to read non-Manichaean philosophy and science, and aspired to synthesize a personal system of his own.[99]

His abiding fascination with astrology and astronomy, which constituted a single field in his time, offered one such outside personal engagement that persisted throughout his Manichaean period (*Conf* 4.3.5).[100] Astrologers neither sacrificed living things nor conferred with demons (*Conf* 4.2.3), and so consultation with them did not violate Manichaean precepts. Manichaeans accepted a limited validity for astrological theory, and had their own distinctive astrological system.[101] But Augustine was drawn toward "mainstream" astrology, the work of "philosophers"[102] whose mathematically derived calculations and predictions seemed to contradict the personified, dramatic explanation for astronomical events in Manichaeism.[103] These issues formed a lasting point of resistance within Augustine to fully identifying himself as a Manichaean.[104]

When Augustine met the proconsul Vindicianus after winning a rhetorical contest, at a time probably prior to any active anti-Manichaean legislation that might have induced him to be circumspect about his faith, it was astrology that he spoke of with enthusiasm, apparently even expressing an interest in making a career of it (*Conf* 4.3.5). Neither the proconsul nor Augustine's Manichaean friend Nebridius could dissuade Augustine from practicing astrology, because, as Augustine says, "the authority of the writers of these books still had greater power over me" (*Conf* 4.3.6). Thomas O'Laughlin has highlighted the way in which this profession of popular astrology marks a point of tension between Augustine's public and private personas, the "difficulty of teaching one thing and claiming adherence to another," and has emphasized "its significance in holding him back from a full acceptance of Mani's teaching."[105] Additionally, through studying Manichaeism and astrology simultaneously, his astrological convictions may have colored his understanding of Manichaean views of responsibility for sin, tending in an even more fatalistic direction than that actually taught by the Manichaeans.[106]

Augustine raised his problems with the incompatibility of the two views of celestial phenomena with members of the Carthaginian Manichaean community. In *Epistle* 55 to Januarius, he relates how he presented the arguments of scientific astronomical calculations to his fellow Manichaeans, to which they responded by pointing out that the view he was proposing would lead to the conclusion that the cosmos was spiritually meaningless (*Ep* 55.4.6). They reminded him that all religions invest celestial phenomena with significance, as, for example, other Christians did by observing Easter according to astronomical calculations. Augustine gives no indication that his Manichaean comrades discouraged his reading in the subject, despite the problems it was causing. Instead, unable to resolve his issues themselves, they urged him to await patiently the return of their long-absent leader, Faustus. He would explain everything, they promised. In the meantime, Augustine appears to have dealt with the unresolved issue for some time by assuming that Mani probably spoke allegorically on these subjects; he seems to have expected the promised explanation from Faustus to involve initiation into the literal "scientific" truth hidden behind the symbolic imagery of Manichaean myth. In short, he still anticipated a resolution of his issues favorable to Manichaeism.

Augustine's astrological interests formed part of a larger concern to understand the order of the universe, as the ultimate truth to which he aspired, by putting Manichaean discourse in dialogue with other ideological sources he valued. The first fruit of these philosophical aspirations was *The Beautiful and the Suitable* (*De pulchro et apto*), written circa 380–381 C.E. (*Conf* 4.15.27). Notably, it is a "philosophical" work, not a "religious" one—that is, it contains no cultic, devotional, or expressly theological subject matter. In other words, the distinction was more one of choosing an established mode of discourse than of indicating any fundamental epistemic divide. Augustine possessed the model of Cicero's philosophical digests, and like the latter *The Beautiful* probably was composed as a dialogue.[107] In it, he filters Manichaean dualism through popular tropes of Greek thinking in what K. E. Lee has characterized aptly as "a demythologization project, a philosophical investigation into the 'truth' symbolized by the Manichaean myth."[108] As such, it appears to show Augustine seeking to provide for himself the sort of rational interpretation of the Manichaean symbolic system he had been awaiting in vain from Manichaean authorities.[109]

Even with due caution with regard to the hindsight coloration of his account of the work,[110] *The Beautiful* can be taken as demonstrating Augustine's strong interest in aesthetics and, even more, that he considered beauty a hallmark of the good long before any exposure to Plotinus. Thus Augustine's equation of the divine with the beautiful is a striking feature of his thinking already present in his Manichaean days and persisting throughout the rest of his life. K. E. Lee has argued that if, as can be shown, this identification predates Augustine's discovery of a similar theme in Plotinus, it can only be Manichaean in its inspiration.[111] The theme of beauty as a manifestation of the divine is indeed woven throughout Manichaean theology, and marks a fairly distinctive trait of this tradition.

Augustine appears to have turned to the Pythagorean tradition as the primary conversation partner with the work's Manichaean foundations.[112] This early engagement with Pythagoreanism persisted into his post-Manichaean years, showing itself in his conviction that mathematics represented the purest form of reason, as well as in his identification of Pythagoras as the purest example of the sage, both expressed in his earliest compositions as an apostate from the Manichaean faith. "Middle" Pythagoreanism, like Middle Platonism, had a distinctly dualistic tenor.[113] Numenius of Apamea contends that in its undetermined, formless, and orderless condition, dyadic matter as Pythagoreanism conceived it "was without beginning and origin" and "should be held to be as old as God," by whom it was "adorned with form and order" and "regulated."[114] The model of the monad and dyad that Augustine applies in *The Beautiful* may derive directly from Pythagorean texts or from a mediating source, such as Numenius or Porphyry's *Life of Pythagoras*.[115] Porphyry reports that Pythagoras "declared that of the opposing powers in the world the better was the monad and light and on the right and equal and enduring and straight, the worse was the dyad and darkness and on the left and unequal and curved and transient" (Porphyry, *Vita Pyth.* 38). The monad is "the reason for unity, and that for identity, and that for equality, and the cause of the union and sympathy of all things and of the preservation of that which remains the same," while the dyad is the "reason for diversity and inequality and everything that is divided and in change and now one way, now another" (Porphyry, *Vita Pyth.* 49–50).

Pythagoras was regarded as the fountainhead of much of the Greco-Roman philosophical tradition, a status reflected in Augustine's *The Academics*, where Pythagoras is cited as the ultimate sage, albeit one who has been appropriated by Platonism. This Pythagorean-Platonic connection was not a new discovery to Augustine in Milan, but one that would have been known to him from his earlier readings in Carthage. An earlier Platonic engagement in Augustine's life would account for the likely derivation of his distinction between the beautiful and the apt from Plato's *Hippias Major* 290A–296E, although more probably mediated by a digest or handbook than read directly from Plato's work.[116] Noteworthy, too, is a similar Pythagorean-Platonist synthesis in the statement of Augustine's Manichaean peer Fortunatus to the effect that the purpose of good's mixture with evil was "to limit contrary nature," echoing Plato's *Philebus* 26E–30E, with its Pythagorean-inspired discussion of the "limit" (*peras*), the "unlimited" (*apeiron*), and the "cause of mixture." This evidence seems to point to a common local trend of appropriating Pythagorean-Platonic philosophy in the Manichaean community of Carthage around 380, similar to the Neoplatonic fad in Milan which Augustine encountered later in the same decade.

So it was that in *The Beautiful* Augustine equated the good and the beautiful with the monad, accord, and rationality. It was, he wrote, a genderless mind (*mens sine ullo sexu*), a manifestation of essential unity evident in human concepts of the rational soul, truth, and the chief good to be striven for (*Conf* 4.15.24). All three of these concepts play a prominent role in his later Cassiciacum dialogues, showing that his basic vocabulary remained intact across the great divide of "conversion." The key shift in his thinking occurred in the way he conceptualized the force opposed to unity. Opposed to the monad from beginningless time, he maintained in *The Beautiful*, was a dyad, a substantially and naturally existent evil (*substantia et natura summi mali*) characterized by discord, irrationality, and the divided genders (*Conf* 4.15.24–27). In making use of these dualistic concepts of monad and dyad, then, Augustine was, in the words of Eugene TeSelle, "only giving a Manichaean twist to a standard Pythagorean theme."[117] Between these two conflicted principles, phenomenal reality was constituted of various attempts at relative order. Augustine characterized our experience of successful balancing and ordering of conditional existence as one of perceived fitness and suitability.[118] The balanced and suitable coexistence of multiple distinct things, or harmony, represented a secondary, derivative beauty (*Conf* 4.13.20; 4.15.24).[119] Unsuccessful attempts at order, on the other hand, yield the perception of unfitness and inaptitude. Within each of these aesthetic experiences, one may discern the dualistic constituent principles that underlie them: fitness suggesting by its attractiveness the perfection of absolute beauty, unity, and wholeness; unfitness pointing toward a more absolute form of ugliness, divisiveness, and defect (*Conf* 4.13.20).[120]

Whoever is able and does not neglect to consider the difference between what is beautiful and what is suitable, something which is in a sense spread throughout the universe of things, sees, of course, what a wide application this question has. For the beautiful is considered and praised in itself; its opposite is the ugly and deformed. But the suitable, whose opposite is the unsuitable, is dependent, as if tied to something else, and it is judged not by itself but by that to which it is linked. (*Ep* 138.5)[121]

This idea merely restates the fundamental epistemological position enunciated by Mani, that from the mixed and imperfect good in nature we can gain intellectual purchase on the unmixed and perfect good that lies beyond this world, and likewise from the partial and restrained evil in the world we can recognize the underlying principle of absolute evil.[122] As pointed out by K. E. Lee, in making his analysis Augustine clearly follows the inductive line of reasoning characteristic of Manichaean argument.[123]

Other correlations with Manichaean teachings accumulate rapidly upon closer analysis of Augustine's report of his first composition. True to Manichaean teaching, Augustine discussed both the soul and evil as material substances, and considered the latter as much as the former a conscious and living force. The dyad was "some unknown substance of irrational life, and the nature of the chief evil, which should not only be a substance, but real life also," animate, and yet not derived from God (*Conf* 4.15.24), exactly as Manichaeism taught. Likewise his idea at this time that the soul itself was identical to the monad that was "the chief and unchangeable good" to be realized (*Conf* 4.15.24) matches the Manichaean identification of the soul with God. Despite its intrinsic divinity, the soul is changeable and led to err by constraint from the opposing force (*Conf* 4.15.26). And since the soul shares a common nature with God, God too must be changeable (*Conf* 4.15.26)—not in his essential goodness, but in other features related to his dynamic responsiveness to the coexistence of evil.

Augustine made the latter careful distinction evidently with the aid of Aristotle's discussion in *Categories*, referred to by Augustine in the immediate context of his report of *The Beautiful* (*Conf* 4.16.28),[124] although he unsurprisingly refuses to grant such an immutability of God's essence in his later polemical characterizations of Manichaean teachings. The materialistic underpinnings of Aristotle's analysis suited Augustine's thought at the time,[125] and Augustine says that he applied Aristotle's discussion (where else than in *The Beautiful*?) to God, "imagining that you were the subject of your greatness and beauty, and that those attributes inhered in you as in their subject, as they might in a material thing."[126] Such substantialist metaphysics dominated the scientific, philosophical, and religious discourses of the time, into which Manichaeism fit comfortably. It was Neoplatonism that represented a deviation from this existing philosophical norm. When Augustine in hindsight faults the materialism of his former Manichaeism, he is attacking the entire sweep of traditional metaphysics in the light of the Neoplatonic revolution he had come to embrace.

None of the individual positions Augustine takes in *The Beautiful* were uniquely Manichaean; all could find correlates in various forms of popular philosophy of the day. It is obvious that Augustine brokered a rapprochement between Manichaeism and the philosophical tradition he knew from his other reading. His synthetic handling of the material indicates the sort of intellectual liberty he had—or took—as a Manichaean, and foreshadows his similar efforts to work Nicene Christianity's basic concepts through philosophical interpretation and development once he had switched his allegiance to that tradition. The evident continuities of his thought from one religious commitment to the next apparently proved embarrassing for him. Takeshi Kato has made a good case for regarding Augustine's claimed uncertainties about the dimensions and fate of his first work as disingenuous, motivated by a desire to obscure its similarity in philosophical themes and arguments to the early dialogues he wrote as a convert to Nicene Christianity. Between the "Manichaean" and "Catholic" philosopher there had been only slight adjustments of overall vision and vocabulary.[127] In Augustine's Manichaeism, then, we find a personalized synthesis built up of a number of sources that Augustine comprehended in light of each other. He sought to discover the philosophical concepts and models that would offer a "secular" version, as it were, of the same apprehension of reality expressed by Manichaeism in suitably "religious" imagery. Believing, at least to a certain degree, that the Manichaean system provided truth, he attempted to understand that truth through the reason-based analyses of reality found in the available schools of philosophy.

An Unsuccessful Self

In not perfectly conforming his thinking to Manichaean propositions, Augustine remained resistant to the complete installation of a Manichaean self. Some of these points of resistance remained insignificant to his ability to live his life as a Manichaean. But to the degree that individual elements of Manichaean teaching and practice supported other elements, and together formed a self-reinforcing coherent system, any "bugs in the system," any "chinks in the armor," left Augustine's Manichaean identity vulnerable to disintegrative pressures. Ultimately Augustine "found no rest" in a Manichaean identity, and came to experience it as only a surface persona that "mouthed the opinions of others" without full conviction (*Conf* 7.14.20).

We can understand this sort of self-alienation in the terms of Harry Frankfurt's discussion of one of the ways in which a person's organization of desires and intentions may be divided against itself.

> It is a matter not of volitional strength but of whether the highest-order preferences concerning some volitional issue are *wholehearted*. It has to do with the possibility that there is no unequivocal answer to the question of what the person really wants, even though his desires do form a complex and extensive hierarchical structure. There might be no unequivocal answer, because the person is *ambivalent* with respect to the object he comes closest to really wanting: In other words, because, with respect to that object, he is drawn not only towards it but also away from it too. Or there might be no unequivocal answer because the person's preferences concerning what he wants are not fully integrated, so that there is some *inconsistency* or *conflict* (perhaps not yet manifest) among them.[128]

I have chosen to use Frankfurt's exposition here because of its way of talking about the self as coming to want and will certain things, rather than coming to know things. What otherwise might be discussed in terms of Augustine not being fully *persuaded* by Manichaean ideas can and should be looked at in terms of his lack of *wanting or choosing to believe* them. When he speaks of accepting Manichaean teachings, he refers rather insightfully to wanting to believe them (*DA* 11), and in adopting Nicene Christianity he will similarly express making a choice to believe rather than knowing it to be true. The exact motives of such a choice may remain as obscure to the person making it as they do to us. What the individual will want is not given in advance, but emerges in the process of self-formation as various configurations of dispositions and intentions are tested against each other, that is, various selves assessed in the environment—partly given by the individual and partly given by his or her sociocultural context— where they will need to operate. All sorts of nonrational factors go into determining whether and to what degree an individual will elect to subject him- or herself to a particular discursive system. Recasting that choice in terms of persuasion largely involves post hoc rationalizations within the new terms of reason given by the adopted system itself; and such rationalizations serve to reinforce and sustain the choice of that system in new ways that would have been impossible when one provisionally chose it as one's self-organizing program.

The intention in making such a choice is to form a power relation to oneself, reproducing the power relation the system presents to the individual by making oneself one's own monitor of compliance. If such a reproduction of power does not take hold, then the person becomes alienated from the system, and the latter retains only the possibility of a coercive relationship to the individual. Manichaeism in Augustine's Africa had no such recourse to coercion; everything depended on his voluntary subjection to Manichaean discourse. In the end, Augustine was an unsuccessful Manichaean because he failed to internalize its teachings and values sufficiently to become a Manichaean self. Both his evident misunderstanding of key parts of Manichaean doctrine as known to modern research and his own self-description lead to this conclusion. It is striking how shallow was his penetration of Manichaean teachings after so many years as an Auditor, and this fact leads one to think that his primary interests rested elsewhere. As Rebecca West remarks, Augustine's limited grasp of a religion he belonged to for more than a decade "can only be explained by supposing that, as so often happens to very gifted people in their youth, he passed through a period of moonish reverie, during which he thought a great deal of Manichaeanism, but not very alertly, and attended at their services regularly but did not listen very vigilantly."[129]

Augustine would later claim that he never "cleaved completely" to the Manichaean faith, and always had some mental reservations about all he was asked to believe as a Manichaean (*BV* 1.4; *UC* 1.2; *Conf* 8.7.17). While he had clear apologetic reasons for saying so, the claim fits other evidence about the way he thought of the quest for truth at this time, namely, as a progressive acquisition of understanding leading to confident trust that one was in possession of truth. Yet as his non-Manichaean reading proceeded unchecked by any restriction (since Manichaeism as far as we know had no such prohibition), he found that he could not reconcile every idea that captivated him to Manichaean tenets.

Now I had read a lot of philosophy, and I retained in my memory a great deal of what I had read. I began to compare some of the things said by the philosophers with those interminable fallacies of the Manichaeans, and it seemed to me that what the philosophers said was the more probable. (*Conf* 5.3.3; cf. 5.14.25)

This emerging sense of dissatisfaction, however, only came to the foreground after about eight years within the Manichaean community, and was tempered by uncertainty that he understood fully or correctly either the Manichaean teachings or the philosophical material he was reading. At least one of his fellow Manichaeans agreed with Augustine's self-assessment of his incomplete commitment to the faith. The Manichaean Auditor Secundinus wrote to him in the first decade of the fifth century charging that Augustine had never been a true Manichaean and remained ignorant of key parts of the religion's teachings (*EpSec* 3). Ironically, the letter arrived even as Augustine was combating accusations made by leading Donatist Christians that he was *still* a Manichaean.

From 373 through 382, throughout his twenties, Augustine remained an active member of the African Manichaean community,[130] living all but about a year of that time in Carthage. He had become a Manichaean at the last opportune time; it was the waning days of an unprecedented period of tolerance that the religion had enjoyed in the Roman Empire since the policy of Constantine and Licinius had established the basis of relative religious freedom in the realm in 313.[131] Augustine's public affiliation with the Manichaeans did not hinder him from winning a rhetorical competition in Carthage before Vindicianus, proconsul of Africa, in 380–381. In a private conversation on the occasion of his victory, the proconsul chided Augustine for his belief in astrology, while nothing was said between the two men about Augustine's Manichaean activities, which he later claimed were notorious at the time.[132] More than a decade after the events, Augustine fixed upon 382 as the year when he began to lose confidence that Manichaeism would fully satisfy his spiritual yearning. Experiencing several points of dissonance, and having difficulty reconciling certain Manichaean teachings with "philosophy," he kept being promised that the Manichaean bishop Faustus would have the answers (*Conf* 5.3.3; 5.3.7). So this long-absent figure was built up in Augustine's imagination to superhuman proportions. In such a situation, disappointment was perhaps inevitable. From his own predilections, his education, his enchantment with the intellectual life of such men as Cicero, Augustine had definite ideas about what to expect and look for in an authority figure who would earn his respect. Against this background, Faustus came as a complete surprise.

CHAPTER FOUR

Faustus

IN THE FACE of Augustine's difficulty in committing wholeheartedly to the Manichaean faith, and his inability to make progress toward fully identifying his self as a Manichaean one, others repeatedly commended Faustus to him as an authority. Implicitly, such a completely informed and fully realized Manichaean self could resolve all of Augustine's issues with Manichaeism, because he had effected a total integration of the system in his own person, and understood how it all fit together and functioned in the path of life Manichaeism proposed and promoted. Hearing this, Augustine looked forward to meeting this paragon and paradigm, and adopting him as his personal mentor in making progress as a Manichaean. In the event, Faustus defied Augustine's expectations, and forced—rather than resolved—the issue of Augustine's dissatisfaction with Manichaeism.

What we know of Faustus comes from three principal sources. The first is Augustine's carefully crafted characterization of his time among the Manichaeans in *Confessions*, composed in the closing years of the fourth century. The second is Faustus's own composition, the *Capitula*,[1] embedded as disarticulated passages in Augustine's refutation of it, *Against Faustus* (*Contra Faustum*). The latter constitutes our third source, containing a number of further reminiscences. Augustine apparently composed it in the first years of the fifth century, *after* the *Confessions* had been completed and circulated.[2] It is noteworthy that, although Augustine alludes to Faustus several times in earlier works, he consistently avoids mentioning him by name before the *Confessions*, using various circumlocutions instead in *The Morals of the Manichaeans, The*

Usefulness of Belief, and elsewhere. Most likely he did not wish to be perceived as naming names in the role of a *delator*, regardless of his differences with the illegal Manichaean community. By the time he names Faustus in the *Confessions*, he appears to have known that his former mentor was dead.

In *Against Faustus*, Augustine introduces Faustus as a native African (*gente Afer*) from the city of Milevis in westernmost Numidia (*Faust* 1.1), born to a poor family (*Faust* 5.5). Faustus himself relates that his family was pagan, as was he before being converted to Manichaeism (*Faust* 9.1; 13.1; 15.1). The fact that he, Honoratus (*UC* 1.2), and Nebridius (*Conf* 9.3.6) had all been pagans before conversion weakens the common assumption that Manichaeism found most of its converts among the already Christianized. Titus of Bostra states emphatically that Manichaeans actively proselytized among pagans as well as Christians (Titus of Bostra 3.1). Peter Brown has noted the degree to which Faustus seeks to appeal to a pagan audience, offering Manichaeism as the "Church of the Gentiles," consciously drawing on the Classical tradition and decrying the semi-Judaism of the Donatists and Nicene Christians[3]—a stance that could well appeal to someone like Augustine who identified himself most with Classical culture.

Faustus says in his *Capitula* that he was attracted to Manichaeism from paganism "solely by the fame, and the virtues, and the wisdom of our liberator Jesus Christ" (*Faust* 13.1), which he saw authentically represented only among the Manichaeans. He provides no indication at what stage of his life his conversion occurred; although he speaks rhetorically of having given up family, we simply do not know if he means that he had actually left a wife and child behind in taking up the life of a Manichaean Elect, or merely had foregone a family life.[4] Like Augustine, his language skills were limited to Latin, and his schooling evidently fell short in comparison with Augustine's (*Conf* 5.6.11). He was familiar with the works of Cicero and Seneca,[5] reportedly fond of poetry, and "began late in life to learn oratory, that he might discourse eloquently on these absurdities; and with all his cleverness, after ruining his health by study, his preaching has gained a mere handful of followers" (*Faust* 21.10). This remark would seem to make Faustus older than Augustine by at least a decade and possibly two. It also suggests that when Augustine knew him, his health was frail, which may account for his use of a horse (*Faust* 21.10) and of a down mattress (*Faust* 5.5), for both of which Augustine chides him as falling short of the standards of some more rigorist Manichaean Elect.

Faustus apparently had already been a bishop for more than a decade

when Augustine met him, since the latter implies that Faustus was the recognized leader of the North African Manichaeans throughout the whole of
Augustine's time in the community (*Conf* 5.6.10). As a bishop, Faustus was in
theory one of only seventy-two leaders of the Manichaean sect, distributed at
this time from India, Bactria, and Sogdiana in the east, across Persia and the
West Asian borderlands, and throughout the Roman realm. We have no way
of ascertaining how many episcopal colleagues he had within the empire—
perhaps no more than a dozen.[6] Faustus's diocese is likely to have included not
only the Africas, but Numidia and Mauretania as well. Thus a Manichaean
bishop occupied a much higher and broader position of authority than his
Catholic counterpart, one which at the same time required extensive travel.
This obligation over a substantial territory possibly offers at least part of the
explanation for the otherwise strange absence of Faustus from Carthage—the
region's political and economic capital— for as many as nine years.[7] Nevertheless, he returned to Carthage in 382 C.E., and was still in its environs four years
later, when he was arrested. One wonders if already before his long absence
he had left his stamp on the Carthaginian community enough for Augustine
to detect an inclination for Cicero which he shared. The Manichaean rhetoric
that Augustine reports attracting him has a distinctly Ciceronian, skeptical
ring to it.[8]

When Faustus finally arrived in Carthage sometime before the start of
Augustine's twenty-ninth year in November 382, Augustine found him to
be a charming, eloquent, modest man. The positive impression he made
stayed with Augustine through the years and is still vivid in the *Confessions*. It is even possible that hindsight permitted Augustine to appreciate
things in Faustus that he had not when he first met him. At the time, he
had been hoping for, and led to expect, a brilliant intellectual able to solve
all difficulties in reconciling Manichaeism to "philosophy." Faustus not only
failed to do this, he declined even to try (*Conf* 5.7.12). Augustine remarks
on "his ability to make good use of his mental powers" (*Conf* 5.6.11), but he
was no intellectual by Augustine's high standards. Despite its love of books
and learning, the Manichaean community apparently gave priority to other
gifts as grounds for promotion to positions of leadership, whether these be
good looks and eloquence, as Augustine freely suggests of Faustus, or spiritual depth and maturity, as Augustine more reluctantly concedes of him.[9]
Surviving Manichaean literature outlines a rigorous scrutiny of mental and
emotional control expected of the Elect. These demands would be all the

more applied to those meant to provide guidance and a role model to the others. Augustine allows that Faustus would be considered a pious man, had he not been a Manichaean (*Conf* 5.7.12), and describes him as a man of common sense and insight. More remarkably, Augustine invokes the classical Platonic praise on Faustus's behalf, remarking that, even if he did not know God rightly, he at least knew himself, and like Socrates was wise in knowing what he did not know (*Conf* 5.7.12).[10] The surprisingly positive description Augustine gives of Faustus leads him to a moment of self-consciousness. He pauses and asks God to confirm the truth of his recollection (*Conf* 5.6.11); he will not deny the good impression Faustus made on him personally, despite the impolitic nature of such an admission.

The long-deprived Carthaginian Manichaean community, and perhaps a good number of the curious, immediately flocked around the charismatic Faustus. Augustine found it difficult to get near him, or discuss his concerns with him in private (*Conf* 5.6.11). While within the camaraderie of the tight-knit sect Faustus showed himself to be an upbeat and generous character, with an "attractive personality" and full of "goodwill," in his public activity he "set about the task of disputation," defending his community and seeking new converts (*Conf* 5.6.11). Augustine attributed his aptitude in this area to natural ability rather than to advanced rhetorical training. "The ease with which he found the right words to clothe his thoughts delighted me, and I was not the only one to applaud it, though perhaps I did so more than most" (*Conf* 5.6.11). We find support for this characterization in Faustus's *Capitula*, as recorded for posterity by Augustine's own *Against Faustus*, as well as in the occasional anecdote Augustine reports elsewhere. Faustus is almost certainly the protagonist of the pragmatic refutation of intellectualist quibbling over the existence and nature of evil Augustine relates in *The Morals of the Manichaeans*.

> For one of the leaders of this heresy, whose instructions we attended with great familiarity and frequency, used to say with reference to a person who held that evil was not a substance, "I should like to put a scorpion in the man's hand, and see whether he would not withdraw his hand; and in so doing he would get a proof, not in words but in the thing itself, that evil is a substance, for he would not deny that the animal is a substance." He said this not in the presence of the person, but to us, when we repeated to him the remark which had troubled us, giving, as I said, a childish answer to children. (*MM* 8.11)

Augustine is careful even amid the polemic of this work to make clear that he understood that such a response was not intended as a serious philosophical one, and should not be judged as if it were. We catch glimpses in the *Capitula* of the flashes of wit that so charmed the young Augustine, and through them we get a sense of Faustus's methods of public disputation. In *Against Faustus* 23.1, for example, Faustus is quoted as recollecting an exchange he had with someone in public in which he playfully toyed with his opponent while displaying his own erudition.[11] Augustine himself at several points in his attempted refutation of the *Capitula* pauses to remark on the rhetorical talent on display in it, as evident in writing as it had been in person (*Faust* 16.26; 21.10; 22.50). Johannes van Oort has made the intriguing suggestion that Augustine's rhetorical characterization of Faustus as "a snare of the devil" (*laqueus diaboli, Conf* 5.3.3; cf. *laqueus mortis, Conf* 5.7.13) may be an ironic play on an expression of praise used of Faustus by the African Manichaeans, describing him as capable of snaring the devil with his disputational skills.[12]

Seen in the pages of the *Capitula* some twenty years later, however, Faustus's aggressive rhetoric seems to have surprised Augustine, who remembered a more modest and pleasant man.[13] Did Faustus display a dramatically different persona in his writings from the one in his personal exchanges within the Manichaean community? Or had he changed through the bitter experience of persecution after Augustine had known him?[14] Perhaps the difference between Augustine's personal recollection and the person he found represented in the *Capitula* may be accounted for best by Augustine's new vantage point on the receiving end of Faustus's attacks. In the friendly circle of believers, he had had the privilege of seeing Faustus's generosity of spirit, private wittiness, and personal humility. When Faustus girded his loins for public disputation, all this disappeared. While Augustine was still an insider, he applauded, "perhaps more than most," Faustus's ability to run circles around opponents of the faith, while knowing his more personable side. But when certain Christian brethren brought him Faustus's *Capitula* almost two decades later, Augustine suddenly encountered the man from the other side. The same rhetorical skill that Augustine had applauded he now had to dissect and condemn as merely clever maneuver.

The *Capitula* is a self-consciously performative work, engaging with opponents outside the Manichaean community,[15] and so can be presumed to provide only a partial picture of Faustus, with only some facets of his Manichaeism on display. Yet, as much as we might expect the Faustus of the polemical *Capitula* to put on a different public face from the one he presented in the intimate company of the tight-knit Manichaean community, we find key continuities between the two personae—enough that we can begin to delineate an historical individual in the intersection of his various self-performances. By correlating characteristics of his literary performance with what Augustine reports of his attitudes in person, the historian discovers a consistent set of values and orientations that governed Faustus's self-presentation, his personality.[16] It turns out that Faustus was no more a "typical" Manichaean than Augustine, that despite his attainment of high position within the community Faustus maintained an idiosyncratic posture in relation to the Manichaean creed. Augustine would come to see his encounter with this man as providential, and a new understanding of the unique stance taken by Faustus allows us to appreciate Augustine's point from the perspective of secular rather than sacred history. If Augustine had not brought his uncertainties to this particular man and elicited the sort of response Faustus was inclined to make to such questions, his path in life would not—could not—have taken the particular course it did.

Faustus's Manichaeism

Faustus's position of leadership in the Manichaean community both attested to, and further motivated, his strong commitment to the faith and his effective realization of its ideals. Faustus makes clear his adherence to the form of Manichaeism developed by its original missionary to the Roman West, "the learned Adimantus, the only teacher since the sainted Manichaeus deserving of our attention," who had "exposed and thoroughly refuted the errors of Judaism and of semi-Christianity" (*Faust* 1.2). This Adimantus, or Adda, had been responsible a century earlier for undertaking the initial acculturation of the Manichaean system to Western religious and philosophical discourse. Much of the Greek terminology adopted by Manichaeism in the Roman Empire probably goes back to Adimantus's discursive choices about how to engage with existing traditions in the region. Evident in the results of this work is his appropriation of Marcionite Christian critiques of the Old Testament,[17] as well as distinctly skeptical rhetoric aimed at various forms of philosophical dogmatism.[18]

Faustus fully adopts, and makes original contributions to, both aspects of

Adimantus's missionary initiative. He clearly knows Adimantus's contrast of the Old and New Testaments, but may have dug further into original Marcionite writings and pursued his own study of biblical literature to bolster his arguments against "semi-Christianity."[19] Some early Protestant theologians felt they could see a kindred spirit in Faustus both in his critiques of Catholic accommodation of pagan practices and in his "biblical theology." His challenge to the integrity of the New Testament text foreshadows modern historical critical approaches.[20] On the philosophical front, Faustus displays a thoroughgoing skepticism remarkable in a religious leader, albeit fitted to a program of religious practice.[21] Indeed, Faustus's own brand and application of skepticism closely corresponds to that of the New Academy of Carneades and Philo of Larissa as it is known to us—and possibly to Faustus—primarily through Cicero.[22]

The intellectual leaders of the Platonic New Academy undertook to solve the interconnected problems of knowledge and action. They called into question the Stoic claim that certain things presented themselves with such convincing reality that one simply knew them to be true. Carneades and his successors argued that no such clear criterion of truth existed, that all knowledge entailed only the probable or plausible (Greek *pithanon*; Latin *probabile*), not the certain. True to skeptical principles, the Academics refused to put forward any dogmas. While accepting the premise that such a thing as truth existed, and conceding that it might be apprehended, Philo of Larissa maintained that human beings have no way to ascertain the difference between an accurate apprehension of truth and an inaccurate one. The senses are not necessarily false, but we cannot determine for sure in any particular case whether they are truly or falsely presenting reality to us (Cicero, *Acad. pr.* 2.32.104–5; 2.34.111). In the face of concerns that such a philosophical position leads to *apraxia*—an inability to act—the New Academy contended that one can and should act on evident truth, even if one does not know truth with absolute certainty. "The wise man will therefore employ whatever is apparently plausible if nothing happens that is contrary to that plausibility, and his whole plan of life will be governed in this fashion" (Cicero, *Acad. pr.* 2.31.99). Thus the standard of truth-likeness (*veri simile*) was that a particular idea or perception was not (yet) contradicted by, and that it showed provisional agreement with, other ideas or perceptions. The main point of this qualified skepticism was that it issued in successful action (Cicero, *Acad. pr.* 2.10.32). Acting successfully on the basis of a provisional assumption was the most reliable test of its truth-likeness. If action proceeded successfully as a result of treating a proposition as if it were true, then that provisional truth met the criterion of thorough testing and continued to show itself truth-like (Cicero, *Acad. pr.* 2.33–34.107–9).

Understanding that Faustus works with this Academic skepticism as a subtext of his arguments helps us to see the coherence of the positions he takes. It permits him both to apply skeptical criticisms to his opponents and to maintain a remarkably liberal stance toward his own religion's ideological propositions. It establishes for him the criterion of successful action, upon which he can assert the truth, or truth-likeness, of Manichaeism by its ability to form new selves and motivate good action. It shapes his entire understanding of what constitutes religion. Faustus sharply directs the focus of religious commitment to action, relativizing the importance of doctrine. He argues in the *Capitula* that religion is defined by practice. Commitment to a particular religion entails enactment of its precepts and living the life its teachings dictate—nothing more and nothing less. To believe is to do.[23] Any other pretense of faith is hypocrisy. This is the case not only for Manichaeism, he contends, but for any religion. Religions that fail to demand concrete results in human conduct, or are unable successfully to motivate people to good actions, do not merit consideration.

Faustus demonstrates his thesis with the example of Judaism which, he maintains, makes promises specifically to those who follow certain practices.

> Remember that the promise of Canaan in the Old Testament is made
> to Jews, that is, to the circumcised, who offer sacrifice, and abstain from
> swine's flesh, and from the other animals which Moses pronounces
> unclean, and observe Sabbaths, and the feast of unleavened bread,
> and other things of the same kind which the author of the Testament
> enjoined. Christians have not adopted these observances, and no one
> keeps them; so that if we will not take the inheritance, we should
> surrender the documents. (*Faust* 4.1)

Judaism clearly offers a valid religious program that demands actions and specifies the consequences of those actions. It cannot be faulted in these terms. Yet, since Faustus prefers the promises of the kingdom of heaven and eternal life, he adopts the conduct suitable to that goal, rather than the prescriptions by which Jews are promised material rewards (*Faust* 4.1;

cf. 15.1). "I, like every other Christian, pay no attention to these things, as being trifling and useless for the salvation of the soul" (*Faust* 10.1). He considers the mainstream Christians of Africa as neither fish nor fowl (literally, "half horse, half man"), failing to follow completely either Judaism or Christianity, but allowing portions of each to undermine the practice of the other (*Faust* 15.1). At least the Jewish Christians (the "Symmachians") are consistent in continuing to adhere to Jewish law while claiming that Christ fulfills it (*Faust* 19.4). Other Christians, by contrast, are hypocritical in retaining the Old Testament while failing to adhere to its commands (*Faust* 19.6; 32.3–4). The God of the Old Testament is explicitly the God of the circumcision, the God of Abraham, Isaac, and Jacob, and so of a limited domain of concern and power (*Faust* 25.1). While neither Manichaeans nor other Christians maintain the practice of circumcision, the latter still try to claim that the God of the circumcision is their God.

> You ask if I believe the Old Testament. Of course not, for I do not
> keep its precepts. Neither, I imagine, do you. I reject circumcision as
> disgusting; and if I mistake not, so do you. I reject the observance of
> Sabbaths as superfluous: I suppose you do the same. I reject sacrifice as
> idolatry, as doubtless you also do. Swine's flesh is not the only flesh I
> abstain from; nor is it the only flesh you eat. I think all flesh unclean:
> you think none unclean. Both alike, in these opinions, throw over the
> Old Testament. We both look upon the weeks of unleavened bread and
> the feast of tabernacles as unnecessary and useless. Not to patch linen
> garments with purple; to count it adultery to make a garment of linen
> and wool; to call it sacrilege to yoke together an ox and an ass when
> necessary; not to appoint as priest a bald man, or a man with red hair, or
> any similar peculiarity, as being unclean in the sight of God, are things
> which we both despise and laugh at, and rank as of neither first nor
> second importance; and yet they are all precepts and judgments of the
> Old Testament. You cannot blame me for rejecting the Old Testament;
> for whether it is right or wrong to do so, you do it as much as I. As
> for the difference between your faith and mine, it is this, that while
> you choose to act deceitfully, and meanly to praise in words what in
> your heart you hate, I, not having learned the art of deception, frankly
> declare that I hate both these abominable precepts and their authors.
> (*Faust* 6.1; cf. 22.2)

He suggests that if the God of the Old Testament has been unwilling or unable to bestow his promised rewards even on "the synagogue, his proper wife, who obeys him in all things like a servant," he can hardly be expected to grant them to strangers who refuse to bend their neck to the yoke of his commandments (*Faust* 15.1). Conversely, he argues, "If a Jew were to claim part in the Gospel, I should justly reproach him with claiming what he has no right to, because he does not obey its precepts. And a Jew might say the same to me if I professed to receive the Old Testament while I disregarded its requirements" (*Faust* 10.1).

Faustus uses the same principle in discussing Christ's relation to the Law. He asks why the Jews thought Jesus had come to destroy the Law, and answers that such an intention was evident in his deeds, by which he challenged circumcision, broke the Sabbath, discarded sacrifices, and made no distinction in foods (*Faust* 17.2).[24] Even if Christians claim to believe that Christ fulfilled rather than destroyed the Law, their own practice shows that they consider the Law destroyed, since they do not obey it (*Faust* 18.1; cf. 22.2). In the final analysis, "fulfilling" and "destruction" seem to amount to the same thing, since in any case the precepts of the Law are no longer observed (*Faust* 18.2).

Faustus similarly criticizes his Christian opponents for directing attention solely to the prophecies of the Old Testament prophets with no regard for how they conducted their lives. Regardless of what they may be said to have believed, the Jewish patriarchs did not act in continuity with the teachings of Christ, Faustus observes. Either the biblical texts themselves are guilty of slandering these figures, or they lived according to different standards of conduct, immoral ones from the Christian perspective (*Faust* 22.1–3).[25] For "it is impossible to gather grapes from thorns, or figs from thistles," and "if the Hebrew prophets knew and preached Christ, and yet lived such vicious lives," then the words of Paul may be applied to them, that "though they knew God, they did not glorify him as God, nor were they thankful, but they became vain in their imaginations, and their foolish heart was darkened. You see," Faustus concludes, "the knowledge of great things is worth little, unless their life is worthy" (*Faust* 12.1).

Faustus sees his own commitment to Manichaeism in the same terms, prioritizing practice as the defining feature of authentic identification with a religious tradition. For him, the ethical precepts of the Sermon on the Mount, encapsulated in the beatitudes, constitute the "gospel" and are the hallmark of the true Christian (*Vides in me Christi beatitudines illas, quae euangelium faciunt, Faust* 5.1).

Do I believe the gospel? You ask me if I believe it, though my obedience
to its commands shows that I do. I should rather ask you if you believe
it, since you give no proof of your belief. I have left my father, mother,
wife, and children, and all else that the gospel requires; and do you ask if
I believe the gospel? Perhaps you do not know what is called the gospel.
The gospel is nothing else than the preaching and the precept of Christ.
I have parted with all gold and silver, and have left off carrying money
in my purse; content with daily food; without anxiety for tomorrow;
and without solicitude about how I shall be fed, or where-withal I shall
be clothed: and do you ask if I believe the gospel? You see in me the
blessings of the gospel; and do you ask if I believe the gospel? You see
me poor, meek, a peacemaker, pure in heart, mourning, hungering,
thirsting, bearing persecutions and enmity for righteousness' sake; and
do you doubt my belief in the gospel? (*Faust* 5.1)

Faustus could make a fairly persuasive claim on the Sermon on the Mount,
since the Manichaean Elect—such as Faustus himself—offered just about the
only literal embodiment of its radical ethic in the religious environment of
North Africa. The other Christian communities of Africa had settled down
to fairly mundane "family values" and had nothing to compare to the ascetic
code of the Elect, involving celibacy, poverty, homelessness, and pacifism.
Only when Augustine and his associates introduced from Italy the new ascetic movement that had arisen within Nicene Christianity could the latter
offer a competing claim to the more radical aspects of Christ's demand on the
believer.

Just as Jesus set the negative example of rejecting the Jewish faith by not
adhering to its rules of conduct, Faustus maintains, so he set the positive example of pointing to his own deeds as the proof of the truth of his religious
claims. Faustus reminds his readers that, when asked by John the Baptist if he
was the Christ, Jesus "properly and justly did not deign to reply that he was;
but reminded him of the works of which he had already heard." Stringing
together a catena of gospel passages, Faustus demonstrates that Jesus consistently tied salvation to the performance of actions, rather than the holding of
beliefs.

Who shall enter, O Christ, into your kingdom? "He that does the will
of my Father in heaven," is his reply; not, "He that confesses that I

was born." And again, he says to his disciples, "Go, teach all nations, baptizing them in the name of the Father, and of the Son, and of the Holy Spirit, teaching them to observe all things which I have commanded you." It is not, "teaching them that I was born," but, "to observe my commandments." Again, "You are my friends if you do what I command you;" not, "if you believe that I was born." Again, "If you keep my commandments, you shall abide in my love," and in many other places. Also in the Sermon on the Mount, when he taught, "Blessed are the poor, blessed are the meek, blessed are the peacemakers, blessed are the pure in heart, blessed are they that mourn, blessed are they that hunger, blessed are they that are persecuted for righteousness' sake," he nowhere says, "Blessed are they that confess that I was born." And in the separation of the sheep from the goats in the judgment, he says that he will say to them on the right hand, "I was hungry, and you gave me meat; I was thirsty, and you gave me drink" and so on; "therefore inherit the kingdom." Not, "Because you believe that I was born, inherit the kingdom." Again, to the rich man seeking for eternal life, he says, "Go, sell all that you have, and follow me;" not, "Believe that I was born, that you may have eternal life." You see, the kingdom, life, happiness, are everywhere promised to the part I have chosen of what you call the two parts of faith, and nowhere to your part. Show, if you can, a place where it is written that whoever confesses that Christ was born of a woman is blessed, or shall inherit the kingdom, or have eternal life. (*Faust* 5.3)

Faustus's emphasis on religious practice belongs in part to a tendency found throughout the Manichaean sect, which conservatively maintained its core system of practice while adapting the expression of its doctrine to local conditions.[26] He carried forward the religion's conservative disinclination for non-literal interpretations of either Christian scripture or the teachings of Mani, treating both as *mandatum*, instructions for conduct rather than bases for speculation. The North African Manichaeans looked upon Mani primarily as a cultic preceptor who guided them as a community of practice.[27]

Yet to this underlying character of Manichaeism in general Faustus added his own predilection for skepticism against any dogmatic assertions. He criticizes the emphasis of other Christians on belief over practice, and particularly belief in certain dogmas, such as the incarnation of Christ, that he regards as entirely unrelated to explaining and justifying the way of life Christ taught, whereas his opponents seem to believe that "confessing that Christ was born has more power to save the soul than the other parts" of the Christian religious system (*Faust* 5.2). Faustus views the Manichaean moral project, just as his colleague Fortunatus would later express it to Augustine, as an *imitatio Christi* justified by the common spiritual nature of the docetic Christ and the human soul. One seeks to be as immune to evil as Christ was, acting as an unencumbered soul, checking conduct against the model Christ provides of what freedom from evil's constraint looks like.[28] The Nicene emphasis on the dogma of Christ's physical embodiment puts the stress on exactly the wrong point, from his point of view, making so much of how Christ might be as we are in our limitation, rather than highlighting the liberty of his spiritual nature to which we should actively aspire.

In a striking skeptical turn to this criticism, Faustus freely admits that the exact character of Christ's incarnation is an open question, and might very well turn out to be as the other Christians say (*Faust* 5.2–3). By arguing in skeptical mode *in intramque parte*, he makes the point that action does not depend on either position one takes on this question. No justification exists for focusing on such a point of belief to the exclusion of actually following the commandments of Christ, over which there is no doubt whatsoever. "Belief in the gospel," then, "consists solely in obedience to the commands of God" (*Faust* 5.2). These commands do not depend on any particular metaphysic, just as the authority of Christ in giving them does not depend on the exact nature of his body. Accounting oneself a Christian is simply a matter of obedience to Christ as the guide of one's conduct. Even if belief and practice are complementary parts of religion, those who emphasize practice take the more difficult part than those who merely believe while neglecting practice.[29] Of course the Manichaeans do believe as well as practice. But, as Faustus presents it, their beliefs involve ideas essential to the authority and salvational role of Christ,

> for we confess that Jesus Christ is the son of the living God; and Jesus declares with his own lips that this confession has a benediction, when he says to Peter, "Blessed are you, Simon Barjona; for flesh and blood have not revealed this to you, but my Father who is in heaven." So that we have not one, but both these parts of faith, and in both alike are we pronounced blessed by Christ; for in one we carry out the works, while in the other we preach without blasphemy. (*Faust* 5.3)

Faustus ventures to set Manichaeism apart from all other religious options of his world by means of a taxonomy of religion.[30] He distinguishes a schism—"those who have the same doctrines and worship as other people, and only choose to meet separately"—from a sect—"those whose doctrine is quite unlike that of others, and who have made a form of divine worship peculiar to themselves" (*Faust* 20.3). He argues that paganism, Judaism, and non-Manichaean Christianity are little more than schisms of the same overarching set of beliefs and practices, whereas Manichaeism alone stands apart as a distinct sect.

> The pagan doctrine is, that all things good and evil, mean and glorious, fading and unfading, changeable and unchangeable, material and divine, have only one principle. In opposition to this, my belief is that God is the principle of all good things, and *hylē* of the opposite. *Hylē* is the name given by our theologian to the principle or nature of evil. The pagans accordingly think it right to worship God with altars, and shrines, and images, and sacrifices, and incense. Here also my practice differs entirely from theirs: for I look upon myself as a reasonable temple of God (cf. Rom 12:1), if I am worthy to be so; and I consider Christ his Son as the living image of his living majesty; and I hold a mind well cultivated to be the true altar, and pure and simple prayers to be the true way of paying divine honors and of offering sacrifices. (*Faust* 20.3)[31]

In Faustus's eyes, pagans, Jews, and other Christians commit the common mistake of a what we might call a *monothelite* cosmology, one that ascribes both good and evil to a single divine will.[32] Non-Manichaean Christians have brought the doctrine of a single principle behind the universe from their own pagan and Jewish heritage, he contends. Only Manichaean dualism represents a fundamental break with this unenlightened error (*Faust* 20.4). What is more, the practice found among popular African Christianity shows it to amount to a thinly disguised continuity of pagan ritual.

> The sacrifices you change into love-feasts, the idols into martyrs, to whom you pray as they do to their idols. You appease the shades of the departed with wine and food. You keep the same holidays as the Gentiles; for example, the calends and the solstices. In your way of living you have made no change. (*Faust* 20.4)[33]

Only Manichaeism represents a truly distinct religious tradition, therefore, by making a clean break from mundane social values and past ritual practices, as well as from the long-established error of viewing deity primarily in terms of power rather than goodness.

Consistently with both this sweeping association of all religions other than Manichaeism and his more specific critique of Judaism, Faustus rejects the notion of a "Judeo-Christian" tradition, adopting a more universalist perspective on religious history. Pagans and Jews occupy equivalent positions as pre-Christians for him. Both had their law and prophets (*Faust* 19.2), which are to be left behind for the new revelation of Christ. He alludes to the Manichaean affirmation of antediluvian heroes, such as Seth and Enoch, to whom it was believed angels already had revealed basic principles of morality: not to kill, not to commit adultery, not to bear false witness, and so forth (*Faust* 19.3; cf. 22.2). It is these primordial instructions that Christ fulfills in the moral system of the Sermon on the Mount, rather than the elaborated superstitious code of the Israelites. By close analysis of Matthew 5, Faustus seeks to demonstrate that Christ fulfilled these more universal antediluvian laws, while rejecting laws directly identified with Mosaic legislation, such as the *lex talionis*, the loving of friends but hating of enemies, and divorce. If God in his mercy saves the Jewish patriarchs, why would he not do the same for the ancient heroes of the Gentiles, whose conduct was no worse? (*Faust* 33.1). The exclusive link of Christianity to the Jewish heritage poses an obstacle to the universal call of faith Christ issued, Faustus maintains, which is only fulfilled by the boundaryless mission of the Manichaeans. The latter stands prepared to make its case on whatever antecedent belief system its audience follows, and at the same time calls for a radical break with all such previous religious outlooks, be they pagan or Jewish.

For Faustus, the orientation toward action in his religious commitments goes hand in hand with what might be called pantheistic elements in the Manichaean view of the world. Action in the world, rather than withdrawal from it, is required by the divine presence that permeates our environment. The externalization of self in action possesses great seriousness when it can potentially inflict harm on the deity itself, the "vulnerable Jesus" (*Jesus patibilis*), "hanging from every tree" (*Faust* 20.2). Within this understanding of the world, all action takes on the seriousness of ritual, just as the entire environment becomes sacred space. To get this point across to an audience of Christians, Faustus informs them that, "your religion resembles ours in attaching the same sacredness to the bread and wine [of the eucharist] that we do to everything" (*Faust* 20.2). Being religious, then, requires the formulation of a self capable of interacting with everything, at all times, with the degree of attention and care appropriate to interacting with the sacred, and required for the salvational processes of which human actions are a part.

What is it, then, that religion calls us to do, and what are we in the process of becoming when we take up a religious program of practice? Faustus answers that true religion provides the means for constituting a new self. He insists that Manichaeism stands apart from the other religions in its recognition that neither we nor the world reflect the state of perfection that should be entailed in a direct, unopposed creation and maintenance of existence by God. The Christian tradition demands an acknowledgment of God as creator. Very well. But creator of what? If Christians mean creator of this world, just as it is, then they are taking a fundamentally *secular* stance, implying that there is no problem to be resolved, no need for the sort of solution religion is meant to provide. Manichaeism, true to its Christian roots, discerns a problem in our congenital condition as human beings, Faustus emphasizes, and summons us to a recreation of our selves.

> For according to the Apostle there are two men, one of whom he calls sometimes the outer man, generally the earthy, sometimes too the old man; the other he calls the inner or heavenly or new man. . . . For there are likewise two times of our nativity: one when nature brought us forth into this light, binding us in the bonds of flesh, and the other when the truth regenerated us in our conversion from error and our entrance into the faith. It is this second birth of which Jesus speaks in the Gospel when he says, "Unless a man be born again, he cannot see the kingdom of God" (Jn 3:3). (*Faust* 24.1)[34]

Emphasis on our creation as embodied beings, like emphasis on the physical reality of Christ's incarnation, places the stress in the wrong place, going against the priorities set forth by Christ himself, who states, "That which is born of the flesh is flesh, and that which is born of the spirit is spirit" (Jn 3:6). There are therefore two kinds of birth that must be sharply distinguished, even opposed.

> In the humiliating process of ordinary generation, we spring from the heat of animal passion. But when we are brought into the faith, we are

formed under good instruction in honor and purity in Jesus Christ by the Holy Spirit. For this reason, in all religion, and especially in the Christian religion, young children are invited to membership. (*Faust* 24.1)

If human beings came into worldly existence as they should be under an omnipotent divine regime, there should be no need to initiate children, at least until such time as they have fallen into sin and need reform. Faustus thus implies a kind of "original sin" that even children have before they have committed any wrong in this life.[35] Of course, for him it is not sin, but a congenital domination of the divine soul by mixture with evil.

For if it is when we are fashioned in the womb that God forms us after his own image, which is the common belief of Gentiles and Jews, and which is also your belief, then God makes the Old Man, and produces us by means of sensual passion, which does not seem suitable to his divine nature. But if it is when we are converted and brought to a better life that we are formed by God, which is the general doctrine of Christ and his apostles, and which is also our doctrine, in this case God makes us New Men, and produces us in honor and purity, which would agree perfectly with his sacred and adorable majesty. (*Faust* 24.1)

For this reason, Paul condemns the Old Man, commands that he be "put off," and speaks of the New Man who is to be "put on" as alone "the image of him who created him in you" (Eph 4:22–24; Col 3:9–11). As Paul himself stresses, this new identity has nothing to do with gender or ethnicity or social status (Gal 3:27–28). "Man, then, is made by God not when from one he is divided into many, but when from many he becomes one. The division is in the first birth, or that of the body; union comes by the second, which is intelligible and divine" (*Faust* 24.1). It is in this self-forming project that religion finds its raison d'être for Faustus, giving him the liberty to relativize and downplay absolute doctrinal claims, even while he assumes certain key doctrines essential in providing rationales for the specific self Manichaeism promoted.

As we have seen, then, Faustus forged his own personal synthesis of the Manichaean faith with other values and ideas that he possessed as a man born and raised in Roman Africa. This personalized amalgam of commitment—which had a remarkably liberal character—apparently had not impeded his advancement into the highest ranks of leadership within the Manichaean community. This circumstance is perhaps indicative of the character of North African Manichaeism that had attracted Augustine in the first place, and probably played a role in retaining his allegiance for so long, despite various misgivings. It is fascinating, therefore, to observe the role this very same liberal attitude had in leading to Augustine's exit from the sect. He had been seeking long enough, it seems; he was ready to find some solid truth. Although Faustus had some solid truths to offer, they apparently were not of the kind Augustine expected or was ready to ingest.

Faustus and Augustine

Whatever Augustine's diagnosis at the time of his inability to "make progress" in Manichaeism, he reports seeking Faustus's answer only to his problems with Manichaean teachings about the causes of the movements of celestial objects. If he had other issues he wished addressed, he does not mention bringing them up. He gives no indication that he sought counseling on moral issues,[36] or that he confronted Faustus with the "Nebridian Conundrum," or that he voiced doubts about the Manichaean teaching that the New Testament texts had been corrupted by interpolations. Even though Augustine would later claim that all of these issues gave him pause in his allegiance to the Manichaean faith, they apparently did not rise to a significant level of concern as long as he held confidence in the Manichaean system as a whole. Rather, it was his keen interest in astrology and astronomy (as previously noted, indistinguishable at the time) that created his chief conflict with the Manichaean system. He had "read widely," he relates, "in the works of philosophers" (*Conf* 5.3.3), by which he means not figures such as Plato or Aristotle, but astronomers and astrologers. He determined that "they have discovered much, and predicted eclipses of the sun's light, or the moon's, many years in advance, indicating precisely the day, the hour, and the extent of the eclipse. And their calculations have been accurate" (*Conf* 5.3.4).[37] This regularity of the cosmos seemed to be at odds with the dramatic explanation of celestial phenomena put forward by Mani, who ascribed such events to the struggles between good and evil, which one might suppose should be neither regular nor predictable. Thus, in the accurate characterization of Thomas O'Laughlin, "the problems posed to Faustus little concerned philosophical or religious issues as we might define them";[38] rather, "the dispute with Faustus is a clash between two materialist cosmologies: ordinary astrological belief on the one hand, and Manichaeism on the other."[39]

A point that at first might seem rather minor, and somewhat marginal to religious commitment, took on wider ramifications for Augustine within the expectations he had of infallible authority. If Mani were wrong about the causative forces behind the motions of celestial bodies, would not the reliability of his entire cosmology begin to unravel, and with it the dualist metaphysical principles on which that cosmology is built? Alexander of Lycopolis had already raised astronomical objections to Manichaean cosmology similar to those Augustine discovered independently (Alexander of Lycopolis 22.30.1 –23.32.9). With the challenge to Manichaean cosmology came a further issue with Manichaean claims that their teachings could be demonstrated—or at least not contradicted—by direct observation of the cosmos. The movement of stars and planets was among those things directly observable. If their defiance of the expectations set up by Manichaean cosmological constructs forced the Manichaeans to resort to an appeal to Mani's authority as a prophet, they forfeited their much vaunted advantage over all those who demanded blind faith in their followers.[40]

Yet when Augustine raised the difficulty over astronomical predictability with Faustus, the latter declined to solve the problem. In this momentous response, we detect a strong correlation between Faustus as Augustine knew him and the author of the *Capitula*. Faustus did not simply come up short on Augustine's particular question; he programmatically declared all such speculative matters to have no importance (*Conf* 5.7.12). Jean de Menasce captures the gap in priorities separating the bishop and the Auditor.

> His preoccupations of a moral and spiritual nature contrasted somewhat sharply with the "scientific" curiosities of the young auditor in quest of a system founded on reason, for whom it was a question of truth that, without being quite at the center of the system, was posed to him in a manner persistently enough to not fade throughout these three years of waiting. Faustus represented by contrast the "evangelic" and personal aspect of the Manichaean religion, to which . . . Augustine was well nigh indifferent.[41]

Missing from Menasce's characterization of Faustus's more pragmatic set of concerns, however, is a recognition that Faustus as much as Augustine grounded his particular stance on a rational basis, one provided by Academic skepticism.

In his reading of Cicero, Faustus evidently had discovered a system of thought he regarded as compatible with his Manichaean commitments, despite significant surface differences. Augustine had detected something of the same spirit, in which both Manichaeans and Academics could say that they conducted inquiries into truth in such a manner "that our auditors may be guided by reason rather than by authority." Unlike absolute skeptics, adherents of Academic skepticism such as Cicero did not deny the existence of a true reality, but only questioned the human capacity to know that reality with complete clarity and certainty (Cicero, *Acad. pr.* 2.32.104–5; 2.34.111). Similarly, Manichaeism taught that the human senses, under the control of evil, constantly bombarded the mind with misleading impressions. Even though the solutions to this dilemma offered by the two systems differed considerably, in both cases the solution was put in service of plans of action. The Manichaean tradition held that divine intervention and revelation empowered human beings to gain some apprehension of truth, and so gain some control over their actions, despite the continuing lure of misleading impressions. The Academic tradition, on the other hand, offered no such divine help, but proposed a systematic testing of impressions against other impressions and in action (Cicero, *Acad. pr.* 2.10.32; 2.31.99). This policy, of course, made some sorts of experience more testable than others, and left much of the more theoretical areas of knowledge out of the range of testable conclusions. Cicero specifically had made speculation about cosmological questions his prime example of unresolvable theoretical questions (Cicero, *Acad. pr.* 2.36.116ff.), and concluded that the sage is not required to answer all the riddles of the universe (Cicero, *Acad. pr.* 2.38.119), inasmuch as impressions one has of them cannot be tested by acting on them in some way (Cicero, *Acad. pr.* 2.34.110).

It can be taken as a direct application of such key passages in Cicero that Faustus felt at liberty to frankly admit to Augustine that he did not know whether Mani or the astronomers had the better explanation of celestial phenomena (*Conf* 5.7.12)—a remarkable position for the head of the African Manichaean community, but consistent with Cicero's assertion that Academics "are bound by no compulsion to support all the dogmas laid down for us almost as edicts by certain masters" (Cicero, *Acad. pr.* 2.3.8). Accordingly, Faustus implicitly critiques some of his own Manichaean predecessors in his *Capitula* (*Faust* 1.2).

There is good reason to suspect that Augustine has integrated traces of Faustus's response to him into his discussion of the respective purviews of religion and science in *Confessions* 5.4.7ff. The sharp distinction between religious and scientific concerns made in this passage expresses an outlook utterly at odds with Augustine's own views in the period he is discussing, as well as those to be seen in his early post-Manichaean writings; and it appears to have found a place in the *Confessions* only by a fairly remote association with the vice of *curiositas*. The earlier Augustine espoused the harmony of "scientific" and "religious" truth—or rather failed to see any relevant distinction—and took astronomical phenomena as significant expressions of the divine will and nature. While the polemical targeting of Mani in the passage certainly belongs to the author of the *Confessions*, the underlying reasoning of the critique echoes the position Augustine attributes to Faustus, namely, that the sort of scientific problems Augustine posed at the time "are not necessary to the learning of goodness and piety" (*Conf* 5.5.8). Faustus could scarcely have found a more exact guideline for dealing with his overly curious pupil than Cicero's statement that the sage, "if a question be put to him about duty or about a number of other matters in which practice has made him an expert, would not reply in the same way as he would if questioned as to whether the number of stars is even or odd, and say that he did not know" (Cicero, *Acad. pr.* 2.34.110).

By no means do I wish to suggest that Faustus adhered to a thoroughgoing Academic skepticism, any more than I would argue that he offered a complete embodiment of Manichaean principles. Both allegiances were qualified, and idiosyncratically hybridized, in Faustus. Faustus's uncertainties about the literal truth of all of Mani's pronouncements did not amount to doubts about his commitment to Manichaeism, as they did for Augustine. Rather, they represented a programmatic choice not to make complete commitment depend on confirming everything first, and not to suspend acting on faith until after every point of doctrine had been scrutinized. Skepticism provided him with a toolkit of principles and arguments with which he rationalized and justified an emphasis on practice he wished to maintain in his own Manichaean identity and to promote in the Manichaean identity of his flock. It allowed him to characterize his pragmatic focus in terms of standards of reason, rather than as an anti-rationalist appeal to faith.[42]

Based on the clues Augustine provides to his own attitudes and interests at the time, he probably had difficulty appreciating the approach to religion being suggested by Faustus. We can be certain that his experience with Faustus convinced him that some of his reservations about Manichaean teaching would go unresolved; it may also have led him to start to suspect that he did not share its values. Faustus clearly had been chosen as a leader for merits other than those Augustine was looking for in an authority figure. His refusal to answer Augustine's questions definitively and with proofs defied the Auditor's expectations of the role of the sage as an intellectual mentor. His abiding intellectual interest in the pursuit of truth may have come to eclipse whatever initial intention he had to implement a Ciceronian program of self-cultivation through the Manichaean disciplinary system. Instead, the issues that weighed upon his mind indicate that he expected the sect to provide a body of knowledge absolutely certain in its every detail, and for that reason capable of being invested with total confidence. This expectation ran up against Faustus, unconcerned to verify every pronouncement of Mani or Adimantus on the authenticity of a verse of scripture, the exact nature of Christ's embodiment, or the causative forces of celestial motion. What mattered for him was the overall ethos of the religion, its compelling character as a value system, and its plausibility as a means of salvation. More than just offering reason before belief, he in effect was proposing practice prior to belief, gradually building confidence and understanding as practice succeeds. Out of this encounter, Augustine would gradually formulate a problem: how can one invest oneself and make progress in a practice unless one first somehow believes in it?

At one level, Faustus appears to break with an intentionalist account of religious action, by which we imagine religious practitioners saying to themselves, "Because I believe that reality and my place in it are such-and-such, I will act accordingly." Faustus proposes in place of this something along the lines of, "Because I wish to act such-and-such, I will believe accordingly," with "accordingly" representing a scenario by which the motivation to act will be engendered and sustained. "Knowledge of great things is worth little," he declares, "unless one's life is worthy" (*Faust* 12.1). Faustus explicitly and actively forwards this position against what he regards as an impotent intellectualism emerging in the Christian mainstream's obsession with orthodoxy. Instead of relegating religious practices to the status of entailments of certain truths about the universe and humanity, the evidence for which remained debatable, Augustine and others Faustus mentored should look to the most immediately observable evidence of truth in their own bodies and mental states. Effective selfhood, measured in capacities and stabilities that reflected Manichaean models of human perfectability, provided its own proof. Teachings that effectively motivated pious conduct and provided a successful framework for moral character proved their validity, their *probability* and *truth-likeness*, within this vale of tears where the presence of the forces of darkness constantly interfered with our ability to perceive certain truth. So, for example, Augustine could resolve uncertainty as to whether Mani or the astronomers were right by noting the former's superior holiness (*Conf* 5.5.9). Was this not what Augustine had sought in the Manichaeans? Was this not a realization of the Ciceronian program of moral advancement to a state capable of apprehending truth?

Faustus was perfectly capable of offering criteria by which Augustine could assess and confirm the Manichaean system of rationales, and so employ them in the usual way as motivations for action. Academic skeptics defined the sage as one who had built up a set of probable truths that have proven themselves, providing a basis for further extrapolated probability (*Acad* 2.12.27; 3.3.5). Correspondingly, Augustine reports that Faustus, and the African Manichaeans in general, took the position, "you believe in what Manichaeus has not proved, because he has so clearly proved the existence of two natures, good and evil, in this world" (*Faust* 32.20; cf. *CEF* 14.17), just as the fact of his achievement of holiness demonstrated his correct grasp of the truths that induce a holy life (*Conf* 5.5.9). Any further doctrines consistent with these relative certainties may be trusted until contradicted by experience. The Manichaean could add to these bases of judgment an innate sense of true and false, right and wrong (*Faust* 32.2), implicitly deriving from the divine origin and connections of the soul—yet another view Faustus would have found echoed in Cicero.[43]

Yet while Augustine could agree that Mani displayed a more spiritually advanced character than astrologers—or for that matter the patriarchs of the Old Testament—he had yet to operationalize Manichaeism successfully as a means of significant spiritual progress in his own life. The effectiveness that Faustus was proposing as proof of the validity of Manichaeism was the very thing Augustine could not personally confirm. He describes his own conduct as a Manichaean as falling short of an ideal disengagement with the world. Sex (albeit monogamous and restrained according to Manichaean principles) and ambition (albeit moderated with a Manichaean concern for virtuous employment), as well as worldly entertainments (albeit as benign as theater and sporting events), continued to preoccupy him. We in fact do not know how much this state of affairs dissatisfied him at the time, since it was not among the issues he took up with Faustus. It could only matter to him to the degree that he aspired to be an Elect or in some other fashion more disengaged with mundane life. He only enunciates this failure of Manichaeism to prove itself according to Faustus's own criterion as part of a polemical contrast he wishes to make to the greater efficacy of the system of teachings and practices he found among the Nicene Christians of Milan. From this later vantage point Augustine faulted Faustus's attitude toward religion, and came to see his encounter with that attitude as a decisive turning point in his own spiritual development. "All the ambition I had to go far in that sect," he later claimed, "simply collapsed once I had got to know the man" (*Conf* 5.7.13).

The impression he wishes to give of that encounter in his *Confessions* confronts a number of other pieces of evidence, however, that give a somewhat different picture of how events unfolded at the time. From what we know of Augustine, we have no reason to doubt that he experienced disappointment with Faustus because of the latter's disinterest in pursuing the fine points of celestial motion. Yet Augustine admits to being impressed and awed by Faustus, and these sentiments appear initially to have muted any chagrin. Faustus's affable manner disarmed Augustine's intellectual zeal for the moment. In the words of James O'Donnell, "it was the modesty with which Faustus failed to live up to his advance reputation that endeared him the more to Augustine, even as Augustine was disappointed with what Faustus had to say." He adds, "there would have been those in Africa who remembered Augustine's growing friendship with the Manichean bishop," even after his refusal to meet Augustine's expectations, as the two read and conversed together over several months.[44]

Faustus, discovering that Augustine was a teacher, asked him to guide his reading of important works of literature. The bishop wanted to improve himself intellectually, and did not confuse his spiritual rank with personal superiority to the lower-ranking and younger Augustine, who obviously had the better education. The look on Augustine's face in this ironic reversal of expectations must have been priceless. All the shallow measures of superiority that he valued at the time, as he later acknowledges in the *Confessions*, were at odds with Faustus's character.[45] Whereas Augustine remarks on his own love of disputation as a Manichaean, and never tires of describing his fellow Manichaeans as "loquacious" (*Conf* 3.6.10, 7.2.3; *DP* 20.53),[46] he makes a point of saying that Faustus did not share this vice (*Conf* 5.7.12), and appears to ascribe the latter's disinclination to address obscure subjects at least in part to this character trait. It is an essential part of the purpose of the *Confessions* as a protreptic appeal to the Manichaeans, as well as an indication of a belated revolution in Augustine's thinking, that Faustus serves in a remarkable capacity as a major hero of the story. Augustine picks his words carefully, ascribing to Faustus the key virtues he wishes to promote in the book: modesty, confession, and that most classically applauded virtue, the Socratic awareness of one's own ignorance (*Conf* 5.7.12). These traits were object lessons Augustine was not prepared to absorb fully at the time, though he recognized them in hindsight.

In that hindsight, Augustine saw Faustus playing a role ordained by God to disabuse him of his devotion to Manichaeism (*Conf* 5.7.13). By being who he was, by displaying an idiosyncratic combination of Manichaean piety and skeptical dismissal of absolute truth, by being *this* person at *this* place at *this* time, Faustus affected the course of Augustine's own formation of self in a way that otherwise would have taken a very different route. The Manichaean Augustine would never have become the later Augustine—perhaps even never would have become the "Catholic" Augustine or the "Neoplatonic" Augustine—if it had been anyone else who showed up in Carthage as the supreme representative of Manichaean identity in 382. Our task as historians is to identify in precisely what way Faustus immediately shaped Augustine in his relationship to Manichaeism and to his larger quest for truth, without assuming that the *Confessions* tells the whole story, or the story at all, as it was experienced by the parties involved at the time of its unfolding. Was Augustine actually self-confident and arrogant enough to reject immediately the spiritual advice of this famously talented and evidently pious man? While speaking of his encounter with Faustus as the point when he gave up all ambition to advance within the sect, he adds the telling understatement, "Not that I broke completely with the Manichaeans" (*Conf* 5.7.13).

In fact, he continued to be a practicing Manichaean for at least another two years, a period that he equates with an ideological skepticism. By establishing the skeptical elements in Faustus's pragmatic approach to Manichaeism, we have come as close as history usually can to laying out a correlation of antecedents to outcomes suggesting something like causality. It is in light of Faustus's own idiosyncratic synthesis of skepticism with Manichaeism as a system of religious practice, therefore, that we can recover the story behind Augustine's introduction to Academic skepticism, as well as his return, full-circle, to his original Ciceronian inspiration for bothering with a religious community and identity at all (*Conf* 5.10.19). It is clear that Cicero's *Academica* provided most of Augustine's information on this long defunct philosophical school, and yet he does not specify precisely where, when, or from whom he learned of it.[47] Given Faustus's own skeptical inclinations and the clear debt he owes in them to Cicero, along with the timing of this new direction in Augustine's philosophical reading, it seems all but certain that Cicero formed part of the extra-Manichaean reading Augustine did with Faustus in the last year of his residency in Carthage. His comment in 386 that the skeptical outlook had held him back from commitment "for a long time" would seem to correlate with this scenario. His remarks several years later in *The Usefulness of Belief* similarly associate his meeting with Faustus with entering into a period in which he was "doubtful and hesitant about what I should hold and what I should forsake" (*UC* 8.20). From the hindsight of the ultimate failure of the skeptical program for him, Augustine only could view it as an exacerbation of his existing doubts, rather than as an effective means for circumventing them. But it took time for him to reach this negative conclusion.

Indeed, abundant evidence suggests that we should credit the Manichaean Augustine with something the later Augustine is loath to confess: that he tried it Faustus's way for a time. This is precisely what we see in Augustine's subsequent conduct: after leaving Carthage for Rome, he continued avidly to observe Manichaean practice, while intellectually pursuing a more skeptical path of thinking, more consciously open to taking theoretical suggestions from other religious and philosophical traditions. With the authorization offered by the attitude of Faustus, he felt free to assess all proposed truths by the principles of the New Academy, "trying to discover if I could in any way convict the Manichaeans of falsehood by some definite proofs." "But this I could not do," he adds (*Conf* 5.14.25), acknowledging that the plausibility of Manichaeism by the standards of reason gave it continuing credibility in his eyes. "Since I had found nothing better than this sect . . . I resolved to be content with it for the time being, unless some preferable option presented itself" (*Conf* 5.7.13). He adopted as his own Faustus's criterion of resultant piety (*Conf* 5.5.9; *Acad* 2.2.5; *Ord* 2.9.27),[48] and one notes that most of his references to participating in Manichaean ritual practices seem to belong to this later period of his membership in the sect.

Parted Company

The author of the *Confessions* is perfectly willing to credit external forces for determining most of the major developments of his life, and as historians we could do worse than follow his example. Faustus's mentorship of Augustine might have produced any number of possible outcomes, but it was cut short by the pressures of persecution. Anti-Manichaean legislation had begun to appear in the years just before and soon after Faustus's return to Carthage, and it was only a matter of time before it was enforced by some zealous new governor of Africa. As we shall see, Augustine chose wisdom over valor and fled into anonymity in Rome in 383. He may have been urged to do so by Faustus, and it appears likely that the nameless traveling companions who accompanied Augustine to Rome served to vouch for Augustine to the Manichaean community there, so that interceptible letters of recommendation would not need to be carried on his person. The Manichaean brethren of Rome took Augustine in, despite the risks, no doubt on Faustus's good word. Faustus remained behind in Africa, choosing perhaps to provide much-needed stability to a community facing tougher times ahead.

It took a few years for the axe to fall. Probably in early 386, the proconsul Messianus acted upon existing anti-Manichaean laws, and initiated the first serious legal prosecution of the Manichaeans in Africa. Faustus was still there at the time, and was accused to the proconsul as a Manichaean, apparently by Christian leaders. Haled before Messianus, Faustus took his stand as the spokesperson for the North African Manichaean community, defending as legitimate the Manichaean claim to the Christian legacy. No circumstance offers a better explanatory context for the formal confession of faith Faustus incorporated into his *Capitula* in the aftermath of his trial. The Roman state had issued a new official standard of religious legitimacy. So be it. But he would show that it had wrongfully drawn the conclusion that Manichaeism fell outside the bounds of that new standard.

The official decrees and creeds defined the limits of the Christian faith on the grounds of belief rather than practice. So Faustus would have to play it their way. The preceding century of intra-Christian debate had pitted Trinitarian theology against non-Trinitarian alternatives. Consequently the new definitions of faith focused on affirming the full divinity of Christ within a Trinitarian model of deity. But Manichaeism had always been Trinitarian in expression (however complex the theology represented by that expression) and stood clearly with Nicene Christians in favor of the divinity of Christ. In these circumstances, Faustus wished it to be known, Manichaeans had every right to be considered a viable, legal religious alternative.

We worship, then, one deity under the threefold appellation of the Almighty God the Father, and his son Christ, and the Holy Spirit.

While these are one and the same, we believe also that the Father
properly dwells in the highest or principal light, which Paul calls "light
inaccessible" (1 Tim 6:16) and the Son in his second or visible light. And
as the Son is himself twofold, according to the apostle, who speaks of
Christ as the power of God and the wisdom of God (2 Cor 1:24), we
believe that his power dwells in the sun, and his wisdom in the moon.
We also believe that the Holy Spirit, the third majesty, has his seat and
his home in the whole circle of the atmosphere. By his influence and
spiritual infusion, the earth conceives and brings forth the vulnerable
Jesus, who, as hanging from every tree, is the life and salvation of men.
(*Faust* 20.2)

While Faustus makes no attempt to censor the distinctly Manichaean elements of this theology, his imitation of Christian creedal form as well as the
Trinitarian edict of Theodosisus seems to mark his intention to have it compared to these other formulations.[49] How could adherents of a theology so
closely approximating the official definitions be justly condemned?

Messianus probably was supremely uninterested in such fine points of
theology. Faustus headed the Manichaean community, an outlawed group.
There was nothing else to be debated. The sentence was death. His accusers,
mindful of creating a martyr, requested a commutation.

Faustus, when shown to be a Manichaean by evidence, or by his own
confession, on the intercession of the Christians themselves, who
brought him before the proconsul, was, along with some others, only
banished to an island, which can hardly be called a punishment at all,
for it is what God's servants do of their own accord every day when they
wish to retire from the tumult of the world. Besides, earthly sovereigns
often by a public decree give release from this banishment as an act of
mercy. And in this way all were afterwards released at once. (*Faust* 5.8;
cf. *CLP* 3.25,30)

Paul Monceaux has identified this amnesty convincingly as the occasion of
the *vota publica* of Theodosius and Arcadius in January 387.[50] Faustus may
have composed his *Capitula* during this short period of exile, allowing the
voice of his leadership to continue even in his physical absence. His fate after
his release is unknown. There is no indication that he returned to Carthage,

which would have been impolitic, and he seems to have died sometime in the subsequent decade, freeing Augustine to name him in the *Confessions* as a Manichaean, after alluding to him namelessly a number of times in earlier compositions. It would be going too far to attribute this reticence to a continuing loyalty or religious sympathy. Some matters of personal honor were above polemics.

Yet we cannot discount the evidence of a lasting influence of Faustus on his erstwhile acolyte. All this evidence comes from Augustine's own pen. Although he constantly reinterpreted the nature of his debt to Faustus, he never reduced this debt to insignificance. For a time, it seems, he attempted to follow the program Faustus proposed as he understood it. Because of Augustine's own intellectualist inclinations, however, the skeptical element of this program outgrew the subordinate place it held in Faustus's own pragmatic program. While remaining unrefuted, Manichaeism gradually lost its allure for Augustine. This gradual lapse into apostasy is the story of the next two chapters. Yet, as we shall see, Faustus's proposals survived Augustine's exit from their original Manichaean context, and found new places within the rearrangement of priorities and commitments that we call Augustine's "conversion," even as Augustine sought to distance himself from his former faith.

CHAPTER FIVE

Exile

In the very period that he would later characterize as one of discontent and disaffection, Augustine had become a veritable Manichaean insider. After nearly a decade of proselytizing, entering into public disputation, and forming discussion groups in support of the Manichaean cause, Augustine was now hobnobbing with Faustus himself, the supreme authority of the faith in Augustine's African homeland. However frustrated he may have been with the dismissal of his curiosity over cosmological questions, he evidently drew close to Faustus. He served his Manichaean superior as a literary tutor, reading with him the books that Faustus had heard merited attention, as well as making a few recommendations of his own (*Conf* 5.7.13). To all of Augustine's peers at the time, he must have seemed to be well embedded in the Manichaean community, a confidant of the bishop himself.[1]

Suddenly, in the summer of 383 C.E., Augustine left Carthage for Rome. He left behind his family, his pedagogical wards (among them his patron Romanianus's son, Licentius, *Acad* 2.2.3), and most famously his mother (*Conf* 5.8.15). "What sudden impulse or sudden circumstance drove him to do this thing to them?" John O'Meara asks. "Impulse it must have been, for no circumstance that we can reasonably conjecture could explain his sudden and irresponsible deceit. It looks as if he wanted to escape from everybody and everything he knew."[2] The suddenness and abandonment involved in Augustine's departure belie his own explanation of the decision as one motivated primarily by personal ambition and petty disgruntlement with conditions in the Carthaginian classrooms—reasons fitted to the psychological themes and the apologetic purpose of the *Confessions*, and just perhaps to a studied deniability of even less honorable motivations. The coincidence of his departure with a major shift in government policy toward Manichaeans was too strong to ignore. Petilian, Donatist bishop of the city of Constantine, later accused him of having fled Africa at a time of persecution of the Manichaeans (*CLP* 3.25.30).[3] It is almost certain that Petilian based his charge on earlier questioning of Augustine's actions by the latter's own colleagues in the emergent African "Catholic" community he had joined.[4] The evidence supporting this accusation, though largely circumstantial, is substantial. It seems likely that Augustine, at some risk as an outspoken if idiosyncratic member of the Manichaean community at Carthage, fled into exile when new imperial edicts were published against adherents of his sect.

Crackdown

Augustine mentions experiencing the restraining conditions of anti-Manichaean edicts in *The Morals of the Manichaeans*, when he says that meetings were prohibited, and so held in secret, in Carthage (*MM* 19.69). The old executive order of Valentinian I (*Cod. Theod.* 16.5.3)[5] against Manichaean meetings, issued on 2 March 372, is unlikely to stand directly behind the restrictions Augustine describes, since it was not issued to a Praetorian Prefect for provincial publication, but only to the prefect of Rome, Publius Ampelius, for local application.

> Wherever an assembly of Manichaeans or such a throng is found, their teachers shall be punished with a heavy penalty. Those who assemble shall also be segregated from the company of men as infamous and ignominious, and the houses and habitations in which the profane doctrine is taught shall undoubtedly be appropriated to the resources of the fisc. (*Cod. Theod.* 16.5.3)

Nonetheless, these provisions may have been incorporated into a lost rescript issued by Gratian from Sirmium sometime in 378, which excepted the Manichaeans (as well as "Photinians" and "Eunomians") from a general allowance of assembly to all other Christian groups (Sozomen, *Hist. Eccl.* 7.1.3; Socrates, *Hist. Eccl.* 5.2; Theodoret, *Hist. Eccl.* 5.2). Even the allowances of the rescript

were revoked by *Cod. Theod.* 16.5.5, issued by Gratian in Milan the following year, on 3 August 379. In an apparent effort to establish a uniform policy
for the entire empire that, with the catastrophic death of Valens, had fallen
to his responsibility, Gratian renewed the general ban on meetings for "all
heresies," that is, most marginal schismatic and heretical groups outside the
still unsorted Christian mainstream. It has been argued with good reason that
Gratian addressed specific provisions of this edict to the Donatist situation in
Africa,[6] and it certainly found publication there. By its invocation of the prior
enactments of both Valentinian and Gratian himself, its proscriptions would
have produced the clandestine character of Manichaean meetings Augustine
describes for part of his tenure with them.

We must get the timing of the African crackdown on Manichaeism right
in order to understand properly how it may have affected Augustine. Nothing
in his account of his attraction to Manichaeism or his enrollment in the community suggests that he saw himself signing on to an antisocial or countercultural program. He perceived Manichaeism as a potential realization of the
eminently respectable Ciceronian project of self-cultivation. In the climate of
the time, Augustine could not have anticipated persecution, at least not of an
officially sanctioned kind. He no doubt was perfectly prepared to be misunderstood by lesser men, or by his mother, and to espouse values foreign to the
general public; but how comfortable was he with the identity of a subversive?
The proscription of Manichaean meetings contained in the laws of 378 and
379 would have posed a minor inconvenience to Augustine, little more. Most
likely, he could still speak out individually as a Manichaean, and rhetorically
demolish non-Manichaean Christian opponents, so long as he was not caught
with his fellow sectarians in meetings.[7]

But Augustine found himself caught up in a rapidly unfolding process by
which the emperor Gratian and his new imperial colleague Theodosius began
to harden sectarian boundaries and establish an official, state-sponsored form
of the Christian religion. On 28 February 380, Theodosius had issued the momentous edict that declared the Neo-Nicene theology to be the only form of
Christian doctrine acceptable to the government, and henceforth considered
"catholic" or universal in its sway. The declaration defined, by creed and by
communion, a "Catholic Church" as an institution committed to Neo-Nicene
Trinitarianism—that is, to a belief in "the single deity of the Father, the Son,
and the Holy Spirit under the concept of equal majesty and holy trinity"—as
defined by the bishops of Rome and Alexandria (Damasus and Peter, respec-

tively). The law had its greatest impact on non-Nicene Christians, who up to that point had considered themselves, and been legally considered, part of the Christian mainstream. Non-Christians were not affected at all, while more marginal Christian sectarians continued largely as before. The place of the Manichaeans on this religious terrain remained unclear. They had kept themselves aloof from the debates over Christian doctrine and polity that had been the focus of state involvement, and were looked upon by all sides of those debates as not really Christians at all. It was up to the imperial courts to clarify how the new religious policy would impact the Manichaeans.

An intensification of legal restrictions on Manichaeans was signaled on 8 May 381, when Eutropius, serving as Praetorian Prefect of a temporarily detached Illyria, received *Cod. Theod.* 16.5.7,[8] ordering him to interdict any transfer of property, through bequest or trade, made by a Manichaean, or any inheritance received by one. Manichaeans were deprived of all legal rights. They could not make wills or conduct business. This was a typical way for the state to go after undesirables. Since the courts were involved in legal transfers of property as well as taxation, they were in a position to confiscate property in transit from one owner to another. But the edict broke legal precedent by also giving the Praetorian Prefect the right to apply this confiscation retroactively, that is, to acts of bequest or trade that had occurred before the law was made. The timing of the law and its locale of application may explain its excesses. The empire was in the midst of a major military crisis, and strapped for cash. The emperors had already squeezed as much out of the existing tax code as they could, and issued major increases across the board and emergency levies on the cities. Now it was time to target individual total estates at the vulnerable point of transference from one owner to another. The Manichaeans, as notorious sectarians, were easy targets for a major revenue-raising campaign, and the law may have been an entirely local initiative aimed at the Manichaeans of Illyria, in order to raise funds for Theodosius's campaign against the Visigoths in the region.[9]

The anti-Manichaean campaign widened the following year, however, with a law, issued on 31 March 382 to the Praetorian Prefect of the eastern empire, Florus (*Cod. Theod.* 16.5.9). While reiterating the previous edict's provision for retroactive application, it went considerably farther.

> Your sublimity, therefore, shall appoint investigators, shall open court, and shall receive informers and denouncers, without the odium attached to informers (*delatores*). No person shall destroy the establishment of

this accusation by means of the usual defense of prescription (of time). No person shall convoke such secret and hidden assemblies; they shall be forbidden in the country, they shall be prohibited within the walls, they shall be condemned in public and private habitations. (*Cod. Theod.* 16.5.9)

The Roman legal tradition had always looked unfavorably on delation, that is, accusation—often anonymous—without legal consequence if proven false. Roman law had imposed legal responsibility on accusers as recently as 380 (*Cod. Theod.* 10.10.12 and 13), making them subject to punishment for making false or unfounded accusations. The law of 382 reversed this tradition, specifically approving the use of "informers and denouncers," and absolving them of all risk connected to their charges. The appointment of investigators at state expense was also unusual for anything except treason. The concern for the whole countryside, not just the cities, and for activities in private homes, not just public spaces, also makes this law out of the ordinary.

The law addresses itself to an apparent countermove on the part of the Manichaeans to the law of the previous year. It records that they were declaring themselves "hermits" and giving their property away (precisely to whom is ambiguous). In other words, strongly committed Manichaeans, faced with the impossibility of bequeathing their assets, were liquidating them and joining the ranks of the Elect. The law seeks to prevent this economically disruptive tactic by disallowing it, and restoring a more orderly legal process to the potential disposition of estates of the accused: only property of persons for whom no legal heir can be identified is to be confiscated for the state; otherwise, the courts are instructed to make sure property is passed to legal heirs, not disposed of arbitrarily. Thus even a property holder under threat of the law as a Manichaean could have confidence that his property would pass to his legal heirs, and in this way not be motivated to dispose of it rather than risk having it taken by the state.

Incidental to the law's purpose, but central to ours, is its gesture toward clarifying the categorization of Manichaeism among the religious pluralism of the realm. Up to this point, Roman law had labeled them simply as "Manichaeans," a distinct group in the general population, and had not specified their relation to any other tradition. The new law now identified a Manichaean as a Christian sectarian, "a profaner and corrupter of the Catholic discipline," and hence guilty of sacrilege, since the "Catholic discipline" was now the state cult. This clarification of Manichaean identity may have stemmed from discussions held around the Council of Constantinople the previous year concerning the standing of various groups in relation to the "Catholic" communion. It forestalled Manichaeans from placing themselves out of the way of internal Christian struggles by presenting themselves as a pagan group. From Antioch, the pagan orator Libanius had penned an argument along these lines some years earlier on behalf of Palestinian Manichaeans, seeking government protection of them from mob action in the backlash following the death of the emperor Julian.

> Those who worship the sun without blood and honor it as a secondary god and chastise their appetites and reckon the last day as gain are very dispersed in the land but few in number anywhere. They harm no one, but are harassed by some people. I wish that those of them who live in Palestine may have your authority for protection and be free from anxiety, and that those who wish to harm them will not be allowed to do so. (Libanius, *Epistle* 1253)[10]

The categories by which Roman legal and public discourse handled religious identity struggled to keep up with the rapidly shifting religious landscape of the fourth century. There could be no concepts of conversion and apostasy unless and until some clearly demarcated boundaries had been defined.

We cannot confirm that Africa received the further proscription of Manichaean meetings in the laws of 381 and 382. Gratian may have issued duplicates to western Praetorian Prefects, which have not been entered into the Code as superfluous copies. Or perhaps not. So it may have been with surprising suddenness that the weight of the law against Augustine as an individual Manichaean finally came in 383, and at one stroke increased exponentially the pressure on him to evaluate the strength of his commitment. Coincidentally, the edict that reached Africa's shores that year marked the first attempt within the new religious policy to address legally issues of conversion and apostasy for the Roman west.[11]

On 21 May 383, Gratian issued an edict for the western empire, addressed to the Praetorian Prefect of Italy, Africa, and Illyria, Flavius Hypatius,[12] which condemned anyone who converted from Christianity to either paganism, Judaism, or Manichaeism (*Cod. Theod.* 16.7.3)—the latter now seemingly treated as a rival religious tradition rather than a Christian heresy. The terms "conversion" and "apostasy" do not appear. Rather, the law speaks of Christians "who turn to altars and temples," or "who have disdained the dignity of the Christian religion and name and have polluted themselves with Jewish contagions," or "who at any time prefer to frequent the nefarious retreats and the wicked seclusion of the Manichaeans." The edict called for such persons to be "pursued constantly and perpetually." But Augustine fell under this law not only as an apostate; it further condemned those "who have deflected unstable minds to their own society," as Augustine had a number of his friends and associates as a public debater and recruiter for Manichaeism. The law left the severity of the punishment to the discretion of judges. When it was enforced in Africa a few years later, it resulted in multiple arrests and capital sentences for a number of Manichaeans, commuted to exile. The same heightened atmosphere of persecution is reflected in a second edict dated 25 July 383, directed to the Praetorian Prefect of the eastern empire, Postumianus, banning both public and private assemblies of nearly a dozen sects, including the Manichaeans (*Cod. Theod.* 16.5.11). Making public speeches in favor of these sects was specifically prohibited. Accusations were encouraged and welcomed from all "Catholic" Christians, regardless of rank or station. Both of these laws mark a decisive turn from primarily fiscal to corporal and capital punishment. From now on being a Manichaean meant risking life and limb.

The arrival of one or both of these laws in Carthage would have made life very dangerous for Augustine. He had lapsed into "heresy" or committed "apostasy" from what was now declared to be the established faith of the realm. By his own account, he was a well-known debater and recruiter on the Manichaean side. The new laws made it possible for any enemy of his, or even a disgruntled pupil, to accuse him without risk. He had a partner and child to think of. He had to leave Carthage, and he hints that his fellow Manichaeans urged him to do so (*Conf* 5.8.14). Do we perhaps detect a reminiscence of the rhetorical particulars of Gratian's edict of 383, when Augustine, in talking about his brush with death later that year in Rome, says that he was nearly carried off to hell "loaded with all the evil that I had committed against you, against myself, and against other men" (*Conf* 5.9.16)?

When dealing with Roman law, there is always a question of how widely it was circulated and to what degree it was enforced. The general trend as the Roman Empire aged was for laws to be enforced less and less consistently, and later laws often include clauses specifying punishments for government officials who fail to enforce them. Bribery was a way of life in the Roman world, and those with means could usually buy themselves out of trouble, as long as they did not directly and personally affront the emperor. Of the four edicts of 381–383 surveyed above, only *Cod. Theod.* 16.7.3 of 21 May 383 certainly reached Carthage. If the earlier edicts preserved as issued in the eastern empire had copies issued in the west, the Proconsuls of Africa in 381–382 (Herasius)[13] and 382–383 (Aemilianus)[14] apparently took little or no action upon them.[15] The edict of 383 was delivered into the hands of the Proconsul Eusignius.[16] Would he act upon the imperial orders? In light of his lack of action against the Donatists, as well as his later involvement in the religious liberalization policy of the Milanese court of Valentinian II, which temporarily reversed the course set by Gratian and Theodosius, he may have been disinclined to pursue religious nonconformists in Africa. Given the prior course of fourth-century religious politics, it would be natural to assume the wind would soon shift again at imperial whim, as it had so many times before; and this assumption would moderate very rigid enforcement of any edict. Local politics and civil order would have priority over declarations from the court that often must have been all but incomprehensible, not to mention vague on application, to the average magistrate.

But Augustine was no political insider. He could not know how swiftly or thoroughly the laws would be carried out in Carthage. All that he knew was that he was at risk. As it turned out, the proconsul Eusignius did not act on the new anti-Manichaean laws. Nor did his immediate successor. Perhaps they were not the sort of people to spoil the civic life of Carthage by enforcing the edicts against Manichaeism too zealously. Augustine had not waited to find out, and his discretion saved him. When a more zealous Proconsul finally arrived on the scene in the person of Messianus in 386, the very law of 383 that had probably put a chill in Augustine served as the basis for a devastating sweep of the Manichaean community of Carthage. Augustine himself was named in the legal proceedings[17] and apparently sentenced in absentia.[18] But he had made good his escape long before events reached a crisis.

But if Augustine intended to flee beyond the reach of the law, would not the capital be the last place he would go?[19] In reality, Rome offered an ideal refuge in the circumstances. He was known as a Manichaean in Carthage, as well as in his home town of Thagaste. Best to get out of Africa altogether. Rome, with roughly a million inhabitants, offered the kind of anonymity he could find nowhere else in the western empire. The city was no longer the center of the empire; the imperial court resided in Trier and Milan. But it was full of Manichaeans who, because of the new laws, had to carry on their religious life "unobtrusively" (*Conf* 5.10.18–19). The pagan urban prefect Q. Aurelius

Symmachus seems to have given them a level of protection.[20] Given his open opposition to the religious policy of the court in Milan, it is no surprise that he ignored edicts on religion entirely, and made Rome a refuge for those faiths out of imperial favor. Faustus was in the best position to know that conditions were safe in Rome. He knew the Manichaean community there, and could provide the necessary connections. Augustine's traveling companions on this trip, about whom he is quite circumspect, certainly were Manichaeans known to the community in Rome and able to vouch for him; otherwise it is impossible to account for the refuge he found among them when he arrived.

Because Augustine got away from Africa well before trouble started there, he later could plausibly deny any connection between his departure and the anti-Manichaean program of Messianus two and a half years later. But the coincidence is too much for the historian to dismiss. Augustine went directly from the Manichaean community in Carthage to the Manichaean community in Rome, traveling with one or more Manichaean companions. Once there he was taken into a Manichaean home (*Conf* 5.10.18–19), and had a position arranged for him by Manichaean patrons. Beyond this set of evidence, there is the fact that in going to Rome he left everything behind: his domestic partner, his son, his patron's son over whom he had guardianship,[21] and his own mother for whom he was now responsible, and whom he left, literally, at the docks. His departure from Carthage in 383 was the only trip out of Africa he would ever take, and the only other time he dared set foot on a seagoing ship was to return home. Despite Augustine's later disclaimers, all the evidence suggests flight.

That is not to say that Augustine fabricated the other reasons for his move to Rome that he gives in the *Confessions*. If we take seriously Augustine's carefully considered position on truth and lies, which he appears to have worked out for himself in the circumstances of replying to the very accusations about his flight we are considering,[22] then we should expect him only to go so far as to withhold information, not to invent it. In answering accusations about his motives in leaving Africa precisely when he did, Augustine needed plausible deniability that anti-Manichaean legislation had anything to do with it. He had it in the fact that, for all the trouble it had started to cause him, Manichaeism represented a secondary commitment for him. Regardless of his connections to the Manichaean community, he gave higher priority at the time to his rhetorical career and intellectual pursuits. That higher priority, among others, prompted him not to risk martyrdom for his faith, something that Faustus felt obliged to do in the crisis his community faced.

Later in life, Augustine recalled in a letter to one Martianus how the two had been friends at a time he remembers being characterized by an indifference to religious matters on both their parts (*Ep* 258.2). Martianus had been among the first to praise Augustine's rhetorical and intellectual talents, and to encourage the ambitions in that direction that in the *Confessions* Augustine counts among his chief motivations for going to Rome. Martianus therefore represents the secular side of Augustine's identity and relationships at the time, and Augustine recalls how the friendship cooled when he began to display a greater interest in religion that Martianus had difficulty appreciating (*Ep* 258.3). Their final alienation apparently occurred only after Augustine returned to Africa from his exile, for the two had still been close when Martianus saw his friend off on his journey across the sea. Despite their primarily secular identity and ambitions, it was evidently to the role Manichaeism was playing in Augustine's departure that Martianus alluded in his cautionary words to him. "Remember what you said to me as I was about to leave," Augustine reminisces, "when you recalled the comic but still most fitting and useful verse from Terence: 'Now this day brings new life, and requires other conduct'" (*Ep* 258.5).

Augustine's Faustian Experiment in Rome

Augustine arrived in Rome gravely ill (*Conf* 5.9.16). A Manichaean Auditor took him in and saw to it that he was well cared for (*Conf* 5.10.18).[23] Considering the fear of disease in the ancient world, Augustine had unusual good fortune to be taken in and cared for by the Manichaeans, rather than abandoned at the docks.[24] Augustine himself mentions that he nearly died. He explicitly confesses that he never even considered baptism during this near-fatal episode. (*Conf* 5.10.18). When he recovered, he did not adopt the "other conduct" urged by his friend Martianus. Instead, he maintained his close association with fellow Manichaeans, and continued to participate in the daily ritual life of the sect, bringing offerings to the Elect and conferring with them on doctrinal and moral matters (*Conf* 5.10.18). He continued to make his regular confession before them, and receive their absolution. Of such activity, James O'Donnell remarks, "it is a sign of how involved in the movement he still was, whatever his doubts."[25] Louis Bertrand, noting how his deep involvement in the Roman Manichaean community supports the suspicion that Augustine had fled Africa to continue his Manichaean life in safety, maintains that at the very least Augustine hid his doubts and presented himself as a fellow-traveler, thus gaining the aid of the community both in financing his teaching in the city and in gaining an important post the following year.[26]

Indeed, Augustine indicates that the Roman Manichaeans formed the almost exclusive social circle of his year and a half in the city. Removed from the company of his African friends, most of whom treated religion as a minor hobby, his engagement with the religious life of the Manichaean community actually intensified in Rome. His engagement with this new and intense social network forestalled one of the most common conditions of apostasy observed in modern studies, the disruption of social ties that comes with relocation.[27] Even though he was now in doubt about several tenets of the Manichaean faith, the connections of community life kept him within the fold, surrounding him with significant others who kept reflecting Manichaean prompts back to him.

It is usually glossed over that in book 5 of the *Confessions* Augustine apparently offers a catalog not just of what he believed when he was a Manichaean, but of what he *still* believed as a Manichaean in Rome in 383–384. Augustine explicitly admits that, despite a growing uneasiness that parts of the Manichaean belief system might be wrong, he continued to adhere to the basic materialistic dualism of the faith. It was perfectly consistent with his new more skeptically oriented attitude that, even while actively maintaining the life of a Manichaean Auditor, he cautioned his host against simply believing the entire set of Manichaean teachings (*Conf* 5.10.19). After all, had not Faustus himself declined to defend some of them? Nonetheless, he retained the operationalized ideology of self and evil, and the practices associated with it, even while giving up some of the more tangential details of the Manichaean myth. He still conceived of the good God and its evil opposite as "two antagonistic masses" (*adverso sibi duas moles, Conf* 5.10.20). He still thought of Christ as a divine being, projected (*porrectum*) substantially from God, rather than incarnated in flesh through Mary (*Conf* 5.10.20). He still found the crude anthropomorphism of popular Christianity unpalatable (*Conf* 5.10.19), and the widely accepted set of its scriptures unreadable (*Conf* 5.11.21). Nothing suggested that non-Manichaean Christianity lay in Augustine's future, or that the unresolved issues he had with Manichaeism would lead to a complete break with that community.

And what of astrology? Thomas O'Laughlin reasonably raises the question, "why, when he had vanquished Faustus with 'the books of the philosophers,' did he not declare his acceptance of that system he had just judged truer," namely astrology, "instead of adopting a quasi-Academic attitude"?[28] The answer is that he had never vanquished Faustus, because the latter declined to enter the contest. Instead, it was Faustus himself who offered the quasi-Academic attitude as the appropriately enlightened stance for people like Augustine and himself. The key proof that this was the case is the fact that Augustine continued to be a Manichaean for a considerable time after his encounter with Faustus. During this time, he appears also to have continued to study and practice astrology, although now led by certain Academic and Manichaean criticisms of it to the point of being "almost persuaded of its falsehood." Besides, in itself, astrology could not speak to Augustine's condition. Its fatalism offered a simple variation on that of Manichaeism, and fell far short of the latter in not even offering a program for self-improvement.

Any number of Augustine's issues with or resistances to Manichaeism might have been resolved by personal adjustments in the form his Manichaeism took, or selective adherence to the sect's teachings such as Faustus seems to have practiced. None of his problems were necessarily fatal to his Manichaean faith. But the solutions and alternatives he was offered failed to satisfy his demand for certain truth, and he appears to have instinctively balked at Faustus's rejection of such intellectual certainty as humanly impossible.

> Often it seemed to me that [truth] could not be found and the great waves of my thoughts were borne into the opinion of the Academics. On the other hand, gazing often, insofar as I could, at the human mind, so lively, so wise, and so clear-sighted, I did not think that truth must remain hidden, but perhaps the manner of seeking it might be concealed, and must be received from some divine authority. It remained to seek what that authority was, when in such great differences of opinion each one promised that he would deliver it.[29]

His reading in popular philosophy and literature had instilled in him a glorification of the human mind and soul and an enthusiasm for its powers that in certain respects Manichaeism reinforced with its own attribution of divinity to the essential self; yet in other respects it critiqued human knowledge and ability in this life in a way amenable to skepticism. Thus none of the terms by which Augustine evidently carried out this internal debate at the time required any new resources beyond the ones with which he had been working for the past decade.

Yet he was beginning to make contact with the limits of those resources. By all his training, Augustine thought the Manichaean myth should represent a preliminary, vulgarized instruction leading to more philosophically precise explanations. He had discovered to his great dismay that it hid no further layers of meaning. He had mistakenly thought that the promise of Faustus's coming meant initiation into the inner meaning. Faustus not only had no esoteric additions to make to Augustine's knowledge of the Manichaean system, he even dismissed the details of the exoteric myth as irrelevant. For Faustus, deeper truth did not necessarily mean more knowledge, as it did for Augustine. Forget stellar mechanics, and work on the New Man, we can almost hear him saying. But those were not the terms on which Augustine had been attracted and initially committed to Manichaeism. He had never intended the cultivation of his New Man to be an end in itself, but only a preliminary preparation of his mental purity and powers for greater things.

Augustine's initial Manichaean commitment had been systematically reinforced by his preceptors through a reasoned course of evidence and proof. Observation of existence easily demonstrated a cosmos in conflict between opposing forces of good and evil. Since only Mani taught such a dualistic understanding of things, his authority alone was rooted in reason. His life as an exemplar of holiness offered an independent confirmation of his worthiness. These two proofs within the realm of the observable and confirmable allowed confidence in Mani's authority in other areas not directly observable or confirmable. Yet Augustine had determined that Mani was wrong in some other areas where direct observation could play an equally confirming role. With this simple discovery, the secure basis of Mani's authority began to collapse for Augustine. For if Mani was wrong about *anything*, he could be wrong about *everything*.

If Faustus had offered compelling counter-arguments in defense of Mani's teachings on celestial phenomena, Augustine's faith might have been reinforced, and the crisis averted. As it happened, Faustus was the wrong sort of person for that task. He appears to have regarded Mani as a human prophet, theoretically capable of error. Mani was, after all, a mixed being like all humans. The limitations of physical existence in this world where truth and falsehood are so entwined cast doubt on all perceptions. As long as we are in the world, we inhabit a partial lie. Manichaeism fully recognized this, and Faustus found the expression of similar ideas in the Platonic Academy, transmitted to the Latin world by Cicero, perfectly fitted to his understanding of the Manichaean view. As an embodied being, Mani's perfection was a relative one until such time as he achieved complete liberation from mixture with evil at the moment of his death. His relative purity of conduct directly indicated the degree of his separation from evil, in mind as well as body. Since such external signs of worthiness were all that were accessible to observation and confirmation, Faustus directed Augustine to such proofs to settle his doubts. Even if Mani proved to be wrong in some minor technicalities of his vast comprehension of the cosmos, his holy conduct alone confirmed the validity of the system of religious practice he taught.

Yet for Augustine, evidently more interested in intellect than in action, and in virtues of character more than in unfailing adherence to a program of conduct, Faustus's argument fell short. If Mani presumed to be an authority on things he actually knew nothing about, such arrogance undermined his moral authority, no matter how pure his conduct (*Conf* 5.5.8). The only thing holding Augustine back from convicting Mani of such a failing was his own uncertainty on the issues he was raising. Evidence seemed to favor the astronomers over Mani; but Augustine could not absolutely prove it. He had to admit Faustus's point that the matters at issue were relatively insignificant compared to the essential tenets of the Manichaean faith, and against the latter Augustine found no compelling argument (*Conf* 5.14.25). Mere plausibility was all Faustus asked for; once that was conceded, he proposed following the practices of Manichaeism and finding in its results the necessary supporting evidence of experience. It should work. We might even presume that Augustine, after a decade of investment, wanted it to work. But for him it simply did not. With intellectual conviction still eluding him after all these years, the heart went out of his commitment.

We are now in a position to understand Augustine's insistence that his time as a Manichaean lasted only nine years, and his exclusion from that period of everything that he did after meeting Faustus. As a man who valued theory over practice, belief over deed, even truth over virtue, Augustine could only consider himself a Manichaean so long as its proposed truths held conviction for him. The additional time he spent behaving outwardly as a Manichaean meant nothing to him without a corresponding belief held with utter confidence. So he is being true to himself and to his understanding of things when he says he was a Manichaean for no more than nine years. For him, everything beyond that period was going through the motions.[30] We should not for that reason simply accept his own accounting; rather, we should keep in mind that "going through the motions" is what usually counts as membership in a religious community. By those standards, Augustine continued to be a Manichaean for nearly three years after meeting Faustus—a year with him in Africa, and nearly two years without him in Rome and Milan.

But Augustine's attempt to be a Faustian Manichaean ran counter to his own apparent predilection for contemplation over action. He considered his thoughts, not his deeds, the true seat of his selfhood. He could not be persuaded by Faustus that action is everything, that a Manichaean or a follower of Christ is one in deed more significantly than in thought. Thought, the Manichaeans contended, is unstable, invaded by doubt and temptation. The Manichaean cultivates virtues and dispositions rather than intellectual propositions. The latter provide rationales, but the Manichaean ethos is sustained by affect. For Faustus, the reasoned truth of dualism takes one as far as necessary to validate the way of life revealed by Christ as the needed response to evil. But Augustine had signed on to Manichaeism as part of a larger intellectual venture. Faustus's stance threatened to drive a permanent wedge between Augustine's intellectual pursuits and the performance of his religious duties. This bifurcation of his identity raised the question of where Augustine would invest most of his energies. His intellectual interests significantly outweighed his cultic ones, and if the former were no longer comfortably embedded in his life as a Manichaean, he would tend to find his thoughts elsewhere even while performing as a Manichaean Auditor.

Attempting to follow the qualified, probabilistic skepticism of Faustus, Augustine found himself lurching toward the precipice of absolute skepticism, and its accompanying paralysis of the will.[31] The Manichaean system appeared to him as plausible as any other (*Conf* 5.7.13), since he could find no means to refute any of it (*Conf* 5.14.25). Yet neither could he establish it with any certainty. Such adherence by default seemed empty to him. Augustine's skeptical crisis developed before he ever heard Ambrose, or read a word of Plotinus (*Conf* 5.10.19).[32] He found he could not be a Faustian Manichaean, although to all appearances he was. Cultic and even moral practice meant nothing to him without an intellectual truth it could serve. He was ripe for a change of allegiance.

A few years later, Augustine gave a purported description of this transition in his life to a former associate in the Manichaean community of Carthage, Honoratus:

When I departed from you across the sea I was already in a state of serious doubt. What was I to hold? What was I to give up? Indeed my hesitation grew greater day by day from the time that I heard the famous Faustus. You remember, his coming to explain all our difficulties was held out to us as a gift from heaven. Well, I recognized that he was no better than the others of the sect, except for a certain eloquence he had. When I got settled in Italy I reasoned with myself and deliberated long, not as to whether I should remain in that sect—for I was already sorry that I had fallen into it—but as how truth was to be found. (*UC* 8.20)

With due allowance for a telescoping of the timing of his resolve to quit the Manichaean community, which by his own account elsewhere did not actually take place until he was in Milan, this passage sums up the state of a person departing from an identity he has held, shuffling the priorities of his discrete commitments, and reconfiguring his self. This change of self began to occur well before Augustine had ever picked up a Platonic book or sat in on the sermons of Ambrose. Those later encounters served to provide new sources of the self to fill the void left by Augustine's loss of identity in his deconversion from Manichaeism.

Deconversion

Augustine's famous conversion to Nicene Christianity in his early thirties necessarily entailed, in the words of John Quinn, "a deconversion, a probing disengagement from Manichaean shackles."[33] This disengagement occurred in stages, beginning with Augustine's self-marginalization within the Manichaean community due to his doubts about its absolute truth. Marginalization of this kind typically takes place when one begins to lose confidence that the religious community has something to offer that the surrounding society cannot provide. The exclusive claims of the community erode as external sources of potential satisfaction become more evident. Based on studies of modern sectarian religion, referred to as "new religious movements," or "NRMs," Eileen Barker draws the following overview.

The reason why members shift to the margins will vary, but it is likely to be the result of some profound disagreement with *part* of the NRM. At the same time, they are also likely to believe that their movement—its beliefs, practices, or members—still has something to offer.[34]

This conflicted attitude can take the form of various rationalizations, such as that the core doctrine is true but has been distorted by misguided interpreters, or that the religion's organization and power structure has become corrupt.

> On the other hand, it may be that the beliefs are no longer
> convincing . . . but that the once literally held beliefs can still provide
> a goal—a direction—toward which people can aspire and which
> is superior to that found in any of the other religions or ideologies
> available in the wider society. Alternatively, it could be that the beliefs
> are completely rejected, yet the friendships that have been built up over
> the years prevent the marginal from completely severing ties.[35]

Augustine displays elements of each of these variations on marginalization observed in modern studies. He began to keep track of failures of the organization to retain the high ideals of discipline it espoused, but with the zeal of a true believer in those ideals. While questioning details of Manichaean cosmology, he still valued some of its core teachings, and found these both impervious to criticism and superior to available alternative explanations of existence. Moreover, his bond of friendship with other Manichaeans was such that he would repeatedly expose himself in reaching out to them long after he had left their ranks. As Barker notes, the high level of tension between a sectarian community and the surrounding society plays a key role in perpetuating marginal membership for individuals despite "tensions both within themselves and between themselves and the core elements of the movement," because continued identification with the positive aspects of the sect "seem to them to be more palatable than the apostate role."[36]

A Failure of Moral Progress

Although they play no role at all in the *Confessions* narrative, failures among his fellow Manichaeans to observe properly the religion's disciplinary code feature prominently in one of Augustine's earliest polemical tracts. The episodes he recounts in *The Morals of the Manichaeans*, written circa 389–390, reveal the frustrations of a person deeply committed to the high morality promoted in the Manichaean community. The same respect for Manichaean moral principles appears in several of his other works. He reports that it was the chief attraction of the sect for his friend Alypius (*Conf* 6.7.12), and credits both Mani (*Conf* 5.5.9) and Faustus (*Conf* 5.7.12) as holy men in their conduct. He acknowledges the sincerity of the moral instruction he received from Manichaean leaders (*UC* 1.3). It troubled him deeply, therefore, when he observed or heard about moral failings within the community, particularly among the revered Elect.

In *The Morals of the Manichaeans*, he rhetorically exaggerates the extent of this problem, rashly asserting, "Through nine full years, while I was your most diligent and devoted Auditor, there was not a single one of the Elect known to me who, according to these precepts, was not either caught in sin or placed under suspicion of it" (*MM* 19.68). The Manichaean Fortunatus would make Augustine eat these words a few years later, when he was forced to admit in the face of Fortunatus's public challenge that he actually did not know first-hand of any serious moral enormity among the Elect (*Fort* 1–3). Should we attribute his earlier rashness to the polemical purpose of *The Morals of the Manichaeans*, to the initially elevated antagonism of a recent apostate, or to a lingering disappointment in a cause failing to live up to the ideals that had attracted him to it? His complaint appears to have been, essentially, that the Elect turned out to be quite ordinary mortals, "full of envy, full of covetousness, full of greed for costly foods, constantly at strife, easily excited by trifles" (*MM* 19.71). He observed senior Elect, in the company of their presbyter, in the theater, and junior Elect quarreling over their favorite actors and charioteers (*MM* 19.72). In other words, for all the stringency of the Manichaean disciplinary code, something was not working to make the New Man every Manichaean, and particularly the Elect, were supposed to become.

> Many were discovered in wine and meat, many washing at the baths. Yet this we only heard. Some were proved to have seduced other men's wives, so that for this reason it was clearly not possible to doubt it. Yet suppose this, too, rumor rather than truth. (*MM* 19.68)

All of these reports are simply hearsay, as he readily admits. By direct observation, Augustine had found little more than the occasional boorish behavior; but it was enough to expose those involved as morally unreformed.

> I personally saw, not alone, but with others who have either been freed from that superstition or I hope will yet be freed—we saw, then, at an intersection in Carthage on a busy street, not one, but more than three

of the Elect following some women with such rude sounds and gestures as to surpass all ordinary shamelessness and impudence. That it was quite habitual, and that they behaved this way among themselves, was sufficiently clear, since indeed no one was deterred by the presence of his associates, indicating that all of them, or nearly all, were affected by this illness. For they were not all from one house, but lived in completely different places, and merely by chance had departed at the same time from that place where all had held a meeting. (*MM* 19.68)

Because Augustine and his companions had met in the same place as the Elect for religious observances as a congregation of the local Manichaean community, they were in a position to know who the men were and how their behavior did not reflect the peculiarities of a close-knit group. He and his friends were sincere and devout enough in their Manichaeism to be shocked by what they saw, and lodged a complaint with an appropriate senior of the community (*MM* 19.68). This action on their part displays the Auditor supervision of Elect conduct central to Manichaean community life. Their own spiritual well-being depended on the sanctity of the Elect who served as fit vessels for the ritual offerings. But while Augustine and his comrades fulfilled their supervisory role, they were disappointed by a failure of leadership in this instance.

But in the end who punished this—I don't say by separation from the church, but at least by a rebuke in proportion to the serious degree of the disgrace? And the only excuse given for their impunity was that, at that time, when their meetings were prohibited by law, it was feared that the punished would report (the Manichaeans to the authorities). (*MM* 19.68–69)

Conditions of persecution apparently loosened internal discipline—a not uncommon phenomenon in religious history. Faustus's return to Carthage may have been prompted by concern for such disintegration of effective authority within the community once it had to go "underground." In any case, this incident was troubling for Augustine in his commitment to Manichaean moral ideals, even if from an outside perspective seemingly minor. His actions at the time reflect not disenchantment, but earnest dedication to the faith and the role of the Auditor as a monitor of Elect conduct; and Augustine repeated his dedication to this role on subsequent occasions.

Augustine says that the same excuse for not following up a complaint was given to him—apparently by Faustus himself[37]—in connection with an incident at a vigil, perhaps on the eve of the Bema festival in March of 383.[38]

> We reported to the very highest authorities the complaint to us by a woman who, in a meeting where she was with other women, and naturally trusting in their holiness, when a number of Elect had entered, and one of them had extinguished the lamp, one of them—just which one she could not be certain in the darkness—reached out to embrace her, and would have forced her into disgrace, had she not escaped by crying out. (*MM* 19.70)

Was the extinguishing of the lamp a normal part of the vigil? Augustine implies that it was not, attributing the act to a jocular mood among the Elect, who were all complicit in allowing it to happen. Such a mood would be particularly inappropriate for the night of the vigil, and that might be Augustine's point in including such a detail. If, on the other hand, it was part of the ceremony (and the fact that others at the meeting did not immediately protest being put in the dark suggests that it was), then this could very well be a case of someone brushing against the woman in the dark, and she, in a heightened state of sensitivity due to the conditions, overinterpreting what was happening. The circumstances are far from clear, and the idea that the individual intended to have sex with the woman surreptitiously in a room crowded with people stretches credulity. Augustine admits that the individual supposedly responsible could not be identified, and that the inability of the woman to identify the person responsible made it impossible to bring him to the bishop for discipline. Augustine apparently had proposed that all of the Elect present be disciplined; but Faustus declined this course of action.

Augustine goes on in *The Morals of the Manichaeans* to report a personal animosity between two Elect whom he knew quite well (one of whom studied the liberal arts with him, as Faustus also did), who were "of sufficiently good reputation, of agile wit, and leaders in their debates," and one of whom "is said to now be a presbyter there," presumably Carthage. This animosity led to an exchange of accusations.

> These two were very jealous of one another, and one accused the other—not openly, but in conversation, as he had opportunity, and in

whispers—of having raped the wife of one of the Auditors. And the other, in clearing himself, brought the same charge against another Elect, who lived with this Auditor as his most trusted friend. Entering suddenly, he had caught this man with the woman, and his enemy and rival had advised the woman and her lover to raise this false report about him, that he might not be believed if he reported it. We were very distressed, and deeply affected, that although there was a doubt about the assault on the woman, nevertheless the jealousy in those two men, than whom we found none better there, showed itself so clearly, and raised suspicion of other things. (*MM* 19.71)

In this incident, too, Augustine conveys his feelings as a Manichaean Auditor, distressed at less than perfect behavior in the Elect who were responsible for liberating the light and bestowing benedictions on their adherents.[39]

He goes on to tell the sad tale of a particular Elect who used to hold discussions in the street of the fig-sellers, who was discovered to have impregnated a female Electa (*virginem sanctimonialem*). Her brother, who apparently was a Manichaean Auditor and for that reason refrained from going to the public authorities with the crime, complained to the leaders of the Carthaginian Manichaean community. In this case, action was taken, and the man was expelled from the order of the Elect and from the community. The brother and some friends added the additional punishment of a beating—to which Augustine appears to have been a witness, if not a participant (*MM* 19.72).[40]

We are not in a position to know whether these incidents actually built up in Augustine's mind and contributed to his disenchantment with the sect, or whether it was only in hindsight that he looked back on them as calling into question the validity of the Manichaean disciplinary practices. It may be significant that all of these incidents appear to date from near the end of Augustine's time in the African Manichaean community. Either he had risen to a level of prominence within the community that caused him to be dragged into these interpersonal conflicts in a way he was not before, exposing him to the seamier side of group existence, or his dissatisfaction with other aspects of Manichaeism made him alert to rumors he had dismissed when more zealously loyal to the sect.

We only can speculate how his growing awareness of shortcomings among some practitioners of Manichaeism fed back into his self-dissatisfaction with his own moral progress. He apparently continued to adhere to the Manichaean moral code for Auditors. Yet he could not bring himself to give up sex, family life, secular ambition, perhaps even three square meals a day, in order to take up the highly disciplined and dedicated life of an Elect. He apparently believed that only as a member of the Elect would he be given the secret philosophical meaning of the Manichaean teachings. He thus was locked in a catch-22 of failure to "make progress." Rome may have given him the time to reflect on this dilemma, temporarily separated from his family as he weighed the indications from Faustus that no further mysteries were forthcoming.

One also might speculate about how the differences between the Manichaeism of Rome and the idiosyncratic version proffered by Faustus may have given Augustine pause. Augustine met a quite different Manichaean bishop there, one who had nothing of Faustus's charm or even his limited education. He was a simple, severe man, admirable only in his moral and ascetic purity: "very rustic and unpolished (*rusticanus atque impolitus*), but somehow, from his very moroseness, more severe in observance of good morals (*severior in custodiendis bonis moribus*)" (*MM* 20.74).[41] Louis Bertrand concludes from such remarks that he "made a bad impression on him from the very outset. This man, he tells us, was of rough appearance, without culture or polite manners. Doubtless this unmannerly peasant, in his reception of the young professor, had not shown himself sufficiently alive to his merits, and the professor felt aggrieved."[42] While Augustine's characterization of the bishop is colored by polemic, it highlights the fact that the Manichaeans did not favor education and culture as much as Augustine did in the selection of Elect to positions of leadership. As in the case of Faustus, Fortunatus, and Felix, other factors could be paramount. The latter three all may be characterized as earnest, passionate, and to relative degrees naturally gifted. But what appear in them as flashes of brilliance may reflect more a well-honed training in the system they are presenting than their own unique abilities for insight. Augustine could hope for no deep philosophical discussions with the Roman bishop. Perhaps this Manichaean leader put a different face on Faustus's promotion of practice above doctrine. If such a man represented the realization of this approach to Manichaeism, Augustine apparently found it unappealing.

A Failure of Intellectual Progress

In the later account Augustine provides in the *Confessions*, intellectual issues with Manichaeism overshadow any complaint about failures in practice among the Manichaeans. There he treats his failure to make moral progress as his own shortcoming, which Manichaeism did nothing to alleviate. But it would be a distraction from his protreptic purpose in the *Confessions* to dwell on a handful of Manichaean miscreants, especially when experience had substantially lowered his initial idealism about practice in the Nicene Christian community. He accepts that ascetic Manichaeans and ascetic Nicene Christians aspire to the same, or closely similar, disciplined lives. He highlights ideological differences between the two religions in order to establish the Nicene advantage in more successfully grounding that common aspiration. Rather than regarding the *Confessions* account as necessarily better or worse information, therefore, than Augustine's earlier treatments of his deconversion from Manichaeism, we should recognize how the story is angled differently every time Augustine tells it from the vantage point of his present concerns.

In the aftermath of his meeting with Faustus, Augustine evidently struggled to adjust his expectations of a commitment to a way of life based solely on reason. Augustine had taken "reason" to be the widely accepted "common sense" of the late antique intellectual environment. Where Manichaeism deviated in its premises from those to which Augustine had been exposed through his schooling and independent study, the sect's teachings met little pockets of resistance. They kept Manichaeism from taking complete possession of his identity, and provided openings to non-Manichaean counter-proposals. When Augustine discovered new sources of self in Platonism or non-Manichaean Christianity that agreed more closely with generally accepted truths of the age, his Manichaean master discourse was compromised and weakened. He reports "much consideration and frequent comparisons" (*magis magisque considerans atque comparans*) of the views of "philosophers" (among whom, as we have seen, he apparently includes astronomers and astrologers) with those of the Manichaeans, leading him to conclude that the philosophers' views were more probable in the areas of "this world and the whole of nature that is within the reach of our bodily senses" (*Conf* 5.14.25). The ability of astronomers to predict celestial events years in advance showed that the heavenly bodies did not operate by arbitrary will, either their own or that of a superior deity, but merely followed present inanimate patterns of motion that could not be changed by ritual or prayer. This was a strike against many theistic apprehensions of the universe, Manichaean and Nicene Christian among them, but was connected with long established views among the intellectual elites of Augustine's culture that regarded God as a source of universal order rather than a responsive personal being. Thus, Augustine's first reaction to "scientific" disconfirmation of his "religious" metaphysics was to bifurcate reality into two separate spheres, a natural one and a transcendental one. Many have followed in Augustine's footsteps in more recent centuries.

By letting go of Manichaean teachings about causes and forces behind the motions of celestial bodies, however, Augustine crossed the first threshold of deconversion. Having done so, he found himself standing upon a slippery slope. The African Manichaeans had based their proselytization of intellectuals like Augustine on the following argument: If the religion's teachings on that which can be confirmed by direct observation and inductive reasoning from such observation are proven true, then its other teachings, not amenable to proof by observation and reason, should be accepted as true. Now, in one of the most directly observable phenomena involved in Manichaean teaching, that teaching appeared to be disproved. It would seem that a reversal of the original proposition should be in order, and that the other teachings not subject to rational proof must fall too.

Yet this consequence did not immediately follow for Augustine. He is careful to note that he considered Manichaeism refuted only in its teachings on the structure and operation of the cosmos; the astronomers offered no ethical guidelines to which Augustine could "entrust the cure of my soul's sickness" (*Conf* 5.14.25), nor any argument that could challenge the fundamental dualistic metaphysics Manichaeism proposed. The latter was similarly left unassailed when Augustine learned possible answers to Manichaean criticism of the Bible from Ambrose in Milan (*Conf* 5.14.24). In short, he yielded segments of Manichaean teaching incrementally and piecemeal, while retaining allegiance to other parts of the faith that still held intellectual credibility for him.

Augustine found a flaw not in dualism per se, but in the character of God it entailed, which he came to consider insufficiently exalted. A God who must do battle, who can suffer seeming defeat and hurt, on either the cosmic or the human scale, seemed less than perfect to him (*Conf* 7.2.3–7.3.4).

> With all my heart I believed that you could never suffer decay or hurt
> or change, for *although I did not know how or why this should be*, I
> understood with complete certainty that what was subject to decay is
> inferior to that which is not, and without hesitation I placed that which
> is cannot be harmed above that which can, and I saw that what remains
> constant is better than that which is changeable. (*Conf* 7.1.1)

This passage rings true of Augustine's thought at the time, despite being written a decade later, because its ideas are found in Augustine's writings of that earlier period. In its unusual candor, absent from those earlier discussions, it exposes the role of arational premises, or intuitions, in opening up objections to ideas the Manichaeans had attempted to cultivate in Augustine's thinking. This particular intuition about a scale of power and relative permanence and invulnerability pervades Augustine's post-conversion writings. He would try out various ways of rationalizing it, none too successful. He simply *knew* that something more powerful, more static, more invulnerable, was better. It was an evaluation deeply rooted in Greco-Roman valuation of power as defining superiority; indeed, omnipotence as a defining characteristic of a god is a fairly widespread premise of theism throughout world history. By deviating from this premise, Manichaeism set itself in opposition to the values of the surrounding dominant culture, putting a higher price on adherence to its teachings than other religions required. As Manichaeism loosened its hold on Augustine's allegiance, he slipped back toward the "common sense" center of his culture.

His recognition of a cosmic order led initially to an adoption of the sort of monistic ideas of pantheism and providence that pervaded Roman popular philosophy.

So I thought of you . . . as a great being with dimensions extending everywhere, throughout infinite space, permeating the whole mass of the world and reaching in all directions beyond it without limit, so that the earth and the sky and all creation were full of you and their limits were within you, while you had no limits at all. . . . I imagined that you were able to pass through material bodies, not only the air and the sky and the sea, but also the earth, and that you could penetrate all their parts, the greatest and the smallest alike, so that they were filled with your presence, and by this unseen force you ruled over all that you had created, from within and from without.[43]

Augustine could shift fairly easily from the Manichaean idea of the divine dispersed in the material world to the notion of an omnipresent divine order in things. This went hand in hand with a move from the Manichaean fatalistic sense of the human condition to a view of human dependence on divine providence that likewise tapped into dominant popular models of reality. Once Augustine found conviction in an immutable, omnipotent God permeating all of nature with his providential control, the Manichaean solution to the problem of evil could not work. Thus, Augustine's newly adopted a priori concept of God necessitated a shift to a different theodicy, which he had yet to discover. Consequently, he temporarily found himself in an unsettled state between the coherent system from which he was extricating himself and the new one he would eventually form.

He continued to consider his inner self as divine and utterly alien to the body. In asserting God's strength to be superior to any possible countervailing force, he raised the issue of the divine soul's abilities. If the soul is God-like, he reasoned, it should be capable of achieving its goals over any resistance just as God did (*UC* 8.20). Perhaps, then, the accounts of bad conduct well established in Greco-Roman ethical discourse sufficed: ignorance of the true good, or of the proper means to achieve it, or laxity in disciplining countervening passions of the body. Did one really need to premise an active, external force of evil?

It cannot be stressed too much that at this point, before relocating to Milan in late 384, Augustine had not developed any dissatisfaction with the materialistic presuppositions of his metaphysical thinking. Why should he, when such materialism was by far the norm in his world? Only when he discovered Platonic immaterialism in Milan did he look back at his prior thinking as defective. In other words, he did not set out to seek a solution to something troubling him in the underpinnings of his metaphysics. He found the solution of immaterialism before he had experienced any problem with materialism, and only perceived a problem from the hindsight of the new position he had adopted. Indeed, from that hindsight he could only describe a prior inability to conceive of anything outside the language and imagery given by the tradition to which he belonged. Michael Polanyi has pointed to such passages in Augustine as indicative of the "logical gap" between conceptual frameworks, such that conversion requires learning an entirely new language and set of presuppositions about what counts as reasonable.[44] In order to articulate a problem not just within the internal coherence of a way of thinking, but with the way of thinking as a whole, one must be provided with terms from outside that way of thinking. Since Platonism came with its own critique of materialism as its theoretical nemesis, Augustine came to associate his own rejected past with what Platonism targeted as erroneous thinking. In doing so, he somewhat arbitrarily deepened distinctions that on the surface were not that great. Although there are key differences between Platonic immaterialism and Manichaean materialism, even Plotinus often lapsed into materialist language and drew conclusions about immaterial reality rooted in materialistic thinking. The same was true of Augustine in his attempts to emulate Plotinus. For this reason, it is easy to make too much of metaphysical distinctions that were largely rhetorical.

Augustine began to think that what had appealed to him in Manichaeism in his youth had done so precisely because he was in his youth, quick to accept ideas that appealed to his vanity and naiveté, judging things by an underdeveloped precision of thought. Of course Manichaeism seemed reasonable to such a person. The Manichaeans were asking to be judged by people who did not yet have the capacity to judge soundly.[45] At the promise of a religion rooted purely in reason, "the human soul naturally rejoices and, without considering its own strength and health, by trying to get the food of the strong which is unwisely prescribed except for the strong, it rushes right into the poison of deceivers" (UC 9.21). Such immature minds are naturally inclined to project onto the divine sensory-based conceptions, or onto the cosmos the division within their own wills (Conf 8.10.22).

Subtly turning the skepticism of Faustus against the more conventional Manichaeans he knew, Augustine in his earliest post-Manichaean writings repeatedly criticized their illusion of having already reached the truth as Auditors (e.g., Acad 2.3.9; Sol 1.12.20). He had always suspected that the Auditors had possession of only an exoteric shadow of truths the Elect reserved to themselves. Even though this suspicion proved erroneous, the basic construct received reinforcement from Faustus, who picked up the Ciceronian emphasis on truth as the end and fulfillment of the journey rather than its beginning and foundation. One makes spiritual progress as one approaches closer to perfect truth through various levels of partial truth, incomplete knowing. Augustine clearly accepted this construal of the human situation—if no longer from Faustus, then from Cicero—and used it against his Manichaean friends who remained in the condition he had been in before meeting Faustus. With Manichaean truth thrown into uncertainty, Augustine found himself back at the beginning of his quest with those friends who shared it with him, as if their entire experience with Manichaeism had gotten them nowhere, and had held them up under the mistaken notion that they had found everything they were looking for.

Prospects

Modern commentators have attempted in various ways to work into this short span of Augustine's life wholesale, if transitional, commitments to Skepticism and Stoicism.[46] Aspects of his earliest surviving writings, as well as later remarks about this period, suggest elements of both in his thought at the time. Yet nothing in this evidence points to formal adherence to either complete system, nor to any sudden novel discovery such as had occurred with his reading of Cicero and would occur with his exposure to the Platonic books. Indeed, it is naive to assume that everything present in Augustine's earliest post-Manichaean writings must have been newly acquired ideas. A person in Augustine's intellectual position would carry forward all sorts of ideas from his past thinking; and if we find traces of Skepticism and Stoicism in his earlier writings that gradually fade away, we can be confident that they represent the vestiges of his eclectic personal philosophy yielding ground to his new system. Both Skepticism and Stoicism belong to the environment of African Manichaeism, the latter as a function of the general materialistic metaphysics of the religion, and the former as the individual philosophical attitude of Faustus. Even as Augustine extracted his thinking and conduct from the Manichaean system, the other elements of his personal philosophy remained operative, ready to be fitted into any new commitments to which he was drawn; and so we see them emerge into high relief as the surrounding Manichaean matrix gets eroded away.

Yet two solid rocks of the Manichaean system remained largely undisturbed: the Manichaean self and its underlying premise of dualism. Still employing a central tenet of Manichaeism, he ascribed his very failure to make progress in the religion to the presence of a dualistic alterity within him.

> It still seemed to me that it is not we who sin, but some other nature within us that sins. My pride was gratified at being exculpated by this theory. When I had done something wrong it was pleasant to not confess (*non confiteri*) that I had done it, a confession that would have given you a chance to heal this soul of mine that had sinned against you. On the contrary, I liked to excuse myself and blame this unknown other thing that was with me but was not me. . . . I did not consider myself a sinner. (*Conf* 5.10.18)

Despite his new thinking about the cosmos, Augustine's experience of self still found resonance with Manichaean models. He could not explain his own interior conflict of wills and intentions without resorting to some concept of opposing forces. It simply was not possible for people to be divided against themselves, without questioning the very reality of self.

Augustine had time to grapple with all these issues, to weigh and try out different solutions to them, while he lived a fairly comfortable life amid the support of the Roman Manichaean community. His comrades in religion had helped set him up as a teacher of rhetoric in the capital, where he experienced the usual pros and cons of working with students. After about a year of this, a new opportunity presented itself in the fall of 384, when Symmachus received a request from the imperial court to identify a suitable candidate for a post as "teacher of literature and elocution" for the city of Milan.[47] Augustine was recommended for the post by his Manichaean friends. Earlier in the year Symmachus had clashed with Ambrose, the Nicene bishop of Milan, over the issue of the altar of Victory, which the senate led by Symmachus had asked to have restored to its place in the senate house. In such a climate, anyone but a member of the newly empowered Nicene community would do for the post in Milan, in Symmachus's eyes. Augustine performed well in a test performance of his rhetorical skills before the Prefect, and was awarded the post.

In leaving Rome, however, Augustine lost the close contact of a strong Manichaean community. He could afford to forego their material support, now that he had a well-paying position; but he could ill afford to lose the reinforcement of identity that they had provided him. The Manichaean community in Milan lived under radically different, necessarily more constrained circumstances. Augustine makes no mention of making any contact with it. In the *Confessions*, he allows his departure from Rome to mark his exit from Manichaeism. It was his *real* reason for leaving Rome to cut himself off from his Manichaean identity, he surmises, even though, as he admits, he did not know that was the reason at the time (*Conf* 5.13.23). Indeed, just as his Donatist opponents would charge that his sudden departure from Carthage a year earlier had been motivated by a desire to flee possible persecution as a Manichaean, so the Manichaean Secundinus would accuse Augustine of leaving Rome out of a self-interested wish to disassociate himself from the persecuted Manichaeans there as an obstacle to the advancement of his career (*EpSec* 2).

The recollections of Augustine and the accusations of his opponents both stem from circumstances in which religious commitments occupy the greatest prominence in retrospectively defining his self. Our own interests have kept this side of his identity in the forefront as well. But at the time these events unfolded, Augustine still lived and made plans on the basis of an identity as a professor and intellectual, for whom participation in a cultic community had secondary importance. There was absolutely no reason at the time to believe that this hierarchy of commitments would be reversed, and that his interests would lead him to define himself primarily in cultic terms. There may have been little clue, even among his intimates, that anything was seriously troubling Augustine at the time. His intellectual inquiries and speculations continued unabated; his cultic activities retained a distinct, somewhat isolated role in his personal makeup. He could go from attending upon the Manichaean Elect in Rome to standing in the crowd in Ambrose's basilica in Milan with barely a ruffle of his demeanor. If he had gone on to be a famous member of the late antique literati, or an accomplished philosopher, we might give little attention to, or not even know for sure, his religious commitments. It is only the self Augustine was to become that makes any of what we have examined so far at all relevant to history. This self was formed in the context of a heightening and hardening of religious definitions of self going on in the society around Augustine at the end of the fourth century, which marked a fundamental change from the terms of self and society into which he had been socialized in his youth.

CHAPTER SIX

The Apostate

Two ENCOUNTERS PROVED decisive for Augustine in Milan: the Nicene Christian community of Ambrose and the "books of the Platonists." Although Augustine had had a passing acquaintance since childhood with African Christianity, the form that the new Nicene "Catholic" communion was taking in Milan under the city's bishop Ambrose was unlike anything he had encountered before. Neo-Nicene Trinitarianism, allegorical interpretation, and liturgical music were as new to Milan as they were to Augustine's experience of non-Manichaean Christianity, reflecting ideas and practices brought to Milan from elsewhere by a highly literate and widely connected bishop.[1] Likewise, although Augustine certainly knew of Plato and various Platonic ideas from his earlier studies, in Milan he discovered the development of Platonic thought initiated by the third-century philosopher Plotinus, referred to today as Neo-platonism. It was something of the latest thing in the city's intellectual circles; the sudden appearance of its elements in the sermons of Ambrose around the time of Augustine's arrival attests to its new ascendency.[2] Augustine entered an environment of novel enthusiasm that proved contagious.[3]

In the *Confessions*, Augustine carefully distinguishes the roles played in his transformation by Christian faith and Platonic philosophy, prompting a long and heated debate in modern Augustinian studies over which influence proved more decisive for Augustine at the time. It is a debate for which Augustine must bear his share of the blame, since it appears quite likely that he distinguishes for his own compositional reasons in the *Confessions* two movements that were considerably intertwined in Milan.[4] I make no attempt here to review ground well covered in other studies on the nature and interrelation-ship of these two movements as Augustine encountered them while residing in Milan between late 384 and summer 387 C.E. Instead, my concern lies with delineating the ideological and affective bridges across which Augustine could pass from a prior engagement with Manichaeism to an attraction to the par-ticular alternatives for self-identification Milan offered. How could a person who had been drawn to Manichaeism likewise be drawn to Nicene Christian-ity and Platonism? How can we best understand as a single historical person someone who makes these respective choices in life?

Augustine in Milan

Augustine came to Milan as a promising political appointee to a highly visible and prestigious position. It was a reversal of his fortunes he scarcely would have been able to predict just a year earlier, and one that put tremendous pres-sure on his continued association with an illicit sect. His secular ambitions were now in the ascendant. He was the principal source of income and con-nections for his family, and it is a testament to his new prospects that he was joined in his new home by not only his partner and son, but also his mother and brother, some cousins, friends, and pupils. After a time, however, the mother of his son was packed off back to Africa, to make way for a marriage more suited to his new prospects (*Conf* 6.15.25). A girl from an appropriately important family was found, but she was only ten years old; Augustine was expected to wait two years before consummating the betrothal. Manichaeism, too, now seemed to be a dalliance he could no longer afford, and it no longer carried sufficient conviction with him to be maintained in secret. He ceased his active involvement with the sect within a matter of months of arriving in Milan.

For all the attention usually given to Augustine's conversion in Milan, it is important to note how quietly, unobtrusively, and undramatically the pre-requisite withdrawal from the Manichaean community occurred. Augustine is absolutely clear that he still considered himself a member of the Manichaean religious community when he left Rome to take up his post in Milan. We know from Ambrose that there were Manichaeans in Milan, and Augustine had no doubt been told with whom to make contact when he arrived in his new home. Yet the responsibilities of his new status and the degree to which it placed him in the public eye appear to provide the context—call it explanatory, if you will—in which he dropped his association with the Manichaeans, which all his prior doubts and disaffection had not brought him to do. Neither "Catholicism" nor "Platonism" had anything to do with this decision, which he made prior to any significant exposure to them. Like the other changes in his private life at the time, I would argue that his dissociation from Manichaeism was largely a move of expediency in his new circumstances.[5]

"I gave up my customary intercourse with those whom I intended to abandon" (*UC* 8.20), he claims in one of his first accounts of his conversion—of course not including such long-established Manichaean friends as Alypius and Nebridius, as becomes clear from his later account in the *Confessions* (*Conf* 6.10.16–17). His decision did not involve any substantial revolution in his thinking, and in speaking of his early days in Milan he even speaks of Manichaeism as continuing to be the religion he "professed" (*Conf* 5.14.24);[6] but his deeply qualified convictions no longer outweighed the potential detriment to his life and career entailed by active participation in an illegal sect. He reports the apostasy from Manichaeism without emotion or hint of turmoil, unlike his characterization of the circumstances of his later conversion to Nicene Christianity. To the degree we can trust his later recollection of events, we may reasonably draw the conclusion that, even after more than a decade, Manichaeism had only a shallow hold on Augustine's sense of identity. A Manichaean self had failed to take root there, as Augustine fully recognized when he declared that he could not progress in his development as a Manichaean. Instead, his identity appears to have been built around his self-perception as an intellectual, open to new avenues to truth he might find among the cultured elite he had joined in Milan.[7]

There was nothing inevitable in Augustine's eventual gravitation toward Ambrose's community. Moving in the circles of the imperial court as well as the civic institutions of Milan, Augustine rubbed shoulders with pagans and non-Nicene Christians as well as Nicenes. Indeed, the rise of zealotry within the latter community as the conflict between Ambrose and the court intensified appears to have put Augustine off. Although he had accompanied his mother to church following her arrival in the summer of 385,[8] he appears to have stayed away during the political showdown between bishop and emperor that occurred in two basilicas around Easter of 386, which he watched with detached fascination from a safe distance (*Conf* 9.7.15). Nor did Augustine form an entirely positive assessment of Ambrose. Although he considered him more cultured than Faustus, he thought him not as gifted a rhetorician as the Manichaean bishop (*Conf* 5.13.23), and too quick to resort to authority or tradition rather than reason.[9] Even when Augustine later placed himself in Ambrose's hands—writing to him in mid-October 386 confessing his Manichaean past and asking for guidance toward baptism—Ambrose's response did not speak to his condition: he recommended that Augustine read the book of Isaiah, which Augustine had to put down after finding it both impenetrable and uninspiring (*Conf* 9.5.13), much as he had in an earlier exposure to these originally Jewish scriptures a decade before.[10]

Ambrose was well aware of the Manichaeans and the challenge they posed to the emerging Nicene orthodoxy,[11] and used his sermons and writings to attack Manichaean positions. Through his exposure to Ambrose's rhetoric, Augustine would have been alerted to what was considered objectionable and unorthodox among the many things Manichaeism promoted. Ambrose objected to the dynamic, responsive God of the Manichaeans as insufficiently transcendent (Ambrose, *Spir.* 2.5.34), and faulted their rejection of Christ's incarnation (Ambrose, *Fid.* 5.8.103–4; *Epistle* 44/42). He chided their view that humans had been created by the forces of evil (Ambrose, *Fid.* 2.13.119; *Off.* 1.25.117; *Hex.* 3.7.32). He did not hesitate to repeat about them rumors of secret sex rituals that had been a commonplace of pagan suspicions about Christians generally only a few generations earlier (Ambrose, *Epistle* 14/50). If Augustine heard any such expressly anti-Manichaean criticisms, they apparently made little immediate impact on him.[12]

Nonetheless he quite evidently respected this imposing and distant figure of authority. "Ambrose I counted one of the happy ones of this world, because he was held in such honor by the great" (*Conf* 6.3.3). In Ambrose he could see power and influence wedded to intellectual mastery, in sharp contrast to the unlettered fugitive Manichaean bishop Augustine had just left behind in Rome.[13] Ambrose and the other educated men who came into positions of leadership in the Italian Nicene community at this time formed a movement that took as its cause the perfection of civil society through the propagation of a truth suitably tailored to the masses, but rooted in the highest philosophy. We cannot, of course, gauge the level of excitement this movement elicited in Augustine; he himself reports that it failed to attract him at first. But gradually he absorbed its implications and came to recognize how much it offered another chance at that community of truth-seekers of which he had dreamed since reading the *Hortensius*. Perhaps there existed an option for fulfilling that dream that did not come at the high cost of social marginalization and breaking so deeply with the Classical tradition.

Yet Augustine acknowledges in the *Confessions* that, even after months of attending Ambrose's sermons as an observer in 385, he accepted the identity of a catechumen in Ambrose's church without conviction. "I did not yet consider the Catholic way the one to follow simply because it too could have its learned proponents, men who were capable of refuting objections with ample argument and good sense; nor did I yet consider the Manichaeism I professed was to be condemned because I had observed that the party of defense could make out an equally good cause" (*Conf* 5.14.24). The term "Catholic" appears here for the first time in the *Confessions*, designating a new kind of Christianity in Augustine's experience, capable of contesting the field of intellectual sophistication with Manichaeism. Unable to prove Manichaeism wrong, he found in Ambrose's reasonable defense of Nicene views further reason to hold to skeptical uncertainty of any truth. He recollected a few years later that, at most, "certain disputations of the bishop of Milan gave me some hope that I might find the answer to many Old Testament difficulties which, because they were badly explained to us, used to offend us. I made up my mind to continue a catechumen in the Church in which I had been brought up by my parents until either I discovered the truth I was seeking, or was persuaded that nothing was to be got by seeking" (*UC* 8.20). His recollection of the same event a decade later in the *Confessions* reads similarly: "I resolved therefore to live as a catechumen in the Catholic Church . . . until some kind of certainty dawned by which I might direct my steps aright" (*Conf* 5.14.25). Dare we reduce the term "conversion" to this act of social conformity and at most mild curiosity? Yet for much of religious history just such a change of venue as Augustine's move from clandestine Manichaean meetings to attendance as a catechumen in Ambrose's church would be taken as constituting conversion. It is largely Augustine's fault if we expect more, conditioned by his refusal to regard this surface conformity as meaningful in comparison with self-transformations yet to come.

Yet we can take the decision he describes in the passages above as marking a definitive moment of apostasy. Indeed, Augustine provides a textbook case of apostasy as it has come to be understood in modern sociological and psychological studies based on fieldwork with living examples of this phenomenon. In the first place, Augustine had gone through a rapid series of changes in his geographic and social location, disrupting his network of personal relationships, and presenting new conditions in which to "be himself."[14] He found himself in a "new life," requiring "different conduct." In the second place, his upward mobility brought him into elite circles and exposed him to different religious options closely connected to those circles.[15] His social network expanded exponentially in Milan, becoming much more religiously plural. We can discern the emergence of new pressures for religious conformity in his betrothal.[16] Although some of his African friends joined him in Milan, the tepid, ambivalent Manichaeism they shared with Augustine provided little reinforcement of the faith in the absence of a more zealous core community. Finally, the rapidly developing political situation raised the stakes on the secular rewards and punishments associated with his religious choices and affiliations.[17] By 386, the cost of being a Manichaean in the Roman Empire had grown frighteningly high for a group of friends who, in Peter Brown's apt characterization, were at most "fellow-travelers," not card-carrying activists in the Manichaean mission.

The focus in Augustine's later accounts on his "religious" associations obscures the degree to which ties to a cultic community were still a relatively minor component of his identity at the time. In "switching"[18] from being a nominal Manichaean to being a nominal Nicene Christian, he persisted in paying most attention to the ideas of "philosophers," whose publicly accessible arguments did not tie them exclusively to any particular cultic or devotional tradition. His initial period in Milan therefore represents an apostasy, a dropping out of his former sectarianism, without any serious replacement by another sectarian commitment that we might term a conversion. Because Manichaeism represented a role peripheral to Augustine's self, one in relation to which he had formed a certain "role distance," it could be abandoned without trauma, because roles more central to his identity continued unaffected.[19] When conversion finally did come for Augustine, it involved a change in his central and primary identity, from a civil service career and family life to an existence in which he devoted all his time and resources to the intellectual and contemplative pursuit of truth, be it a "philosophical" or "religious" profession.

Familiar Points of Attraction

Augustine had been drawn to Manichaeism as a community that seemed geared toward fulfilling philosophical counsels to rise above the body, senses, and passions toward the purity and truth of the soul's divine nature; he found a quite similar orientation in the rhetoric of Ambrose and Platonic literature. Paul More noted a century ago, "There is much in the *Enneads* of Plotinus to render the transition from Manichaeism easy."[20] Ambrose shared many of the same late antique themes that Augustine had first absorbed through a Manichaean lens. Modern interpreters emphasize a contrastive note of cosmic optimism in the ideologies to which Augustine was attracted in Milan, because Augustine himself plays that note in setting forth the new insights to which he has been brought by them. But we must reckon with the fact that he came to these insights only after substantial exposure to bodies of thought to which he had been attracted for other reasons. If we wish to contrast monism to dualism, or a pro-cosmic attitude to an anti-cosmic one, we must be sure how much such seemingly divergent premises mark a difference at the surface of the respective systems' discourse that might have been obvious to an Augustine considering his options.

In seeking to understand Augustine's situation in Milan, we must come to terms with how humans process novel information, regardless of the particularities of their distinctive cultures. A person encountering a new set of ideas and experiences inevitably will see them through the lens of prior conditioning that directs his or her attention to certain features of the new experiential environment and away from others. It is a commonplace of human experience that we hear and read selectively, passing through successive phases of inattention and alertness. We understand the words of another against a background of our own distinctive preparation. We contribute readings that wear down the rough edges and inconsistencies of our sources. It does no good for modern scholars to point out patiently the many differences between various systems of thought and orientation that make them incompatible at some level, and requiring a clear choice between alternative apprehensions of reality. The fact is that people regularly dodge this intellectual either/or, and conflate supposedly incompatible systems by "blinking" at the jagged seams between them.

Augustine shows no immunity to this tendency to partial reading of his sources of self, and it is well known that he spent the second half of his life brokering a marriage between Platonic philosophy and Christian faith that many modern researchers regard as awkward at best. It is neither accident nor inspiration that these two systems provided the major components of Augustine's synthetic project, since they dominated the intellectual discourse of the elite he joined in Milan. He merely signed onto an existing intellectual fad, and his initial impression of compatibility between Christianity and Platonism derived from the confidence of others around him, who in turn drew upon two centuries of experiments in bringing them together. Because of our considerable uncertainty about how much exposure to either Ambrose or Platonism Augustine actually had, we do best not to rest too much on small details or subtle nuances of their respective systems (as much as they can be called systems) that Augustine could have missed easily. Robert O'Connell has rightly raised the question of just how well equipped Augustine was to work his way through the intricacies of Neoplatonic thought the way modern researchers labor to do.[21] Nor should we expect any further advance in our understanding of Plotinus to help us substantially with Augustine's own rendition of his philosophy. We must reckon with *Augustine's* Plotinus and Ambrose, however partial and defective they be compared with modern academic reconstructions of the thought of these two figures. We can neither presume nor predict which of their major or minor themes will catch Augustine's attention, and be reset out of all proportion to their place in their original source.

Augustine's later sense of greater debt to the Platonic books than to Ambrose may stem from the fact that he actually read the Platonic books, whereas his exposure to Ambrose came mostly in the oral medium, which he could not analyze with the same precision.[22] His Ambrose is mostly a matter of memory, which impressed upon him only a few key ideas and ways of thinking. In his sermons that have survived, Ambrose tends to stitch together his various sources with minimal effort to resolve their divergences. We might reasonably expect Augustine, in hearing them, to favor one line of thought over another with which it was in tension, or to harmonize conflicting passages by reading them in light of a construct in which the disharmonies were submerged. Platonism may have served in this role, although the sources of this tradition known to Augustine presented interpretive problems of their own, undoubtedly exacerbated by translation and Augustine's only partial exposure to the system as a whole. The notorious difficulties modern researchers have had in isolating the exact source of Augustine's particular ideas arise from this context of creative misprision, in which he went back and forth between standing in Ambrose's audience and engaging in reading circles around Platonic tracts. Indeed, his remarks suggest that Ambrose's sermons made only a minor impression on him until he began to listen to them with ears ringing with Platonic phrases.

A great deal of what Augustine found in both the Platonic books and the sermons of Ambrose would have sounded quite familiar to him; and it is in such familiar material that we must seek the bridges between the pre- and post-conversion Augustine. Both Ambrose and Plotinus tended toward familiar cultural dualisms of the self, contrasting soul to body, the mind to the passions. True human identity resides in the soul for both Ambrose and Plotinus, just as it did for the Manichaeans.[23] Ambrose follows traditional Platonic emphases in stating that the body is only a something used by the soul, put on and taken off like a piece of clothing. "We are souls; our limbs are clothes" (Ambrose, *Isaac* 8.79). Life in this world is punishment, and the body a prison (Ambrose, *Cain et Abel* 2.9.36), a tomb (Ambrose, *Poen* 2.8.71; *Bono mort* 5.16), or quite simply the enemy of the soul or mind (Ambrose, *Bono mort* 7.26). For Plotinus, the soul could not serve evil instead of good if it were not combined with matter in a body, with the consequent subjection to matter's darkening effect and passions (Plotinus, *En* 1.8.4). Unreservedly plagiarizing Plotinus, *Ennead* 1.4, Ambrose explains that true happiness is the stable contentment of the soul, not anything that the body can provide (Ambrose, *Iacob* 1.7.27–28). The pleasure of the mind brings happiness, and this is achieved by detachment from the body and its passions. Perfection comes through reason, not the senses, and this reason is a human soul's most intrinsic property, and so inalienable (Ambrose, *Iacob* 1.7.29; cf. Plotinus, *En* 1.4.4). Through reason, the individual transcends the fortunes and misfortunes of the bodily and sensible by recognizing that they have nothing to do with the true self (Ambrose, *Iacob* 1.7.31–32; cf. Plotinus, *En* 1.4.5–6). "Virtue that has been perfected remains always amid adversities and pleasures; adversities do not take away anything from its perfection, nor do pleasures add anything" (Ambrose, *Iacob* 1.8.35; cf. Plotinus, *En* 1.4.7). Our purpose in this life below is "by the use of reason to bring under subjection the irrational emotions of our bodies" with which the soul had come to be commingled (Ambrose, *Cain et Abel* 2.9.36).

In common with most ideologies of late antiquity, including Manichaeism, Neoplatonism affirmed the divine character of the soul, and its derivation from the ultimate good by a process of emanation or procession. "To turn inward, as Plotinus and Augustine do, means looking for the divine in the self (and of course specifically in the soul)," Phillip Cary reminds us, "and therefore requires a view of the soul and its relation to the divine that would make sense of directing one's attention that way."[24] Augustine evidently crossed from Manichaeism to Platonism across this bridge of essential human divinity, which he affirms in his earliest post-conversion writings (e.g., *Acad*

1.1, 1.3, 1.11). This was one of the points where Manichaeism accorded with the "common sense" position of the culture, to which Augustine as an apostate resorted, as Cary observes:

> In other words, for Augustine at Cassiciacum the divinity of the soul is an old familiar song, not a sudden, passing fad brought on by an overly enthusiastic reading of "the books of the Platonists." It has deep roots in a decade and a half of his thinking about the relation of God and the soul as a Ciceronian philosopher and as a Manichaean believer as well. It is the sort of thing one takes for granted in the cultured milieu of ancient thought, and at Cassiciacum Augustine treats it as a rather straightforward implication of the common definition of "human being" as "rational mortal animal."[25]

Augustine leaves us in some doubt as to whether he initially recognized any tension between Platonism and Ambrose's Christianity on this subject; but he fairly quickly (perhaps as a result of his catechetical instruction in the spring of 387) dropped language that emphasized the soul's divinity for more conventional Christian expressions of the created nature of the human being, burning one of his intellectual bridges behind him.[26]

Regardless of any differences on the precise origin of the soul, both Ambrose and Plotinus shared with Manichaeism the idea that the soul's predicament results from its descent from a transcendental realm into material existence. It was simply the image of descent, and not any particular theory of its cause, that had ubiquitous popularity in Augustine's culture. We find distinct causative theories between different schools of thought, and even within them. Whereas the Manichaeans strongly adhered to the "sent" scenario, and Ambrose clearly articulated the "fall" scenario, Plotinus reflected the ambivalence of the Platonic tradition on the cause and purpose of the soul's descent.[27] Likewise, the descent could be viewed either as a collective event in primordial time (the mythic version), or an individual occurrence behind each human life (the moral version). Ambrose himself vacillated between these options, depending on the sources he was drawing upon at the time;[28] the latter usage comes closer to Plotinus's "fall" scenario, whereby souls rather than falling collectively are seduced one by one into overengagement with material reality and disorientation of their attention from their proper good, and in this way fall into time itself. Augustine appears to have been somewhat overwhelmed by the nuances that distinguished the different conceptions of the soul's descent, and employs the theme liberally around the period of his conversion without sorting out the distinctions in a definitive manner. But he evidently was drawn to Plotinus's image of an original and essential unity of souls fragmented and isolated by descent into materiality,[29] which strongly resembled the Manichaean account of the soul's origin and character.

Augustine's past and potential sources of self-understanding shared the goal of the soul's escape and ascent from the material world.[30] He would have found in both Plotinus and Ambrose echoes of Faustus and Cicero on the need for moral purification from the world prior to any clear grasp of reality and truth (e.g., Plotinus, *En* 1.2.3–5). In words that would be welcomed in any of the communities competing for Augustine's adherence, Ambrose asks, "What do the just accomplish in this life but to divest themselves of the contagions of the body, that bind us like fetters?" (Ambrose, *Bono mort* 3.9). For all these contemporary systems, a properly lived life amounts to a disengagement from the world as much as practicable while still living an embodied existence.[31] We must "free the feet of our soul from the bonds of the body," Ambrose insists, "and clear our steps from all connection with this world" (Ambrose, *Poen* 2.9.107),[32] in anticipation of even greater freedom hereafter.

> Since the life of the soul remains after death, there remains a good which is not lost by death but increased. The soul is not held back by any obstacle placed by death but is more active, because it is active in its own sphere without any association with the body, which is more of a burden than a benefit to it. (Ambrose, *Bono mort* 4.13)

Therefore death is not to be mourned, but celebrated, because it is escape from "this lie," and "releases and frees the soul from this union with the flesh" (Ambrose, *Bono mort* 4.14; cf. Plotinus, *En* 1.7.3).

Augustine would have found in Neoplatonism an account of the soul's moral predicament couched in terms very similar to those employed by the Manichaeans, hemmed in by constraints, and struggling to master its own liberty. In its own nature, the soul is free in the only true sense of the word,[33] the freedom to pursue the soul's proper destiny in the immaterial realm (Plotinus, *En* 1.1.5). Taking the same position as the Manichaeans, that the inherently good soul can make only good choices when acting entirely in its own character, Plotinus considered that any bad choices are not "free" in the same way,[34] occurring only when the mind is confused by its circumstances of contact with material reality.

> This entry into matter is the fall of the soul; this, and the weakness which ensues because matter, invading the soul's domain, and as it were forcing her to narrower bounds, does not permit all her powers to be actualised, but filches away a part and makes it evil, until it have strength again to escape upwards. Matter is thus the cause both of the soul's weakness and of her vice. (Plotinus, *En* 1.8.14)

As in Manichaeism, so in Plotinus's thought different bodies will have constitutions more or less prone to passion, determining in this way how much of a fight a soul has to free itself of bodily control (Plotinus, *En* 1.8.8).

> Now when the soul is without body it is in absolute control of itself and free, and outside the causation of the physical universe; but when it is brought into body it is no longer in all ways in control, as it forms part of an order with other things. Chances direct, for the most part, all the things round it, among which it has fallen when it comes to this middle point, so that it does some things because of these, but sometimes it masters them itself and leads them where it wishes. The better soul has power over more, the worse over less. For the soul that gives in at all to the temperament of the body is compelled to feel lust or anger . . . but the other soul, the one which is good by nature, holds its own in these very same circumstances, and changes them rather than is changed by them. . . . When therefore, the soul is altered by the external causes, and so does something and drives on in a sort of blind rush, neither its action nor its disposition is to be called free; this applies, too, when it is worse from itself and does not altogether have its impulses right or in control. When, however, in its impulse it has as director its own pure and untroubled reason, then this impulse alone is to be said to be in our own power and free; this is our own act, which does not come from somewhere else but from within from our soul when it is pure, from a primary principle which directs and is in control, not suffering error from ignorance or defeat from the violence of the passions, which come upon it and drive and drag it about, and do not allow any acts to come from us any more but only passive responses. (Plotinus, *En* 3.1.8–9)

Both the Neoplatonists and the Manichaeans identified this interior director with the *nous*, which aids the soul in its liberation from entanglement in the material world and its ascent to its divine origin, by enlightening the individual human mind.[35] We can confirm the fatalism inherent in such material as an additional bridge in Augustine's passage from Manichaeism to Platonism by the fatalistic remarks scattered throughout his earliest post-conversion writings, which evaporate from his rhetoric within a couple of years.

Nor should we allow the significant differences between Manichaean and Neoplatonic metaphysics to obscure the prominence of dualistic rhetoric in the latter, particularly in passages of Plotinus known to Augustine at the time of his conversion.[36] Plotinus characterized matter as eternal and unchanging (Plotinus, *En* 2.4.6; cf. 3.6.7, 3.6.13–14). Far from being the culminating emanation from the One and the Good, it represents the radical otherness beyond the limit of that otherwise monistic procession of being. Identifying this matter with evil in *Ennead* 1.8, Plotinus argues that, "if evil occurs accidentally in something else, it must be something itself first, even if it is not a substance. Just as there is absolute good and good as a quality, so there must be absolute evil and the evil derived from it which inheres in something else" (Plotinus, *En* 1.8.3). He thus arrives at a polarization of two antithetical principles.

> So there must be something which is unbounded in itself and absolutely formless and has all the other attributes which we mentioned before as characterising the nature of evil; and if there is anything of the same sort posterior to this, it either has an admixture of this or is of the same sort because it directs its intention towards it, or because it is productive of something of this kind. So that which underlies figures and forms and shapes and measures and limits, decked out with an adornment which belongs to something else, having no good of its own, only a shadow in comparison with real being, is the substance of evil (if there really can be a substance of evil); this is what our argument discovers to be the primal evil, absolute evil. (Plotinus, *En* 1.8.3)

For Plotinus, all material things, including the human body, are evil in so far as they participate in matter, and he expressly invokes Plato's language of "disorderly motion" (*ataktos kinēsis*, *Timaeus* 48E-53C),[37] as did the Manichaeans, as a property of matter that leads to its mutability, the tendency of material things to destroy each other and to hinder the soul in free activity (Plotinus, *En* 1.8.4).

Plotinus even employs the same Neo-Pythagorean categories of the limited and unlimited (Plotinus, *En* 2.4) as those Augustine uses in his own Manichaean-period treatise *The Beautiful*, both authors identifying the unlimited with matter and taking unlimitedness as the measure of something's badness: the more unlimited, the more bad the thing is (Plotinus, *En* 2.4.15).[38] Matter in itself lacks goodness, thought, virtue, beauty, strength, shape, form, and quality. "Must it not then be ugly? Must it not be utterly vile, utterly evil?" (Plotinus, *En* 2.4.16). Yet in the same way that the unlimited does not cease to exist when something is limited in some way, nor does matter disappear when it is endowed with form.[39]

Plotinus insists, in agreement with Mani, that "we must not be assumed to be the beginning of evil, as being evil by and from ourselves; evils are prior to us. Those that take hold of men do not do so with the latter's consent; but there is an escape from the evils in the soul for those who are capable of it, though not all men are" (Plotinus, *En* 1.8.5). Evil matter must be present to work a corrupting effect on the pure soul, which otherwise would not err (Plotinus, *En* 1.8.11–12). The "ugliness" of the soul come from the "addition of alien matter."

> So we shall be right in saying that the soul becomes ugly by mixture
> and dilution and inclination towards the body and matter. This is
> the soul's ugliness, not being pure and unmixed, like gold, but full of
> earthiness . . . . In the same way, the soul too, when it is separated from
> the lusts which it has through the body with which it consorted too
> much, and freed from its other affections, purged of what it gets from
> being embodied, when it abides alone has put away all the ugliness
> which came from the other nature. (Plotinus, *En* 1.6.5)

Plotinus can at times speak of an active agency, a "rebellion" of lower existents (rooted in nonbeing) as the cause of the soul's alienation from the One (Plotinus, *En* 6.4–5, esp. 6.4.15), or of the irrational soul as a distinct other which dwells in the body with the rational soul and tries to subjugate it (Plotinus, *En* 1.2.5–6). These dualistic aspects of Plotinus's thought—although far from the whole story[40]—would have appeared initially consistent with Augustine's prior Manichaean indoctrination into both the causes of human affliction and the potential for escape from the limitations of material existence.

Given this broad set of affinities between Manichaeism and Platonism, we have no trouble in seeing how a person first attracted to one could make a smooth transition to adherence to the other. Such a transition was, for Augustine, *making progress*. Yet he did not see in Platonism a more refined and sophisticated Manichaeism. Perhaps had he encountered Plotinus a few years earlier he would have seen in him precisely such a complement to the more popular and mythological expressions of Manichaean devotion. But in history timing is everything. By the time he read the Platonic books, he had lost interest in intellectual patches for a fundamentally Manichaean garment. The irony of Augustine taking Neoplatonism as a route of exit from, rather than a reinforcement of, Manichaeism has been noted by a few perceptive commentators.[41] Why should exposure to a system of thought so amenable to the Manichaean world view have been taken by Augustine as providing the means for a decisive break with the religion, rather than an opportunity to return to it with new understanding? The historian lacks a large piece of the picture involving Augustine's affective situation at this crucial moment in his life. His limited commitment throughout his dalliance with Manichaeism and his record of disappointing experiences with them may provide much of the answer. We must also consider the exact timing of his exposure to Platonism, *after* he had already broken with Manichaeism. The company he was now keeping no doubt colored his absorption of Neoplatonism. Even if this company included non-Christian Platonists, Milanese Christian Platonists played a key role in bringing Augustine to this new set of ideas. Plotinus came to Augustine in a certain environment, then, and framed within a particular reading that accommodated it toward Nicene Christianity rather than any other religious system.

New Horizons

Despite the common construction of conversion as a radical repudiation of one's former values, therefore, it is my contention that the presence in both Ambrose's sermons and the Platonic books of familiar themes Augustine already valued formed a likely source of attraction for him. The continuities between Manichaeism and the new options he found in Milan permitted him to be open-minded to these alternative apprehensions of reality, precisely because to some degree they confirmed and reinforced the reality to which he was already conditioned by past commitment. But these familiar elements did not exist in isolation; they came accompanied by other, novel elements to which Augustine was now exposed. He had identified himself with the Manichaean system because it possessed the characteristics he valued in a truth-discourse, along with other features of which he was not so sure. Now he encountered many of those same characteristics coordinated and interconnected in new arrangements with other ideas and practices.[42] While maintaining his allegiance to his strong interests and commitments, he could swap out elements of less conviction for new options, resituating his core beliefs and values within a new *episteme*.

In encountering close parallels to Manichaean discourse about the soul's affinity to God, its descent into the world, its battle to resist the senses and the passions, and its aspirations to ascent, Augustine also discovered new settings for these themes framed by alternative metaphysical premises. He eventually decided that these alternative *epistemes* could potentially fulfill his spiritual and intellectual aspirations as well as Manichaeism had, if not better. Back in Africa, only Manichaeism had appeared to offer the life in pursuit of truth and detachment from worldly entanglements to which August felt himself beckoned by Cicero. After a decade, he had given up on Manichaeism as a failed identification of his self-project. Now Milan presented more options for pursuing this project, carrying over the more successful commitments of his Manichaean period and testing their compatibility with new propositions.

While recognizing that Augustine had problems with some details of the Manichaean system, we should resist imagining that he had been searching for alternatives to such basic Manichaean premises about the world as materialism and dualism. The frustration he expresses with being unable to think in any other terms at the time (*Conf* 5.10.19, 5.11.21, 7.1.1–2) belongs to the narrator of the *Confessions*, not to the experience of the earlier self he purports to be describing. We have no good reason to suppose that he saw anything wrong with a materialist metaphysics until Platonism told him to view it as problematic. As with any ideology, Platonism came with its own account of errors, a diagnosis of wrong thinking as a foil for its own solutions. In being persuaded to a Platonic outlook, Augustine accepted its diagnosis of error as his own pre-conversion story. What Platonic discourse critiqued *must have been* the very mistakes in thinking that subjected him before his Platonic breakthrough. Accordingly, he treats materialistic thinking as the root of all his limitations as a thinker: "it was principally the corporeal thinking about those masses that held me fast and stifled me" (*Conf* 5.11.21). It distorted his understanding of the nature of God (*Conf* 5.10.19),[43] minds or souls (*Conf* 5.10.20),[44] and evil (*Conf* 3.7.12).[45] He ascribes materialistic thinking to a reliance on sensory experience that he associates with Manichaean inductive approaches to knowledge and truth, now to be replaced with deductive methods. "For as my eyes were accustomed to roam among material forms, so did my mind among the images of them. I could not see that this very act of perception, whereby I formed these images, was different from them in kind. Yet my mind would never have been able to form them unless it was itself a reality, and a great one" (*Conf* 7.1.2).

But when Augustine diagnosed his own error as materialistic thinking, he at the same moment condemned a viewpoint shared by the vast majority of people of his age, Christian, Manichaean, and pagan. In fact, materialism, in its Stoic permutation, was no less than the accepted "science" of the day. It was simply taken for granted that "anything not a body was nothing whatsoever" (*Conf* 5.10.19). Materialism had ruled both metaphysics and epistemology for centuries, in part due to its accessibility as "common sense"; analogies offered effective teaching aids, and reasoning followed an inductive course from observed phenomena to invisible counterparts and sources. Even Middle Platonism had largely conformed to this way of viewing reality. The Neoplatonism of Plotinus, however, opted for a radical transcendental alternative that could not be arrived at through the inductive scientific method. Believing in a dimension of being that somehow grounded all material existence and yet had nothing in common with it required a leap of faith, indeed.

Yet the idea of an immaterial reality did not necessarily entail a rejection of dualistic constructs of the universe; in fact, to some degree the contrast of the immaterial to the material could find expression in dualistic imagery. Nevertheless, at some point Augustine encountered a nondualist account of evil associated with the immaterialist conception of ultimate reality. Plotinus had assayed Aristotle's definition of evil as a privation of good, but rejected it as inadequate, despite its apparent good fit with his view of reality as a scale of being, descending from the ultimate good to that which lacks any good qualities. It may have been precisely this obvious suitability to other aspects of Plotinus's thought that led some of his interpreters to overlook the master's own reservations about the privation theory of evil. Ambrose was one of those interpreters.[46]

Commenting in his *Hexaemeron* on the reference to "darkness" in Genesis 1:2, Ambrose rejects the idea that this could refer to the powers of evil. "The reason is, of course, that evil is not a substance, but an accident and that it is a deviation from the goodness of nature" (Ambrose, *Hex* 1.8.29). On this basis he could synthesize Christian and Neoplatonic themes of the goodness of all things. "For God is the author of all good things and all things which are, are his. Nowhere is there evil there, and, if our mind dwells in him, it does not know evil" (Ambrose, *Isaac* 7.61). The very things that tempt and entangle the soul to its detriment are in their own nature good (Ambrose, *Bono mort* 6.22).

Ambrose expressly saw his treatment of the subject of evil as a pointed response to Manichaean dualism (Ambrose, *Hex* 1.8.28, 30; *Fid* 3.6.42), and he used it to reinforce the traditional free will account of evil that had become accentuated within mainstream Christianity (both Nicene and non-Nicene) through that very encounter with Manichaeism. "You yourself are the cause of your wickedness," he declares, "you yourself are the leader of your own crimes and the instigator of your own misdeeds. Why do you summon an alien nature to furnish an excuse for your sins?" (Ambrose, *Hex* 1.8.31). Augustine closely echoes these phrases in characterizing his attitude as a Manichaean (*Conf* 5.10.18). He doubtless heard Ambrose emphatically stress individual moral responsibility against the more fatalistic ethical discourse of Manichaeism.

> Evil is not a living substance, but is a deviation of mind and soul away from the path of true virtue, a deviation which frequently steals upon the souls of the unaware. The greater danger is not, therefore, from what is external to us, but from our own selves. Our adversary is within us, within us is the author of error, locked, I say, within our very selves. (Ambrose, *Hex* 1.8.31)[47]

> Evil arose from us, and was not made by a creator God. It is produced by the lightness of our morals; it has no prior right over any created thing, nor has it the dignity of a natural substance. It is a fault due to our mutability and is an error due to our fall. (Ambrose, *Hex* 1.8.30)[48]

The Devil, he says, "received the power to tempt us but not the competency to subvert us, except when our weak and unassisted will falters" (Ambrose, *Paradiso* 2.10). Similarly, even though the body may be assaulted by all kinds of misfortunes and passions (because it had been placed in the hands of Satan), nevertheless the soul is able to withstand sin through vigilance (Ambrose,

Poen 1.14.74–77). Sin occurs only with mental assent to temptation. "Our mind is the cause of our guilt. And so the flesh is innocent, but is often the minister of sin" (Ambrose, *Poen* 1.14.73). The body is a passive instrument at the beck and call of the soul, either to good or evil.[49] "Why do we blame the flesh, as if it were weak? Our members are the tools of wrong and the tools of right. . . . And so the passions are the authors of guilt, and not the flesh, for the flesh is the servant of the will" (Ambrose, *Iacob* 1.3.10). Drawing on his expertise in Roman law as well as the Greek ethical tradition, he contends that guilt attaches only to that which one chooses to do, not that which one does under coercion by some other power.

> It is not that we can attribute our trouble to anything but our own will. No one is held to guilt unless he has gone astray by his own will. Actions which are imposed on those who resist contain no fault; the malevolence of sin follows only upon actions perpetrated voluntarily, and this fault we would divert to others. Christ chooses for himself the volunteer soldier; the devil buys for himself at auction the volunteer slave. He holds no man bound to the yoke of slavery unless such a one has first sold himself to him at the purchase price of his sins. (*Iacob* 1.3.10)[50]

We find in Ambrose, therefore, an exact anticipation of the combination of free will with a privation theory of evil that Augustine settled on in the years immediately following his conversion. The close match of the two on this subject raises questions about Augustine's claim in the *Confessions* that he learned the privation theory of evil not from Ambrose but from the "books of the Platonists." Indeed, Augustine himself contradicted this version of events toward the end of his life, at which time he did acknowledge his debt on this subject to Ambrose.[51] Though Plotinus mentions the privation theory of evil in a passage Augustine probably read, he gives stronger endorsement to the alternative (and much more "Manichaean") idea that matter exists as a substantial cause of evil (Plotinus, *En* 1.8). Evidently Augustine read Plotinus under the influence of Ambrose's constant rhetorical reiteration of individual moral responsibility over an insubstantial evil. Indeed, Ambrose appears to "predigest" Plotinus for Augustine in the *De Isaac*, where he reviews much of Plotinus's treatment of the problem of evil in *Ennead* 1.8. Within a few lines he alludes to both the privation theory ("What is wickedness but the lack of good?") and the attribution of evil to matter ("Vices of matter darken the grace of the soul"), before proceeding to explain why both views have some degree of validity.

> Ignorance and concupiscence are illnesses of the soul but are ascribed more to form than to matter. The flesh is matter, ignorance and concupiscence form. Then why is the flesh blamed when there are such great blemishes in the form? Because the form can do nothing without the matter. Indeed the form accomplishes nothing in the case of those who are tranquil because they are without the matter. For what would concupiscence be if the flesh did not enflame it? . . . Evils, then, arise from goods, for there are no evils but deprivations of goods. . . . Thus the lack of good is the root of wickedness . . . (*De Isaac* 7.60; cf. Plotinus, *En* 1.8.1)

This attempt at a harmonization of the two explanations of evil, explicitly cited by Augustine late in his career (*Iul* 1.9.44), is far from clear, and appears to do little more than juxtapose them. It does succeed, however, in undermining Plotinus's own emphasis on matter as a cause by reiterating that matter, even for Plotinus in his usual characterization of it, is passive, even inert. So in the process that generates evil, it attracts the soul and sullies it, and therefore is a cause of evil, but not actively so. Ambrose, and Augustine following him, correctly discerned that logically one must place responsibility on the active party in this encounter, namely, the soul that makes the free choice of yielding to matter's attractiveness.

But there is a problem. Soul without connection to matter is considered to be equally inert, as Ambrose notes. It abides in a tranquil, static condition and cannot act without a material medium. Thus one faces a classic chicken-or-egg conundrum where in theory neither the soul nor matter should be able to initiate action, yet one or the other in some sense does. The Manichaeans did not share this problem of reciprocal inertness in their account of the origin of evil. As we have seen, Alexander of Lycopolis reports their employment of Plato's concept from the *Timaeus*, attributing to matter a "disorderly motion" (*ataktos kinēsis*) of its own. For the Manichaeans, then, evil has motion and a kind of blind and directionless will, and is fully capable of initiating contact with the realm of light and the souls that inhabit it. In fact, evil is this disorderly motion, rather than matter per se. But Augustine was not in the frame of mind to compare these alternative accounts for strengths and weaknesses on an even plane. We should not think of him being persuaded by arguments coherent within the existing terms of Manichaean discourse, and even less within some neutral frame of reference. Rather, it makes better sense of his conversion to think of it in terms of a *re-discoursing*—an attraction and habituation to a package of novel phrases and models within which the issues, experiences, and themes that mattered to him were rearranged.

The facile either/ors of pessimism and optimism, materialism and idealism often expressed in connection with Augustine's conversion largely evaporate in the face of both a better understanding of the nuances of Manichaeism and a more precise accounting of the ideological exchange taking place in Augustine in Milan. If we think that Augustine was in a position consciously to choose optimism over pessimism, idealism over materialism, or even to know that such options stood before him, we credit him with full participation in a discourse of which he had only heard rumors. Augustine comes as close as any convert ever has to conveying the absence of rational comparison and deliberative assessment in his change of heart. Yet we still have difficulty hearing what he has to say. He confronted a number of not just incompatibilities, but incomparabilities between the alternative systems before him. Manichaean dualism refused to abide by the "common sense" soul-body dichotomy that pervaded Augustine's culture, and as a result he appears to have mistaken it for the latter sort of conventional Western dualism, in a way perhaps fatal to the system's motivating ethos. Platonism refused to speak in terms of the "common sense" materialism of antiquity, and consequently struggled—as Augustine would struggle—to find coherent ways to express itself. Augustine was awash in isolated bits of meaning from fundamentally different discourses about reality. By what logic was he supposed to sort out, weigh, coordinate, and systematize them for himself? With one leg in Manichaeism, even as an apostate, and one leg in a new world of first impressions, what was there to serve as a basis for decision?

Augustine's prior commitment to the Manichaean *episteme* had required the adjustment of exceptions, qualifications, "common sense" patches, which eventually overburdened the plausibility of the whole. As an apostate, then, he had let go of this *episteme* as the master discourse of his life and experience, while retaining a number of its individual elements that still held meaning for him. These were the various isolated concepts, explanatory schemata, and plans of action that commanded his primary loyalty, in comparison with which their epistemic frame held secondary importance. In identifying new, potentially compatible frames for the uncompromised truths which retained their value for him, Augustine initiated a kind of private Kuhnian paradigm shift. The consequences and entailments of the new paradigm had yet to be tested for their satisfactoriness, or for the price they would exact from the still firm convictions Augustine sought to carry forward from his past. For the moment, everything was under-determined possibility.

Man on Fire

Both the writings contemporary with Augustine's change in thinking, and his later reflections on that change in the *Confessions*, agree that it was books of Platonic philosophy that initiated the process of intellectual revolution for Augustine, and characterize their effect on Augustine as setting his mind on fire.[52] The ample sympathy between Manichaeism and Neoplatonism in a number of areas offers a context in which to understand the appeal of both systems to the same person. Yet Augustine conveys a sense of exciting novelty as well. He had evidently found a new intellectual discourse that furthered many of his customary ways of thinking about the world, but did so completely apart from the now problematic Manichaean tradition. He had discovered an alternative system for pursuing Truth—one that entailed mastering a new set of terms, models, and self-conceptions. He had, in a manner of speaking, changed his mind.

Yet adopting Neoplatonism would no more have required a break with Manichaeism for Augustine than adopting Skepticism had necessitated a break with the religion for Faustus. If he had been so inclined, he could have integrated and synthesized the attractive new philosophy with his prior thinking, all the more since he had misprised key parts of Manichaeism in a direction more amenable to accommodating Platonism. As a cultic system, Manichaeism could be combined with a variety of philosophical allegiances, and in various permutations drew close to Stoicism, Platonism, Pythagoreanism, and Skepticism. It is only insofar as Augustine took his commitments to Manichaeism as loyalty to more than a cult, to an entire *episteme* of coordinated metaphysical, ethical, and ritual discourses and practices, that Platonism presented potential incompatibilities with it. Perhaps, if he had not already been disenchanted with key aspects of Manichaeism by the time he encountered the books of the Platonists, they might have never provided sufficient reason for him to abandon his former faith. Indeed, hearing Ambrose's sermons and reading Platonic books, Augustine did not find himself called to a fundamentally different sentiment about life and the world from that which he held as a Manichaean. He did not experience a call for a significant shift in his values. Instead, he found the same basic outlook shorn of some of the more baroque features of the Manichaean myth—features that were not, as the Manichaeans had initially promised, based solely in reason. Augustine's conversion, then, was not a change between two radically different views of life, but a transfer from a system that failed sufficiently to ground that view of life for Augustine to one that could because it better met his standards of judgment.

Just as the new ethos he had derived from reading Cicero's *Hortensius* inspired him to identify with the Manichaean community (*Conf* 3.4.8), so Augustine found reason to link Neoplatonic ideas with the Nicene Christian value system as he began to understand it in Milan. It was precisely in Milan, and only because of relatively unique conditions in Milan, that Augustine learned that there was more to non-Manichaean Christianity than hellfire motivation for a prudish morality. The elite culture of that city moved comfortably between secular and cultic settings where roughly complementary nondualist cosmologies and the related idea of an all-encompassing and unopposed providential order to things found emphasis. Augustine put his finger on this common ethos when he intuited that commitments to both Platonism and the Nicene ethical and cultic system were compatible.

It was primarily to the degree that Milanese Christianity involved a credible engagement with the philosophical world Augustine prized, I suggest, that it held appeal for him and gained his attention. Through the sermons of Ambrose, personal contact with men such as Simplicianus and Manlius Theodorus, and any number of books circulating in Milan, such as those of Marius Victorinus and Celsinus, Augustine encountered a tradition of philosophical theology and philosophically oriented allegorical biblical interpretation that derived from Basil of Caesarea, Origen, and ultimately Philo of Alexandria. This tradition of thought stood for a Platonic completion of Christian premises. This synthesis tended toward rejection of materialism and dualism; emphasized God as ultimate being, and his transcendence of material and sensory categories; taught the creation of all from nothing, and therefore the grace of existence from God; dismissed natural evil and located the cause of sin in human free will; and envisioned the individual as primarily soul, fallen through error and sin and seeking to reascend to proximity and likeness to God. Augustine would adopt this set of positions wholesale in his decision formally to join the "Catholic" communion in Milan in early 387, the culmination of a rapid series of exposures to new options in the preceding two years.

A decade before, Augustine had looked to the Manichaean community in Carthage to provide the sort of organized, collective quest for truth among like-minded intellectuals that he was inspired to seek out from his reading of Cicero. It worked for a time among his casually committed little group of sophisticated dabblers. But in the end, in the person of Faustus, Augustine discovered that he was dealing with what was, after all, a *religious* community, for which intellectual pursuits were at best a resource to be used in support of a cultic system. Now, in Milan, he encountered another potential community of inquiry, another form of Christianity that seemed to offer an atmosphere of sublime philosophy in which he could feel at home. He considered Ambrose more educated than Faustus precisely because the former was more thoroughly versed in Cicero and Varro and the other classics which were never far from Augustine's thoughts. If the Manichaeans were the best African Christianity had to offer, he had now found an even more impressive body of sophisticated intellectuals in Milan. As he relates in the *Confessions*, once he and his fellow former Manichaean companions in Milan—Alypius and Nebridius—had determined that non-Manichaean Christians—or at least its "learned exponents"—did not teach all that the Manichaeans had ascribed to them, they asked themselves, "Can we, then, hesitate to knock where other truths may be opened?" (*Conf* 6.11.18).

Even as this new door opened to Augustine and his companions, events unfolded in the summer of 386 that cut into any lingering sentiment for Manichaeism among them. Word arrived in Milan of the failure of an experiment in communal living among the Manichaean Elect of Rome (*MM* 20.74). Augustine seems to have been aware of the project from its inception,[53] and apparently had aspirations to emulate it with his friends in Milan (*Acad* 2.2.4; *Conf* 6.14.24).[54] In post-conversion hindsight, Augustine treats the event as a failure of the Manichaean system of conduct. But before we join him in that judgment, it is important to recognize that Manichaeism did not approve of monasticism. According to the precepts of the Elect, they were to lead an itinerant life, lodging in the homes of the Auditors on whom they depended for their sustenance. Augustine offhandedly confirms the maintenance of this original model of Elect life in his reports of incidents in Carthage, where the Elect came together for a meeting from "different houses," and where an Elect lived in the home of an Auditor (*MM* 19.67–73). The interconnection of Elect and Auditor was the essential bond of the community, and the Elect were strictly prohibited from isolating themselves. But monasticism was a growing cultural trend in the fourth century, and attracted the interest of a particularly influential Auditor in Rome, Constantius, who launched the experiment and presided over its demise.[55]

Augustine credits Constantius with being "quite equal to the Elect in their far-famed abstinence,"[56] and attributes his worthy undertaking to both his liberal education and his zeal in defending the Manichaean faith,[57] in light of which he "took it very ill that he had cast in his teeth the vile conduct of the Elect, who lived in all kinds of places, and went hither and thither for lodging of the worst description"—in other words, practiced the itinerancy enjoined for the Elect by Mani, but apparently at odds with the aristocratic sensibilities of the Auditor when many of his peers were becoming involved with a more socially respectable form of ascetic monasticism in their elite homes in the city. "He therefore desired, if possible, to assemble all who were willing to live according to the precepts in his own house, and to maintain them at his own expense" (*MM* 20.74).[58] He had some trouble finding Elect willing to adopt this innovation, or persons of sufficient authority within the community to authorize it; but he finally persuaded a Manichaean bishop to do both.[59] The bishop's lack of the refinements of actual and want-to-be aristocrats highlights the rougher edge of the ascetic movement that Manichaeism retained, and the poor fit between this outsider religion and the pretensions of mainstream Roman society with which Augustine identified with renewed ambition.

The recruited bishop agreed to supply the authority for the monastic experiment, and a number of Elect joined under his aegis. The host may have used the argument that, since the Elect would in fact be lodging in the home of an Auditor, the precept for itinerancy was technically being followed, albeit collectively rather than individually as intended. The plan the Auditor and bishop agreed to involved taking "the rule of life in the epistle of Manichaeus" as the governing rule of the monastery. Some of the Elect who had come to hear about the experiment objected to the novel application of this document, and refused to participate. Others chose to give it a try, with the owner of the property filling the expected role of the Auditor to scrutinize the conduct of the Elect and ensure adherence to the precepts, "zealously enforcing everything on everybody."[60]

Nevertheless, this arrangement was a radical inversion of normal Manichaean practice.[61] Where typically many Auditors would monitor the conduct of a few Elect, now a single Auditor assumed a kind of observational authority over many Elect. The latter, used to dwelling with Auditors rather than with each other, had trouble making the adjustment, and began to complain about each other's conduct. Augustine insists that the charges made against each other were "vile beyond description," but conveniently leaves them undetailed in his account. The situation finally came to a head; the Elect met with their host and asked for modifications to the rules. Augustine characterizes this as "sedition." "The Auditor stated his case in the most concise terms, that either all must be kept, or the man who had given such a sanction to such precepts which no one could fulfill"—that is, Mani himself—"must be thought a great fool" (*MM* 20.74). The bishop, recognizing the failure of the experiment, packed up and left. Malicious rumors of his own clandestine arrangement to receive extra supplies while in residence followed him.

We should give prime importance to this incident in affecting an Augustine still swayed by Faustus's criterion of moral effectiveness. It was so significant to Augustine that he took the trouble to inquire into the facts of the matter when he returned to Rome in 387, *after* his baptism into the Nicene Christian communion. Jean de Menasce has identified this incident as the straw that broke the camel's back for Augustine, by adding to his existing theoretical doubts the first strong challenge to the moral and ascetic claims on which Faustus rested such significance.[62] He heard the first rumors of this failed experiment at about the time he began to hear reports of Christian monastic experiments in Egypt and elsewhere.[63] These tales were more edifying, and deeply affected him. If non-Manichaean Christians could truly and voluntarily lead such disciplined and ideal lives, when the Manichaeans could not, perhaps there was something to the faith of these other Christians after all—something that helped people make the moral progress that Augustine thought Manichaeism could not. What if, after all, the discipline of the Elect was impossibly difficult to fulfill?[64] The "Catholic" communion, he learned, more reasonably asked each individual to live according to his or her abilities. Meanwhile, Manichaeism could only offer as an alternative to the rigorous life of the Elect the role of Auditor, which Augustine apparently determined to be insufficiently demanding to instill fervent commitment and inspire consistent moral reform.

A second occurrence would have put an even greater chill on any backward glance Augustine and his colleagues may have been inclined to make. Back in

Africa, a proconsul had finally arrived bent on enforcing the anti-Manichaean laws that had appeared so threatening to Augustine three years earlier. Unlike his predecessors, Messianus came from the zealous circle around the eastern emperor Theodosius.[65] Before his arrival, the Manichaean bishop Faustus had been able to operate with relative freedom in Carthage. But now, he was arrested.[66] Accused by Christian leaders in Carthage, and condemned to death by the proconsul, Faustus had his sentence commuted to exile on an island.

During the trials conducted by Messianus, one of Augustine's former Manichaean associates "named names" in an effort to shift blame away from himself, and Augustine was listed in absentia as a Manichaean, perhaps even as an active proselytizer, in the official acts.[67] As much as Augustine might complain about the prejudgment involved in condemning him simply for being accused without a trial,[68] Messianus apparently issued a warrant or judgment that included Augustine, either explicitly or implicitly, given the appearance of his name in the official acts.[69] Word of this warrant would have reached Augustine in the summer of 386, about the same time that news arrived of the very first execution of "Manichaeans" (actually the Spanish Christian holy man Priscillian and some of his associates) at the court of the emperor Maximus at Trier.[70] With so many possibilities opening up for him in the intellectual elite culture of Milan, and the increasing defamation of his Manichaean associations, there was no shortage of motivations for Augustine to consider a formal act of initiation into the sanctioned ranks of the Catholic Church.

Augustine's African enemies later claimed that his transformation from a "Manichaean" to a "Catholic" had all too conveniently occurred overseas, far from reliable witnesses, and under conditions that made his motivations questionable. Biographers, theologians, and religious historians have not been inclined to credit such accusations, persuaded as many of Augustine's contemporaries were by the powerful account Augustine gave of the internal journey of his soul. In the self-presentation he would provide, as well as more theoretically in other works, Augustine called into question the ability of a facile sequencing of external facts to capture the truth about a person's plans, motivations, and purpose—about the state of a person's soul behind the appearance of his or her actions. Yet that self-presentation—the *Confessions*—was written a decade after the events that form its climax, under specific conditions and with a particular purpose. Since it is not a journal from the period with which we are concerned, it overwrites the events of that time with hindsight. In it, he practically invents the term *conversion*, by a handy appropriation of a Neoplatonic image, and claims such an experience as the motivation of the actions he took and the plans he made in and around Milan in the second half of 386 and the first half of 387. His actions could not be explained by motives related to his prior Manichaean self, he averred, because in conversion that self had been utterly replaced by a new, "Catholic" self, with a distinct set of orientations, attitudes, values, and aspirations. It is this claim about the nature of conversion in general, and Augustine's in particular, that we must now assess.

CHAPTER SEVEN

Conversion

CONVERSION TENDS TO be thought of and discussed as a sudden, dramatic, and complete transformation of the self, instantly creating a new person changed at the core.[1] The paradigm owes not a little to Augustine's dramatic account of his own sudden decision to change his life one late summer day in 386 in the garden of a friend's home in Milan (*Conf* 8.6.13–12.30). But if anything like the famous scene in the Milanese garden ever occurred, it was only a point along the course of a conversion *process*. By the time he writes his *Confessions*, Augustine sees his entire life—not without good reason—as that conversion process, a continuous remaking of self. His literary gifts in constructing the garden scene, however, have obscured this larger theme for many of the work's readers. While acknowledging Augustine's insight into the necessarily protracted character of self-transformation, the historian must be a bit less teleological than Augustine could afford to be. Even though Augustine's change from a "Manichaean" to a "Catholic" identity made a tremendous historical difference, there was nothing inevitable about it.

As it happens, Augustine's uptake of Manichaean models of selfhood proved inadequate and incomplete. As it happens, his reservations were met not with a dogmatic challenge of an either/or choice, but by the liberal skepticism of Faustus, who directed Augustine toward a practice-oriented construction of selfhood rather than an intellectual one. As it happens, certain characteristics in Augustine's antecedent self resisted the neglect of intellectual satisfaction entailed in Faustus's proposal. These historical accidents produced the conditions under which a process of deconversion and apostasy from

Manichaeism could occur. Augustine committed himself to Faustus's skepticism initially, but apparently found the reorientation to practice hollow without intellectual conviction. While remaining a practicing Manichaean in the world of visible conduct, he gradually found greater intellectual satisfaction on some issues in non-Manichaean sources. He drifted out of the Manichaean community, eventually finding his way into the Nicene churches and Platonic reading circles of the elite strata of society he had joined in Milan.

Writing in the *Confessions* more than a decade later, Augustine maintains that he felt compelled to supplement his intellectual interests with membership in a religious community.

> I decided that I must leave the Manichaeans; for in that time of doubt, I did not think I could remain in a sect to which I now preferred certain of the philosophers. Yet I absolutely refused to entrust the care of my sick soul to the philosophers, because they were without the saving name of Christ. I determined, then, to go on as a catechumen in the Catholic Church—the church of my parents—and to remain in that state until some certain light should appear by which I might steer my course. (*Conf* 5.14.25)

We can compare this statement to another made at the time of the events themselves, in *The Academics*, where Augustine declares his resolve not to abandon the authority of Christ in the face of changes in his metaphysical commitments away from those he held as a Manichaean (*Acad* 3.20.43). It has been all too easy heretofore to ignore the fact that he had been conditioned to this high valuation of Christ's authority not by Nicene Christianity, but by Manichaeism, which alone had maintained his tenuous interest in anything remotely "religious," and which had even built on the foundation of his attraction to its rationality a respect for spiritual authority.

In writing *The Academics* and the other works coinciding with his conversion process, Augustine shows clearly that his interests still fall primarily on epistemological, cosmological, and metaphysical questions, and secondarily on ethics; the devotional rhetoric and references to cultic activity typically thought of as "religion" in his day make no stronger appearance in these writings than they do in Cicero's literary gestures to conventional piety. Augustine's deference to Christ attests less to a radical individual choice than to the triumph of Christian culture in the late fourth century, whereby all of Augustine's viable options had some connection to the Christian tradition. The "saving name of Christ" featured so little in Augustine's discussions with his friends at this point that his close companion Alypius could propose it be left out altogether from the polished version of his writings (*Conf* 9.4.7). Could Alypius have so profoundly misunderstood his friend? Augustine, however, deigned to make a few passing references to Christ in those works, identifying his teachings with those of Pythagoras (*Ord* 2.20.53–54) and in general regarding him as "a man of outstanding wisdom" capable of perceiving truth directly (*Conf* 7.19.25). If this was the Christ Augustine was hearing in the sermons of Ambrose, he was hearing it through a heavy gauze of preconception, steeped in traditional philosophical discourse. Alypius's suggestion therefore reflects the actual priorities of the group around Augustine, for whom any religious reference was a gesture toward popular discourse. But either the expectations of their broader culture, or the conditioning of a decade among the Manichaeans, motivated them to adopt a new cultic association in place of the now abandoned one.

By his own characterization, Augustine chose Ambrose's church as a suitable cultic community more or less by default. When he took on the role of a Nicene catechumen—and let us be clear, this entailed no more than saying that he was and attending church regularly—he took the path of least resistance, fitting into the dominant element in Milanese society, and pleasing his mother. In fact, newly arrived in Milan in such a prominent position, the safe anonymity and indifference of Rome gone, he had to declare his association with one religious identity or another. People would ask about his parentage. The leading families with which Augustine sought connections, and among which his mother sought a suitable bride for him, nearly all belonged to the Nicene party. If we treat the saint as we would any other historical figure, his assumption of the role of catechumen in this setting requires no further motive or explanation.

While Augustine initially may have thought that he was rejoining the communion familiar to him from his childhood, and dutifully marched off to its sermons with very low expectations, he appears to have been pleasantly surprised by Ambrose's intellect and sophistication, qualities reflected as well in other members of the clergy and laity. The possibility of a real intellectual community, delivering what Cicero had called for and what the Manichaeans had failed to provide, opened up before him. Add to this the fad for Platonism, both inside and outside Christian circles, and one may conclude that

Augustine found himself in a highly stimulating intellectual and spiritual environment that he could draw on in reconfiguring his identity. Things may have taken a logical course from there; but, as it happens, they were hastened along by other external accidents of circumstance.

The western Roman Empire seemed filled with talk of Manichaeans in the spring and summer of 386 c.e. A major embassy arrived in Milan from the court of the emperor Maximus at Trier, led by Maximus's brother Marcellinus, bringing with it news of Maximus's zeal in defending the "Catholic faith" from "Manichaeans." The Spanish Christian holy man Priscillian, along with several associates, had been executed as Manichaeans in accordance with the laws issued by Gratian and Theodosius in 382 and 383. Maximus wrote to Siricius, the bishop of Rome, declaring his action the suppression of a Manichaean cell (*Coll. Avell.* 40.4). News of this first execution of a Christian as an act of defending the faith raced through the empire, its implications anxiously discussed. With the opening of sea travel for the year came word of similar anti-Manichaean actions by the government in Africa, perhaps brought by Augustine's patron Romanianus, who arrived in Milan seeking to appeal a legal dispute to the imperial court.[2] The African proconsul Messianus had acted to enforce the same laws used against Priscillian, and accepted *delationes* of notorious Manichaeans from the Christian leaders of the province. Faustus had been accused, tried, and convicted. Ominously, Augustine had been named by some of the Manichaeans on trial (*CLP* 3.16.19). Augustine no doubt learned that a warrant for his arrest awaited him back in Africa (*CLP* 3.25.30). Thus accumulated the elements of the "inconvenient coincidence" between a renewed anti-Manichaean crackdown and the timing of Augustine's conversion.[3] Around the same time came word from Rome of the scandal over the failure of the monastic experiment within the still protected Manichaean community there.[4] Although Augustine had already ceased associating with the Manichaean community, we may suspect that all these developments increased his sense of isolation and added to the burden of his own identity crisis. In *The Soliloquies* written shortly afterward, Augustine speaks frankly and painfully of his loneliness away for three years from his African friends—who were mostly Manichaeans, of course—and of anxieties about the poor health that plagued him (*Sol* 1.9.16).[5] He also struggled with the disruption of his previously stable sex life at this time, as he found himself taking up with a mistress while he waited for his fiancée to come of age (*Conf* 6.15.25).[6] In short, his network of significant others had been significantly disturbed, and his identity consequently had lost some of its key engagements. Coincident with this state of anxiety and unhappiness, he developed respiratory problems (*stomachi dolor*, *Ord* 1.2.5; cf. *Conf* 9.2.4). All the signs point to a man overwhelmed by his circumstances and conflicted desires.[7] He unburdened himself to Romanianus, as he reminds him in *The Academics* written later that year, pouring out his desire to be rid of the responsibilities of career and family, and to live, literally, "in philosophy"—a life that Romanianus proposed to sponsor and join Augustine in pursuing (*Acad* 2.2.4; cf. *Conf* 6.11.19, 6.14.24).[8]

His confession of his own agitated mental and emotional state at this time invites psychological analysis of the conditions of his conversion and engagement with the extensive modern research on this subject. Leaving that task to others, however, our concern here will be to understand not *why* Augustine changed, but *how*. From what, and to what, did Augustine convert? What constituted the changes in his life? Can these changes, furthermore, be ascribed to a sudden and complete transformation of his selfhood? Or are they rather part of a developmental process on which has been imposed an artificially heightened drama?

In the Garden

When modern historians speak of Augustine's conversion, they usually mean to refer to the famous scene in the garden in Milan (*Conf* 8.6.13ff.), which Augustine places in the late summer of 386. Yet several incidents before and after this one would qualify as "conversion" moments in someone's life, if they were not overshadowed in the *Confessions* narrative by Augustine's compositional choices. More than a year earlier, Augustine had quit the company of the Manichaeans, started attending the public liturgy of the Nicene Christian community, and begun to consider himself a catechumen of that faith. It was several months after the garden scene that Augustine made the decision to submit his name for baptism; and then, of course, a few months after that came the baptism itself, which marked the formal act of public conversion. Augustine actively had to make decisions at every one of these steps, and we should avoid the temptation to fix on any one of them as *the* decisive change with an exclusive right to be called "conversion." The incident in the garden that he chose to emphasize in the *Confessions* was the least public of these acts; in fact, there is no substantial textual trace of it before the *Confessions* itself.

Naturally, the historian has issues to deal with here. It might be worthwhile to raise the question whether this incident had all the properties of conversion Augustine attributes to it in his text. If the truth was that he became a Nicene catechumen out of indifference and political expediency (which he admits), that he found Ambrose's sermons impressive, but not enough to persuade him of the truth of non-Manichaean Christianity (which he also acknowledges), that he found books of Platonic philosophy much more exciting (which he further reports freely), and that he decided to accept baptism as the beginning of a new disciplined ascetic life that would formalize his commitment to the cultivation of the intellect (which would seem to be the implication of his discussions at the time), then we already have a complete account of his "conversion" without any dramatic scene in the garden, albeit lacking the very internal drama that Augustine has conditioned us to look for in such an experience.

We may suspect that Augustine felt pressured by expectation and literary precedent to come forward with a dramatic conversion story for his African audience, something akin to the stories he reports hearing just prior to his own conversion experience in the *Confessions*. The literary art detected in the account of that experience, from parallels to the stories that precede it, to subtle modeling on conversion scenes in the gospels and book of Acts, supports the idea that the event in the Milanese garden has either been concocted or extensively elaborated by an Augustine with considerable more resources at his disposal than he had at the time of the events.[9] A long list of researchers over the last century have uncovered an array of literary antecedents and allusions.[10] Augustine himself well knew that, because his narrative is primarily an internal one, no one in his own time or in ours would be in a position to dispute it (*Conf* 2.3.5, 10.3.3). Only a couple of its elements would have been discernible even to Alypius, who was supposedly on the scene at the time. As a series of private thoughts, free of the constraint or influence of any other's recollection, Augustine's experience would be particularly vulnerable to reconstruction in his own hindsight. The parallelism between what happens to Augustine in the garden and two stories of conversion he reports hearing in the period immediately before[11] does not require us to doubt Augustine's account as complete fabrication; what he had heard may have served to form his own expectations of what a conversion experience would entail and helped to shape that experience as it unfolded. At the same time, it is impossible to accept the *Confessions* account as a report untouched by both rhetorical and ideological redressing.

As Augustine tells it in the well-known account, he was in a highly agitated state, full of doubts and uncertainties. The tale of Anthony tugged at his own vacillation about how to spend his life, and made him alert for signs of guidance. In his case, it was a child's voice from over a garden wall: "Take, read!" Augustine latched on to this as a command, picked up a copy of Paul's letters that was at hand, and engaged in *sortes biblicae*, reading the first passage to which it opened. It was the sort of thing that in a calmer moment Augustine criticized as rank superstition.[12] But in the moment, it served as a sign that God himself cared about what Augustine would do.[13] This sort of affective release from uncertainty and indecision is characteristic of what we usually mean when we talk comparatively of conversion experiences, and Augustine seems to have shared this sense of the phenomenon.[14]

Assuming that there is at least some underlying basis in events on which Augustine has constructed the details of the "Garden Incident," what can be said to have happened at this moment in Augustine's life, based on a judicious weighing of closely contemporaneous evidence for changes in his life along with his later account? It was not, after all, a decision to be a Nicene catechumen in the informal sense; Augustine had already decided that and was actively attending church. He had done so, he admits even in the deeply apologetic *Confessions*, on a trial basis, while waiting for something more persuasive to come along. Nor was what occurred in the garden a decision to submit his name for baptism; that occurred some months later after the retreat at Cassiciacum—a retreat he took, as he explicitly states, to resolve certain issues that held him back from trusting Christian teachings as truth. Nor, for that matter, was it the discovery of a new way of thinking, which had already occurred in his Platonic readings over the summer.

The incident in the garden, rather, appears to have involved a decision to *make progress* in ordering his life according to his preferred priorities, to make the commitments he wanted to make and become the sort of person he wished to be. This meant abandoning worldly ambition and marriage urged on him by the conventional wishes of his family—and of his own lesser self, as he regarded it—and becoming a "philosopher." As Ann Matter has emphasized, "It seems an inevitable conclusion that Augustine is speaking more clearly of a change to a life of ascetic renunciation of the flesh than of the single, dramatic moment of change from the wrong to the right that seems the starting point of the modern definition of conversion."[15] In the *Confessions*, he wishes to present it as the fulfillment of a long-standing desire to take up the "narrow way" (*uia angusta*) that in Manichaean terms was a code expression for the discipline of the Elect life (*Conf* 8.1.1; cf. *TebCod* 9.8). He introduces the story by saying, "Now I will relate how you set me free from a craving for sexual gratification which fettered me like a tight-drawn chain, and from my enslavement to worldly affairs" (*Conf* 8.6.13), and concludes it by announcing that he was "no longer seeking a wife or entertaining any worldly hope" (*Conf* 8.12.30).[16] Some lines later, he speaks of his mind being "free at last from the gnawing need to seek advancement and riches, to welter in filth and scratch my itching lust" (*Conf* 9.1.1).

One problem with the *Confessions* narrative of this decision, however, is that Augustine has *already* reported being persuaded by his Manichaean friend Alypius not to go through with his arranged marriage for the sake of their aspirations to follow the life of philosophy (*Conf* 6.12.21). Whenever that conversation and decision is supposed to have occurred, it forms no part of the events in the garden as Augustine gives them. He appears to borrow the outcome of that separate decision and add it to the garden scene in order to play up the ascetic and ethical aspect of his decision for the protreptic purposes of the *Confessions*, aimed at demonstrating how commitment to the Nicene Christian faith fulfills the Faustian criterion of ethical outcome. Augustine could not legitimately claim to have newly discovered in the garden the *desire* or even the *determination* to be chaste; but, after recounting his first encounter with tales of successful calls to chastity within the Nicene Christian tradition, he could fairly depict a man reaching conviction that he had found an *effective means* to maintain it.

By the time he recounts his transformation in the *Confessions*, Augustine has adopted the rhetoric of being turned to God at this moment (*conuertisti enim me ad te*, *Conf* 8.12.30), exactly as he had been turned to God by his reading of Cicero's *Hortensius* (*Ille vero liber mutavit affectum meum, et ad te ipsum, domine, mutavit preces meas*, *Conf.* 3.4.7). In both cases, he conveys a response of attraction to something he perceives being presented as available to him, the emergence of a desire and an aspiration to alter his priorities toward the acquisition of that to which he is attracted. Put in the terms offered by Harry Frankfurt's model of commitment, Augustine determined on a second-order desire to reorganize his first-order desires in such a way as to subordinate and harness other wishes, plans, and faculties to a primary, self-defining orientation and set of goals.[17] But where does God come into it? For Augustine, God is synonymous with truth, an identification he had found confirmed and reinforced in Manichaean rhetoric. In turning to God he is turning to Truth, which is another way of saying he is turning to *philosophia* as his culture understood that term: as a contemplative way of life whose full realization required withdrawal from public and family affairs.

But for this point, too, the scene in the garden apparently scavenges elements drawn from other, separate deliberations. It recasts a meditative moment Augustine first related more than a decade earlier in *The Academics*, wherein he imagined gazing like a lover upon the beautiful face of *philosophia*, wishing to fly with his soul to her, if it were not held back by the vices and errors that entangle it (*Acad* 2.2.6; cf. *BV* 1.4; *Sol* 1.13.22). This earlier account is as much a literary construct as the later one, built on culturally provided stock images.[18] In the *Confessions*, Augustine replaces beautiful *philosophia* with fair *continentia*, as part of a shift of emphasis from knowledge to self-discipline in the import of the conversion (*Conf* 8.11.27). The presence of a volume of Paul on the scene presupposes Augustine's caprice to compare the ideas of the Platonists with something similar in ethos he vaguely recalled from reading Paul (as a Manichaean), recounted in the previous book of the *Confessions* (*Conf* 7.21.27). There, he claims that he detected in the ideology of detachment from the world enjoined in Platonism an intellectually respectable underpinning for the moral discipline both Manichaean and non-Manichaean Christians drew from Paul; and it is as inspiration for a disciplined, continent life that Paul features in the garden (*Conf* 8.12.29). That moral angle is missing from his mention in *The Academics* of his investigative review of Paul excited by "certain books" (*Acad* 2.2.5), which leads directly into his yearning for *philosophia*, absent any inspiration by tales of Christian moral heroics or any voice over the garden wall. Augustine added considerable drama and specifically religious themes to his later version of these apparently extended ruminations.[19] He replaced an earlier Classical image of desire for wisdom with a later Christian one of pursuing chastity, both intended to convey within their respective discourses the same decision: to accept the constraints on conduct he considered entailed in his new intellectual project, just as he had similar codes in his Manichaean venture.

The life of the philosopher, as Augustine understood it from his culture, certainly entailed an ascetic withdrawal from the enervations of family life and politics, and this does seem to be the decision made definitively in the garden. Robert O'Connell captures the tenor of this cultural trope as Augustine would have encountered it:

> in exhorting his readers to *philosophia*, Cicero was not recommending that they sign up for a few extension courses . . . he was urging them to abandon the life of worldly life altogether . . . . He was urging them to adopt the contemplative *lifestyle* of study and meditation: to become, in a word, a kind of secular monk.[20]

Such a decision meant taking up a physical and mental discipline that Augustine had grown accustomed to deriving from religious sources from his time among the Manichaeans. The "books of the Platonists" offered at best vague exhortations to withdrawal from the sensory and material, not a concrete code of conduct. In the *Confessions* narrative, all but one of the motivating examples for Augustine's decision come from the new Christian ascetic movement, providing a kind of apologia for resorting to a code that takes its inspiration from popular cultic zeal rather than elite intellectual principles. But it works, as Augustine hears to his dismay that others are committing to and succeeding in the disciplined life he desired for himself. He expresses his exasperation to Alypius: "The untaught (*indocti*) are rising and taking heaven by storm, while we with all our dreary teachings are still groveling in this world of flesh and blood!" The one exception to this pattern completes the point: the rhetorician and philosopher Marius Victorinus, Augustine's *Doppelgänger*. He claimed to be a convert but would not really be such until he climbed down off his high horse and joined in with the practices of the ordinary believer.

Christianity comes into Augustine's decision because he assumes—has assumed since the decision to join the Manichaeans—that "philosophy" and "religion" must intersect on the "narrow way" of a life dedicated to truth. In accord with most writers of his age, he was convinced that both literal intellectual discourse and symbolic cultic language referred to the same truth. There existed some reason to think that cultic codes of purity and conduct supplied the specific means for achieving detachment from the world and passions that "philosophers" enjoined. In the writings he produced at the time, Augustine indicates the primarily disciplinary role he sees Christianity playing in his life, repeatedly ascribing to Nicene Christian initiation and moral teaching the function of purifying his mind so that he could successfully and correctly follow a Platonic path of intellectual progress. His desire to make a commitment to the detached life of a philosopher needed the support of a code of self-discipline that would keep lower-order desires at bay. That meant that he had to make a prior commitment to rules of conduct in order to embark on his identification with philosophy.

Here again, we discern where his priorities stood. Ascetic self-discipline of the sort Augustine decided to adopt formed no part of the requirements for entry into the Nicene Christian community. In fact, such *enkrateia* had a closer association with Manichaeism at the time. Indeed, Augustine himself relates that his patron Romanianus had made just such a self-willed commitment to chastity as a Manichaean: "When you were . . . situated with us in a most destructive error, you corrected yourself from that vice (of sexual activity) by a will full of self-control" (*Ep* 259.3).[21] Although no longer interested in pursuing such ideals within the Manichaean community, Augustine retained his commitment to them and continued to see progress in self-perfection in these terms. It was mere coincidence that the new Christian asceticism coming out of the eastern empire, unheard of in North Africa, gained a foothold in Italy at the time Augustine lived there, and offered for the first time a viable alternative to Manichaeism for a person interested in that sort of lifestyle for reasons inspired more by Cicero than by Christ. But, of course, Augustine had learned throughout the previous decade to associate the distinct calls away from worldliness these two figures represented. Whatever the reason Manichaeism had failed to provide for Augustine a context within which to take up a complete withdrawal from domestic life and worldly career, he leapt at another possible avenue to the same end, willing to see if it proved more successful. He did not choose a fundamentally different ideal for this life from that which he had held as a Manichaean, but instead transferred his loyalties to a new system for achieving it.

With this resolve made, he and Alypius "went in and told my mother" (*Conf* 8.12.30). But told her what? Augustine is remarkably vague. Monnica is said to rejoice, but in what? He already had abandoned Manichaeism, much to her joy (*Conf* 6.1.1), and had gone on to take on the role of a catechumen in the church his mother regarded as her own. Dedication to asceticism and celibacy scarcely would have been welcome news to her; besides the Manichaean associations of such a lifestyle, she had worked hard to procure a good marriage for her son. Indeed, she had looked upon her son's approaching marriage as the route to his eventual baptism (*Conf* 6.13.23). Anyway, he had already been persuaded by Alypius to forego this arranged marriage (*Conf* 6.12.21). It is equally evident that he had not yet decided to be baptized; he would reach that decision only after resolving certain doubts in Cassiciacum some months later. As for conversion to "philosophy," that was his dream, not hers. What is left for his mother to have rejoiced in?

All that remains of the incident to explain Monnica's joy—if it is not simply a pious fiction—is the apparent sign from God: "when we went on to describe how it had all happened, she was jubilant with triumph and glorified you." She had long displayed belief in signs and portents, and now her beloved Augustine had received one as well. More than that, he had recognized and accepted it as a confirmation of God's providential care for him in a way consistent with the Christian setting of his mother's own faith. This may be all that the incident was originally about, but it became recast as *the* moment of "conversion" after subsequent events unfolded in such a way as to lead him to baptism. Yet when he packed his bags some weeks later for his long-dreamed-of philosophical retreat, such an outcome was far from certain.

The Character of Augustine's Conversion

The undeniable divergence between Augustine's account of his conversion in the *Confessions* and a reconstruction of his thought in 386–387 from the sources of the time has produced scholastic hand-wringing for well over a century. Efforts to harmonize these divergent sources have provided little more than fruitless exercises in apologetics and essentialism. With these two textual embodiments of Augustine we find ourselves, in the words of Louis Gourdon, "in the presence of two conversions and of two different men."[22] Weighing up a string of inversions in emphasis between the way the story is told in the *Confessions* and the impression given by Augustine in his earliest works, Paula Fredriksen concludes of the latter, "This is a different conversion, one viewed not as the struggle of the will, sin, and grace, but as progress in philosophy."[23] Such major discrepancies between the two sets of sources on Augustine's conversion naturally raise grave doubts about the historicity of the *Confessions* account. "The bluntest question is the historian's," James O'Donnell offers. "Is Augustine telling the truth?"[24]

With this intractable question, the historian confronts the performative location of self. Augustine's literary productions offer such performances of self, crafted extensions of a similarly performative personal conduct visible to those who knew him. Such literary extensions afforded Augustine more control over his self-performance, presenting as much as possible an ideal embodiment of the character and commitment with which he identified. At an even greater remove, he could formulate a "retrospective self" in the *Confessions* that projected his current ideal back upon an earlier stage of aspiration, accentuating whatever in his past had a future in his present self.[25] It is only in this limited sense that the evidence from the time of the conversion can be taken as a more reliable witness to the events than that provided by the *Confessions*: both sets of material are products of performative craft and manipulation, but the earlier works with the repertoire actually available to Augustine at the time, while the later draws upon resources of which he as yet knew nothing. Rather than thinking of Augustine revealing more of himself in the *Confessions*, we might consider whether there is more of him to reveal at this later date; and if the later account tells a deeper story than the urbane table-talk of the earlier dialogues, it is a depth that has formed gradually, not one formerly concealed. It cannot be altogether ruled out that Augustine downplayed his Christian interests in 386–387 as a public stance, just as it is difficult to deny that he played up the place of Christian concerns in his past a decade later. In both instances, he was presenting the way he wished to be seen by others, and so in a very real sense who he wanted to be. He neither completely conceals his new engagement with Nicene Christianity in his early writings, nor makes a concerted effort to hide in his later writings his earlier prioritization of philosophical interests.[26] It is not the presence or absence of these commitments that is in question, but their relative priority at any given time.

Augustinian scholarship had been embroiled in a protracted debate over Augustine's relative reliance on "Platonism" or "Catholicism" at the time of his conversion ever since Prosper Alfaric, in his epochal *L'évolution intellectuelle de saint Augustin I*, published in 1918,[27] argued that Augustine could be more fairly considered a Platonist than a Catholic in the years prior to his ordination to the priesthood in 391.

> When he had received baptism, he accorded such little importance to this rite that, in his writings of this period, where he speaks frequently of himself and of all that interested him, he never makes the slightest allusion to it. . . . Without doubt he accepted the Christian tradition, but he only considered it as a popular adaptation of Platonic wisdom.[28]

Alfaric's position—often reduced to caricature in the last century's discussions—is merely that Christianity as a devotional and cultic commitment was *secondary* for Augustine at the time of his so-called conversion, and was approached through a primary engagement with Platonism.[29] In other words, just as I have argued for Augustine's Manichaean period, prior and higher interests and identifications took precedence for him. Does any evidence from the time suggest that these relative priorities had changed by 386–387? After surveying the positions Augustine enunciates in his earliest post-conversion works, Alfaric concluded that they are determined more profoundly by Platonic ideas than by anything he had yet learned of Nicene Christian teachings, which was precious little.

> The doctrine which comes to be sketched out proves itself to be essentially Neoplatonic and inspired above all by Plotinus. It modifies appreciably enough the doctrine of the Master in order to adapt it to the teachings of the Catholic faith. But it transforms Catholicism still more in order to bring it into accord with Plotinian philosophy and considers it only as an inferior form of wisdom, good only for those who are of feeble intelligence or still novices.[30]

The strongest argument in support of Alfaric's characterization of Augustine the convert comes from the lips of Augustine himself; for, as radical as this characterization may seem to be to some, it is little more than a paraphrase of what Augustine says himself in his earliest writings (e.g., *Ord* 2.5.15–16, 2.9.26; *VR* 7; *CEF* 4.5). Even in the deeply apologetic and devotionally phrased *Confessions*, moreover, he unequivocally ascribes the key breakthrough in his thinking to "some of the books of the Platonists," in which he found a philosophically refined view of a perfect God, his omnipotent agency in the cosmos, and the hierarchical harmony by which all things cohere (*Conf* 7.9.13–15; cf. *Acad* 2.2.5)—ideas missing or insufficiently emphasized in either the African Christianity of his youth or Manichaeism. Moreover, the revived Platonist tradition of Plotinus propounded the idea that being itself occupied an incorporeal, intelligible dimension utterly removed from physical experience, thereby rejecting the predominant materialist metaphysics of the time. This was a truly revolutionary proposition in its day, and it is understandable that it would strike Augustine that way.[31] It was apparently enough that nothing he heard from Ambrose directly contradicted these new insights, fostering the anticipation that the intellectual and cultic systems would prove compatible.

Alfaric himself cautions against trying to account for everything in Augustine's early thought by means of Platonism. Augustine was more widely read than that, and could draw on broadly shared intellectual assumptions common to much of the Greco-Roman intellectual tradition as it was known to fourth-century culture. He made use of Stoic and Academic arguments, as well as the eclectic thinking of Cicero and Varro.[32] Alfaric insists that Augustine used Christian and Platonic ideas to explicate and complete one another, and it was never the case that he followed either tradition purely to the exclusion of the other.[33] He finds plenty of examples where Augustine displays Christian readings overlying Neoplatonic positions.[34] He correctly observes that Augustine himself regarded these adjustments of Plotinian thought to Christian principles as trivial, "some transposition of words and formulas," as he put it (VR 7).[35] Nor should we consider Augustine a perfectly informed Platonist, any more than we would regard him as a thoroughly indoctrinated Nicene Christian, at a point in his life mere months after substantial exposure to either system.[36]

It is certainly true that as he studied both Nicene Christianity and Neoplatonism in greater detail, Augustine began to see that the two were at odds on certain points; and it is equally true that such discoveries led to rejection of those aspects of Platonism that did not conform to Nicene faith where the latter had spoken definitively, while more generally he tended to put Nicene Christianity and Platonism in dialogue where he could.[37] Augustine naively assumed that Ambrose and his circle represented the mainstream, even the whole truth, of Nicene Christianity, rather than a particularly Platonized wing that glossed over disharmonies between their preferred philosophy and some of the essential implications of the Christian world view. The mistake made by subsequent assessments of Augustine, Alfaric suggests, is reading what Augustine eventually embraced later in life back into his earlier period as a new convert, and in doing so missing his development as a thinker[38]—a development Augustine is the first to acknowledge.[39]

Seventy years after Alfaric, R. A. Markus seconded his essential point. In recounting what he regards as the four principal conversions of Augustine—to rationalism and Manichaeism in the 370s, to a Neoplatonic view of cosmic order and goodness in the 380s, to a Pauline emphasis on the disability of human willing in the 390s, and to an eschatological rejection of hopes for sociopolitical perfection after 410—he passes over entirely and deliberately Augustine's conversion to Christianity. The latter, he suggests, was not a conversion in the sense of a disenchantment with previous commitment, but was a progression of his attraction to Neoplatonic optimism.[40] But many others have opposed Alfaric's reconstruction vociferously, in no small measure because it seems to them to imply that the author of the treasured *Confessions* is not being honest about his earlier thinking and motivations when he reflects on them later in life. To accept an as yet undeveloped Christian in the earlier period appears to them to entail the acceptance of a dishonest one later. But in the years since Alfaric wrote, several new perspectives on the issues involved point the way toward amelioration of this dilemma, and a more nuanced understanding of Augustine's situation at the time of his conversion than the stark either/or of "Platonist" or "Christian."

The first advance out of the interpretive impasse was provided by Pierre Courcelle. By pointing to the high degree of integration of Neoplatonism and Christianity among the key figures of the church of Milan at the time of Augustine's conversion, Courcelle argued that the distinction between "philosophy" and "religion" imposed on Augustine's situation by modern scholarship is largely an artificial one.[41] Augustine himself would not have been confronted by, and would not have recognized, an either/or dilemma in his commitments.[42] The Neoplatonism he adopted was that of Ambrose, Simplician, and Manlius Theodorus, suggests Courcelle—that is, one already in conversation with Christianity.[43] To be sure, Courcelle overstated and oversold the amalgamation of Platonism and Christianity in Milan.[44] But, as stressed by Robert O'Connell,[45] Courcelle's point amounts to a revised view of what Christianity was at the time of Augustine's conversion. There was absolutely no barrier to a person being simultaneously Christian and Platonist, and the typical approach of such hybridized thinking would have been to cull selectively from either tradition what appealed and harmonized, neglecting the rest. We can see in a figure such as Augustine's pupil Licentius the characteristic embodiment of the rather easy-going elite Christianity that was emerging in the second half of the fourth century. We need to take seriously the implications of Licentius—highly praised as a complete embodiment of Augustine's ideals in 386, and roundly criticized as a disappointment a decade later. Licentius had not changed; Augustine had. Licentius represented what Augustine would have been if his facile, intellectualist early Christian faith had never been subjected to the vastly different conditions of Africa or the polemical focus of the Manichaean challenge.

James O'Donnell has proposed a different corrective to the problem of Augustine's loyalties. Drawing attention to the historical and categorical fallacies of regarding the Christianity of the 380s as primarily an intellectual system, O'Donnell has suggested that it and Neoplatonism were distinct kinds of commitment for Augustine to make that never entailed an either/or choice. "All parties seem to have agreed unthinkingly on the principle that 'Christianity' is in the first instance a body of intellectual propositions," such that "movement into and out of 'Christianity' is a matter of intellectual discussion and assessment, ending in assent or disagreement."[46] But what exactly, O'Donnell asks, did it mean for ancient people to go through an initiation such as baptism and to begin to participate in the religious activities to which that initiation entitled them? "For Augustine, and for late antique men and women generally, religion is cult . . . . The central decision he makes in the period narrated in the *Confessions* is, not to believe the doctrines of the Catholic Christians (that is important, but preliminary), but to present himself for cult initiation—and the threshold there is a matter not of doctrine but of morals."[47] Christianity was not a philosophy, but a cult, and there could be—and there were—Neoplatonic Christians, Stoic Christians, Aristotelian Christians, as well as the vast majority of wholly unphilosophical Christians. The faith did not dictate philosophical outlook, and placed few limits on wholesale adherence to such intellectual systems *alongside* full membership in the Church, just as adherents of traditional Roman religion included every shade of the philosophical spectrum. Augustine's own intellectual bent, and relative lack of interest in cultic matters, have shaped his report of his conversion, obscuring the degree to which for the people of his time such a conversion would signify almost nothing about his philosophical or metaphysical commitments. The events have been read as a matter of doctrine, an intellectual development, because Augustine presents them that way in the *Confessions*, which lays over the cultic commitment of 386 the doctrinal allegiances of Augustine more than a decade later.

A third adjustment of a different sort away from the interpretive dilemma has been offered by Paula Fredriksen. Drawing on more sophisticated models of selfhood and memory than those applied previously to the issue, Fredriksen has mitigated the onus of lying from the contradictions in Augustine's various accounts of his conversion.[48] Writing some fifteen years after the events, with a mind and sense of self irrevocably altered by subsequent experience and growth, Augustine was bound to inject his present attitudes into his past and, as even careful historians do, to accentuate those elements of the past that had a future in who he had become. Implications unknown to him at the time were naturally a part of what he could see with the advantage of hindsight.[49] He could change the story, in effect, without any intention of falsification, simply because he projected his current self into the past he was recalling. He both understood Nicene Christianity and Platonism better, and had reordered their priority in his thinking in such a way that the elements of each that were significant for him at the time of his conversion had been replaced with those that mattered to him now. Only that which he had known before that had a future, either in what he thought now, or else as a direct counterpoint to what he thought now, had sufficient relevance to form a part of his past self as he recalled and made use of it in telling his story.

A fourth reframing of the nature of Augustine's conversion can be added from more careful attention to the learning curve of the new convert, well documented in contemporary sociological studies but so far highlighted in only a few discussions of Augustine.[50] While most researchers readily acknowledge a more general progress and change in Augustine's thought and self-conception after his conversion, there has been little scrutiny of just where he stood in relation to his knowledge of Nicene Christianity at the point of his decision to convert. Conversion typically occurs at a time when individuals have had only a limited degree of exposure to the principles and practices of the community they are joining. Moreover, depending on the motivations and circumstances of conversion, individuals may engage with only a certain level of the new faith that attracts and interests them, or is functionally sufficient for a recognized commitment. A great deal depends upon what the community requires or expects of its converts. In Milan, Ambrose identified unacceptable conduct, encouraged certain attitudes toward the world, and warned against particular metaphysical positions he considered incompatible with membership in his community. But his church had no apparatus or system by which it sought to monitor the thinking of its adherents. Conduct alone determined continued membership in the community.

Modern studies of conversion have shown, according to Robert Hefner, that "some individuals engage the truths of their religion only long after their general identification with the tenets of the faith."[51] Even if we assume that Augustine joined the Nicene Christian community out of attraction to its teachings, rather than as a cultic or moral community, it remains true that to some degree "religious conversion always involves such authoritative acceptance of as yet unknown or unknowable truths."[52] The new convert has much yet to learn, and Augustine openly admitted at the time that he had accepted on authority many teachings of Nicene Christianity of which he did not have even the slightest understanding. We have nothing to compel us to

conclude that Augustine had read any significant amount of contemporaneous Christian literature that would have given him a sense of precisely what
he was committing to as a late fourth-century "Catholic." While excitedly
reading the "books of the Platonistis," along with—as we shall see—rereading
Cicero, his engagement with Christianity took place through weekly attendance on Ambrose's sermons and some private conversations. We should not
let our own interest in points of ideological convergence with Platonism in
these sermons obscure the fact that the bulk of what Augustine heard would
have been moral exhortation. Both the disparity in Augustine's attention and
the different interests engaged between these two discourses must be taken
into account in determining what it can mean to identify Nicene Christianity
as the object of Augustine's conversion.

Frederick Van Fleteren has issued the judicious appraisal that "Augustine's
conversion to Christianity was sincere insofar as he, a Christian neophyte,
understood the faith he was about to embrace."[53] This careful qualification of
what conversion *could* mean for Augustine in his exact circumstances makes
all the difference in clarifying the terms of our analysis. It is only from the
long view from the end of Augustine's career that it may be justified to say,
as Gerald Bonner says of Augustine's connections to Neoplatonism, that, "he
adopted it only when it harmonized with Christian doctrine."[54] Augustine
clearly did not have a sufficient command of Christian doctrine in the 380s
for it to act as a check on that which he would or would not appropriate
from Neoplatonism. Furthermore, many of the areas of doctrine to which Augustine applied Neoplatonism had no corresponding Christian position with
which to be compared; Nicene leaders had yet to extend dogma into those
areas, and might never have done so, if not for Augustine. As primarily a cultic
entity, the Christian community that Augustine joined tended to settle dogma
more on the grounds of practical implications than in service of a systematic
truth. Over the course of his career, Augustine would venture into new areas,
and seek to define orthodoxy for them for the first time, through a process of
combat with those who had different ideas about how to fill in the gaps of
the Nicene creed. That Augustine was intent on substantial engagement with
philosophia in connection with his cultic activities tells us something about the
way his character differed from those content to participate in cultic practices
without seeking to test their implicit metaphysics against the more systematically developed models of the philosophical schools. Indeed, Augustine's
"character" in this regard may reflect his conditioning by Manichaeism, which

was furlongs ahead of Nicene Christianity in elaborating a detailed metaphysics, regardless of the wide variation there must have been among individual Manichaeans in engaging with it fully.

Augustine's prior commitment had been to a Manichaeism that, despite all of its shortcomings for him, offered a *complete system*. In it, Augustine had found a powerful metaphysics and a compelling anthropology linked with a clear value system and—perhaps most important of all—a meaningful project for human existence. Platonism, for all of its intellectual sophistication, offered no more than an implicit attitude toward the options life presented. It presented a way of knowing and thinking about the universe, and one's place in it, but no spelled-out practical program for self-cultivation. At some point he came to see the Platonists as "the ones who see where to go, but do not see how" (*videntes quo eundum sit nec videntes qua, Conf* 7.20.26). Platonism *needed* Christianity—or some other apparatus of practice—in order to offer a full replacement for what Augustine was giving up in Manichaeism. Given the way events unfolded, it seems reasonable to surmise that Augustine discovered within himself a need, despite his intellectualist proclivities, for a disciplinary regimen to put his life into some order. We may even read the narrative pattern of the *Confessions* as symbolically conveying this realization, with Augustine's effort at mental ascent succeeding only after the breakthrough of personal commitment to a self-discipline he identifies as Christian in inspiration. It is on this point that Alfaric overreaches when he contends, "Morally as well as intellectually, it is to Neo-Platonism more than to the Gospel that he is converted."[55] Christianity formed a part of Augustine's conversion in 386, I would argue, precisely because it provided a moral regimen he considered necessary and complementary to the Neoplatonic intellectual system. Only the practical and disciplinary component that Christianity provided kept Platonism from being merely another passing influence on Augustine's independent bent of mind, and produced the sort of lasting change that the term "conversion" represents.[56] The synthesis evidently jelled, and created something effective and lasting for Augustine's identity.

The reason that Augustine had a copy of Paul's letters with him in the garden, it turns out, was that he thought the successful conduct of moral life reflected in the Christian apostles must be based on the same aspiration to transcendence beyond the sensory world as that embodied in Platonic writings; for "those men would never have been able to do such great things, nor would they have lived as they evidently did live, if their writings and doctrines were opposed to this so great a good" (*huic tanto bono, Acad* 2.2.5).[57] Augustine did not realize the degree to which he was reading Platonism into the biblical text, a process abetted by his preference for the wisdom books in his early readings in the Bible. His companion in conversion Alypius could comfortably identify the ideas they then held with those of Pythagoras—namely, the pursuit of a virtuous life toward the goal of obtaining a vision of God rooted in order and harmony (*Ord* 2.20.53)—and have Augustine blithely accept this identification (*Ord* 2.20.54).

We can find no indication that Augustine had ever intended to depart from the mainstream intellectual traditions and values of his culture; he had joined the Manichaeans with the idea that they best epitomized the community of withdrawn philosophers he had felt summoned to by Cicero's *Hortensius*. Many of the points of resistance in him to a Manichaean self derived from his prior education and ongoing non-Manichaean studies, and offered ready avenues by which the dominant cultural values could reassert themselves in his life. Augustine discovered in Milan an intellectually respectable form of Christianity that had not been available to him as an option a decade earlier in Africa. His polite and politic attendance at Ambrose's sermons in 385–386 began to expose him to allegorical interpretation of the Bible in line with a view of providence and cosmic order that reflected the common world view of most philosophies of the day.[58] For the first time, a door was opened to a non-Manichaean form of Christianity that satisfied Augustine's taste for sophisticated thinking, and at the same time did not carry the burden of cultural subversion attached to the Manichaean sect.

As Dennis Trout has argued, Augustine's conceptualization of his choices was limited by what culture—and for Augustine particularly, elite culture—offered as ways to think about his desire to take up a life specially dedicated to contemplation.

> Thus at the very time of his life when his spiritual development engendered criticism of his chosen profession and he was dissatisfied with his secular aspirations, Augustine encountered a variety of models for retirement which could also offer intellectual and social justification for the renunciation of worldly honor. The interplay between these models and Augustine's own thought and emotions was of course complex, and perhaps not fully understood by Augustine himself.[59]

The sharp differences between the extreme asceticism of an Anthony and the *otium* of the Roman gentleman may have gone uncrecognized by Augustine, as it did for many of his contemporaries.[60] Christianity had developed new models of selfhood to accommodate elite routines, allowing Augustine and many of his contemporaries to transfer their elite aspirations from the secular to the religious forum. Marius Victorinus represented the mainstream intelligentsia Augustine so admired, and in his story of conversion, relayed to Augustine by the Milanese priest Simplician in 386, we see an example that Augustine states proved compelling to him at the time. In close parallelism with the way Augustine would like his own conversion to be seen by the time he writes the *Confessions*, Victorinus had already been persuaded intellectually of the truth of Christianity, but had not taken the step of joining the Christian community or in other ways made an appreciable change in his conduct in life, and Simplician had called him on it (*Conf* 8.2.4).[61] Finally, exhausted by the vacuity of intellectualism, he submitted with humility to the authority of what most certainly were in elite terms of estimation *lesser men*.[62]

Augustine came to understand such submission to authority as an exercise in humility necessary even for the most capable and advanced intellectual, because reason alone, without an attitudinal adjustment, could get no sure footing (*Ord* 2.9.26; *UC* 10.24). Hence the Platonists "see where to go, but do not see how" (*Conf* 7.20.26). The failure of his Manichaean experience had taught him that spiritual progress required a closer integration of intellectual attraction and personal conduct, a commitment of the whole self. For all his mental ability, Augustine expressed frustration that he could not alter even his own day-to-day conduct. Yet people all around him of lesser intellect were changing their lives in a manner consistent with the Platonic call to detachment from worldly things, of which they were not even aware. While Augustine found himself burdened with still unresolved metaphysical questions, "other people are given wings on freer shoulders, people who have not worn themselves out with research, nor spent a decade and more reflecting on these questions" (*Conf* 8.7.17–18). There must be something to the method they were employing; and he apparently concluded that, since it produced results consistent with Platonic goals, the two systems must share the same underlying truths. Not that Manichaeism did not teach or evidently produce detachment from the world, at least in the Elect. But it did not produce this result for *him*. Without his ultimate goal changing or being fundamentally reconfigured, therefore, Augustine was ready to try a different method for attaining it.

Augustine thought that Platonism and Nicene Christianity were ultimately compatible, and he fully believed that Platonism was the intellectual explication of the same truths symbolically garbed in Christianity.[63] "Augustine's presiding *intention* is from the first sincerely Christian," Robert O'Connell concludes, "it was a 'Neoplatonizing Christian' that he most deeply aspired to be, and was convinced he was being. But the order of intention and aspiration is one thing, the order of achievement and result quite another."[64] Augustine had been exposed to and had accepted various phrases and images that he could *think*, but not yet *think with*. He had yet to operationalize the various concepts to which he had been introduced by arranging them into a reasonably coherent set of interrelationships. As O'Connell has further observed, "it is not a question of what Augustine 'believed'; he firmly willed to believe what the Church believed. The question . . . was what that belief entailed, how one was to 'understand'."[65] Augustine could not yet know all that his decision would demand of him, were he to maintain it, because, as Robert Hefner notes, "the allegiance professed early in conversion may be preliminary to a more radical and unanticipated resocialization." Indeed, "converts may only later discover that their religion has moral and intellectual entailments greater than they had realized," arrayed according to a "hierarchy of commitments," that may at some point "require repudiation of ideals or desires once regarded as consistent with religion's truth."[66]

From Subject to Subject

We arrive, then, at the crux of what Judith Butler poses as a paradox: how can there be a subject to initiate a commitment to a subject-forming discourse, before the discourse has formed the subject with the particular desires and capacities to act as a subject?[67] The answer in Augustine's case lies in stepping back from the level of theoretical abstraction at which the paradox is posed, to the actual situation of pluralistic societies where individuals are engaged from birth in subject-forming discourses and systems of *habitus* formation. Even though one's initial socialization occurs more or less involuntarily, at various points alternative identifications present themselves, offering varying degrees of complementarity or contrast with one's prior self-conception. Such "convergence with other discursive regimes" creates, Butler suggests, a "discursive complexity" that "undermines the teleological aims of normalization" within the original—or indeed any single—regime of subjection.[68] Before Augustine acted to enter into either the Manichaean or the Nicene Christian systems of subjection, he was born and raised in a larger, involuntary social order, that instilled in him a background, "common sense" subjection, upon which more systematic schemes of subjection were overlain by his deliberate acts of engagement with them, which amounted to a chosen and opportunistic resistance to certain values and priorities in his larger society. Augustine did not live in a self-enclosed monoculture, but belonged to a complex, cosmopolitan society whose means of surveillance and reinforcement of the socially conditioned self were inadequate to produce involuntarily the same level of subjection that more systematic, organized, and managed schemes of subjection achieve through the voluntary submission of individuals. But this involuntary background self derived from his broader culture served Augustine as a necessary enabler of his subsequent self-selections, conditioning to a degree the choices he entertained and the inclinations he had, and in the process making one scheme of voluntary subjection more palatable and amenable than another.

Augustine's acculturation to Roman values through his upbringing and his education created points of incompatibility with and resistance to the Manichaean scheme of subjection. Some he overcame out of his own desire to distinguish himself from his larger society; to others he yielded. In apostasy, he resorted to some degree to the background "common sense" of his broader culture, which had always remained as a kind of "psychic remainder" at the limits of a Manichaean formulation of his identity. We should not resort to imagining in this place an essential, pre-social Augustine who could or could not accept certain identities, and kept searching until he found his "true self," however much he adopted such a script first from the Manichaeans and then from the Nicene Christians. In any given iteration of "Augustine," the most relevant "psychic remainder" will be from prior subjections, now broken up and capable at most of thwarting some aspects of the new demands represented by the next formula of self-formation.[69] In retreating to the paradigms of his general society, Augustine necessarily carried with him fragments of his failed Manichaean self, and it was from this complex field of conflicting purposes that he scouted for other self-forming projects capable of making a whole from the parts. Despite his tendency to view his Manichaean venture as a long detour back to his original starting point, he stood on substantially new ground, constituted only of those values and views from his broader culture that he had sustained through the challenge of Manichaean alternatives. But having already successfully brokered some accommodations between Manichaean concepts and attitudes and those of his broader acculturation, he did not need to abandon everything he had learned about himself, or everything he had made of himself, through the tropes provided by Manichaeism.

In this way, it may be useful to follow carefully what Michel Foucault means in suggesting that resistance is an effect of the *very power* that it opposes. His proposal only works if we understand power in the broadest sense of everything originally external to the individual, everything that confronts and places demands upon the individual, in however uncoordinated a manner. For the multiplicity of power's manifestations in discrete apparatuses of subjection gives the self a space in which to negotiate its own constitution as an effect of power. Augustine confronted and engaged with not a single monolithic power, but a field of several conflicted forms of power, all eager to reproduce themselves in him, but by different means and oriented around different articulations of purpose. Each stage of Augustine's journey entailed the novel demands of these programs running up against the remains of accommodations of the prior demands of other programs. At any given point, I would like to suggest, Augustine embodied the outcome of these juxtaposed investments. The temporal, iterative quality of the self conceived in this way would involve a constant modification of one's relationship to this larger field of possible engagements with power, that is, with what in a pluralistic society can only be a collection of competing formulas for subjection.[70]

Augustine came to neither Platonism nor Nicene Christianity, therefore, as a blank slate, as a pre-self; and in effecting this new subject in Augustine, these new sources of his self had to contend with partial yet deeply rooted commitments and identifications, which, though no longer arranged according to the Manichaean system, had to be accommodated somewhere in what would take the latter's place. Augustine abetted this reorganization of self by discarding his own prior resistances to Nicene Christianity, first by disavowing the systematic resistance represented by his commitment to Manichaeism, and then by gradually shedding those isolated points of resistance that either predated his Manichaeism or had been instilled by it. He offers a protracted account in *Confessions*, books 6 and 7, not of gradual conversion, but of preparation for conversion through the loss of such resistances to it. And even as we leave the Milanese garden with him in book 8, we are in the company not of a convert, but of someone who has had an impulse he has not yet been expected to sustain—who has made a promise (to himself) he may or may not be able to keep.

CHAPTER EIGHT

Rationalizing Faith

AUGUSTINE NOW OCCUPIED the same place with respect to Christianity that he once did to Manichaeism. He had been swept up in the attractiveness of a faith, and a community practicing that faith, largely by his own attribution and embellishment of expectations. He expected "great and hidden goods" (*Ord* 2.9.26) in the one as he had in the other, but he did not yet know specifically what they would turn out to be. He perforce had to accept the authority of those who keep the mysteries before he was allowed to receive them. This authority set out the prerequisites of initiation: a code of conduct producing perfection of life and worthiness to receive the mysteries. When training has rendered the individual docile, when the body is transcended and the mind quieted, then the superior person may see beyond the surface of discipline and cult to the transcendental truths hidden within them, which in turn leads to an understanding of the nature of intellect, which contains or is the sum of all things.[1] Finally, one ascends to comprehension of the nature of the source of all things. The construct is pure Plotinus; but in place of the latter's rather vague advice to begin with a flight from the senses Augustine had hit upon the idea of substituting the specific regimen of the Nicene Christian communion.

Yet in his new attraction to Nicene Christianity, Augustine risked merely repeating his experience as a Manichaean, holding back with mental reservations, bifurcating his conduct between intellectual pursuits and cultic activity, never allowing them to form a single identity capable of displacing his unreflective personal habits and preferences. He could easily find as many problems with Nicene Christian doctrine as he had with Manichaean teachings. He had his doubts. We can safely conclude this, not only from his own clear statements to that effect (*Ep* 1.3; *Acad* 2.3.9, 2.9.23), but from the fact that he did not rush out to be baptized,[2] or even to sit at the feet of a Nicene preceptor. He chose instead to gather his thoughts, and to try to articulate them as a coherent picture of the new universe he had up to this point only intuited, in order thoroughly to persuade himself of its validity. We might consider Augustine's retirement to Cassiciacum a trial run of the kind of future he was then imagining for himself, fulfilling an attraction to the life of the mind he had toyed with for a decade. The offer of a colleague for the use of his small country estate allowed Augustine to make plans to realize a kind of summer-camp version of his dream of a philosophical community, which he had been entertaining off and on for some time with his Manichaean compatriots Alypius, Nebridius, and Romanianus.

Unfortunately, other factors complicate this promisingly straightforward picture. Although I have sought to stress the active appropriation of power by Augustine in voluntarily submitting himself to self-forming systems, it would be a mistake to allow this to obscure completely the more familiar face of power as an external force with mechanisms of coercion at its disposal. With Augustine's withdrawal from Milan we encounter another of those "inconvenient coincidences" that litter his career.

As we have seen, sometime in the summer of 386 C.E., Augustine received word that he had been named in the prosecution of Manichaeans in Carthage, and that an indictment or judgment against him, having the force of a warrant, had been issued. Augustine's fate depended entirely on how far this warrant reached outside Africa—a difficult question for us to answer. Yet Augustine had already displayed a tendency to take such legal matters very seriously, perhaps more than they realistically deserved. It is therefore difficult to avoid drawing a correlation between this judgment against Augustine back in Africa, and his sudden departure from Milan and resignation of his position, since it so completely repeats his pattern of reaction from three years earlier. It is true that he offers a perfectly plausible motivation for his retirement to a country estate in his desire finally to implement his longstanding plan for a sort of ascetic intellectual commune. But this explanation leaves a number of details of the situation unaccounted for.

The first of these details is the secretive character of his plan to depart, which he is at some pains to explain in the *Confessions* (*Conf* 9.2.2–3). Why was it important that his plans be kept secret from all but his inner circle, mostly of other former Manichaeans? Second, what of the "coincidence" of his supposed ill health (*Conf* 9.2.4)? Such an excuse was a classic ploy of politically advisable retirement. In Augustine's narrative, it seems to offer yet another fully plausible motivation for retirement, without the need to appeal to a supposed conversion experience. Third, it bears noting that, while most if not all of his companions at Cassiciacum came and went freely from there to Milan both during the autumn holiday and in the months afterward, Augustine appears never to have ventured back into the city the entire time. Instead, from a safe distance and perhaps not even indicating his whereabouts, he wrote to bishop Ambrose and "notified him of my past errors," as a Manichaean, "and of my present intention"—apparently, to convert formally to Nicene Christianity (*Conf* 9.5.13). Curiously, this significant letter is missing from Augustine's collected correspondence, despite the fact that the collection begins with other letters from 386. If the intention he conveyed to Ambrose was to accept baptism—something we have no way of confirming—it offered the only possible way out of danger for a wanted Manichaean, taking refuge in its absolution of his past errors.

Yet as quickly as danger had arrived, it departed again with the issuing of a general amnesty (the *uota publica* of Theodosius and Arcadius of January 387) that freed the Manichaean exiles, Faustus among them, and would have negated the warrant against Augustine.[3] This amnesty allowed Augustine to venture off the private estate at Cassiciacum for the first time in over five months, and to return to Milan in safety, where he would indeed submit his name to be baptized into the "Catholic" Church. The combination of the amnesty and baptism also freed him at last to return to Africa, safe from the anti-Manichaean laws, and he set out to do so within a few months.

We cannot now determine whether these external developments swirling around Augustine had the character of coincidences or causes in relation to his decisions and actions. But their number and rather exact timing with moves on his part must give us pause. It might be safest to speak in terms of a possible confluence of motivations, some internal and some external in origin. But that will not make it any easier to reconcile two very different pictures of Augustine as an actor at this time. Wherever we settle on this question, Augustine experienced several months of self-imposed exile from Milan, followed by an intense period of indoctrination into Nicene Christianity in preparation for baptism. In the meantime, he produced a remarkable set of literary dialogues chronicling his reorientation to a new reality, a new set of terms, images, and models by which to know himself within a meaningful cosmos.

Otium liberale

Augustine's retreat to the country villa of a friend at Cassiciacum commenced with the autumn vacation (*feriae vindemiales*), which freed him temporarily from his duties (*Conf* 9.2.2, 9.4.7).[4] Besides family and private pupils, he was accompanied by his fellow Manichaean apostate Alypius, the one who had talked him out of marriage expressly for the purpose of taking up the life of *philosophia* (*Conf* 6.12.21), and joined him in his resolve in the Milanese garden to commence such a life. The perennially doubting Nebridius did not join them, expressing his reservations about Augustine's new thinking by correspondence from Milan. He would decline likewise to join Augustine in being baptized the following spring (*Conf* 9.3.6). Besides Monnica, the only baptized Christian on the premises was the fellow Thagastan Evodius, a former government agent who would stick close to Augustine throughout the rest of his time in Italy (*Conf* 9.8.17).

As the autumn vacation drew to a close in mid-October, Augustine realized that, for various reasons, he could not yet return to Milan. He sent a letter to the court formally resigning as rhetor of the capital, no doubt citing ill health as his reason—a cliché so standardized that taking it literally would have been the last thing to occur to its recipients. At the same time he wrote to Ambrose, "notifying him of my past errors" as a Manichaean, and seeking spiritual guidance (*Conf* 9.5.13). Ambrose's suggestion in reply to study the prophet Isaiah ill suited Augustine. Leo Ferrari suggests that Ambrose's choice of Isaiah was intended to confront the former Manichaean with clear proof that the New Testament and the Old Testament spoke with one voice, particularly in the prophet's predictions of the coming messiah. Referring to Ambrose's recommendation as "the proverbial acid test of the sincerity of Augustine's claimed conversion to Catholicism," Ferrari adds, "If such were indeed Ambrose's motives behind the recommended reading of Isaiah, then Augustine failed the test."[5] He could make no sense of this work, and put it aside, returning instead to the familiar ground of the Roman classics. Specifically "religious" material apparently would continue to play a secondary role in Augustine's intellectual pursuits, which seem to have gotten seriously under way only after the end of the vacation and his resignation.

Augustine was guiding his pupils through Virgil's *Aeneid*, while the serious philosophy under discussion derived almost exclusively from readings in Cicero: *Hortensius* (*Acad* 1.1.4, 1.3.7, 3.4.7, 3.14.31; *Sol* 1.10.17), along with the *Academica* (*Acad*, passim), and quite probably other works by the same author.[6] Even the "books of the Platonists" are conspicuously and puzzlingly absent as direct inspiration for the proceedings.[7] Indeed, many of the positions Augustine takes in the Cassiciacum dialogues come straight out of the *Hortensius*. It appears that Augustine was rereading the work with fresh eyes, free from the assumption that its ideas found their natural complement in Manichaeism, and beginning to see a better consonance between them and a Platonic Christianity. The only Christian texts in evidence were memorized hymns from Ambrose's public liturgy—sung in the toilet.

The literary dialogues that poured forth from this setting—*The Good Life* (*De beata vita*), *The Academics* (*De Academica*),[8] *Order* (*De Ordine*), and *Soliloquies*—do not offer manifestos of a fully worked out position. They reflect instead Augustine's own characterization of his purpose at the time, namely, to resolve issues that were *holding him back* from completely and confidently adhering to Platonic philosophy and Christian faith. These new resources appeared attractive and promising; but Augustine had been down that road before with Manichaeism, and we can easily imagine a man unwilling to lose another decade to what might prove to be a dead end. In fact, Augustine states that he entered upon his Cassiciacum retreat still an adherent of Academic Skepticism, his efforts aimed apparently at determining whether Platonic and Christian positions could be sustained within a skeptical epistemology. "When in my retirement in the country I had been pondering for a long time just how the plausible or the truth-like can defend our actions from error, at first the matter seemed to me nicely protected and fortified, as it usually seemed when I was peddling it" (*Acad* 3.15.34). Well after the Garden Incident, he declares that, "*up to now* I have arrived at no certainty, but have been impeded in my search by the arguments and disputes of the Academics. Somehow or other they persuaded me of the probability . . . that man cannot find the truth" (*Acad* 2.9.23; cf. 2.3.9).[9] While *The Academics* deals with a special hurdle to Augustine's intellectual progress, all of the Cassiciacum dialogues show us Augustine working out issues that pose an immediate challenge to the path he contemplates taking; and insofar as portions of these works may have been written as late as spring 387, after Augustine had returned to Milan to submit his name for baptism and enter into the training of a *competent*, they inform us of the results of more than six months of weighing his options.[10]

Nonetheless, the Cassiciacum dialogues do not represent private ruminations. They are self-conscious performances, dedicated and sent to key figures in Augustine's life at the time.[11] We encounter in them a dialogic articulation of self. Conversations both external and internal, both imagined and real,[12] gave Augustine access to his conflicted desires and ways of thinking so that he could scrutinize and assess them, determine their priority in his affective reaction to them individually and the self-image they collectively constituted. Most operate within Ciceronian models of dramatic dialogue. *Soliloquies*, however, takes the form of an internal dialogue between the vacillating, uncertain, and yearning "Augustine" and his higher self, his *ratio* securely embedded in the intelligible world and serving as spiritual guide. This internal dialogue partner reflects the Neoplatonic concept of an unfallen part of the soul at the same time as it profoundly echoes the Manichaean ideas of the *nous*, twin, or form of the individual soul, similarly unfallen and serving as the conduit of truth.

The inclinations and decisions expressed in these works testify to a plan "to betake myself to philosophy" (*Ord* 1.2.5; cf. *Acad* 1.1.3; *BV* 1.4), rather than any requirements of a conversion to Nicene Christianity; the latter required him to forego neither family life nor secular career.[13] Thus, among the paradigms Augustine's culture offered him by which to understand and organize the focused devotion to knowing ultimate truths he wished for himself, he selected that of "conversion to philosophy," long domesticated within the image of the elite man of leisure. "By presenting his life at Cassiciacum as a life in *otium*," observes Dennis Trout, "Augustine placed himself firmly within a venerable social and literary tradition, a tradition that had the potential to fulfill his intellectual needs without compromising his social position."[14] Imitating Cicero, he calls his readers to this life (e.g., *Acad* 2.2.3). He shows no inclination to the life of a cultic devotee, which previously would have been equated with a particularly "religious" turn in life. He is more likely to have understood the new Christian ascetic movement he had been hearing about within the paradigm of philosophical retirement, rather than in terms of the cultic professional, such as a priest or Elect. The ascetic self-discipline of the latter was still closely integrated with cultic activity, compared to the more freestanding asceticism emerging in the Nicene communion with only a tangential relation to ritual. It therefore would have presented a closer parallel to philosophical programs of self-development to someone like Augustine steeped in the literate traditions of Rome. He construed his interests in the philosophical terms of truth-seeking and happiness that his reading in ancient authors provided, rather than the popular religious terms of devotion and salvation.

Yet these very distinctions were eroding all around Augustine. He was caught in the middle of a shift of paradigms in the late antique structuration of several closely related forms of specially dedicated ways of life. For the path he was mapping out for himself, he considered "philosophy" and "religion," reason and authority, to be two complementary methods of attaining to the same truth (*Ord* 2.5.16; *QA* 7.12; *UC* 9.21–10.24). In his book *Order*, Augustine explains that to make progress in understanding truth requires a procedure that both regulates life and directs reason (*Ord* 2.8.25). Humans require a code of conduct whose purpose is to purify the mind of its addictions to the material and the sensory. This accomplished, the mind becomes able to advance in its perception of the spiritual.

> In point of time, authority is first; but in the order of reality, reason is prior. What takes precedence in operation, is one thing; what is more highly prized as an object of desire, is something else. Consequently, although the authority of upright men seems to be the safer guide for the uninstructed multitude, yet reason is better adapted for the educated. (*Ord* 2.9.26)

"Augustine here tells us that the role of authority is to give man the moral precepts by which he can become teachable," observes Frederick Van Fleteren. He continues, "After he has attained moral purity then man can begin to understand the reason present in the moral precepts which he followed previously."[15] Such was certainly the full extent of Augustine's original idea of the complementarity of the Christian moral and Platonic intellectual systems. He makes it clear that Christianity on its own, without the Platonic project of ascent, has no appeal for him, even though the culturally given idea of many paths to the same truth allows him to postulate that it advances the liberation of the souls of the less capable masses.

> But as to those who are content to follow authority alone, and who apply themselves constantly to right living and holy desires, while they make no account of the liberal and fine arts, or are incapable of being instructed in

them: I know not how I could call them happy as long as they live among men. Nevertheless, I firmly believe that upon leaving the body, they will be liberated with greater facility or difficulty according as they have lived the more virtuously or otherwise. (*Ord* 2.9.26)

Exactly what form Augustine imagined this post-mortem liberation "with greater facility or difficulty" would take remains suggestively vague. As a Manichaean, he had been taught that souls progress over multiple lifetimes, and go through various kinds of purification in the transition from one life to the next. Pythagoreans and Platonists also generally assumed some sort of transmigration of souls. With studied imprecision, Augustine offers no more than the suggestion that advancement in virtue alone, which the authority of Christian moral precepts provides, improves the soul's condition in a limited way, preparing it to achieve the clear apprehension of truth on the other side of death to which it failed to advance on this side.

But Augustine's position subtly developed—perhaps as a result of his exposure to Ambrose's philosophical rhetoric in his catechumenal instruction—into ascribing more than just a moral function for authority. He soon concluded that reason pursues truth on the basis of authority-derived premises, and finally achieves full understanding of ideas accepted initially without understanding (*LA* 2.5 ff; see also *Sol* 1.12–15). Whereas reason offers truth naked, and as such is difficult for most to grasp, authority clothes truth in images accessible to the many, but whose inner meaning must await rational interpretation (*Ord* 2.5.15–16).[16] Although expressed in the abstract terms of a theory, Augustine's reflections on the rational gap between inclination toward a system and understanding it express, in my opinion, his attempt to manage the peculiar position of the convert, to perform a self that is not yet a self.

Motives Without Reasons

J. Kevin Coyle has insightfully stressed Augustine's tendency to leap before he looked, to make a sudden commitment to a community of faith based on a superficial resemblance of its tenets and practices to something that had moved him deeply in his reading.[17] This had occurred with his embrace of Manichaeism immediately after reading the *Hortensius* in Carthage, and should be seen as well in his turn to the Nicene Christian community after reading the

Platonic books in Milan. We must guard against assuming that in either of these instances Augustine could have consciously chosen the whole of the respective religions' teaching and tradition at the time of his conversion. In both instances, he actually knew very little of it, and learned with varying degrees of interpretation and resistance over the years. Augustine himself recognized, and incorporated into his early writings, the problematic of conversion and commitment. He argued that believing without proof or understanding, on the basis of compelling authority, must precede understanding of the content of faith. This is so because in order to understand one must commit oneself to the way of life entailed in belief, which purifies and conditions the mind not simply to reason, but to reason well and effectively, so that true understanding rather than misconstrual results. He was perfectly prepared to learn as he went.

Augustine's conversion did not result from the ability of either Platonism or Nicene Christianity to make a better case for itself within the epistemological and metaphysical premises he held as a Manichaean. Conversion for him entailed the adoption of an entirely new set of such premises, a new *episteme*. Therefore he did not reason his way from Manichaeism to Nicene Christianity, and we should not buy into his own construction of such a course of reasoning in the post-conversion stage of his development, culminating in the *Confessions*. Rather, alert to the learning curve of converts, we should look for just what it took for him to identify himself as a Nicene Christian and a Platonist in the months leading up to his baptism.

It has seemed to some that the necessary corollary of considering Augustine honest is to treat the *Confessions* as a kind of journal, recording stages in his mental development. Most researchers now recognize the falsity of this corollary, and conclude that the *Confessions* is written from hindsight, and in large part as a rationalization of Augustine's experiences and choices. Perhaps less widely acknowledged is the implication that even the intellectual problems Augustine identifies in his past thinking are shaped by hindsight, and are those presupposed by the solutions he has come to embrace. We need to be alert to the ways that particular discourses, religions among them, suggest various problems that they undertake to answer—straw-men, if you will, that set up the teachings of the school or sect as solutions. There is nothing to say that a particular problem might have been recognized by an individual apart from and prior to an encounter with a discourse that poses it only as a foil to its own proposed answers.

With Robert O'Connell, "One might wonder how explicitly Augustine formulated his need for a more 'spiritual' way of thinking about spiritual realities *before* he 'read the answers,' so to speak, in those Platonist books."[18] O'Connell can suggest no more than that Augustine's inclination for mathematical abstraction and his detection of conceptual infelicities in the materialist account of evil the Manichaeans offered made him amenable to the more "spiritual" modes of thought to be found in Platonism. Perhaps. Yet it is equally possible that Augustine found himself attracted to other, more "common sense" aspects of Platonic thought, and accepted its immaterialism as part of the package, only gradually making sense of it. The hierarchical models of reality he deploys repeatedly in his early works postulate the mind and soul as "better" rather than "other," and it takes some time for him to engage the full implications of the Platonic postulate of intelligible reality. Not all of a system's components possess equal initial attractiveness to the would-be convert, and not all of the problems it proposes to solve are necessarily given priority or even perceived in the mental, emotional, and practical life of the candidate for conversion. Once sufficiently motivated to convert, however, one is likely to be encouraged to come to see the entire set of solutions as relevant and compelling, and consequently to recast one's own past in the problematic terms given by the system as representing its negative shadow.

Intrinsically connected to Augustine's moral and intellectual transformation in the mid-380s was a dramatic shift in the way he thought about the human capacity to know. His writings around the time of his conversion are dominated by one discovery above all, namely, that reason, which he had so long valued above all else, requires a starting point that it itself cannot provide. This theme runs strongly from *The Academics* (386) to *The Teacher* (389), and has been explored in dozens of studies in the last half-century. Efforts have been made to trace its source back to Cicero, Plotinus, and Porphyry, but none has been able to make an exclusive claim.[19] This puzzle has led Frederick Van Fleteren to suggest that we should be looking for a negative source rather than a positive one. He argues that Augustine's idea—that authority is necessary as a starting point of reason—is his own novel reversal of the Manichaean promotion of reason as the basis of religious conviction.

> The evidence gathered from the *Confessions* and the Cassiciacum dialogues indicates that the dialectic between authority and reason dates back as far as Augustine's Manichaean days. The teaching of the

Cassiciacum dialogues is a reversal of his Manichaean experience: now Augustine asks for the acceptance of authority before an attempt at rational understanding. Thus, the terms seem to be Manichaean, but the notion a Christian one based upon Augustine's notion of conversion to Christianity as an acceptance of faith.[20]

Augustine repeatedly alludes to Manichaeans as those who have prematurely applied their reason to the quest for truth, precociously leaping past the necessary disciplining and purification of the mind that must prepare it for valid reasoning. While Van Fleteren is certainly correct that Augustine saw his prioritizing of authority over reason as a reversal of the Manichaean position that had failed him and—in his opinion—others, we need to be cautious about taking this as the whole pedigree of his new position.

For one thing, there is a more direct, positive antecedent for the construct in Augustine's particular experience as a Manichaean. In chastising the Manichaeans for presuming to have reached truth already (e.g., *Acad* 2.3.9; *Sol* 1.12.20), Augustine was beating them with a stick with which Faustus had provided him. We know that Augustine's Skepticism preceded by several years his discovery of the necessary place of belief; and it has become clear from our analysis of Faustus's own idiosyncratic synthesis of Skepticism and Manichaeism that the latter offers a likely source for Augustine's own engagement with Skepticism. It is clear from the bits and pieces of Faustus's teachings preserved for us that he, like the post-conversion Augustine, believed that self-discipline preceded and enabled ascent to truth. On this point, Augustine did little more than apply Faustus's program to a different system of thought and practice. Faustus had proposed that the moral authority of Mani and Jesus be accepted on the basis of rationally derived proofs, such as their own personal achievement of virtue or the correctness of their teachings in areas amenable to empirical assessment. Augustine only heightened the concession already made in Faustus's approach to the place of authority, and made more explicit that reason must wait until discipline received on authority had rendered one capable of knowing truth when one saw it. Augustine emphasizes this insight as his momentous discovery in all his early post-conversion works, and signals in this way the breakthrough that enabled conversion itself.

Faustus had taught Augustine when and why to default to authority in the absence of rational certainty. Augustine accounts for his uncertainty over giving up Manichaeism entirely by citing both principles suggested by Faustus: Mani could be proven right about some things, and so presumably was right about others, and the truth of his teachings could also be vouched for by the spiritual quality of the life those teachings produced. At the same time, Augustine had not been able to commit himself fully to Manichaeism because, by those very same standards, it seemed to fall short of proving itself: Mani was evidently wrong about some things, and Augustine certainly was not succeeding in attaining to a life of satisfactory spiritual quality. His education and extensive reading apparently enabled him to grasp that any two systems of thought may be perfectly consistent in drawing conclusions from their respective premises, but may have premises totally incompatible with one another. Each system is therefore self-contained in its reasoning, and no objective standard exists by which either set of premises can be shown to be better. In realizing this, Augustine had reached the brink of despair over finding truth.

But he went from seeing this state of affairs as a predicament, to seeing it as an insight into the nature of intellectual progress, through a reconsideration and rejection of the whole approach to self-development he had experienced among the Manichaeans. He may have found the solvent of his intellectual blockage in his favored master Pythagoras, to whom was attributed the very formula Augustine now adopted: *auctoritas* must supply the precepts by which one is prepared to receive teachings demonstrable by *ratio*.[21] Indeed, according to David Sedley, this formula reflects the typical expectation found in all philosophical schools of late antiquity, namely, that disciples commit themselves to the truths of the particular school on the basis of the school's authority, and proceed to work out the proofs, meaning, and implications of those truths by reason.[22] In other words, this expectation would constitute yet another "common sense" position of Augustine's culture to which he had recourse in his apostasy. An encounter with this sentiment through Neoplatonic sources, at the same time as he was reviewing the arguments on either side of Skepticism in Cicero's *Academica*, may have constituted one of those confluences of disparate sources whose role in novel insights we should not discount. Augustine performs a remarkable misprision on Cicero, taking up many of the dogmatic criticisms of Skepticism Cicero reports without embracing the latter's own rebuttal of them. In a word, then, Van Fleteren is right that Augustine embraced (even though he did not originate) a reversal of standard Manichaean priorities. He did so, however, not by any novel formulation, but by returning to a mainstream construct of the novice's relation to the authority of a master or master discourse already touched upon in Faustus's own idiosyncratic Manichaeism engaged with that very construct.

These philosophical reconsiderations set the stage for Augustine's fresh encounter with non-Manichaean Christianity, whose demand for faith had originally affronted him in his youthful passion for reason, and been one of the sources of his sympathy with Manichaeism. Somehow that same demand seems to have made sense in the more sophisticated form in which he encountered it in Milan. For Augustine expressly states that the *Catholic Church*—not Platonism—teaches that faith must precede understanding,[23] and reinforces that point with the only verse he seems to have taken away from his abortive venture into the book of Isaiah: Unless one believes, one cannot understand (*Nisi crediditis, non intelligetis*, Isaiah 7:9 LXX et Vetus Latina). He had been directed to Isaiah by Ambrose, and as it happens Augustine's construct of the complementarity of authority and reason appears in Ambrose's sermon "Jacob and the Happy Life" in a discussion of the means of obtaining the happy life—precisely the rhetorical context in which Augustine employs it in his earliest writings. "Virtue is teachable," Ambrose declares, but requires the combined use of the "good discourse" of authoritative instruction with the exercise of reason to allow such instruction to penetrate the mind. Authoritative discourse admonishes, but persuasion requires reasoned reflection (Ambrose, *Iacob* 1.1.1).

While Augustine's take on the question differs slightly, it shares Ambrose's overarching point that either authority or reason without the other is problematic. Like Ambrose, Augustine regards reason as an essential engagement of the mind that leads to intellectual enrichment and progress. He prioritizes authority over reason only in temporal order, not in ultimate worth. He concedes that reason is superior to authority, "higher" in his ascending hierarchy of reality (*Ord* 2.9.26). But it must be ascended to from the fallen condition of humans, which requires moral training and a faith that directs reason in its ascent (*Ord* 2.8.25). He believes that a few may be able to ascend by means of reason alone, but seems gradually to accept that he himself is not among that number. From his original disparagement of authority and blind faith, Augustine had come to value the *certainty* it provided to keep reason from degenerating into interminable and insoluble disputation.

But how did Augustine get across the gap between the skeptical collapse of confidence in the human ability to know and a willful belief in that which cannot be proven? Why should he have accepted the truth of Ambrose's allegorical interpretation of the Bible, or of Plato's and Plotinus's teachings on the nature of reality? As historians we have the greatest difficulty with precisely this sort of change in a person's commitments, because it entails things invisible in the historical record. It cannot be given an ordered account, complete with solid reasons, because that is not how it occurs. Augustine does better than most in trying to capture the transition, speaking in various places of being "on fire" with the affective impact of fresh new ideas. What can anyone add in more sober terms without obscuring the nature of the event?

I wish to suggest that Augustine's own emphasis in his earliest post-conversion writings on the bankruptcy of unassisted reason recapitulates in a theoretical form a gap in rational discourse that Augustine encountered in his effort to capture and convey discursively his own conversion process. The rhetorical discourse in which he had been trained would dictate a narrative or argument of persuasion. The convoluted discussions of the Cassiciacum dialogues show a man as yet incapable of producing one. By training and inclination a rationalist, Augustine found himself in the awkward position of defending a resort to sheer trust in authority. Having neither reasoned his way to truth, nor received any divine revelation himself, Augustine confronted the dilemma that his access to a hypothesized divine truth would be mediated by human individuals and institutions. He was fully aware of this dilemma, and perfectly willing to concede that humans must take on faith that which is transmitted by purely human authority, regardless of its ultimate source. He pointed out that we rely on such authority every day, in our acceptance of any fact or event of which we are not direct observers. "Nothing would remain stable in human society if we determined to believe nothing that we could not empirically establish" (*quod non possumus tenere perceptum, UC* 12.26).

Yet his tidy theory that authority precedes reason could not hold. He was forced to concede Faustus's point that one must utilize reason to identify valid authority (*Ord* 2.9.27; *VR* 24.45–46; *UC* 9.21), and we can observe him in the months and years following his conversion trying out various criteria by which he proposed to validate Nicene Christian authority. He initially had no new ideas on this subject, and tentatively repeated (without crediting his source) the twofold criteria of valid authority repeatedly stressed by Faustus: that one give preference, in the words of Augustine's recapitulation, to "those men who propose various proofs for their teachings, insofar as the mind of the unlearned can grasp them, and who do not live otherwise than how they prescribe that one ought to live" (*Ord.* 2.9.27).[24] He soon began work on an attempt to demonstrate that the Nicene Christians succeeded and the Manichaeans failed to meet these criteria.[25] But we must pause over the fact that he began to work out such a persuasive demonstration only *after* he had fully committed to Nicene Christianity, and with resources that he did not have at the time of his conversion. In other words, he was generating reasons for conversion that were not involved, or at least not articulated in these terms, in his own conversion. The post-conversion Augustine started to produce rationalizations for choices made on other grounds, and over time these rationalizations completely displaced and obscured any motives of which Augustine may have been aware at the time of his conversion.

A few years later, back in Africa, Augustine adopted a new set of criteria justifying belief better fitted to what he considered Nicene Christian advantages, and presented them in *The Usefulness of Belief.* Valid authority, he contends, can be established on three bases: (1) miracles (*UC* 16.34), (2) public assent (*UC* 16.34; 7.17), which includes historical priority (*UC* 14.31; cf. *Faust* 11.2), and (3) the power to cause people to live a moral life (*UC* 17.35).[26] We can see immediately that the first two criteria are more specific formulations of his earlier standard of *proofs*, and the third criterion a carryover of his second standard of *conduct*. He later elaborated on the first two in *Against the Fundamental Epistle*:

> To say nothing, then, of the wisdom that you do not believe exists in the Catholic Church, there are many other things that most rightfully hold me in her bosom. The agreement of peoples and nations holds me. The authority begun with miracles . . . and strengthened with age holds me in the Catholic Church. The succession of priests . . . right up to the present episcopacy holds me in the Catholic Church. Finally, the name "Catholic" holds me in the Catholic Church It was not without reason that this Church alone, among so many heresies, obtained this name. . . . But among you, where there are none of these things to invite and to hold me, only the promise of truth is heard. To be sure, if the truth is revealed so clearly that it cannot come into doubt, it ought to be preferred to all the things by which I am held in the Catholic Church. But if it is only promised and not revealed, no one will move me from that faith which binds my mind to the Christian religion by such great bonds. (*CEF* 4.5)

The questions we must ask of these developed "proofs" favorable to Nicene Christianity is how much they are built upon Augustine's own experience, to what degree they may have factored in his own conversion, and to what extent they are post-conversion rationalizations of choices made for other motives and reasons.

Was Augustine affected by his perception of the miraculous toward a favorable orientation to Nicene Christianity? Although he relates in the *Confessions* Ambrose's discovery in the summer of 386 of the relics of martyrs, and the subsequently reported miracles confirming their sanctity, his writings from the time of his conversion put little stock in such things. In *Order*, while acknowledging Christ's miraculous deeds as a matter of faith, he insists that Christ demonstrates "of what little value he considers these things, and commands us not to be bound by the senses, to which these things seem marvelous, but to fly to the intellect" (*Ord* 2.9.27). Similarly, in *The Usefulness of Belief* he will not commit himself to the continued occurrence of miracles in the post-apostolic age. We see another side of Augustine, however, in his report of resorting to *sortes* as a means of determining God's will in the Milanese garden (*Conf* 8.12.29), and in his frequent allusions to his illness as a chastisement from God (e.g., *ME* 18.33; *Fort* 37; *Conf* 5.9.16). Illness commonly plays a part in the circumstances of conversion, whether it be as a psychosomatic indicator of an identity conflict or as a disruption of routine that invites reconsideration of lifestyle. Even though these reports of noting signs come from the more devotional discourse Augustine has learned by the time of the *Confessions*, it remains plausible that the same Augustine who had placed stock in astrology also found meaning in falling ill or in how a book happened to fall open. Rather than thinking of these things as miraculous in Augustine's eyes, therefore, we might consider their relation to the way he tended to think of the world at the time. His consistent attention to such signs suggests an inclination to see the world as ordered in a way that the Nicene Christian stress on divine omnipotence closely matched, while Manichaeism, with its more agonistic themes, did not.

Augustine displays far less ambivalence when it comes to the persuasiveness of public assent. In the months preceding his conversion, he had observed Ambrose's triumph over the impotent imperial court, largely on the strength of the overwhelming majority of Nicene Christians in Milan, in what Ambrose had asserted were universally-recognized and ancient privileges of authority. Augustine appears to have adopted rather gullibly and wholesale such strategically exaggerated claims to the antiquity and universality of the "Catholic" form of Christianity. While it does no credit to Augustine as a thinker, he never grows tired of employing such arguments *ex consensu gentium*, well established in the Roman intellectual tradition and part of Augustine's rhetorical training. He repeatedly appeals to the argument of success: the universality of the "Catholic Church" is the proof of its validity over against regional heresies;[27] the wide geographical distribution of the scriptures validates their authority against challenges to the integrity of their transmission (*Conf* 6.5.8).[28] Augustine appears most at home with this resort to "common sense" in his early post-conversion writings, indicative of the very different status of the Nicene Christian option from that held by Manichaeism in general society by the late fourth century.

But it was the criterion of successful conduct that Augustine would choose to highlight in his *Confessions* narrative—not coincidentally the very standard impressed upon him by Faustus. Once Augustine's attention had been narrowed to this single criterion by his Manichaean preceptor's advice, he seems to have taken greater note of imperfections in the conduct of his fellow Manichaeans, Auditors and Elect alike. Most important, momentarily dissuaded by Faustus from the distraction of his endemic metaphysical curiosity, his attention may have been drawn more forcefully to his own lack of development toward the ascetic ideal promoted by Manichaeism. The religion was not proving itself effective for him in the way it should according to Faustus's own standards.[29] In the *Confessions*, Augustine mentions several reports of personal moral reform inspired by Christianity that came to his ears that summer before his conversion. These reports included not only tales such as the conversion of the rhetorician and philosopher Marius Victorinus,[30] but specifically word of the new ascetic movement that seemed to show Nicene Christians matching the very Manichaean standards that Augustine had found it impossible to meet as a Manichaean.[31]

Augustine's *The Academics* appears entirely dedicated to resolving the means of successful conduct in the face of a rationally irrefutable skeptical challenge to certainty. This is what Augustine means when he says he composed the work to deal with how Skepticism "held me back" from an opportunity he perceived to make progress. John O'Meara traces the work's peculiar shortcomings as a philosophical dialogue to its entanglement with unarticulated issues in Augustine's own conversion.

> The *Contra Academicos* cannot be recommended as a valuable
> contribution to the theory of knowledge, nor even as an answer to
> scepticism. It is a personal work, written by Augustine to meet his own
> needs, and addressed to a friend of his. It is true that Augustine had
> some confidence in his arguments, and that the work was published;

nevertheless, it bears too deeply the traces of experience to be in any sense an objective discussion of epistemology.[32]

Augustine writes to rationalize positions he has already come to for motivations he does not reveal—or may not even know. The result is poor philosophy burdened with the personal nature of that which Augustine chooses to discuss in pretended philosophical abstraction. While affirming the validity of skeptical epistemology, he attacks what he sees as its pragmatic consequences in a turn in his argument (in *Acad* 3.15–16) that David Mosher has astutely identified as reflecting a subtle anti-Manichaean polemic.[33]

As we have seen, the Academic holds to the necessity of acting on the basis of merely probable truth, since it is impossible to know anything with certainty. The sage therefore acts while withholding mental assent to the truth of the proposition on which he or she acts. Yet in following the probable as the best one can know, Augustine contends, one necessarily gives tentative assent to it.[34] To act while claiming not to give assent to the basis of one's actions is only to deny any responsibility for one's actions. Moral responsibility means being committed to the bases of one's decisions to act. Therefore one must assent to what lies behind actions in order to act, however provisional or incomplete one's knowledge or one's assurance of the truth of these bases of action. Mosher sums up the argument as follows:

> If it is morally reprehensible to withhold assent to the probable in the interest of escaping blame for error and sin, then it is morally obligatory to give assent if one is to accept responsibility for one's actions. Hence wisdom can be achieved only if one has the moral courage first to believe what one is trying to understand. If the skeptics are not willing to take this step even in the case of the "probabilities" . . . then they will never be in a position, morally or otherwise, to advance from there to the truths which bring genuine virtue and happiness.[35]

In this way, Augustine shapes his critique of Skepticism to coordinate with his unsatisfactory experience of Manichaeism, including both the religion's theoretical avoidance of personal responsibility and the consequences that theory had for Augustine's own lack of decisive commitment and self-discipline.

Of course, Manichaeism primarily employed skeptical arguments in its polemical tool-kit, without representing a truly skeptical tradition.[36] But Faustus had raised this skeptical rhetoric to a veritable centerpiece of his own prag-matic approach to religion. That approach had not worked for Augustine, but it had brought Skepticism and Manichaeism close together in his mind. He came to see his own dilemma as a failed Manichaean reflected in the position of the Academics. He drew connections between the latter's claim to act on the basis of knowledge one regards as only probable, with mental reservation, and his difficulties as a Manichaean—both his tendency to disassociate himself from his bad actions by recourse to the Manichaean theory of evil, and the in-tellectual malaise of his uncertainties about what to believe. Augustine's anti-skeptical arguments, therefore, do not effectively target Manichaeism itself, but do reflect issues that had arisen for Augustine as a Manichaean exposed to the Skepticism of Faustus.

Augustine had lived as a Manichaean in the absence of wholehearted be-lief, as he awaited rational proof. This apparently proved an obstacle to invest-ing himself fully in the Manichaean way of life. He was unable to trust in the affects and effects of Manichaean practice because he had been promised scientific reasons for their efficacy which he never received. Without his full confidence and investment, they could not transform him in the way he came to think religious practices were meant to do. If he persisted in approaching any new sources of knowledge with the same mental reservations he had as a Manichaean, Augustine ran the serious risk of repeating the same experi-ence of ineffectuality and inability to progress toward the spiritual perfection promised by that source, be it Neoplatonism or Nicene Christianity. He real-ized at some point—dramatized in the Garden Incident—that he must act without reservations to change his self effectively. He decided that a moral system could not be effective without the kind of certainty he had been miss-ing, and that certainty reason apparently could not provide (*Acad* 3.16.35–36, 2.9.22). The Christianity he encountered in Milan demanded obedience to authority without proof or reasons. While this could be looked at askance as a line unworthy of thoughtful people, Augustine had come to recognize a certain advantage in it. The individual had to choose conformity or resistance, trust or doubt, at the beginning without caveat or qualification. Only by such a radical act of submission, Augustine believed, could the person's defective will be reformed. Only in this way would the rebellious human will not be coddled and reinforced. To believe meant to think with assent to the object of thought. The one who wished to make spiritual progress could not afford the skeptical withholding of assent.

Augustine makes the resort to authority appear to be the logical, necessary process of taking reason to its own endpoint. Reason is made to yield an authoritarian conclusion that negates reason's own claims to priority. But plenty of comments by Augustine reveal that he did not engage in such a reasoning process until *after* he had decided for authority. He had made his decision for affective reasons or, more exactly, for reasons of effectiveness. "What is the matter with us? . . . These men *have none of our education*, yet they stand up and storm the gates of heaven while we, *for all our learning*, lie here groveling in this world of flesh and blood!" (*Conf* 8.7.18). The new asceticism revealed an effectiveness of moral purpose and self-transformation that did not seem to rely on a worked-out philosophy. *Lesser men* were succeeding,[37] while the intellectuals floundered in ineffectuality. Theory be damned, Augustine decided, let's go with what works.

But how was this move on Augustine's part any different from the program Faustus had proposed to him? In substance, it was not. As we have seen, Faustus's heightened Skepticism simply developed a critique of the human capacity to know found in Manichaeism generally. The presence of another, evil mind within us undermines the reliability of what we think. We require the initiative of a divine infusion of reliable knowing to set us on the right path, and ever after we must remain on guard against surreptitious revivals of the evil mind under the guise of our thinking processes. Which mind is in control determines how the senses are used in support of either good or bad intentions. It is against the background of this theory of human intellection that Faustus proposed to assess knowledge by its outcome in action. Ideas, perceptions, plans of action that produce good conduct demonstrate a truth value, a truth-likeness, regardless of how well they convey literal absolute truth.[38] Faustus merely brought into sharper relief a fundamental Manichaean emphasis on the role of will, assent, decision, and resolve in marking the axis of one's identity and determining one's orientation to good or evil. Knowledge provides a resource of selfhood, but selfhood itself is made by mastering the decision-making process and putting that knowledge into effect in action.

We can observe, then, how Augustine uprooted a distinctive orientation around the role of the will and assent in both knowledge and action from its Manichaean ground and transplanted it to Nicene Christian soil. Epistemological and moral cautions about the material world and the senses through which it bombarded the soul were a pervasive attitude of Augustine's cultural environment. But from Manichaean teachings, such as the text of the *Funda-*

mental Epistle he heard read out, he had learned about the centrality of desire to defining one's ultimate identity and destiny—whether it was the awakened soul's relentless yearning for liberation and return to its heavenly origin, or the dissolute and intoxicated soul's attraction to the poison of darkness.[39] On this foundation he had added the lessons of Faustus's Skepticism, with his reinforcement of Manichaean doubts about the capacity of humans to recognize truth within the deceptive prison of their own bodies, and his resort to the pragmatic verification of successful moral action. By this very criterion, Augustine had deemed Manichaeism a failure, at least for himself, and Platonic Christianity a better choice for motivating moral action. Now the Christian emphasis on faith instead of reason appeared in line with the skeptical discrediting of reason, and its free-will rhetoric seemed to carry through with greater consistency the place of assent in determining both truth and action.

Augustine's subsequent focus on the role of the human will grows directly out of this earlier period of grappling with Skepticism and Manichaeism and examining the crucial role in both systems of *assent of the will* to things that appear to be true. Since knowledge remains uncertain due to the limitations of human perception, it cannot play the critical role in salvation. It is rather the will that assents or does not assent to a path of life that will prove to be the right or wrong one.[40] And this will to believe what one cannot certainly know is an act of humility by which one demonstrates a correct orientation of the lesser self to the greater God. In a sense then, several core ideas of Augustinian thought begin to unfold out of his repositioning of emphases from his pre-conversion background into the new setting of his converted self.

His decision that unassisted reason is bankrupt and authority the necessary starting point of knowledge signals a dramatic turn in Augustine's thinking, and launches a remarkable program of rationalization. From this point forward, he will not seek to arrive at any belief (or practice) on reason. Since human reasoning does not possess sufficient assurance to form the basis of spiritual commitment, he will insist, authority alone may determine in every instance what is to be believed. The role of reason, then, will be to justify belief, in other words to rationalize it, both by finding arguments to support it and by construing it in such a way that it can be defended as reasonable (*Acad* 3.20.43; *Ord* 2.5.16, 2.9.26; *ME* 2.3).[41]

At the time, Augustine regarded his recognition of the priority of authority over reason as *the* key breakthrough in his thinking. Yet by the time he composes the *Confessions*, he has little use for it. In yet another key inversion between the earlier and later sources on Augustine's conversion, the *Confessions* exactly reverses this breakthrough, describing an intellectual conversion through reason (book 7) *before* a conversion of will that ends his resistance to authority (book 8).[42] In the later work, Augustine depicts reason as picking away at his concerns and doubts, resolving each issue as others remain, and gradually working toward a sufficiently complete reformation of his thinking to provide certainty and freedom from doubts.[43] He is no longer willing to portray this breakthrough as he did in 386–387, as a *resolve* to accept whatever authority will teach without yet knowing how it will address his concerns.[44] The moment of resolve is still there, but in the wrong place: the Garden Incident now follows all the rational exploration of Platonic and Nicene Christian premises that our earlier sources show taking place after Augustine's conversion. The other experiences in Milan Augustine relates in the *Confessions* that plausibly contributed motives to his conversion—Ambrose's successful claims to authority by tradition and popular support, the widely published reports of miracles connected to the discovered bones of martyrs—have become detached from an argument for authority in the retelling, perhaps because Augustine had detected weaknesses in using them for that purpose. But more than this, Augustine seems to have abandoned—at least for the purposes of this work—his earlier model of belief taking root prior to any understanding. Either out of his own changing convictions, or as a strategic decision to offer some sort of model of reasoned conversion, Augustine reverses the prioritization of authority and reason in the *Confessions* narrative, providing an account of many good reasons leading up to the conscious construction of a "Catholic" self in place of a "Manichaean" one.

I want to suggest something quite different from the stark either/or of accepting one or other of these accounts as the "true" one. The freedom with which Augustine construes and reconstrues the central moment of self-transformation, I contend, points to a break-point, a gap, across which his performative repertoire could not reach. Because his act of commitment to a new identity had occurred just beyond the threshold of the mental space he now inhabited, he lacked any other terms with which to think about it than those provided by his current commitments in their developed form. Just as his Manichaean self embedded a caricature of non-Manichaean Christianity and what commitment to the latter would entail, so his post-conversion self could construe his former Manichaeism only in the terms provided by the new discourses in which he now functioned. He had surrendered many of the constructs by which he could convey what it meant to him to be a Manichaean, let alone an apostate at loose ends as to where his priorities should lie. Into this gap of self-knowing, therefore, Augustine was free to pour whatever contents were currently available to him as the post facto significance of the leap across it. Augustine's earlier writings give us a closer reading of his conversion than his later ones only because they reveal the more limited repertoire he had in his possession at the time with which to construe the meaning of his commitments. Even these earliest sources are already too late to catch the moment of decision that we like to mark on a calendar and refer to as Augustine's conversion. But that moment itself, for all its apparently decisive role in determining history, carries no significance in itself, but only that with which Augustine endowed it, both in keeping the promise it entailed, and in reconstruing its meaning as an essential part of who he kept becoming. Until his choice was performed, until it was rendered intelligible by taking up available models of self-presentation, there was no "conversion." The conversion we have been looking for is not in the garden, but in the months and years that followed as Augustine acquired facility with an originally alien system of being himself.

Initiation

I have speculated that Augustine's time as a Manichaean had conditioned him to the idea of the complementarity of intellectual and cultic projects. This may help to explain why he turned to the Nicene Christian community in Milan for ethical formation appropriate to his larger quest, on the analogy of his prior project of self-development. What we know with certainty is his decision, with his friend and fellow Manichaean apostate Alypius, to accept Nicene Christian initiation. They returned to Milan sometime after the first of the year and submitted their names (along with that of Augustine's son Adeodatus) to the list of candidates for baptism (*Conf* 9.6.14). Augustine's comrades at Cassiciacum had come and gone during the six months of Augustine's sojourn there. But Augustine had not ventured back to Milan in all that time, perhaps out of concern for his uncertain legal status. The amnesty connected to the *vota publica* of Theodosius and Arcadius in January 387 put an end to any such concerns, and within weeks of its promulgation Augustine returned to Milan.

Both Ambrose and Augustine considered the annual Easter-time baptism of new converts "the mysteries." Since the peace of Constantine, Christian instruction and baptism had appropriated the model of the pagan mysteries, with mass baptisms occurring at a particular date on the calendar as part of the Easter holy days, with a period of purification prior to this initiation, and with boundaries of participation and vows of silence over the details of both the initiation itself and the rites open to the initiate for the first time.[45] In making the decisive move from a *catechumen* to a *competent*, Augustine entered upon an intensive preparation for the coming initiation. He passed the scrutinies (examination of candidates to ensure the absence of Satan and presence of an authentic personal reform), observed the Lenten fast, received moral instruction twice a day, and participated in rites symbolizing the purification of the senses. A week before Easter, Ambrose imparted to him and the other *competents* the *traditio symboli*, the creedal core of Catholic doctrine, for memorization. Sometime during the eve of Easter, 24 April 387, Augustine received baptism.

His purification empowered Augustine to undergo an additional ritual sealing and blessing, some of which would have closely resembled his initiation as a Manichaean Auditor, while other aspects would have suggested the privileged ordination of the Elect. He was told that the sealing bestowed seven virtues on the initiate: wisdom, understanding, counsel, strength, knowledge, godliness, and fear (Ambrose, *Mysteriis* 7.42). He and the other initiates were then led out, presented to the congregation, and partook for the first time in the eucharist (Ambrose, *Mysteriis* 8.43). Augustine could scarcely avoid comparing his experience of this ceremony with his participation in Manichaean rituals. The similar symbolism and staging would have suggested that he now stood in the place of the Elect: purified, sanctified, displaying virtues, consuming the sacred meal—and for him exceptionally, if not for most of the other initiates, a personal vow of celibacy. Certainly such parallels gave added impetus to his sense that he was finally *making progress*.

These details of Augustine's probable experience of Christian initiation have been culled from Ambrose's exposition of the mysteries as performed in Milan. Of all this Augustine makes at the time a single allusion to the preparatory instruction. "All these things are passed on to us with more secrecy and strength by these sacred mysteries into which we are being initiated. In these mysteries the life of good men is purified with utmost ease, not by the circumlocution of disputations"—a slap at the Manichaeans as he had come to caricature them—"but by the authority of the mysteries" (*Ord* 2.9.27). The trope of the greater power of nondiscursive initiation is a Classical one, the predilection for esotericism and the high expectations of revealed knowledge a recurring part of Augustine's outlook. In the *Confessions* he says even less—*et baptizati sumus* (*Conf* 9.6.14)—adding only that the ritual implied for him release from all his former sins, a fairly direct recollection of Ambrose's scripted declaration that, "now no offences pollute the baptized" (Ambrose, *Mysteriis* 7.41). Perhaps he found significance in the enunciated finality of the baptismal purification in contrast to the Manichaean expectation of recurring "eruptions" of sin and the necessity of repeated confession and absolution. He seems to imply that he had not been successfully released from any prior sins through all the daily, weekly, and annual rites of absolution given in the Manichaean community, perhaps because all that time he had never really thought they were *his* sins. We might read this implication within the themes of the *Confessions* narrative, by which Augustine had to learn first to take responsibility for his sins before he could attain the necessary orientation to have them purged. But this is Augustine of Hippo talking, applying his theme that *conversio* is *confessio*. Augustine of Milan says only that the purification bestowed by the mysteries clears the mind from its bodily and sensory distractions so that it can reason properly. As noted before, Alypius apparently regarded their training as *competents* and baptism as "unworthy of mention" in Augustine's compositions at the time (*Conf* 9.4.7). Based on the unpolished state in which Augustine's *The Immortality of the Soul* escaped his hands, we may suspect that Augustine added such cultic and devotional references to his writings as part of their literary patina, rather than constituting an essential part of their substance.[46] In the end, such references as Augustine included in his initial post-conversion works were subdued, and perfectly in line with the pious asides of writers such as Cicero.[47]

Yet once ensconced within Nicene Christianity, Augustine never visibly questioned his allegiance to it, but progressively surrendered various concepts that had formed effective and affective bridges for his thinking in the process of conversion that he came to consider no longer essential to his developing thought and practice. His attitude in this regard corresponds to observations on the binding power of conversion in other cases made by Robert Hefner, involving the consequences to self-identity of making a new religious commitment a "social fact" by public declaration.

> Even when converts discovered that Christianity has entailments other than those they had expected, they could not revert from their faith.

Public profession of the faith had inspired an interior rationalization quite unlike anything that would have occurred on a purely individual basis. The faith of these young men and women had been made practically compelling by their public declarations and the intense self-legitimation those declarations inspired.[48]

By accepting initiation into the "Catholic Church" and publicly performing speech-acts drawn from its standardized discourse, Augustine had made himself answerable for this commitment of his identity. Such answerability provides a principal motive force for further engagement with and mastery of the system to which one has made an initial commitment. Conversion was an ongoing process for Augustine, as it is for any convert, involving gradual conformation to a system as one learns it more thoroughly, and keeps adjusting one's sense of self accordingly.

It would indeed take Augustine another decade to understand and embody what conversion would mean *for him*, to make of himself a "Catholic" self. There is some sense in which Augustine acknowledges this time-lagged conversion when he composes the *Confessions*, for in that work he projects all of the decade's worth of progress he has made since back into the circumstances of the original moment of conversion, forcing it into the mold of an ideal, life-changing decision that comes as the *culmination* of a process of persuasion, rather than as an unproven impulse that might not have worked out. If the disproof of Manichaeism lay in its inability to enable Augustine to make progress, the proof of his newly adopted faith would have to await those very signs of progress, and could not possibly be invoked at the beginning of a process of verification. Once it had proven itself *to work* for Augustine and actually effect a transformation of self that he found upon reflection in some way satisfying, hindsight allowed the author to assume that ultimate success and all that supported it in the initial providential step.

CHAPTER NINE

A New Man?

By THE STANDARD tropes of conversion, and by Augustine's own later occasional, if inconsistent, portrayal of his story, we expect to see a new man embodied in his writings of 386–388, transformed by a breakthrough of new commitments and identifications. Yet even Augustine in his *Confessions* admitted that he could see continuities between the persona he takes in these materials and his pre-conversion preoccupations (*Conf* 9.4.7; cf. *Retr* 1.1.1–1.4.4), just as the earlier convert acknowledged being at the beginnings of faith. The faith that must precede understanding—the faith of the convert—involves becoming open and receptive to a system of thought and action, trusting it enough to begin a process of assimilating that system to one's predispositions, and reciprocally conforming one's dispositions to the expectations of the new paradigm. The new sources of one's self gradually supply elements that displace or integrate with previously existing convictions and habits. The initial "take" of a new faith, therefore, will be syncretistic, gradually yielding in varying degrees to a permeation of the self by the adopted system.

This is decidedly not the way many religions portray conversion; they have motivation to prefer the model of an instantaneous and total creation of a new self, completely cut free of its past. Augustine puts his own story in the service of this cliché in the *Confessions*, displacing to the *pre-conversion* part of the narrative the process we see under way in his early *post-conversion* writings of a tentative, incremental assimilation of brave new ideas into an existing grid of personal assumptions and preferences. In this way, he seems to leave the garden fully supplied with the full set of insights into his new faith that he has at his disposal as he writes the *Confessions*, erasing the intervening decade in deference to the ideal of an instantly completed and static "Catholic" self. But his writings of the intervening period betray this image as a fantasy, and reveal how Augustine gradually rationalized the discrete set-pieces of the new amalgam of past identity and present commitment, putting them into dialogue with each other, finding ways to make them consistent with one another, inter-referential, and in this way a *system* of consistent self-performance. Just how systematic or thorough such an integration of discrete commitments becomes will vary greatly from one person to another; but in Augustine we have someone very intent on this process.

We should bear in mind the performativity of religious identity, that is, the unavoidable limitation of assessment of religious commitment by external, visible behavior, both physical and verbal. One is not a convert unless and until one acts and speaks the part. And as in all such learned behavior, it involves a process proceeding from the outside in, as performance deepens from a script introduced from outside oneself, to a carefully referenced mimicry of the script, to a gradually habituated unselfconscious embodiment of a tradition of selfhood as the most efficient arrangement of a consistent self-performance. Because conversion occurs publicly from the first taking up of the script of the convert, it entails no more than a decision to declare one's intention to proceed with the learning process within the particular community; and no one can say how far the individual convert may go in internalizing the performance. For that reason, Robert Hefner observes, "conversion need not reformulate one's understanding of the ultimate conditions of existence, but it always involves commitment to a new kind of moral authority and a new or reconceptualized social identity."[1] It entails taking up a role and a set of performative expectations, and putting oneself at the disposal of an epistemic apparatus as a reproduction and transmitter of its self-ordering system. Only such a decision of self-subjection is required; the rest follows from the convert's own desire and effort to take oneself as "an object of knowledge and field of action,"[2] as Foucault phrases it, knowing oneself in confirmation of the supplied paradigms and enacting a replication of the given models of self-realization.

Much of what Augustine has to say at the beginning of this process about the new ideology with which he had come to identify, therefore, cannot be regarded as much more than rote repetition of stock phrases or, at best, piecemeal clusters of concepts that do immediate work for Augustine without being carefully integrated into a coherent discourse or identity. We are witness in these texts to a process in which Augustine begins to forge an initial rough mix of set pieces—some old, some new, some reimagined—into a unified discursive apprehension of reality to which he could not only commit rhetorically, but also act upon in his own conduct. His self-identification with the Nicene Christian community placed him in a situation of "self-legitimation,"[3] "self-verification,"[4] or "answerability,"[5] by which he was motivated to conform his speech-acts and other conduct more and more to the ideological and practical system with which he had associated himself and in which he saw himself defined.[6]

Augustine had already begun in Cassiciacum and Milan to rationalize interconnections between Platonism and Nicene Christianity, supplemented by additional elements drawn from a variety of sources from the broader Roman intellectual tradition. His feverish dialogic explorations of his new ideological identity continued apace after his return to Rome in the summer of 387 C.E. Whether he had already decided on a return to Africa, now that the amnesty of Theodosius had lifted any obstacle to it, or was prompted in such a direction by the unraveling political situation in Milan, he made it only as far as the port of Ostia, where his mother Monnica died, before turning back to Rome, where he remained for another year.[7] There he produced *The Quantification of Soul* (*De quantitate animae*), seeking to clarify the implications of the immaterial concept of the soul distinctive to Platonism, and *Whence Evil?* (*Unde malum*), eventually known by the expression for the solution to the problem he there defends as *Free Choice* (*De libero arbitrio*), attempting to construct a coherent account of the origin of evil within nondualist terms that yet somehow preserve God from responsibility for it.[8] He also began work on what would eventually be *The Morals of the Catholic Church* (*De moribus ecclesiae catholicae*),[9] his first venture into subject matter that would be regarded as "religious" by his contemporaries, defending Nicene Christianity as a legitimate embodiment of the ethical teachings of Christ in continuity with the values found in the Old Testament.

All the works Augustine produced during his second sojourn in Rome display a heightened attention to the specifically anti-Manichaean dimensions of his new commitments, no doubt brought to the surface by his renewed contact with the Manichaean community in Rome, now as both an apostate and a promoter of a rival ideology.[10] In the latter role, he defined himself as much by what he rejected as by what he had adopted. This implicit dialogue with both his past Manichaean self and his current Manichaean or former-

Manichaean friends, rather than any desire to become a polemicist, explains the elements in Augustine's earliest writings identified in previous scholarship as an anti-Manichaean subtext.[11] He employs the speech-act repertoire of the apostate, not the polemicist: his references to Manichaean teachings, rarely very explicit, serve primarily as a means to define himself over against the other of his past self. Certainly, Augustine puts himself forward publicly and endeavors to enunciate persuasive ideas. But his literary efforts do not have sufficient doctrinal specificity to constitute Nicene Christian or even Platonist propaganda or effectively to define an interreligious debate. For some time to come, in fact, Augustine would display considerable discomfort with the role of polemicist. In laboring to define himself within a new world view, he vacillates between attacking the Manichaeans and trying to make that new world appreciable to them. "This preoccupation with a certain audience," Robert O'Connell speculates, "introduces a further twist into Augustine's assimilation of Plotinus"[12]—as well as, it would seem, of Nicene Christian discourse. Foremost among that audience at this stage was himself.

New Sources of the Self?

How much had really changed for Augustine as a convert, either from his former Manichaeism or from abiding loyalty to the "common sense" of his broader culture? Many of the positions Augustine initially takes as a "convert" come straight out of the *Hortensius*. There Augustine read that the practice of philosophy produces in the individual a reorientation of self away from degrading desires and toward desiring only proper goods;[13] that one is directed toward the happiness of truth via the contemplation of the order and beauty of the cosmos;[14] that the soul must be prepared through a disciplined life before it can attain true knowledge;[15] that only the orientation of the mind is within our power, all else being subject to necessity;[16] that the body is a burden to the soul, given as a punishment for past sin;[17] that in this life we find relative happiness in the pursuit of truth, even if it cannot be found with certainty.[18] Augustine seems to have questioned only the last of these propositions, and did so in light of an escape from it provided by Cicero himself in his *Academica*. It appears that Augustine was rereading *Hortensius* with fresh eyes, free from the assumption that its ideas found their natural complement in Manichaeism, and beginning to see a better consonance between them and a Platonic Christianity.

Already during his association with the Manichaeans, Augustine had professed a commitment to the one God, to Christ the divine revealer and savior, to Paul the true apostle, to the authority of New Testament writings, to an ascetic ethic, and to a conception of the self as an exiled soul longing for a return to God. The presence of any of these elements in Augustine's literary productions in the 380s proves nothing in itself about the rapidity or depth of his indoctrination into Nicene Christianity. Instead, we are witness to a gradual adaptation of these prior *symboli* to their meaning within a new pattern of interrelationship and application. When Augustine says that his new commitment to Platonism as his rational discourse will not alter his resolve *not to depart* from Christ as an authority (*Acad* 3.20.43), he signals a self-understanding by which he has *already* been committed to Christ as a Manichaean.[19] He perhaps intends to make clear that his conversion is not to the Porphyrian anti-Christian variety of Platonism, but to a kind reconciled to the unavoidable authority of Christ in the late fourth century.

Distinctly Nicene Christian concepts such as "Trinity" and "Incarnation" represent little more than slogans in Augustine's early post-conversion compositions, for which he offers only tentative applications.[20] In many ways, the God in whom Augustine had now chosen to believe looked much like the God of the Manichaeans. His acceptance of Ambrose's neo-Nicene Trinitarianism would not have demanded any significant shift from Manichaean theology, which was likewise homoousian in character and Trinitarian in expression.[21] Augustine frankly admitted that he did not yet understand the nuances of Nicene theology; the Trinity expounded to him in Ambrose's sermons and catechetical instruction "is as yet conceived by me in faith rather than understood by reason" (*Acad* 2.2.4), and his few Trinitarian references show just how interchangeable Nicene, Neoplatonic, and Manichaean conceptions of the divine economy could be.[22] Nor did the concept of God as creator and orderer distinguish the Nicene position from the Manichaean, which equally held that "the whole of the world, which is called heaven and earth, had God and a good god for its author and maker" (*ME* 10.16). Moreover, Plotinus and Manichaeism shared a rather distinctive identification of the divine with the beautiful,[23] even if Augustine labored to differentiate the Neoplatonic idea of intelligible beauty from the materialist categories of Manichaean aesthetics. Augustine likewise still considered perfectly valid Manichaean criticisms of crudely anthropomorphic conceptions of God, and insisted that in converting to Nicene Christianity he had not embraced such popular delusions (*ME* 10.16–17).[24]

In the *Confessions*, Augustine will fault himself for a time when he had held Christ to be "no more than a man, though a man of excellent wisdom and without peer" (*Conf* 7.19.25). This time was not his Manichaean period, during which he had considered Christ to be an emanation of God, a supramundane intellect bringing the pure revelation of truth unobscured by material evil. Rather, this greatest-of-sages Christ appears in his initial post-conversion writings, where he comfortably compares Christ to Plato, Pythagoras, and Plotinus as sources of wisdom, not distinguished in kind, but at most in degree of "participation in wisdom" (*Conf* 7.19.25).[25]

Augustine appears to suggest that he was hearing an exposition of the incarnation of Christ for the first time during his Lenten preparation for baptism in the early spring of 387 (*Ord* 2.9.27). He apparently struggled with how the intelligible and material could be bridged in such a way as to bring intelligible truth clearly before the perception of materially bound humans in order to provide some foundation for an intellectual ascent—a problem for which Platonism offered no help (*Conf* 7.9.13–14). Indeed, one spots an unexamined contradiction in Augustine's simultaneous commitment to an incarnate Christ and his view of physical embodiment as inherently imperfect and corrupting. Once he had accepted Christ as the divine Word, that is, the essence of Truth itself, he could not help seeing his incarnation as a "debasing," albeit a gracious, voluntary one. His emphasis on the immutability of God, which served as a necessary contrast to the Manichaean view he had abandoned, for a long time proved an obstacle to developing a fully articulated understanding of Christ's incarnation. Augustine's friend Nebridius apparently held to the loftier Manichaean view of the docetic Christ, retaining it even after their break with Manichaeism in Milan (*Conf* 9.3.6). Alypius reportedly struggled to appreciate Nicene Christology as well (*Conf* 7.19.25).[26]

Augustine's gradual indoctrination into Nicene Christianity brought him back to the sort of "higher" Christology he had been taught as a Manichaean, reintroducing him to a belief in Christ's divinity shared by Manichaean and Nicene Christianity against a variety of "lower" Christologies of the time. Whatever the incarnation meant to him as a conveyance of God's "power and wisdom" (1 Cor 1.24)—a favorite Manichaean identification of Christ that appears repeatedly in Augustine's early writings (*Acad* 2.1.1, 2.1.2; *BV* 4.34; *QA* 33.76; *ME* 13.22, 16.28)—Augustine essentially assigned Christ to the same primarily pedagogical and exemplary role found in the Manichaean view.[27] In identifying Christ with the Plotinian *nous* or *intellectus*, Christian Neoplatonists such as Augustine committed themselves to understanding him primarily as an awakener and informer just as the Manichaeans did, and not as a sacrificial redeemer. The cross finds no place in the thought of Augustine at this time.[28] When he offers characterizations of Christ drawn from the Bible, he appears to draw mostly upon his Manichaean liturgical experiences.[29]

Similarly, in his early post-conversion use of the New Testament, and Paul in particular, Augustine appears to rely heavily on his prior exposure to these texts as a Manichaean.[30] He had enough mastery of the Manichaean biblical repertoire to identify confidently which passages they accepted, and which they rejected, from the gospels and the letters of Paul.[31] He persists in the Manichaean fondness for "right hand" language in connection with divine intervention in the human condition (*BV* 5, 18, 20; *Ord* 1), and employs other biblical catch phrases that he expressly identifies as Manichaean favorites (e.g., *ME* 17.31)—"Seek and you shall find" (Mt 7:7–8—*Acad* 2.3.9; *Sol* 1.1.3; *ME* 17.31; *LA* 2.2.6), "The truth shall set you free" (Jn 8:31–32—*Acad* 1.8–9; *LA* 2.13.37)—that sum up their appeal to reason in place of blind faith.[32] Robert O'Connell has suggested that Augustine actually organizes *The Academics* 1.5.13 to 2.3.9 as an inquiry into the proper interpretation of these divine imperatives stressed by the Manichaeans[33]—that is, whether indeed commitment to a way of life must be based upon the certainty of reasoned proof, and "Seek and you shall find" as interpreted in this way by the Manichaeans should have priority as a divine command over other salutary instructions.

Although Augustine claimed to have turned to the letters of Paul in the first flush of his conversion, and to have "read through all of it with the greatest attention and care" (*Acad* 2.2.5; cf. *BV* 1.4; *Conf* 7.21.27), his use of Paul over the next half-dozen years does not bespeak either intense interest in or depth of understanding of the Apostle. In a series of studies, Leo Ferrari has demonstrated effectively the near total absence of the key Pauline passages cited in the *Confessions* from Augustine's works prior to his encounter with the adept Pauline exegesis of Fortunatus in 392.[34] While a turn to Paul would have been an ingrained reflex of Augustine's Manichaean training,[35] and the Pauline letters would have been the one scripture accepted among the Manichaeans easily available to him in Ambrose's Milan,[36] we must reckon with the distinct possibility that both his claim to have read Paul at the time, and the lack of significant Pauline ideas in his immediately subsequent writings, are equally factual, and that Augustine simply was not a very perceptive reader of Paul at this time. He apparently picked among the Apostle's passages and found some that connected to what he was thinking. But at this time he failed to grasp some of Paul's more profound ideas, at least as judged by their impact on his later thought.

The truly new source of Augustine's self as a Nicene Christian was the Old Testament. Augustine's conversion involved accepting the Nicene inclusion of the Old Testament in its biblical canon, overruling his personal disdain for it, as well as the Manichaean criticisms with which he had become familiar. This rhetorical deference to the Bible involved Augustine in a purely illocutionary act, a declaration of allegiance to one of the prime icons of the Catholic community without any immediate intellectual ramification. As stressed by James O'Donnell, "Faith comes *first* as faith in the authority of scripture; not in any doctrines taught by or through scripture, but just in scripture itself . . . as the necessary preliminary to learning any doctrine from the Scriptural text."[37] Augustine's actual use of much of the Old Testament was contingent upon a particular, allegorical interpretation of it that enabled him to bypass deeply troubling elements in the text's apparent literal meaning. Manichaean criticisms of the Old Testament's apparent literal meaning retained a certain validity; but this only pointed out that the true meaning must lie elsewhere. Anyone so naive as to take the Bible literally fully deserved such criticism as the Manichaeans leveled; but the Manichaeans fell prey to the very same error in refusing to take the text any other way (*ME* 17.30). Acknowledging that not all leaders of the Nicene community were equally informed about or able to employ allegorical interpretation, Augustine still insisted that the community possessed and transmitted this correct method of reading at the hands of its more sophisticated representatives (*ME* 1.1). The harmony of the two testaments would become clear to those Manichaeans who taught Augustine their incompatibility, if only "you listen to the learned men of the Catholic Church with as peaceable a disposition, and with the same zeal, as I had when for nine years I attended on you" (*ME* 18.34).

Yet Augustine's own attendance on Ambrose's biblical exegesis yielded limited results. He had the same difficulty understanding or appreciating the book of Isaiah recommended to him by Ambrose (*Conf* 9.5.13) as he had had with respect to the books of Moses a decade earlier. He had not yet learned the proper interpretive method, but could only passively receive its results from others. Left to his own amateur devices, he could only come away from his effort with the enigmatic proverb, "Unless you believe, you shall not understand" (Isaiah 7:9 LXX—*LA* 1.2.4, 2.2.6.). His earliest post-conversion writings show significant familiarity only with the wisdom books[38] and the Psalms,[39] to which he appears to have gravitated for their accessibility as spiritual poetry. He had acquired only a few allegorical solutions to the specific problematic passages highlighted by the Manichaeans, but assumed that the others must have similar esoteric meanings. So, "having already heard many parts of the sacred books explained in a reasonable way and acceptable way, I came to regard those passages which had previously struck me as absurd, and therefore repelled me, as holy and profound mysteries" (*Conf* 6.5.8). In this way, he shows the same culturally conditioned assumption as had led him to await the inner meaning of the Manichaean myths for so long; his new faith in the mysteries of the Nicene Christians ran closely parallel to his prior faith in those of the Manichaeans.

Yet once he had opened himself to the Old Testament, Augustine unavoidably altered the context in which he would understand the New Testament. The sharp dualisms of the latter, so amenable to a Manichaean interpretation, recede when conjoined to the overwhelming dominance in the Old Testament of the theme of God's complete, irresistible control of the world, and his causal role in all that occurs. Once he accepted on authority the equal canonical status of the Old Testament, he could be led to see the undeniable continuities of theological and ethical outlook between the testaments (*ME* 1.2), and the substantial body of such parallels he could cite in *The Morals of the Catholic Church* probably derives from his instruction as a *competent* in the spring of 387. The virtuous conduct that Nicene Christian and Manichaean alike considered the manifestation of one's love of and devotion to God is enjoined, he argued, in the Old and New Testaments alike (*ME* 16.26–29, 19.35–25.46). Nonetheless, Augustine familiarized himself with the Bible only gradually and selectively, and how much his use of it amounted to meeting performative expectations rather than his own deep investment must remain an open question. In his *Retractationes*, Augustine repeatedly excuses weaknesses in his use of the Bible in his early writings on the grounds that he was not very familiar with its content at the time. Biblical verses fail to enter into his private correspondence until after his ordination as a priest in 391

The Augustine of the Italian dialogues confidently airs the opinion that he has established himself within a clear moral program by which he thinks he can both discipline his body's desires and purify his mind of its delusions. As a Manichaean, Augustine had never felt the calling to adopt the celibate life of the Elect. From the Manichaean point of view, the individual need not take the step of commitment to celibacy in this immediate lifetime, as there would be future lifetimes in which to advance toward moral perfection. For this reason, Manichaeans did not demand celibacy of those who were not ready for it (*Faust* 30.4). Augustine's interest in being free of the burdens and responsibilities of family, consonant with Cicero's valorization of the repose of singleness for philosophical reflection, had been held in check by his attachment to sex, his secular ambitions, and a lack of complete conviction in the ideological underpinnings of the Manichaean disciplinary and ritual system (*UC* 8.20). As a Manichaean, he had believed "that continence must be achieved by one's own strength, a strength of which I was not conscious in my own case" (*Conf* 6.11.20).[40] Still believing that moral discipline was self-willed, he now discovered within himself the ability to will himself not to take a wife (*Sol* 1.10.17). The theory of will and responsibility available to Augustine as a convert and essential to the system he put together at the time made it difficult for him to conceive of his transformation as an act of grace, as he later would when supplied with new conceptual resources (*Conf* 6.11.20).

A greater urgency for moral perfection entered Augustine's thoughts. In Ambrose, Augustine was dealing with, as Peter Brown expresses it, "the most enthusiastic advocate of absolute virginity, 'the one thing that separates us from the beasts'."[41] This ascetic strain in Ambrose's rhetoric, coupled with the idealization of singleness in the *Hortensius*, which Augustine was rereading in 386, certainly helped to shape his conviction that conversion and baptism would necessitate celibacy for him—an ideal common to "philosophers," Manichaeans, and ascetically inclined non-Manichaean Christians alike. J. Kevin Coyle observes that "as a Manichaean he had tried to live as an 'ordinary believer' and it had not worked"; now, "he would make an all-out effort to be an 'electus' of Christ."[42]

In analyzing the difference between the Manichaean and Nicene ethical programs, Augustine later would conclude that the rules dividing the conduct of the Elect from that of Auditors were too absolute and intimidating, whereas in Nicene Christianity all were encouraged to take up the degree of ascetic discipline they could manage (*ME* 33.71–73). This voluntary scale of practices was more encouraging and flexible, Augustine contended, and therefore easier to approach and attempt. Somewhat contrived, this rationalized contrast nonetheless may reflect the way Augustine actually experienced things at the time, finding in the Nicene Christian community an attitude toward ascetic conduct that made it less fraught with implications of commitment. A Christian voluntarily observing ascesis did not, by the occasional indulgence of wine or even sex, lose his or her place in the community. Ascetic achievements were applauded, while lapsing into the ordinary ethic of the broader community was viewed as a return to normalcy between exceptional performances. Manichaean Auditors could follow the same pattern of periodic ascetic observances with no problem. But membership among the Manichaean Elect required a perpetually ascetic lifestyle that placed an all-or-nothing demand on the individual.

At the same time, Augustine acquired a new model of the self that may have facilitated moral decisiveness. John Mourant has stressed the centrality in Augustine's conversion story of his rejecting the Manichaean account of the divided will.[43] Augustine had interpreted Manichaean teachings on the dualistic character of the self to mean that he was personally exonerated for his moral failures and weaknesses. The concept of a unified, monadic soul found among Neoplatonists and non-Manichaean Christians may have provided some sort of workable model by which Augustine could make moral demands upon himself that he apparently could not as a Manichaean. It is precisely in finally taking responsibility for all sides of his own internal dialogue that Augustine appears to have found the will power to commit to the change of life to celibacy and detachment from worldly gain.[44] He saw in the ascetic ethic he had adopted "the life by which we become worthy of knowing what we believe" (*ME* 20.37). As we have seen, Augustine reaffirmed the skeptical reservations about the human ability to know to which both Cicero and Faustus had urged him, and with that decision rejected as "perverse and preposterous" the notion that knowledge "will make us perfect, when this is the reward of those already perfect" (*ME* 25.47). We must accept on authority the moral instruction that will train and prepare us to become effective knowers.

While Augustine articulated a clear role for ascetic discipline in his new identity and program of self-development, the same cannot be said of religious ritual. Augustine makes no mention of attending church services or participating in Christian ritual after the week following his initial baptism and communion in April 387 until his visit to Hippo in 391, either in the works he composed at the time, or even in the *Confessions*. This silence, while proving nothing with certainty about his conduct, indicates a disinterest in religious ritual as a means of forming himself as a subject. Augustine viewed his initial baptism and eucharist as a rite of initiation into the Christian mysteries, providing purification from mental fixation on the material world. At the time of Augustine's ordination to the priesthood four years later, he confessed to bishop Valerius that he had little familiarity with church ritual (*Ep* 21.1–2). He assumed that all such liturgical rites were symbolic representations of inner truths rather than efficacious acts, and that they functioned as alternative means of instruction for the less philosophically inclined.[45] Such a view, shared by his initiator Ambrose, stands in stark opposition to Manichaean ritual theory. Yet it was so embedded in cultural models of the mysteries that we must wonder if Augustine had only started to think along these lines as a convert, or if his attitude toward ritual offers another example of his conversion marking a return to the values of the broader culture from which he had been expected to deviate as a Manichaean, but without really taking to it.

In place of ritual, which was the proper purview of priests, Augustine the philosopher planned to support ethical and intellectual self-development through literary pedagogy. In the immediate aftermath of his baptism, he drafted plans for a corpus of digests on the liberal arts, intended to provide a complete curriculum of mental training (*Ord* 2.14.34ff.; *Sol* 2.34–35). He began to outline and compose treatises on grammar, dialectic, rhetoric, music, geometry, arithmetic, and philosophy.[46] These subjects would serve to help train the human mind to withdraw from the world of sense into the intelligible principles which provided the world's order and were more properly the object of the mind's contemplation.[47] The literary program, therefore, can be understood in the context of his commitment to Neoplatonic conceptions of the soul's state and its need for cultivation. Yet the particular program is not specifically Neoplatonic in inspiration,[48] but finds antecedents in Varro,[49] in the skeptical New Academy (reported by Cicero in his *Academics*, a major part of Augustine's reading at this time),[50] and in the Pythagorean tradition.[51] Indeed, given the eclecticism evident in Augustine's *Order*, we may be witness to another point where Augustine brought together a number of distinct sources, finding in Neoplatonic writings an affirmation of Pythagoras as the ultimate source of philosophical wisdom that accorded with his own preexisting engagement with Pythagorean material, dating back to his Manichaean years, in such areas as aesthetics, metaphysics, mathematics, and astronomy. Now, as a convert to Platonism and Nicene Christianity, he maintained his high regard for Pythagoras unabated, identifying him as the paradigmatic sage (*Ord* 2.20.53–54) in the immediate context of outlining his own liberal arts program (*Ord* 2.11.30–16.44).[52] In fact, Porphyry's *Life of Pythagoras* 46–47 contains the main elements of the scheme of spiritual progress Augustine planned.

Augustine fully recognized that substantial continuities existed between his former Manichaean allegiances and his new Platonic and Nicene Christian ones. Indeed, in *The Morals of the Catholic Church* he self-consciously outlined the common set of premises about the conditions and aims of human existence he regarded as shared by Manichaean, Platonist, and Nicene Christian alike: human beings, constituted of a soul that uses a body as an instrument (*ME* 4.6), strive to obtain a permanent and stable happiness in the good (*ME* 3.4); we rely for our existence and our aspiration for happiness on the existence of a God who is concerned at least with the fate of our souls (*ME* 6.10); the soul strives for betterment in reasoning and learning (*ME* 5.8), which depends upon moral improvement and the acquisition of virtue (*ME* 6.9) learned from a superior being, either a sage or a god, but ultimately from the one God who provides the assurance that the instruction is certain (*ME* 6.10), since the ordinary human mind is obscured by ignorance, and so cannot directly perceive God or truth; we must be guided by such authority to any truths beyond these basic premises until we are made virtuous enough to perceive truth for ourselves (*ME* 7.11) by our faith in spiritual authority and our adherence to moral precepts (*ME* 7.12). By his conversion, Augustine had questioned none of these premises that reflect Manichaeism of a specifically Faustian variety, but had discovered a system of thought and practice by which he seems to have thought they could be better realized.

In the same early post-conversion period, Augustine surveyed a long list of "matters most abstruse" he considered as yet unresolved in his thinking. The list reads as a litany of Manichaean challenges to Nicene Christianity of the sort Augustine had learned to deploy to differentiate himself from non-Manichaean Christians:

> How so many evils come to pass, although God is omnipotent, and effects nothing evil; for what purpose did he make the world, though he had need of nothing; whether evil always was, or began in time; and if it always was, then was it under God's control; and if it was, then whether this world also, wherein the evil is curbed by divine order, always was; but if the world had a beginning sometime, how was evil held in check by divine power before that time; what need was there to construct a world in which evil, which divine power had already controlled, was included for punishment of souls; if, however, there was a time when evil was not under God's dominion, what suddenly happened which had not happened before throughout the eternal years? (*Ord* 2.17.46)

How should we understand a "Catholic" Augustine who does not yet have "Catholic" answers to such questions, answers which could have played no part in his attraction and conversion to either Platonism or Nicene Christianity? What, other than such issues, had been at stake in his conversion, then? While Augustine goes on in *Order* to indicate that he no longer considers the Manichaean answers, at least in their mythic form, intellectually respectable, he is not yet in a position to pose alternatives. His commitment to Platonism and Nicene Christianity preceded his awareness of any definitive position they had to offer on these questions. Rather, that prior commitment decided the limits of where he would henceforth look for answers.

The Setting of Salvation

Augustine's conversion entailed placing his self-conception in a larger universe different from that provided by the Manichaean world view. In the words of Robert O'Connell, Augustine came to see that all the difficulties in his intellectual progress were "*of a kind* which the Manichaean style of thinking was unable to furnish; their minds worked far more comfortably along lines of mythical and imaginative conceptions than with the incorporeal mathematical abstractions and metaphysical realities familiar to the Platonists." He came to see, from the hindsight perspective of an exciting new world view, that he had been hindered by "the need for changing his whole *manner* of thinking."[53] This change in his thinking had two principal features: the disenfranchisement of materially based concepts of reality, and a nondualist affirmation of God's providential omnipotence. These two key shifts in the way he conceptualized the environment of selfhood had the effect of removing the chief obstacles to his confidence in his ability to make spiritual progress. By isolating God and the soul in an intelligible dimension distinct from the rest of reality, and at the same time projecting God's control throughout the rest of reality, and thereby denying the existence of any serious impediment to God's will, he adopted a presumption of inevitability to the soul's liberation from its current existential predicament, reducing that predicament to a matter of the soul's own free choice of orientation. It is in this respect that Augustine's conversion can be accurately characterized as an "optimistic" turn.

Augustine famously declared that he wished to know only God and the soul, nothing more (*Sol* 1.2.7). With these words he signaled a continuation of the identification of the human being with the soul rather than the body that he already displayed as a Manichaean,[54] and a conviction that, as souls, we bear a uniquely close connection to God. As Phillip Cary has noted, "Every philosophy that Augustine had any deep interest in at the time of his earliest writings taught that the soul is in some way divine."[55] As either a Manichaean or a Platonist Christian, Augustine could express belief that the soul preexisted in a state unsullied by materiality, and would return to that state in the end (*Acad* 2.9.22).[56] He retained the idea that individual souls derive from a single or collective entity,[57] even as he struggled to reconceptualize it from its earlier Manichaean materialist setting to a Platonic one premised on the indivisibility of the immaterial soul.[58] The soul free of the body would manifest its inherent likeness to God in its immortality, and even in a certain kind of immutability characteristic of the intelligible (*IA* 10.17; *Liber XXI sent.* 19).

Such optimism concerning the soul's possibilities did not bring with it any less pessimism about the ultimate valuelessness of the material universe, despite the tendency of modern scholarship to highlight positive rhetoric about the world in Augustine's early writings. He continued to believe that most of the limitations he experienced in his own being were the result of embodiment, a common trope of his culture reflected equally in Manichaean, Nicene Christian, and Platonic discourse.[59] The soul suffers in conditions of imprisonment, limitation, and ignorance in its embodied state (*Ord* 1.10.29). In its vulnerability to such bondage, the soul—unlike God—is "often mistaken and deceived" (*DQ* 1). What is good about the soul is to be found in acts of mentation removed as far as possible from everything that possesses physicality. For "all authentic value begins only when the soul takes its distance from the mortal body and its defilement, learns to hold body and bodily creation in contempt and to reserve its love for its own true, incorporeal self" (*QA* 33.73; cf. *Ord* 1.1.3).[60]

In shifting the basis of the soul's identification with God from a common essence or substance to a common immateriality, Augustine might be said to simply adopt a different language to express the same basic idea, that the soul belongs with God rather than with the rest of material reality. His early writings show him struggling, just as Plotinus struggled, to purge the concept of immateriality of lingering materialist ways of thinking. He had to overcome the counterintuitiveness of the very idea of the immaterial.[61] Nonetheless, he seems to have regarded the change of epistemic setting as significant in its implications for the way he thought about the relationship of the soul to God.

Augustine signals his intended departure from a materialist metaphysics by an appeal to the paradigm of mathematics. The purely abstract intellectual quality of numbers and equations provided a clear example of something distinct from the realm of the senses. In the world, reason takes pleasure only in beauty, "and in beauty, design; and in design, dimensions; and in dimensions, number," and by comparing the base sensory datum to the intellectual principles that render it pleasing, reason determines that "nothing which the eyes beheld could in any way be compared with what the mind discerned" (*Ord* 2.15.42; cf. *Ep* 3.40). Mind is distinguished from mere sensory apprehension by its level of abstraction, working with the discernment of pattern, order, or harmony, rather than such individual physical stimuli as smell and taste (*Ord* 2.11.32–33). In this way, the human mind connects with the stable reality of the Platonic forms which underlies the illusion of meaningful, identifiable things in the flux of sensory data. Since that which is physical is subject to continuous change, it cannot ever be known with the same permanent meaning as a mathematical equation possesses; knowledge, properly so called, requires a stable existent as its object (*DQ* 9). True knowledge, therefore, involves apprehension of the permanent and unchanging element in phenomena that only reason can discern. While Manichaeism, too, reasoned inductively from pleasing properties of things perceived through the senses to the first principle of the good (and correspondingly from displeasing properties to the first principle of the bad), Augustine is undeniably correct in discerning a fundamental shift in thinking from the materialist and aesthetic premises of Manichaean phenomenalism to the abstract formalism of Neoplatonism.[62]

The concept of the immaterial allowed Augustine to disparage and negate physical reality as beside the point. Although the things of the material world, like those of the intelligible world, have been created by God, and "are wonderful and beautiful when considered by themselves," nevertheless "in comparison with the things that truly exist, they are as nothing" (*QA* 33.76). God created the material world as an inferior order of being, meant to be subject to human souls; but by admiring and desiring what was beneath them, rather than God who is above them, souls went astray (*ME* 21.39). The soul properly is to love only God, "and as regards all other things, must either rule them as subject to himself, or treat them with a view to their subjection" (*ME* 24.44). Accordingly, he rejects the idea that animals and plants possess souls, or that an exchange of souls between them and humans takes place through transmigration. He ridicules "tree-huggers"—to use a modern phrase that captures his sentiment—who subscribe to "a certain kind of utterly crude perversion which is more wooden than the very trees it takes under its wings, and which believes that the vine suffers pain when a grape is plucked, and that such things not only feel it when they are cut, but even that they see and hear" (*QA* 33.71). From the Manichaean who would not tolerate harm to "so much as a fly," Augustine had become someone who insisted that no community of rights pertained between humans and animals or plants (*MM* 13.27, 18.52), that they are not entitled to our empathy (*MM* 17.62) even though they do suffer pain (*MM* 16.52).

Even when it came to human suffering and death, the concept of the immaterial freed Augustine from addressing such experiences within the problem of evil. He considered human death as punitive because unnatural for the soul, not for the body. The death of animals as of the human body is not evil, but natural as part of the mutability of material things. The soul's fall into connection with the body causes it to undergo the unnatural experience of death through its vicarious attention and attachment to the body; but the soul itself does not die, and Augustine defines happiness as entirely a matter of the soul's ultimate condition, irrespective of the fate of the body (*BV* 2.14; *ME* 5.8). The ultimate irrelevance of mortality to the soul's destiny allowed Augustine to dismiss from consideration any natural evil, and to define evil exclusively in terms of the soul's self-inflicted degradation by its orientation toward material things, including an erroneous material conception of its own identity.

Nicene Christian doctrine fairly clearly taught the physical resurrection of the dead. But Augustine demurs, uncomfortable in accepting such a teaching literally.[63] His earliest post-conversion writings lack any substantial reference to the last judgment, or the eschatological kingdom of God. In continuity with his belief as a Manichaean about the soul's ascent apart from the body, he prefers the Platonic scenario of a return of the soul to its original disembodied and static state (*Ord* 1.8.23–24; *Sol* 1.2.4, 1.6.12–1.7.14, 1.13.23; *QA* 33.76),[64] even if he rapidly comes to qualify that ultimate perfection as not being "entirely what [God] is, but in nearness to him, and in wonderful and immaterial contact with him, and in being inwardly illuminated and occupied by his truth and holiness" (*ME* 11.18). Augustine envisions this nearness in terms of the Platonic intelligible world, which he considers the reality expressed behind Christian language of the Kingdom of God.[65]

Augustine found what he regarded as a natural coordination between moral aspirations to detachment from the physical world, shared across many traditions in his environment, and a metaphysics that identified the realm of truth with a purely immaterial dimension. He interpreted the common religious and philosophical rhetoric of his time enjoining disregard for material things as entailing a metaphysical distinction between one's self and material reality per se. He reasoned, "the mysteries carry the injunction that whoever desires to restore himself to the state in which he was made by God, that is, like to God, should condemn all corporeal things and renounce the whole world, which, as we see, is corporeal" (QA 3.4). "God then alone is to be loved" as that to whose likeness we desire to return "and all this world, that is, all sensible things, are to be despised," just as Paul tells us to look to things unseen rather than those seen, implicitly condemning as error veneration of the physical world, such as the Manichaean reverence for the sun and moon (ME 20.37). The wise person worships God alone, "bringing in no creature as an object of adoration whom we should be required to serve," and turning one's back on "everything made, everything liable to change, everything under the power of time" (ME 30.62). Inquiry into material reality is a vain pursuit that breeds pride, a false confidence in one's knowledge, and the mistaken idea that all things are material or material-like (ME 21.38).

While acknowledging in his former Manichaean associates an authentic aspiration to ascetic withdrawal from the worldly concerns that entangled ordinary people, he concluded that their good intentions could not be successfully realized within a Manichaean world view that had failed to transcend a materialist apprehension of reality. Faustus had been wrong, therefore, to consider a virtuous life in itself sufficient in the absence of certainty of the ultimate form of metaphysical Truth. Progressing in virtue necessitated a foundation on a correct understanding of the nature of reality by which the role of virtue could be defined.

> But whoever is still a slave to his passions or is keenly desirous of perishable goods, or, *even though he flee from these and live a virtuous life*, yet if he does not know what pure nothing is, what formless matter is, what a lifeless informed being is, what a body is, what species in a body is, what place and time are, what "in a place" and "at a time" signify, what local motion is, what non-local motion is, what stable motion is, what eternity is, what it is to be neither in a place nor nowhere, what is beyond time and forever, what it is to be nowhere and nowhere not to be, what it is to be never and never not to be—anyone who does not

know these matters, and yet wishes to question and dispute about even his own soul, let alone investigating about the most high God, who is better known by knowing what he is not, such a one will fall into every possible error. (*Ord* 2.16.44)

Here Augustine pitches Neoplatonist principles against the inadequacies of Manichaeism as a means to transcend the world. Manichaeans entered into their notorious disputationness[66] with a deficient materialist repertoire of concepts, while via the skeptical reserve promoted by Faustus treating an ethical system as an end in itself.[67] The latter involves the merely civic virtues of the material world, whereas philosophical concepts provide the soul with the wings by which it will fly back to its supercelestial home.

Augustine had happily abandoned the crude anthropomorphisms of the Christianity of his youth in favor of the Manichaean proposition that the likeness of humans to God was in the soul, not in the physical form. Yet the Manichaean teaching that God and soul shared a substantial connection ran counter, in Augustine's opinion, to the natural hierarchy of being by which the soul cannot be all that God is.[68] He perceived a danger in focusing exclusively on shared attributes between God and the soul, that one "should fall away by pride from him to whom it should be united by love" (*ME* 12.20). He identified such pride in himself as the obstacle to his own self-disciplinary reform, since he viewed his soul as naturally saved in its divinity, and waited passively for this salvation to work itself out.

It is impossible to overestimate the significance for all of Augustine's later thought of his conversion to an understanding of the human soul that differentiated it from God's nature. His conviction that the human soul is a created thing established the essential limiting premise that constrained Augustine's otherwise free use of Platonic ideas of immateriality in his exploration of the nature of the soul. He decided that humans are animated not by a portion of the divine, but by a sustaining act of God that functions immaterially. That is, nothing substantial is imparted, but a force is exerted that maintains us in existence.[69] This new understanding of the soul's relationship to God reorients it from a partnership to a dependence, in which God looks upon the fallen soul not in sympathy but in judgment.

In the end, however, all of Augustine's rational argumentation for the Platonic premise of the immateriality of the soul came up against the insurmountable empirical observation that lizard tails keep moving after they are severed from the body. If the soul were not a *quantum* that could be divided, how could this observation, which directly contradicts Plotinus's assertion that life cannot be broken into parts (Plotinus, *En.* 6.4.3), be explained? (*QA* 31.62). Augustine and Alypius had made a similar observation of worms in Liguria—when bisected they continued to live separately, and touching one did not provoke a reaction in the other separated part. Augustine, frankly unable to account for this phenomenon, despaired that one little worm would undermine all the reason he had marshaled in support of the thesis of the immaterial soul (*QA* 31.63–64)—the complaint of a deductivist whose first principles are confronted with an incommensurable datum. He could only beg that the problem be deferred (*QA* 32.68), although in the remaining forty years of his career he would never return to solve it.

Augustine considered himself to have taken in his conversion a progressive step to an understanding of God more advanced not only than the popular anthropomorphism he already disparaged as a Manichaean, but also than the one he had held himself as a Manichaean, believing that God exists in space, that he moves from one place to another, and even the "wild profanity" that he changes (*ME* 10.17). Whether we think of Augustine's shift from a materialist concept of spiritual substance to an immaterialist one in terms of monism, or of omnipresence, or of timelessness—all of which had significance for Augustine at various points of his developing theology—its primary initial value to him concerned God's transcendent immunity to any other force or will in the universe. He considered the Manichaean idea of an evil force able to disturb God as equally offensive to intellectual and popular concepts of God. "But if you say that evil has been troublesome and, as it were, antagonistic to God—as very many think—no learned man will repress his laughter, and every unlearned man will be indignant" (*Ord* 2.17.46). Augustine recontextualized persistent features of his theology from a dualistic to a monistic setting that offered a providential order of all things in line with a single, unopposed will (i.e., what I term a *monothelite* cosmology).[70] He could successfully coordinate Nicene Christianity and Neoplatonism on their common conception of a universe completely in the power of a single divine source of being and order. He systematically downplayed dualistic elements in Plotinus, perhaps assisted in this by the existing dominant interpretive tradition within both Neoplatonism and Platonic Christianity. He had not come to fundamentally new ideas of God's character and purpose, but only of his power, eliminating the uncertainty of human destiny entailed in theoretical dualism; creation *ex nihilo* and the goodness of cosmic order follow as corollaries to this primary premise of omnipotence. Augustine regards as sacrilegious, "no sooner stated than to be condemned," the Manichaean idea that God could not automatically have his way, lacked complete freedom of action, or might in some way be vulnerable (*Conf* 7.2.3). A vulnerable God would be no God at all (*Conf* 7.4.6). "Thus," Scott MacDonald concludes, "Augustine's mature understanding of the divine nature was not merely incompatible with the Manichaeanism of his youth but a pointed rejection of it."[71]

With the cosmic "optimism" of defining God in terms of uncompromised power, Augustine *temporarily* found a new epistemic setting for his longstanding belief in providence and determined fate, whether he had expressed that belief in the terms of astrology or of Manichaeism; so such ideas carried over briefly into his post-Manichaean thinking. At first this takes the form of a return to familiar Greco-Roman rhetoric concerning fortune, which Augustine employs throughout his early post-conversion writings (e.g., *Acad* 1.1.1, 1.9.25, 2.1.1, 2.3.9, 3.2.2, 3.2.4; *Ord* 2.9.27), much to his later discomfort (*Retr* 1.1.2, 1.3.2). Consistent with this traditional discourse, as well as his previous Manichaean fatalism, he at times expresses acknowledgment of the happenstance character of the condition and circumstances in which one finds oneself in life, "because of our desserts or because of the exigency of nature."[72] He argues in *The Academics* that fortune is a necessary condition of wisdom, because it can so shape an individual's life and state that the acquisition of wisdom is either possible or impossible (*Acad* 3.2.2–4).[73] Yet he opens the work offering to propound to his Manichaean patron Romanianus a "philosophy" that "in declarations of doctrines most fruitful and far removed from the understanding of the uninitiated . . . promises to make clear" the idea that "what is commonly called 'fortune' is governed by a secret ordinance . . . and nothing is either helpful or harmful to the part which does not turn out to be helpful to, and fit in with, the whole" (*Acad* 1.1.1).

Augustine as a Manichaean had already been exploring models of cosmic order. The adherents of Mani were taught that the relative order discernible in nature reflected God's active efforts to limit and control chaotic evil in a dualistic universe, in this way qualifying God's providence within the context of the well-established Christian belief in a powerful, sometimes personified force dividing the cosmos and alienating it from God. In a dualistic universe, all that occurs does not need to be rationally harmonized to a single master purpose; indeed, dualism is a compelling solution to the irreconcilable nature of the contradictions in events, and their inability to be fitted into the intention of a single will. The Manichaeans recognized that a dualistic universe would necessarily produce accidental outcomes, and that the capacity of any individual to comprehend the truth and adhere to the liberating disciplines would be contingent on forces beyond the control of the individual or even of God. By his conversion, Augustine clearly chooses to leave behind this sort of fatalistic indeterminism for a more secure providential order of things.

Augustine had employed this Manichaean identification of the divine good with cosmic order in his Manichaean-period treatise, *The Beautiful*, synthesizing it there with Pythagorean models. The constructs he now employed in his post-Manichaean work *Order* were in striking continuity with that earlier work. In both texts, he identified order as a secondary state pertinent only to this world, where it was necessary to harmonize and balance the differentiated content of the cosmos. When all things are equally good, order is unnecessary. Order arises as an abiding echo of oneness in the multiplying complexity of the phenomenal world. Since that complexity entails widely divergent degrees of goodness, its coordination is by definition hierarchical (*Ord* 2.1.2). In fact, "this orderly arrangement maintains the harmony of the universe by this very contrast" of good and evil. As a Manichaean, Augustine had been taught that the order in the universe reflected God's successful mastery of an agonistic situation; but now he had come to see it as something more foreordained and unopposed. "In this way the beauty of all things is in a manner configured, as it were, from antitheses, that is, from opposites" (*Ord* 1.7.19).

By drawing out the monistic implications of his own earlier Pythagorean studies, therefore, Augustine breaks decisively with any dualist background to his understanding of the purpose and nature of order. There is no more opposition to be reconciled. God's omnipotence precludes anything occurring outside or in defiance of order. Order therefore includes the totality of cause and effect (*Ord* 1.6.15). In a probably deliberate anti-Manichaean rhetorical gesture, Augustine declares that, "Both good things and bad are in order" (*Ord* 1.6.16), subsuming the stark dichotomy to a sliding scale of better and worse (*Ord* 1.7.19).[74] The notion of such a decisively controlling order, rather than just the intention of order that the Manichaean God strives to assert against an opposing force of disorder, makes all the difference to Augustine's sense of the sure possibility of liberation from the material world. This optimistic sense of providence, rooted in the concept of God's omnipotence, marks one of the points where Augustine chose an element in his Christian sources that accentuated difference from his former Manichaeism.

Those who have stressed a fundamental continuity between Augustine's earlier and later thought have pointed to the clear presence of such ideas of fate and providence in his earliest post-conversion writings, and compared them to the themes of determinism and grace that begin to take center stage in his writings decades later. They overlook, however, the near total disappearance of such concepts in works from the intervening period, and in fact Augustine's programmatic rejection of deterministic elements from the theory of human moral responsibility he developed between 388 and 396. As Augustine rationalized his new beliefs, developing their systematic character and sharpening their contrast to Manichaeism, the value of free choice as a nonessentialist explanation of evil pushed notions of providence to the margins of his commitments. Only when the Manichaean Fortunatus, in their public debate in Hippo in 392, demonstrated to him the superior Manichaean reading of both human experience and the words of Paul was Augustine forced to reconsider the erosion of providence from its once prominent place in his world view.

By embracing the idea of an omnipotent God who providentially governed the universe, Augustine adopted a programmatic orientation toward experience that simply denied the possibility of real evil. All injury is self-inflicted in this new universe; nothing that happens to us can in any real sense be tragic or unjust. Augustine had not gone out in search of a new conception of evil, but came to one as a logical consequence of other, more central commitments to beliefs about the transcendent nature of God and the soul. We might apply usefully to this "optimistic" choice Augustine presents in his early post-conversion writings the concept of "systematic healthy-mindedness" coined by William James in his classic *Varieties of Religious Experience*, by which he means a programmatic self-orientation and discursive strategy within which a person "deliberately excludes evil from its field of vision."[75] As James indicates, selective censorship of sensitivity to evil can "grow into a deliberate religious policy, or *parti pris*."[76] By its conscious, systematic character, "The deliberate adoption of an optimistic turn of mind thus makes entrance into philosophy."[77] Adopted consciously, as a matter of policy, it is injected into the self, into the psychological realm, from discourse. Through this activity, we can see the thin perimeter of discursive selfhood working on both interior states and external conditions to bring both into conformity with its optimistic viewpoint.[78]

Consistently with this orientation, Augustine argues that evil, from one perspective, is no more than an uninformed and excessively narrowed focus on events. From God's vantage point, all is in good order. For "whoever narrow-mindedly considers this life by itself alone is repelled by its enormous foul-ness, and turns away in sheer disgust. But if he raises the eyes of the mind and broadens his field of vision and surveys all things as a whole, then he will find nothing unarranged, unclassed, or unassigned to its place" (*Ord* 2.4.11). Peo-ple, Augustine explains, "on account of their feeble mentality, are unable to grasp and to study the integral fittingness of things. They think that the whole universe is disarranged if something is displeasing to them, just because that thing is magnified in their perception" (*Ord* 1.1.2).[79] By this epistemological theodicy, there actually is no such thing as evil. Given Augustine's otherwise starkly negative view of material existence, we might expect him to join ranks with other ascetically oriented people of his time in a morbid assessment of human experience in the world as overburdened with evil. But in seeing hu-man engagement with the world as ultimately meaningless and valueless, he could afford to dismiss evil as barely more than a disappointing half-emptiness to a soul intent on filling its glass. There is nothing in Augustine more non-Manichaean than that stance.

Augustine did not find an alternative to the Manichaean materialist, dual-ist account of evil ready-made in Plotinus, despite what he appears to claim in the *Confessions*.[80] Rather, he engaged in a highly selective reading of Plotinus on the question of evil in light of other ideas to which he gave greater atten-tion and importance. His uptake of Plotinus's treatment of evil appears to have been shaped by his initial preference for the epistemological solution just discussed. Consequently, he misread—or performed a misprision on—Plotinus's account of evil. Such a partial reading of Plotinus is not altogether surprising, given the tensions in the latter's system, which most of his follow-ers demonstrate a desire to resolve in a manner that purges some of its more dualistic imagery.[81] Augustine is no different in this respect, and may have de-pended in part on the previous efforts at touching up Plotinus in the century that separated the two men.[82]

In the circumstances in which he encountered Neoplatonism, however, Au-gustine perceived it to offer a powerful alternative to Manichaean dualism. In Plotinus's consideration of the Aristotelian account of evil in terms of a privation of good, Augustine discovered an alternative way to talk about evil that avoided attributing to it the positive characteristics of a being. Although Plotinus uses "being" and "non-being" as value labels, rather than strictly ontological categories (e.g., *En.* 1.8.3),[83] Augustine apparently misread this evaluative rhetoric ontologically by, in a sense, reading through Plotinus back to his Aristotelian source.[84] Augustine's confusion between literal nonexistence and the kind of indeterminateness of substance by which it lacks any particular identity has been noted several times before.[85] Plotinus had appropriated Aristotle's characterization of matter as a way to describe evil, while rejecting Aristotle's own definition of evil in itself as mere privation of good.[86] Whereas Plotinus equates matter and evil, Augustine reseparates the two as part of his avoidance of overtly dualist constructs. When he speaks of *matter*, then, he returns to Aristotle's understanding of it as just a substrate, consistent with Plotinus's more monistic way of handling matter as the furthest point of descent from being, without itself being nonbeing or nonexistent (e.g., Plotinus, *En.* 1.8.7). Matter is for Augustine the least good thing in the universe, but still a good thing, because created by God. Because of this commitment to God's creation of matter, Augustine cannot bring himself to associate it directly with evil as Plotinus does in his more dualistic passages. So he separates the two. All that is left of evil, then, when matter is intellectually extracted from it in this way, is the abstract principle of privation, which nonetheless can still be talked about with Plotinus's language of nonbeing if that language is taken literally, rather than evaluatively as Plotinus himself used it. With this new rhetorical repertoire, Augustine simply finds new ways to garb the standard fourth-century anti-Manichaean Christian denial of ontological status to evil that he no doubt learned in Milan.[87]

From this reworking of his sources, Augustine drew the conclusion, "evil is nothing except a privation of the good" (*malum non esse nisi privationem boni, Conf* 3.7.12).[88] There was, in effect, no room left for evil in a cosmos pervaded by God's order. His literal reading of Plotinus's identification of evil with nonbeing was facilitated by his identification of God with Being itself, in place of Plotinus's assignment of the divine One to a realm "beyond being." Evil cannot be identified with matter, or even exist, without deriving its existence from God,[89] and to ascribe evil's origin to God was impossible for Augustine—either as a Manichaean or as a Nicene Christian. Nor could he accept the existence of something utterly deprived of every modicum of goodness, for such a thing would be in a condition invulnerable to any harm, since it would have nothing good to be harmed. This rather striking conclusion illustrates Augustine's enthrallment to power valuations. He considered the immunity from any further loss that such an utterly deprived thing would possess to be a logically disallowed superiority to the myriad of relatively more good things that still had something to lose (*MM* 5.7). Such a thing's theoretical invincibleness trumped any other measure of its (lack of) goodness in Augustine's hierarchical construct of value.

Yet there remains something profoundly *substantial* about this seemingly immaterial concept of evil. As Olivier du Roy has pointed out, Augustine appears to assume that it has always existed, and that God has had to exert himself to get it under control.[90] William Babcock characterizes Augustine as stuck in a way of talking about evil dictated by Manichaean challenges to God's omnipotence and invulnerability which he had to answer in defining his new faith over against his old one.[91] The Manichaeans posed the problem of evil in a directly theistic context: Why did God create the world in which evil existed? If as a means to contain and control evil, as they taught and as Augustine continued to say in a striking departure from typical Nicene discourse, then what prompted God to this solution? If God already had evil under control, what explained his shift to a new, global strategy of control that entails human suffering? As Babcock assesses the issue,

> The Platonic notion of evil as privation, although certainly at work in both *De ordine* and the *De libero arbitrio*, held no resources for the reduction or the solution of this puzzle. It served well as a weapon against the Manichaean claim that evil has an independent ontic status . . . [and] served the purpose of reducing evil to a parasite upon the good. . . . But it does not account for the origin of evil; and above all, it does not capture the active force of evil as a power exerting itself in opposition to—even if wholly constrained by—the divine design.[92]

In other words, Augustine was working with piecemeal solutions to isolated issues that he had yet—if he ever could—to reduce to a consistent system. He would find temporary relief from this "muddle" by resorting to a free-will account of evil provided by Nicene Christianity.

The Responsible Self

Our picture of Augustine's new identity would be incomplete without a consideration of his own understanding at the time of the limits of answerability, the degree to which human beings are accountable for manifesting their commitments in performance. On this subject we encounter perhaps the most appreciable shift in Augustine's outlook to follow from his conversion, and perhaps also the most significant one in terms of its immediate determination of his self-image and self-expectation. Neoplatonism had little to contribute directly to staking out a distinct position on human agency and ethical answerability,[93] as Augustine apparently discerned. His Manichaean experience may have raised his expectations that cultic discourse would speak more directly to such concerns; and he would have found these expectations met in Ambrose's promotion of a free-choice version of the care-of-self discourse of late antiquity.[94] Consequently, Christian propositions had to do more work for Augustine in this area, and it is the circumstance of turning his attention to it that J. Kevin Coyle has noted in terms of the appearance of a rapid Christianization of Augustine's discourse during his year in Rome, in comparison to his prior post-conversion writings.

The free choice account of evil had become the standard non-Manichaean Christian answer to dualism in the fourth century.[95] The free will position addressed the nature of evil, its cause or origin, and its solution in a systematic way that offered a clear alternative to the equally comprehensive Manichaean position, whatever one's opinion of its cogency. From their considerable common ground within the Christian tradition, Manichaeism and the emergent mainstream orthodoxy had in part developed and come to define themselves in distinction from one another on this subject. Indeed, in the face of its Manichaean rival, Titus of Bostra treats the nondualist definition of evil as human moral failing as the primary doctrine of Nicene Christianity (Titus of Bostra 1.1, 1.3), and, similarly, Julian of Eclanum reminded Augustine late in life that "The greatest difference between Manichaeans and Christians has always been this . . . that we attribute all sin to a bad will, they to a bad nature" (*Iulimp* 1.24). While in Milan, Augustine had heard Ambrose teach "that the cause of evil is the free decision of our will, in consequence of which we act wrongly and suffer [God's] righteous judgment," even if at the time, "I could not clearly discern this" (*Conf* 7.3.5).[96]

One might propose, therefore, a certain inevitability in Augustine's adoption of this quintessential Nicene position on human agency. Yet, as in so many other aspects of his new faith, Augustine discerned an intuited, nonrational, and nondiscursive conviction at the heart of his conversion to the concept of a free will. "I was as much aware that I had a will as that I had a life. And when I willed to do or not to do anything, I was quite certain that it was myself and no other who willed," from which developed the rationalized commitment to the Nicene understanding of sin: "I came to see that the cause of my sin lay there" (*Conf* 7.3.5). Only a year or two earlier, he had been just as sure that when he willed badly, it was not he himself who willed, but some other. Conversion had been enacted in changing what he believed to be true, adopting a new context within which to understand his own conduct, without immediately providing him good reasons to support his new belief.

In Rome in 388, Augustine undertook a deliberate rationalization project to find such good reasons for localizing evil entirely within human choice of action. The preliminary results of his inquiry appear in the first book and a half of *Free Choice* (originally titled *Whence Evil?*), and in notes on the same issue of a more explicitly anti-Manichaean character later incorporated into *The Morals of the Manichaeans*.[97] Although at one point he suggests that the work is meant to recapitulate the thoughts that had led him to his new faith, this appears to be a rhetorical fiction that he frequently employs in those works meant to lead others to his faith. Elsewhere in the work he states that he is working out a rationalization of positions he holds on faith, and he confirms this actual purpose of the work toward the end of his life: "We were to try if possible to let rational argument demonstrate to our intellects what we already believed about the matter on divine authority" (*Retr* 1.8.1). There is no pretense of open inquiry here, since key premises will be accepted without question: God is good; God is just; the universe is governed by God's providence. Denial of these premises is ruled out from the beginning as "sacrilegious" (*nam et hoc negare sacrilegium est, LA* 1.1.1).

In his efforts to solve the problem of evil within these premises for himself and for his readers, Augustine takes a rather "kitchen-sink" approach in his early works, trying everything he can think of without particular concern for consistency. He attempts in one way or another to have an omnipotent, all-creating God who somehow stays out of the picture where evil occurs. He tries, for example, to suggest that God creates only things, not acts or events (*VR* 20.39). Or perhaps God does cause acts and events, too, but these are only misconstrued as evil when they are actually good—such as instructive warnings or the just punishment of sinners which the latter, naturally, experience subjectively as evil. Or perhaps God only causes things and attributes to exist, but is not involved in their passing into nonexistence, and evil can be reduced to this tending to nonexistence (*MM* 2.2–3, 4.6). In fact, Augustine expresses concern that "there is no way of solving the religious question of good and evil" (*MM* 7.10) without somehow moving evil out of the category of things that can be said to exist, since everything that exists, exists from God. That is why knowing what evil is must take priority in solving the problem of its origin (LA 1.1.1; cf. MM 2.2), because one must first characterize evil in such a way that it fits within the premises of Augustine's adopted beliefs; only then can the origin question be addressed within the safe limits of acceptable possible answers.[98]

Augustine made the problem more tractable by fundamentally shifting the grounds of the issue—distinguishing the evil that we do from the evil that we suffer, and denying that the latter counts as evil (LA 1.1.1; cf. VR 12.23, 20.39; GL imp 1.3; Fort 15; Adim 26; Conf 7.3.5). With this surgical division, he removes the bulk of the human experience of evil from consideration, and relieves himself of the burden of accounting for it as anything other than a misunderstanding. Perhaps drawing on his own life experience,[99] Augustine identifies the concept of *punishment* as appropriately fitting the description of something that is experientially evil, and yet from an ultimate perspective good. In his view, such experiences cannot essentially harm the good soul, immune as it is to all occurrences in material reality. The suffering of God's punishment therefore has a pedagogical quality, warning us away from attachment to our physical experiences and circumstances. With all such experiences dismissed from the issue, Augustine had disposed of "natural" evil, and confined the problem to individual human action.

Manichaeans came at the problem of evil from the opposite direction, placing "natural" evil at the center of their exposition of the subject. They could not accept Augustine's epistemological reassignment of some of the human experience of evil to good because they defined evil by the experience of suffering itself.[100] For the Manichaeans, evil is something one suffers, at the hands of either external or internal "others." They insisted that the evident pains and injustices of the world were irreconcilable with God's goodness. God could not be omnipotent master of the forces by which innocents suffered and evil often prevailed in the cosmos. Nor could they accept a God who could only help or instruct people with the crude methods of the switch-wielding schoolmaster. Suffering can only be explained by the presence of something other than and contrary to God with which he is forced to contend.

Even with a large segment of the experience of evil dealt with by Manichaeism set aside as actually the good of just punishment, explaining personal acts of moral evil within the confines of his conception of unresisted order still presented a "difficulty for the mind," Augustine realized. "If sins originate with souls which God has created, and which therefore have their origin from God, how are sins not to be charged against God at least mediately?" (*LA* 1.2.4; cf. *Conf* 7.3.5). He mentions elsewhere that he used to recite this very objection as a Manichaean (*Conf* 4.15.26). He did not yet have an answer. As A. W. Matthews has observed, "Augustine's inability to explain rationally this difficulty does not lead him to lose faith in the premise."[101] At best, he could strive to insulate his transcendent God from responsibility for the failings of that which he has created, even if logically ultimate responsibility is inescapable. In the words of William Babcock, "If God is the author of souls and souls are the authors of evil, then only a narrow interval, a tiny space, separates God from responsibility for evil."[102] Augustine strives to widen this space separating God from the faults of his creation and fill it with the autonomy of the human mind in its free choice of either good or evil.

The broad brush-strokes by which we label Augustine's early theory one of "free will," and the Manichaean theory he was countering "deterministic," obscure what was in fact a very narrow and technical disagreement about relative degrees of agency possessed by the human soul or mind. Augustine and the Manichaeans were staking out differentiated ground on the exact interpretation of standard models of the time on the limitations of human agency in a world shaped by forces beyond human mastery. Most people in the ancient world, recognizing the contingency of their own lives and their inability to control circumstances, accepted varying degrees of determinism. In the classical formulation of the Stoic Chrysippus, events are determined through two complementary channels: the determination of external conditions, and the determination of the nature of the agent. "If auxiliary and proximate causes are not in our power it does not follow that even impulse is not in our power . . . For although assent cannot take place unless it has been prompted by a presentation, yet . . . assent has this (presentation) as its proximate, not principal cause." Whatever is presented to the mind for assent cannot instill assent into the mind, but only elicit an assent already potentially there in the nature or character of the mind to which it is presented. "Just as someone who pushes a drum forward gives it a beginning of movement, but not its capacity to roll, so the visual object which presents itself . . . will mark its image on the mind; but assent will be in our power and . . . once it has been given an external stimulus it will move itself for the rest by its own force and nature" (Cicero, *Fato* 41–43; cf. Aristotle, *De anima* 3.10–11). Our assent to any external determination of conditions depends upon a corresponding *volubil-*

ity (literally, "rollability") in our nature, which amounts to a kind of internal determination, since we will always act in accord with our nature. "Each of the things brought about . . . comes about compulsorily, in accordance not with the necessity that results from force, but with that resulting from its being impossible for that which has a nature of that sort to be moved at that time in some other way and not this" (Alexander of Aphrodisias, *De fato* 181.18ff.).

Manichaean "determinism" simply lays a dualistic construct of reality over this Stoic, "common sense" understanding of human agency.[103] The person is constituted of two distinct natures, either of which may "surface" depending on which nature prevails over the person in that moment—determining the presentations to which one gives attention, prompting impulses, managing the reasoning process that generates assent, and carrying forward actions. By bifurcating the human being, the Manichaeans complicated the Stoic distinction between external and internal realms of determinacy by considering much of our internal space, so to speak, as external space. In opposition to ancient and widespread religious ideas about spiritual pollution, which imagined it to be a contamination of the exterior of the body that could be washed away ritually, Manichaeism taught that the body was insurmountably vulnerable to penetration by the polluting forces of evil. Through eating, respiration, and other metabolic functions, the body was constantly going through reformulation according to the elements it was taking in from its environment;[104] and since the soul, too, had a material nature, it was equally implicated in this constant mixing with other forces in its environment. Consequently, things happened within the person just as they happened in the world around, as effects of various causes that the human will could do nothing about.[105] Although this condition can be characterized as "deterministic" in that a person's state is determined by factors outside his or her control, from another angle we might better term it "indeterministic" or "fatalistic" in its largely random and accidental character.[106] This ongoing vulnerability of the soul to environmental influences gave the path to salvation an agonistic, back-and-forth quality expressed ritually in the Manichaean practice of confession and absolution.

Ontological Freedom

The various ways in which Augustine regarded the soul as not simply other than, but also apart from and immune to, material reality had the effect of cutting off any possible coercive role for a substantial evil, and bringing the locus of sinfulness back into the soul itself. Such a view correlated well with the non-Manichaean Christian emphasis on free will.[107] Continuing earlier ideas he had developed in his Manichaean treatise *The Beautiful*, Augustine assumed that order is a distinctive trait of a world where good and evil—or, put within the more monistic terms of his new thinking, better and worse— coexist, brought into a shadowy reflection of the perfection of the good by being harmonically arranged and managed in a fashion Augustine conceives of as a hierarchy. In his early post-conversion writings we find both this hierarchical concept of order and the convertibility of that hierarchy to power relations descending from the ultimate power of the omnipotent God. Since God's creation must be in order, he argues, and it is contrary to order for the better to be subject to the worse, the mind must be able to command emotions such as lust, and cannot be unwillingly overcome by such desires. Its failure to maintain itself aloof to passion, therefore, must be an act of free choice. Anything strong enough to coerce the human will must necessarily be better in this hierarchical scale of value, and as better would never coerce the will toward the bad (*LA* 1.8.18–11.21). By the simple, unexamined equation of "better" with "more powerful," Augustine can reject the model of external compulsion he understood to be the Manichaean position.[108]

To this more common "scale of being" construct, Augustine added the particular Platonic concept of the immaterial nature of the soul. The soul cannot be coerced to sin, not only because it is "better" and therefore stronger than any physical influence, but also because it occupies a dimension of reality completely different from the material and sensory. By denying the materiality of the soul, Augustine created a fundamental disjunction between the soul and body, to the degree of giving the soul something akin to God's invulnerability, should it not voluntarily forfeit it. The body, he held, cannot unilaterally stimulate the soul, since the two parts of the person have no direct contact. The soul becomes affected by the body only by turning its attention to it, away from its own private introspection of eternal things (*Mus* 6.13.39–40). The soul's isolation from material reality gives it freedom of action, which it could only lose by its own initiative, becoming so entranced by what it is looking at that it, as it were, travels the distance to the object of its gaze and loses its detachment from it. Augustine follows Plotinus in favoring sight as the most suitable paradigm for the soul's contact with material things, since it requires the initiative of the soul and allows it to be affected at a distance where no immediate impingement is possible.

Since the soul is immaterial and cannot be impinged upon or coerced by any material thing, any defective movement it initiates must come from its own free exercise of attention. In this way, Augustine wove into the existing free-choice position of the emerging Nicene Christian tradition the specific fall scenario offered by Plotinus, involving the audacity (*tolma*) of souls, "delighting in their own independence (*autexousion*), and making great use of their self-movement, running the opposite course" and putting themselves in subjection to material things to which their nature made them superior (Plotinus, *En.* 5.1; cf. 6.8). Augustine settled on this particular account of the soul's descent only after sorting through the various alternatives. Around the time of his conversion, Augustine could say no more than that the soul has entered the material realm because "God or nature or necessity or our will or some combination of these has cast us into the world" (*BV* 1.1). By the time he composed *The Quantification of Soul* a year later, he reported that Nicene Christianity teaches that the soul was given to the body to control and direct it (*QA* 36.81); yet he did so with a notable lack of conviction in the doctrine that perhaps betrays a recognition of its proximity to Manichaean teachings (e.g., *Menoch* 186). While Plotinus at times also envisioned this more positive, directed descent scenario, in other instances he maintained that souls had fallen into material existence through error and audacity (e.g., Plotinus, *En.* 5.1; 4.8.3–5),[109] an idea that bore a surface resemblance to the idea of a fall in some strands of the Christian tradition, and typical of allegorical readings of the creation account.[110]

Augustine shows no specific knowledge of the Plotinian concept of *aversio* until his extensive plagiarization of Plotinus in *The Immortality of the Soul* (*IA* 11–12), composed in Milan in the late spring of 387.[111] But from that point forward he latches on to this more "pessimistic" Platonic explanation of the soul's background and its Christian parallel, and ignores in both traditions the alternative "optimistic" account that had a Manichaean analogue. Perhaps this choice should be understood in part in light of Augustine's preference for omnipotence as the defining characteristic of God. If the soul had acted obediently and well in its descent into materiality, God should not permit it to suffer for this descent, and would be in no way constrained to do so. Logically, the scenario of a sinful fall made better sense of the soul's continued predicament under the premised regime of an all-powerful deity. Or perhaps mere reaction to his prior Manichaean understanding of the soul's descent, and a simple desire to distinguish his new commitments as much as possible from his old ones, drove Augustine to his preferences.

For Augustine, people perversely give themselves over to the passions and the glitter of material things, and become so habituated to them that they may appear to be held in the grip of something more powerful than they are. The soul experiences itself to be "dominated by lust, spoiled of its resources of virtue, drawn hither and thither in abject poverty," while "the cupidities exercise their dominion tyrannically and disturb the man's whole mind and life with varying and contrary tempests"—in short, all the experiences to which the Manichaeans point as signs of domination by an alien evil force.

> Wherever it turns it can be restricted by avarice, wasted by luxury, bound by ambition, inflated by pride, tortured by envy, enveloped in sloth, excited by wantonness, afflicted by subjection, suffering all the other countless emotions which inhabit and trouble the realm of lust. Can we think that a condition like that is not penal, when we see that it must be undergone by all who do not cleave to wisdom? (*LA* I.11.22)

In other words, in the fact that sinful people experience sin as overpowering, while good and virtuous people who "cleave to wisdom" remain immune to temptation, we see the proof that these two conditions reflect a moral judgment and a just management of human affairs by God. God permits those who yield to sinful promptings to fall into the ever-tightening grip of a cycle of sin. The Manichaeans are mistaken to see this as a conquest of the will by a more powerful evil other.

Yet the fall of the soul into embodiment only exacerbates the bombardment of tempting presentations from material (ir)reality. It does not alter the fundamental human capacity to say no to these presentations, because the monadic individual soul remains intact and endowed with the capacity for free choice with which it was created. Although Augustine accepts from Christian moral discourse the idea that humans deal with the inherited consequence of mortal embodiment, especially the inrush of sensory experience, he does not recognize any change in the human will and its capacity to operate freely after the fall of Adam and Eve.[112] William Babcock locates the core moral ethos of Augustine's position:

> What shows that we are willing companions of cupidity is not that we once deserted our former virtue, but that we now fail to attain a virtue which we could achieve "with perfect ease," simply by willing it

([*LA*] 1.13.29). Since the will is fully under its own control (1.12.26), he argues, our failure to embrace virtue is not a sign that our moral agency is diminished or impaired. It is rather itself an unimpaired exercise of moral agency, itself the uncompelled choice that marks our cupidity as sin and warrants as just the penalties that follow in its train. Thus it is not our former moral virtue but our present moral failure that vindicates the scheme of sin and penalty in Augustine's thought.[113]

This particular emphasis appears to have been motivated by a desire on Augustine's part to formulate a solution to the problem of evil that did not depend on the idea of the soul's preexistence and the possible causes of its descent. Not all articulations of free will within the Christian tradition shared these Platonic premises of the soul's transcendence, nor for that matter did they necessarily work with the concept of the soul's preexistence and descent. Although evidently inclined toward such ideas, Augustine either did not want to deal with all the issues they entailed, or did not wish to exclude other possible scenarios of the soul's origin. For such reasons, he found it necessary to map a common ground sufficient to accommodate the diverse ways of treating moral responsibility within the traditions with which he now associated. So he worked out a free will argument that would apply equally with or without preexistence. "He locates our decisive exercise of moral agency not in some pre-embodied state, but precisely in the willing that we do, or fail to do, as embodied souls acting in time and history. The morally decisive moment does not occur off stage."[114]

Regardless, then, of any difficulty caused by mortality or the limitations of embodiment that may have occurred as a consequence of a fall of a preexistent entity, the soul or mind remains free, even in a body debilitated by sin, and the individual is able to work toward righteousness (*VR* 15.29). To "believe in God and turn from the love of visible and temporal things to the fulfillment of his precepts" is something that "all have in their power if they will" (*GCM* 1.3.6).[115] Even if sinful desires and affections might be attributed to the physical senses or the promptings of the body, they depend on the will, that is, the consent of reason, to be acted upon (*VR* 14.28). "What obstacle then remains to hinder the soul from recalling the primal beauty which it abandoned, when it can make an end of its vices?" (*VR* 39.72).

Augustine's ontological argument for free choice, however, runs him into some difficulties. By imposing the concept of hierarchy on the Platonic distinction of the intelligible from the material, Augustine creates a muddle of conflicting models of reality. To speak of God and soul as superior on some gradient of being to material things implies continuity rather than distinction between the intelligible and the material. Likewise, the equation of superiority with power leads Augustine into an ill-conceived attempt to demonstrate that the principle of evil as the Manichaeans conceive it would be superior in its invulnerability to their vulnerable God. Since the evil principle possesses no good of which to be deprived, he argues, it is impervious to harm, which by definition is the loss of good.[116] But this line of argument actually turns Augustine's hierarchy of relative good on its head, for by positing invulnerability as a good in itself, rather than in terms of securing a possessed good, Augustine by implication makes everything with less good better, because relatively less vulnerable to a loss of good. Certainly a stone is less vulnerable to being deprived of the few goods it has than a person is to the possible loss of his or her richer store of goods. As James Wetzel points out, in a universe ordered by the principle that inferior things can never subordinate superior things, the soul's voluntary choice can only explain things going wrong by violating that very principle.[117] The soul should not be able to subordinate itself to material things, even if it wishes to, for this would constitute a violation of its nature, like air being able to make itself heavier than water. Moreover, Augustine's anti-Manichaean assertion of the goodness of all things leads him into the predicament of being forced to describe evil in terms of the good soul's turn toward other good things. His hierarchical thinking trumps his monistic reaction to Manichaean dualism, and he simply substitutes a scale of "better" and "worse" in the same evaluative role as that played by the Manichaean polarity of "good" and "evil."

Forensic Freedom

The free choice position Augustine adopted as a convert and developed so carefully in this-worldly terms involved a rather straightforward correspondence with the dominant forensic theory of Greco-Roman law and society, widely enough shared to be considered the *consensus gentium*. If humans did not have free will, then the entire premise of legal systems would be destroyed, and no one could ever be justly punished. Rather than call the mundane principle of human crime and punishment into question, Augustine affirms it as the modus operandi of God himself. Because Augustine believes that God punishes, he must also believe that those who are punished bear culpability. "Every evil man is the author of his evil deeds," because such deeds "would not be justly punished unless they were done voluntarily" (*LA* 1.1.1).[118] Since Augustine has settled a large portion of the problem of evil by explaining it as punishment, he needs a state of affairs that justifies punishment, and according to the familiar legal and ethical paradigms of his culture that means a crime voluntarily, informedly, and willfully committed. Without human guilt by those standards, the whole problem of human suffering, or "natural" evil, looms up again.

Aristotle had framed the Classical forensic criterion for human responsibility, namely the capacity to do otherwise. If a person could not have acted other than he or she did—if one was constrained by circumstances or ignorance of the moral quality of a choice—then no culpability could be assigned to the person (Aristotle, *Nic. Eth.* 3.2–3, 3.5; *Eud. Eth.* 2.6, 2.8–9). Nor can sin be attributed to some overpowering influence that takes away a person's ability rationally to choose what to do. "If the defect we call sin overtook a man against his will, like a fever," Augustine hypothesizes in response to a well-known Manichaean trope, "the penalty which follows the sinner and is called condemnation would rightly seem to be unjust. But in fact sin is so much a voluntary evil that it is not a sin at all unless it is voluntary" (*VR* 14.27).[119] Within the traditional ethical theory on which this version of the free choice position rests, the self must have liberty to choose and full knowledge of what it is doing to bear responsibility for its choices. Augustine maintained that the soul had both necessary conditions in the circumstances of its original decision to turn away from God and subject itself to material interests, and retains both conditions sufficiently freely to choose the good and, with God's helpful facilitation of external conditions, to act upon that choice. Before its fall, the soul has both freedom of choice and freedom of action; after its fall into engagement with the material world, it retains freedom of choice, but not freedom of action. That situation does not fundamentally change the soul's ethical situation, since only what goes on within the soul or mind truly matters. "For what is so completely within the power of the will as the will itself?" (*LA* 1.12.26). All other things one wills to possess can be taken away or denied by circumstances, but no one or nothing can deprive us of will itself (*LA* 1.13.28). Augustine takes the forensic interest in the intent behind acts as indicating the locus of ethical reality. God assesses the intent of the soul or mind, not the carrying through of that intent in action, which may be constrained for good or ill by external circumstances. Action in the material world is irrelevant, which is why Augustine can speak sometimes as if there is no impediment to carrying out our will, and other times as if this is not a given of our current state.

Free agency is necessary not only for accountability in doing wrong, but equally so for credit in doing right. "An action would be neither sinful nor righteous unless it were done voluntarily" (*LA* 2.1.3). Instinctive or coerced good acts are as ethically irrelevant as bad ones of the same sort. Augustine therefore reasoned that God had to bestow free will on humans for any act to count as good, just as the same capacity was necessary to judge any act bad. In other words, according to Augustine's logic, God is constrained by an apparently universal principle of ethical and legal assessment to do things in a particular way. But why must God adhere to such conditions for crediting people with good; or, put in more starkly Manichaean terms, why does God's love for people depend on judging them? Normally, Augustine considers it unthinkable that God *must* do anything; yet here he is contending that God *must* give free will in order to exercise just judgment. But why must God be a judge at all? Why is judging the paramount concern in God's ordering of the cosmos, rather than securing the greatest amount of happiness possible? Why is endowing the soul with free will more important that instilling in it inherent and unshakeable goodness? If God gave free will for the good purpose of crediting individuals for their choice of the good, why could he not endow such a will with the capacity to choose only the good, so that the soul would be credited with good, without being left vulnerable to the derangement of evil choices? "But don't you think that if it was given for the purpose of well-doing," Augustine has his interlocutor ask, "it ought not to have been possible to convert it to sinful uses?" (*LA* 2.2.4). Augustine finds no way to answer this challenge.

Freedom was for Augustine a good in itself, reflecting transcendence from constraint or material reality, and so a kind of power that unfree things did not possess. But by defining that freedom in the Aristotelian terms of *freedom to do—or at least to choose—otherwise*, Augustine put himself in the awkward position of defending freedom *from* the good as equally a good as freedom *for* good. The Manichaeans Augustine encountered could never understand such a position; for them, only choosing the good is a good, while choosing the bad logically could not be. So the freedom to do otherwise, if it meant a freedom to choose to sin, had no intrinsic value for Manichaeans, and they regarded it as impossible that a good God would endow humans with the capacity to choose and do wrong. Whereas in Stoic and Manichaean understandings of the self, its nature determines its choice, for libertarians like Augustine in his early post-conversion years the self seems to possess no inherent nature, no confidently predictable orientation. Its possession of freedom constitutes a kind of power that places it above unfree things in the cosmic order, but this power is not intrinsically directed toward any particular purpose. Freedom in itself is amoral; and it is the logical consequence of a free will position in a monotheistic setting that God considered this amoral freedom a more important attribute to instill in human beings than goodness itself.

Nor did Plotinus provide as compatible a dialogue partner as Augustine might have wished on the forensic side of his free will theory. Since according to Plotinus the soul cannot be acted upon by the material, it would seem to be a contradiction in terms ever to speak of the soul acting "unwillingly" (Plotinus, *En* 3.2.10). Yet, because the mind's judgment is clouded by its distraction with the material world, it can be considered to act without the intention of doing wrong, and therefore "unwillingly," when it errs. Plotinus thus applied the Aristotelian exception of ignorance or error in judgment to the issue of responsibility, holding that no one would do wrong voluntarily, that is, fully informed and utterly free of outside inducements.[120] In doing so, he took a position much closer to the Manichaean appropriation of Classical moral discourse, only identifying acts in accord with reason as truly the soul's, and allowing for "other agencies" in human action for which the soul proper is not responsible. "Thus the causes of unwisdom are not in ourselves; and it may be that they are right who ascribe this kind of conduct to destiny, if by destiny they intend a principle of causation affecting us from without" (Plotinus, *En* 3.1.10).[121] Putting his own spin on the common intellectual pastime of balancing moral responsibility with cognizance of deterministic constraints on human agency,[122] Plotinus found it logically impossible for the superior soul to be acting in its own right when it put itself at the disposal of the material vicissitudes of change with which it mistakenly identifies. "For everything which goes to the worse does so unwillingly, but, since it goes by its own motion, when it experiences the worse it is said to be punished for what it did" (Plotinus, *En* 4.8.5). Augustine therefore had to forge his own synthesis of a Plotinian ontology of freedom with an Aristotelian forensics of freedom, ignoring Plotinus's own rendition of the latter in a direction much more accommodating to the Manichaean position.

Remaining Problems

Augustine places in the mouth of his interlocutor in *Free Choice* several key Manichaean objections to his free will position that redirect it to the question of *unde malum*:[123] How does such an awful state of sin come about in a being created by God perfect and for happiness? (*LA* 1.11.23). How can it be that we have chosen servitude to sin and so deserve to suffer this captivity in sin? (*LA* 1.12.24). If everyone wills to be happy, why do some fail to obtain the happy life? If the will remains free and the happy life is so easy to obtain, why do not those who experience unhappiness reverse their course and immediately obtain happiness? (*LA* 1.14.30).

These questions echo those attributed to Alypius in *Order*, by which his fellow former Manichaean raised doubts about how easy ascent sounds in Augustine's new optimistic universe. He noted the human tendency, even after consciously accepting divine instruction, to revert to past habits of bad behavior. Representing a view he had learned as a Manichaean, he stated the opinion that those who manage to avoid falling back into sin must be either divine themselves or have divine aid (*Ord* 2.10.28). In the face of this reality check, Augustine acknowledged, "for anyone who has advanced towards objects of sense, it is difficult to return to himself" (*Ord* 2.11.30), and elsewhere seems to share Alypius's views on the necessity of divine aid: "Hence it is that man's reformation is dependent on the mercy of him to whose goodness and power he owes his formation" (*QA* 28.55). Yet he is at pains to reject any selectivity in God's aid as unjust. He believes God extends salvation to all, stating, "divine assistance fulfills its office of mercy in favor of all peoples, and more abundantly than many imagine" (*Ord* 2.10.29). By implication, the degree of receptivity of this universal grace is a matter of individual ability and effort, and most of all of free will.

Now, a year later, Augustine maintains in *Free Choice* that those who attain happiness (that is, liberation from the material world) do so because they not only wish it, but also act on that wish and live rightly, as the wicked are not willing to do in order to obtain happiness. "It is not surprising that unhappy men do not obtain what they wish, that is, a happy life. For they do not at the same time wish its accompaniment, without which no one is worthy of it, and no one obtains it, that is to say a righteous life" (*LA* 1.14.30). Their will to goodness is somehow incomplete or insufficiently resolved.[124] If one *really* wanted to be good, one could be. And if good, then happy, because properly oriented to God and no longer subjected to any significant punishment. Augustine does not accept that a truly virtuous person might not be happy, because that would constitute an injustice on God's part. Of course, unhappiness due to impinging external circumstances, such as lack of food, clothing, shelter, love, and so forth, does not count, because the properly oriented soul should put no stock in such things. Happiness is to be found in virtue alone, not in the satisfaction of the necessities of life in this world. Such suffering is meaningless for the wise person detached from the world who accepts whatever happens as God's will.

We can delineate a discourse by its limits, by the sort of questions it rules out, and must rule out because they threaten to reveal the arbitrariness of the discourse's reading of reality. When Augustine runs up against such limits in his efforts to work out a rational account of the free choice position, we detect the circularity of reasoning on which he depends.

> If it is certain that [God] has given it, we ought to confess that, however it was given, it was rightly given. We may not say that it ought not to have been given or that it ought to have been given in some other way. If he has given it his action cannot in any way be rightly blamed. (*LA* 2.2.4)[125]

Here Augustine assumes the key point at issue, namely, whether what is being discussed in terms of free choice is indeed something given by God for the purpose of doing right, since we see—says the interlocutor, employing the Manichaean inductive method—that it can be used to do wrong (*LA* 2.2.5). In other words, the phenomenon called "free choice" either cannot be traced back to God, if one wishes to insulate God from responsibility for the evil use to which the free will is put, or else it fails to offer a theodicy, if one ascribes it to God despite the evil that results from it. How do we know that free will is what it is claimed to be? How do we know it is not a mistaken description of two independent wills in conflict within a person, wrongly attributed to a single entity? Augustine again has no answer. He brusquely reminds his interlocutor—and his readers—that the free will position is not up for debate, but is a premise that must first be believed and then rationalized to the best of one's ability (*LA* 2.2.6).

The anthropological implications of a free choice account of evil suited Augustine's "optimistic" turn toward the possibility of spiritual progress and ascent. He had the consistency of mind to realize that such a theodicy works only if everything essential to moral choice and goodness is at the disposal of the human individual. If a person depends on any external power for moral awareness and the ability to assent to either good or evil, then the free will theodicy collapses. For this reason, Augustine's lingering sentiments toward ideas of fate and fortune rapidly evaporated from his exposition of the soul's circumstances, as his rationalization work forged a more systematic coordination of interdependent concepts.

Augustine later recognized that he had been pushed deeper into what he came to regard as an overly one-sided reliance on free will by his efforts to support this established answer to Manichaeism. His unqualified free will position in *Free Choice* "was necessary for the purpose I had in view in that discussion," namely, to mark out a clear alternative to the Manichaean explanation of sin (*Retr.* 1.8.3). He came to realize that, in carrying out the project, he had been diverted into unproductive lines of argument. William Babcock has suggested that, because Augustine was aware that the Platonic (and Manichaean) idea of the soul's preexistence did not find universal acceptance within the Catholic community, he held back from making explicit use of this scenario in *Whence Evil/Free Choice*; this tactic in turn may have served to marginalize full acknowledgment of the soul's post-fall debility.[126] But the stance he chose to take strategically in his efforts to define himself over against his past Manichaeism—in being articulated, elaborated, defended, repeated—worked its way into his habits of self-expression and came to determine his thinking. He became locked within his own construct of what commitment to Platonic Christianity *must* mean in terms of a model of his own, and any person's, agency, and he found that model confirmed everywhere he looked—in human experience, in secular and sacred literature, in "common sense."

Only a fresh encounter with the Manichaean Other, the rejected alternative discourse on human nature and agency, would shake Augustine out of his mental box, reopen his set of possible perspectives, and prompt a new rationalization of faith in different terms. That encounter lay just a few years down the road, back across the sea in his African homeland. Over the next several years, Augustine would progressively displace the vestiges of his Manichaean self as he incorporated more and more Nicene Christian and Platonic constructs into his performative repertoire. He would find ways to articulate his identity almost completely free of Manichaean discourse. Yet he would discover that total freedom from it eluded him; and in pressing its demands on his self-reflections anew, Manichaeism would continue to challenge the meaning of Augustine's conversion.

Conclusion

When Augustine put the finishing touches to his *Confessions*, he made his conversion the climax of his narrative, as if that one act of reidentification contained implicitly within it all he would become as a Christian and as a man. He proceeds to end his tale at the harbor of Ostia, as it were looking out across the sea toward his African homeland, pointing to the completion of his journey of self-discovery through conversion, apostasy, and conversion again. The metaphor of the journey had great currency in late antiquity, usually as an image of venturing forth only to return home again. Accordingly, Augustine portrays his own journey as ending with his return to the very same faith he had learned as a child. It is a historically fallacious characterization, regardless of whether or not Augustine himself believed it when he said it. Already in his earliest compositions as a convert, he described himself as "looking back from the end of a journey" (*Acad* 2.2.5); only at that time he imagined it as one across the perilous sea of uncertain opinion to the safe harbor of "philosophy" (*BV* 1.4). His companions on most of that journey had been the Manichaeans.

Attracted to the life of the mind, he had found in the Manichaean community the seriousness and mental self-discipline to shake off what he regarded as the unquestioning superstitiousness of Christianity in his African homeland. Manichaean discourse and practice, however secondary a part of Augustine's life at the time, instilled in him a regard for religion as a vital, necessary component of his identity. The conditioning of his expectations by this Manichaean experience shaped the way he came to view religion, the role it played in self-development, and the sort of commitment entailed in identification with it. Having learned to enact Manichaean practices, utter Manichaean discourse, and finally think Manichaean thoughts, Augustine did not shed his Manichaean identity easily, and his sense of self became permanently marked by this apostasy. For the rest of his life, his new commitments—whatever they might be—were defined over against this Manichaean background.

The hindsight consequences of his Manichaean conditioning justify in a limited way Augustine's retrospective alteration of his past priorities. Because of who Augustine has become by the time he writes the *Confessions*, he presents his past in terms of religious identity and commitment. He is now primarily a Nicene Christian; what was he before that contrasts with that current identity? A Manichaean. Yet this construal of his life remakes his past, because in his younger days he actually gave religion only secondary importance. He was a rhetorician, a teacher, a family man, and an amateur astrologer. His bookshelf was lined with volumes of Cicero, Seneca, Virgil, Aristotle, and Pseudo-Pythagoras. He also read a little Mani, and took initiation as a Manichaean Auditor. That meant that his social life included, besides the classroom, the theater, and the sports arena, some time spent in Manichaean meetings and reading groups. It meant following a code of conduct that included birth control, prohibition of alcohol, and avoiding harm to animals. It meant attending on itinerant holy men in ritual settings, singing hymns, and reciting prayers. It meant public argument in which he defended Manichaean interpretations of events and experience. Peter Brown, writing at the height of the Cold War, chose the apt phrase "fellow-traveller" for Augustine and his like-minded friends. He was a sympathizer and supporter who signaled this by adjusting his life in largely symbolic ways. He admired the greater zeal of the austere Elect—from a distance, probably never seriously considering becoming one himself. Instead, half a dozen years into his association with Manichaeism, he contemplated becoming a professional astrologer. Perhaps the most successful way in which Augustine rewrites his past in the *Confessions* involves defining himself in terms of religious identities which seem to have been rather secondary to his interests at the time, and were only emerging into sharp definition in the culture around Augustine as he himself went through his self-identifying journey.

He was by no means persuaded that the Manichaeans had it entirely right. After all, the predictable orderliness of the cosmos seemed to belie the dramatic cosmic combat depicted in Manichaean myth. Because of the many things about Manichaeans that attracted him, he assumed that these myths must be symbolic and allegorical, clothing philosophical principles in garments suitable for mass consumption. That was the standard view of myth in his day. But his uncertainties kept his time among the Manichaeans from being as fruitful as he wished; he sensed a lack of personal growth, of progress toward the enlightenment and truth that Manichaeism promised. When he raised his concerns with more advanced Manichaeans, they advised him to wait for the return of Faustus, the bishop, from his long absence. When Faustus finally arrived, however, he proved to be anything but a conventional religious leader, dismissing Augustine's desire for dogmatic certainty and forcing him, against his own inclinations, to prioritize practice over theory.

Both Faustus and Augustine provide examples of an individualized uptake of religious systems in dialogue with other traditions present in their common cultural environment. Faustus found a way to accommodate a dogmatic system built upon the authority of a recipient of divine revelation to a skeptical perspective on the limitations of human knowledge drawn from another system of thought, and by combining them to reinforce and help to reproduce the Manichaean program of religious practice and self-transformation. His rise to high authority within the religion despite his unorthodox handling of its traditions demonstrates the bargain made between such institutions and those who can further their dissemination and success. Augustine was well on his way to emulating Faustus in this kind of negotiated partnership with the Manichaean tradition when slight differences between their backgrounds and predispositions sent Augustine in a different direction, toward an alternative personal intersection of complementary commitments. Not yet as fully integrated into the Manichaean community as Faustus, and under far less pressure of observability, Augustine found in his other interests more engaging objects in which to invest himself.

Augustine's apostasy presupposes some accumulation of dissatisfaction with the way Manichaeism as a system, or the Manichaeans as a community, supplied him with the tools he needed to process experience, find meaning, and direct his labors toward satisfying outcomes. As long as the amount of experience Manichaeism succeeded in harnessing to its models of reality outweighed the handful of anomalous frustrations and disappointments, Augustine had no impetus to throw over one paradigm for another. That impetus eventually came from outside this rational discourse, in social factors and subconscious pressures that were able to move Augustine because Manichaeism was a secondary factor in his identity that had been weakened, first by the limitations of its effectiveness, and then by the way in which Faustus refused to deal with his issues in the manner Augustine had been conditioned to expect. His apostasy came first, before any significant attraction to another system, and in fact set the stage for his exploration of those other options.

Augustine's life between his encounter with Faustus in 383 C.E. and his retirement to Cassiciacum in 386 offers a textbook case of the typical conditions of apostasy: successive relocations, disruption of his prior social network, rapid socioeconomic advancement, close engagement with an elite class associated with another religion, and the rising potential costs of affiliation with a socially deviant group.[1] We do not need any of Augustine's later claims about the unsatisfactory premises of Manichaeism to explain his exit from the faith. And since many of those criticisms depend on the vantage point of other, competing premises Augustine did not know at the time, we should discount them as hindsight. He became an apostate from Manichaeism before he knew anything that Platonism or Nicene Christianity had to offer. By minimal performative definitions of conversion, it might be claimed that Augustine converted sometime in 385, when he started accompanying his mother to Ambrose's church. The inadequacy of such a claim reveals itself in the way his reference to this reentry into the Christian catechumenate practically yawns from the page of even such an apologetic work as the *Confessions*; even if that yawn is a self-conscious pose, it shows Augustine unwilling to put forward that event as conversion. His expectations were set so low that he was bound to be mildly impressed by Ambrose's ability to preach philosophically informed self-discipline under the clever guise of allegorical interpretation of the Bible. He gradually established close ties to the new Christian elite of Milan, participating in their civic events, attending their dinner parties, sharing their reading lists, and becoming engaged to one of their daughters.

But of course Augustine had yet to be persuaded to believe anything he was hearing from Ambrose. He had been unable to disprove Manichaeism, even though he found other explanations of parts of experience somehow more compelling (*Conf* 5.14.28). He expressly talks about choosing some of these alternative premises without being able to articulate or explain how he knew them to be better than Manichaean views (*Conf* 7.1.1). In these recollections, he puts his finger on the arational nature of conversion. Heeding unaccountable preferences, he found Platonism an attractive alternative to Manichaeism. It shared many of the themes and values that had attracted him to Manichaeism, but differed in areas where Augustine had been uncomfortable with the Manichaean position. He could go from being a Manichaean to being a Platonist without questioning his belief in an all-good God who providentially manipulated a universe that nonetheless contained an evil alterity to God's goodness, and without changing his belief in a soul that once dwelt in the divine realm free of bodily constraint but had somehow fallen into material reality and there found itself hemmed in and corrupted by the needs of a body that passed itself off as the locus of human identity. He found in Platonism the same desire for ascent out of this world, and the same conviction that mental and physical restraint provided the preliminary means of that ascent. Besides these major common themes, the two systems shared a dozen other points of similarity, much of which belonged to the accepted "common sense" popular metaphysics of Augustine's age. The bridge was there. The question is only how much Augustine could make out of the other side before crossing over.

In crossing over Augustine went not just to Platonism, but also to Nicene Christianity. Certainly he was able to discern compatibilities between these two systems; but we need to attend to why Augustine even considered taking on a new cultic affiliation at the same time as he adopted Platonism as the intellectual tradition within which to do his thinking. As James O'Donnell has remarked in his commentary on the *Confessions*, the assumption in Augustine's day was that a religion was primarily a ritual cult, and this was true of the African Christianity Augustine knew growing up. When he was first attracted to the life of "philosophy," the Manichaeans were the only community in Africa—"philosophical" or "religious"—that seemed to offer in an organized form what that life called for—a program of self-mastery through which one could discipline the mind's relationship to the body and senses. He adopted Manichaeism as a "philosophy," only to discover it to be a "religion." But before he could find an intellectual tradition more purely representative of what he imagined "philosophy" to be, the Manichaeans had shown him the merits of a systematic, community-based approach to shaping a person's character toward particular standards of self-mastery and ideals of perfection.

Augustine did not depart from his primarily intellectual interests, but maintained his connection with Manichaeism as long as it supported them. Nevertheless, his decade-long Manichaean experience altered his expectations, inculcated new desires and preferences in him, and conditioned him to certain assumptions that made possible his attraction to Nicene Christianity as a complement to Platonism, not the least of which was a very Manichaean commitment to Jesus conceptualized as the uniquely authoritative conduit of truth. But more generally his observation that Platonists seemed to have a sense of what truth is, but had no program for getting there, bespeaks his conditioned expectation that a self-disciplinary regime is a prerequisite for freeing the mind. The recent arrival of the new Nicene Christian asceticism in Italy coincident with his sojourn there gave Augustine the first viable alternative to Manichaeism for this component of his self-making enterprise.

As a convert to Nicene Christianity, Augustine believed in Christ, the Church, and the Scriptures as authorities guiding personal conduct and making available truths awaiting decipherment. He believed in Platonism as "the one true philosophy" (*Acad* 3.19.42), the discursive system with the most accurate view of the universe, compatible with and reflected in the Christian mysteries behind the veil of symbolism (*Ord* 2.5.16). He believed in a preexistent, divine-like soul, originally inhabiting the intelligible realm but now fallen into association with the body, the senses, and the material. He believed in an intellectual return to the immediate presence of God, and accepted Christian texts, teachings, and rituals as popular disseminations of the moral prerequisites for such a spiritual ascent. He believed in the incarnation of Christ as a divine intervention in human degradation for the purpose of giving humankind, in the flesh, a completely reliable sage whose words could be trusted to guide them to truth. He believed in a way of life that eschews the bodily and cultivates the pure soul.

Yet with no place for the sacrificial death of Jesus, for a physical resurrection of the dead, or an apocalyptic world judgment, Augustine's thinking at the time of his conversion lacked many of the classic biblical elements of the western Christian tradition. His views of God, the nature of the soul, and the need for ascetic restraint required little or no immediate adjustment from his Manichaean to his Nicene Christian commitments. Doctrinally, the key differences lay in whether God was considered to be in control of the universe, or battling for its control, and in whether the soul was intrinsically divine itself, or only potentially so as the full realization of its created promise. Interpretively, they were to be found in whether one had a unitestamental or bitestamental Christian scripture, and whether one read that scripture literally or allegorically. Practically, they involved whether one belonged to a secret cell at odds with broader social mores, or became part of a politically sanctioned social institution.

If Augustine had been an ordinary convert, and had never written a word, the limited degree of his internalization of tenets and attitudes associated with his new public commitments would have gone unnoticed, both in his time and historically. No doubt there were many superficial converts in the communities of Milan and Rome. Ambrose and the other Nicene leaders of his time promoted, inculcated, and expected more of their membership, but they lacked the means to observe, enforce, and ensure the desired outcome. As long as one maintained the surface performance of the expectations of the Nicene Christian self, one was one. By that standard, those modern commentators who insist that Augustine was unequivocally a "Catholic" or a "Christian" from the time of his baptism are correct: by the entirely external criteria of the time, he was. But that is settling for a very minimal standard, indeed; and nothing that Augustine was at that minimal level is at all historically significant.

Of the eight compositions Augustine produced in his first two years as a convert to Nicene Christianity, and the half-dozen more he planned during that period, only one addressed "religion" proper: *The Morals of the Catholic Church*. All the others he devoted either to the liberal arts or to questions of epistemology, cosmology, or psychology in which specifically Christian premises barely feature. His specifically religious references in these writings offer mainstream, abstract Roman intellectual theism, no more "religious" than Plotinus's own remarks in this vein, and in key ways cutting across the grain of the more dramatic God of the Bible. Augustine retained his assumption that cultic and devotional language packages scientific and philosophical truths for mass consumption, and presumed that over time he would get the "mysteries" propounded in Ambrose's church to open for him with a Platonic key (*Ord* 2.5.16). Augustine himself reports in the immediate aftermath of his conversion and baptism that the stock phrases of Christian discourse as yet had no meaning for him, including such fundamental concepts as the trinity, the incarnation, the sacraments, and the eschaton (*Acad* 2.2.4; QA 33.76). He can repeat the terms but, he says, he has no understanding of them. He can say that they are true, because on the assumption that they are true, reason will find a way to make sense of them.

The *Confessions* narrative offers a considerably different depiction of events from one that can be reconstructed on the basis of Augustine's earliest writings, and that means we actually have a choice between two paradigmatic conversions when it comes to Augustine, either one of which might prove useful for thinking about the concept of conversion. The most important difference between these two paradigms of conversion relates to the role of reason. Augustine gives the impression in the *Confessions* that the ground for his conversion was prepared by reasoning his way to more persuasive premises about the nature of God, humanity, and the universe. But this is, of course, pure fantasy. No one can reason his or her way to new premises, because reason depends on premises, rather than the reverse. And Augustine knew this perfectly well. Indeed, he took precisely this point as the central revolution in his thinking at the time of his conversion: that belief in premises accepted on authority is a prerequisite of reasoning. At the time of his conversion, Augustine not only admitted, but emphatically argued that belief must precede understanding, that reasoning simply flounders around until given direction by commitments made without benefit of good reasons, that is, commitments made on bases other than rational ones. Here is where Augustine's historical conversion and the way he presented it at the time connect with modern studies of conversion, which have confirmed time and time again how little any conscious weighing of the plausibility of different doctrinal constructs has to do with decisions to convert. Such rational comparison actually takes place too late to play a role in conversion, as part of the verification stage of the new convert, who is in the process of constructing a narrative of him- or herself as an apostate from one belief system to another, critiquing past commitments from within the premises and paradigms of the new one.

The poverty of Augustine's discursive reasons for preferring Nicene Christianity to Manichaeism or any other option will perhaps help us get over a natural resistance to the conclusions of modern research that the causes of conversion operate elsewhere than in the fully conscious exercises of rationality. Michael Polanyi, studying paradigm shifts in the sciences, found in Augustine a good comparative example of the "logical gap" separating one paradigm from another, and the role of nonrationalized desires in inducing transference of allegiance from one system of belief to another.[2] Thomas Kuhn's development of this idea of a "paradigm shift" is well known. Such revolutions in thinking involve changing the rules of the game, and settling on new criteria for determining what will be accepted as a valid fact:

> paradigm debates are not really about relative problem-solving
> ability, though for good reasons they are usually couched in those
> terms. . . . The man who embraces a new paradigm at an early stage

must often do so in defiance of the evidence provided by problem-solving. He must, that is, have faith that the new paradigm will succeed with the many large problems that confront it, knowing only that the older paradigm has failed with a few. A decision of that kind can only be made on faith.[3]

Isolated observations and experiences remain constant across paradigms, but yield different interpretations when set within different systems of premises and rules of reasoning. The game pieces are arranged and used differently. Conscious, rational, discursive thought operates only within each successive game, as Kuhn explains:

> whatever its force, the status of the circular argument is only that
> of persuasion. It cannot be made logically or even probabilistically
> compelling for those who refuse to step into the circle. The premises
> and values shared by the two parties to a debate over paradigms are not
> sufficiently extensive for that. As in political revolutions, so in paradigm
> choice—there is no standard higher than the assent of the relevant
> community.[4]

Stanley Fish has discussed the same phenomenon in terms of competing inter-pretive communities.[5] The transition from one school of thought, one game to the next is something akin to blinking between realities, unable to account for the passage from point A to point B—a situation as acutely frustrating to the typical historian as to those who posit substantial continuity of self in human beings.

In the *Confessions*, Augustine tries to present a different story from this, one in which reason gradually leads him to new ways of thinking, and per-suades him to Platonic and Christian truth. In this story, it is his conscious, ra-tional mind that races ahead of his ability to commit, rather than commitment paving the way for reasoned understanding. This reversal in the *Confessions* of the order of authority and reason, belief and understanding, evidently has a protreptic purpose. Augustine employs exactly the same reversal in several of his earlier anti-Manichaean works, where he expressly says that he is putting reason first to accommodate the Manichaean mode of discourse, which preco-ciously requires rational analysis before faith. In its overall design, the *Confes-sions* follows this specifically Manichaean-engaged plan, modeling conversion as motivated by fully informed rational persuasion culminating in submission to the new winning paradigm.

Yet the odd detail of the sequence of events he offers retrospectively defies his literary construct. His more strategic self-presentation cannot completely master remnants of his past selves. He recalls details of his conversion experience with sufficient vividness to discover new things in it. He recalls the controlling character of premises, and how it was impossible for him to articulate problems with the Manichaean world view in the absence of alternatives he could mentally entertain. He also remembers the impingement on his thinking of sentiments and preferences that he could not at first rationally justify.

Augustine's conversion arguably did not involve a change to a radically different view of life; he still thought of himself as an exiled soul yearning to transcend a kind of bondage in the material world. But by converting he transferred his allegiance from an ideological system that failed sufficiently to ground that view of life for him to one that could, because it better met both discursive standards of judgment and certain unarticulated preferences more closely conformed to the traditions of his broader society. He continued to affirm a set of interests and orientations that predated his conversion, and still looked upon his earlier conversion to Manichaeism as a progressive step that stalled at a relatively premature point of understanding.[6] He had adopted in principle the whole of the Platonic and Nicene Christian *epistemes* without knowing either particularly well. He had yet to identify all the implications of his new commitments that he would eventually discover, and it would be simply anachronistic for us to consider those later conclusions to be implicit in an Augustine to whom they were yet to occur.

By keeping strictly to this earlier Augustine "without his futures," we allow his conversion to be analytically informative, rather than theologically normative, providing an extremely well documented example by which to understand better where the convert stands between past and future selves. As Robert Hefner sums up recent studies on this question,

> The most necessary feature of religious conversion, it turns out, is not a deeply systematic reorganization of personal meanings but an adjustment in self-identification through the at least nominal acceptance of religious actions or beliefs deemed more fitting, useful, or true. In other words, at the very least—an analytic minimum—conversion

implies the acceptance of a new locus of self-definition, a new, though not necessarily exclusive, reference point for one's identity.[7]

Augustine no more adopted and internalized the full system of either Platonism or Nicene Christianity than he had that of Manichaeism. Even if religious leaders strive for total duplication of their system in each individual adherent, religions do not require it in order to be sustained from generation to generation. Certain minimal gestures of adherence from each member of the community allow the system to go on, with its various elements taken up in different ways valued by the participants. The religion as a whole is a collective construct, a generalized outcome of many individual choices and accommodations. Augustine brought with him into his new identity the conditioning of his prior commitments, as well as even more deeply seated predispositions, both of which shaped his attention and interest in ways he could not always consciously control. Consciously or not, he worked over the discourses presented to him, hearing selectively, recombining creatively, understanding mistakenly. Where discursive options presented themselves, we see him often making choices that tend toward differentiation from Manichaean options, rejecting alternatives within his sources or diverging from them entirely whenever they appear to accommodate Manichaean views. His identity as a convert takes shape in no small part from his situation as an apostate.

Many have characterized the tendencies of Augustine's conversion as a brand of optimism. Although I have argued that this description requires significant qualification, it certainly applies to Augustine's theoretical pragmatics in his initial post-conversion period. He now conceived of the universe as not only ordered to facilitate liberation, as in Manichaeism, but completely devoid of forces oppositional to that liberation. He now considered his soul intact rather than fragmented, immune to material impingement rather than buffeted by it, capable of immediate realization of its intention rather than compromised in its free agency. All these viewpoints can be usefully contrasted to more "pessimistic" apprehensions of existence to which Augustine had been exposed as a Manichaean, whether or not he ever actually accepted them as his own. From a critical vantage point, we might regard the particular constructs of Augustine's new-found optimism as wishful thinking. In key respects, Manichaean discourse better captures some of the harsh and morally challenging aspects of human experience. Yet such an assessment does not negate the historical force of Augustine's optimism, both in effecting desired changes in his own life, and in propelling him toward those future Augustines who would play a much larger role in shaping the world than he ever did as a Manichaean.

The force of the new paradigms Augustine explored in Italy showed itself in the way they propelled Augustine forward and allowed him to make progress in self-mastery, in aligning formerly conflicted desires and aspirations into a focused program for his life. Ironically, then, Augustine's experience had proved Faustus right: doctrines that successfully motivate right action thereby prove their "truth"; that is, by working for the one who gives them provisional assent, concepts reinforce that assent or belief, anchoring identification with both the belief and its pragmatic outcome so that one becomes defined by adherence to this theory-practice complex and by association with its other adherents. Truth is the constructed reality within which a community of such adherents understands itself and operates, as its various individual members learn and gain further facility with its discursive and practical systems.

Yet within the pluralism that characterized Augustine's culture, such truth-communities could not secure their members from exposure to alternative rationalities or the larger "common sense" of the mass society of the Roman world. The adherents of these systems could not be totally bound within their respective sectarian rationalities, but constantly had available to them the larger perspective of general society from which they had the opportunity to reflect critically on their commitments. It is in such circumstances, as George Mead perceived, that individuals can step beyond the local logic of their primary group and, taking an outside or larger perspective, recognize and critique the very premises within which they have previously thought. One can "think outside the box" if there is another or larger box from which one can realize that one was in a box to begin with. Thus it turns out that Augustine had available a larger perspective from which to assess the paradigms identified with his own particular sectarian community, and it was to this more popular consensus that he withdrew from the specific program of the Manichaeans. We can assume that this larger *consensus gentium* had retained some place in Augustine's thinking even as a Manichaean, based on his earlier conditioning to it, his only partial engagement with the Manichaean system, and his likely construal of some aspects of that system in terms given by the broader culture.

In certain significant respects, the trend discernible in Augustine's conversion as he expresses it at the time is *reversion* back to the norms of the social and intellectual traditions in which he had been born and educated, giving up commitments he had made to Manichaeism that had necessitated a break with the dominant models of reality and value held by the intellectual elite of Roman society, traditionally pagan but increasingly Nicene Christian. Augustine goes back to providential omnipotence in place of agonistic dualism, back to matter as qualityless substrate in place of matter as an active evil agency, back to forensic free will in place of the debilitated will and divine grace, back to the simple equation of soul with self in place of complex interior conflict, back to allegorical interpretation of myth in place of literalism.

In other respects, his conversion reflects his divergence from those traditional norms in the direction of new options in his immediate environment. He joins the Neoplatonic revolution over Stoic, Academic, and Middle Platonic constructs of reality with which Manichaeism was more closely associated. He adopts monism over a variety of dualist formulations, divine and psychic immaterialism over a consistently materialist metaphysic, dogmatism over skepticism. He embraces the equally novel propositions of Nicene Christianity, in which he found valuable differentiation from his unsatisfactory experience with Manichaeism. He commits to a gulf of createdness separating the human soul from God, to the divine accommodation of incarnation, to a less formal ascetic regime.

These partial uptakes, misreadings, and recombinations yielded a microsystem unique and personal to Augustine, fitted to his past conditioning and preferences, still adjusting to the juxtaposition of its severable parts. Questions about the orthodoxy of this conglomeration of ideas have scarcely any historical relevance. No one was paying attention. Augustine simply was not important enough to have his utterances closely scrutinized by the guardians of institutional power. As a layperson and new convert, he stood at the margins of the Nicene Christian community. The intellectual genre in which he worked, which engaged religious doctrine rather allusively, afforded broad leeway to the expression of ideas. Augustine fit comfortably among the classically trained literati finding their way into the new "Catholic" Church, tolerated in their resort to the familiar tropes of non-Christian expression. To the degree that anyone in authority, such as Ambrose or Simplician, bothered to note Augustine's contributions, they were still too engaged in yesterday's theological disputes over Christology to look closely at anything else. They might have raised an eyebrow at Augustine's initial comparison of Jesus to Pythagoras, but probably chose charitably to consider its context one of *praeperatio evangelica*.

Augustine's early post-conversion writings strongly suggest that, at the time, he made commitments of whose entailments he had not the slightest inkling. Certain specific, isolated ways of expressing things offered by Platonism drew his interest; accepting the system as a whole was a corequisite of making use of those individual elements, just as accepting the entire ritual and symbolic system of Nicene Christianity was a corequisite of acting on his attraction to its revealer figure and moral-disciplinary system. It would wait for Augustine's futures for some of these pieces to be fitted together in a way that was coherent and functional for him, while others would have to be discarded for the sake of that coherence and functionality. In the process of mutual accommodation of subject to system, many individual elements would be negotiated. While the phrases might be the same in the mouths of Augustine and other members of the Nicene community, the meaning ascribed to those phrases varied from person to person, and changed from their initial rote recital to integration into an operationalized personal system of meaning. It is safe to assume that these processes go on to a greater or lesser degree in all converts. Augustine's case matters more than most because he became an especially important point of articulation for the Nicene Christian system as a whole, successfully reproducing his particular permutation of that system as one of its dominant paradigms.

This, then, is the Augustine I have sought to bring to light for closer examination. He is not simply the narrativized self of the *Confessions*, repackaged and elaborated into contemporary intellectual respectability. I have presumed to second-guess Augustine's own account of things—of which he certainly had more direct experience and greater knowledge than I—because I have another Augustine to play off against him, the convert who made public pronouncements that the bishop was unable to take back. I also have other information provided by Augustine and others about the character of the Manichaean community with which he associated, and even some of the key Manichaeans with whom he interacted. Thus Augustine cannot have the last word on his own story.

There are those who contend that Augustine was already a deeper and more thorough "Catholic" than his own utterances of that earlier time reveal. Charging that those who minimize Augustine's indoctrination into Nicene Christianity at this time rely too much on the apparent Augustine of the texts he produced, these "maximalists," if you will, have appealed to another Augustine, hidden from the historian because not made public in his writings of the period.[8] The evidence for the existence of this earlier invisible Augustine, they argue, derives from the later Augustine's recollection of his existence at the time. The problem with this position is that the public, textual Augustine of 386 and 387 not only fails to manifest this posited hidden Augustine, but actually displays ideas and attitudes incompatible with the existence of such a private self. A close reading of his utterances at the time reveals him expressly denying that he understands the very things the maximalists wish to ascribe to him, and shows him to be actively and publicly working with a system of belief that has no place for things he later held to be vital commitments of his Christian identity. Why would he so misrepresent himself? And if we hypothesize such a deliberate obscuring of his personal interests and commitments in his early writings, how are we permitted to assume anything more transparent to his inner self in his later works? To redeem the later Augustine from being a liar, they are forced to make the earlier Augustine a hypocrite. Augustine may have been either, or both. But less speculative for the historian is to give most weight to Augustine in his performative presence in the historical record, in all its vicissitudes.

We would do well to attend to the way the earlier Augustine sloganeers, deploying terms and phrases he has heard as conventions of speech without investing them with particular meaning or function in the active, operationalized portion of his current thinking. Later, he invests these same terms and phrases with meaning and function, or redeploys them with new significance, creating the illusion of continuity and consistency of thought. He may even have fooled himself in this way, if his comments in the *Retractationes* are not consciously misleading. It is easy enough for those working on specific aspects of Augustine's thought simply to duplicate his own efforts to find logical continuity between his earlier positions and his later ones, between the self he had become and the self he had been. That such logical continuity can be constructed is beside the point; it is a construction, a construal of the earlier Augustine from the vantage point of his futures. All such teleological history arbitrarily picks out details of a past that turned out to have a future, regardless of how minor those details were in their own time, or how much their meaning and setting within larger *epistemes* have been changed by the course of events. But even with all the reinterpretation of his past utterances Augustine makes in the *Retractationes* to deprive his critics of legitimate points against his shifting positions, he frankly confesses there that his thinking has changed, that he no longer agrees with some of the things he said before, that he found some of his choice of phrasing quaint, and that at times he simply does not remember what he meant by what he said.

In this important way, Augustine becomes a prime witness to the transilience of the self, and the challenges such a self poses to popular constructs of essential, continuous identity. Those very constructs map the goals cultural and social systems take as one of their primary tasks. That is, the self is a project, not a given, in human existence. "To breed an animal with the right to make promises," Nietzsche declared, is "man's true problem"—to find a way to manage oneself according to one's own desired priorities and identifications, and fulfill the commitments such identifications entail. Augustine found in both Manichaeism and Nicene Christianity models and technologies for doing precisely that, and discerned within himself a desire to order himself accordingly.

This may very well be the bargain religions, as systems of discourse and practice, make with potential adherents, by which they attract sites of reiteration that constitute their historical continuation. And the human need for self-intelligibility and -mastery may constitute the other side of this bargain, "a primary vulnerability to the Other," as Judith Butler puts it, by which "the price of existence is subordination" to an originally external system of power that promises to provide the means to satisfy those needs.[9] I would like to suggest that the examples of both Augustine and Faustus reveal the capacity, perhaps even the inevitability, of an individually negotiated embodiment of an adopted religion, which is undoubtedly one of the primary forces behind the historical process by which religions change. Each new convert represents an axis around which a religious system makes a slight adjustment toward its as yet undetermined future, collective form.

If Augustine's case were only normative within a particular tradition of selfhood, it would not help us understand more widely shared features of human experience. But I have approached this study confident that his story of conversion and apostasy is more broadly informative, not only about the particular historical confrontation between Manichaean and Nicene Christian construals of selfhood, but also concerning the ways in which meaningful and effective selves may emerge from an apparently voluntary and sought-after subscription to religious systems.

Augustine's experiment in having Manichaeism serve him in this way, although ultimately unsuccessful, offers the most fully documented case of an individual Manichaean, and of the way individual elements of the religion were or were not engaged in a particular example of embodying the system. As such, it may tell us a great deal about Manichaeism, not just as a proposed system, but as a lived religion in its successes and failures. The details of Augustine's subsequent conversion to Nicene Christianity are equally informative about the extent and character of the commitments such an act of public identification entailed.

There may be some merit in considering conversion and apostasy as arbitrarily isolated segments of a constantly adjusting self, highlighted and scripted by institutionally provided conventions retrospectively imposed on a person's self-orienting memory. Yet the constructs of conversion and apostasy may just as much mask continuities of self, and stake claims on a self-transformation that under closer scrutiny turns out to be rhetorically exaggerated. We have seen reason in Augustine's story to support both of these qualifications of our subject, and to recognize that the illocutionary repertoire of self-identification Augustine had at his disposal was inadequate as a way of signaling very complex, ongoing changes. He may have no longer identified with Manichaeism, but that religion had marked its claim on certain isolated concerns and perspectives now subordinated as subjected discourse within the overall orientation of a Nicene Christian, as he understood and enacted it. In the unfolding of Augustine's futures, these traces of the Manichaean construct of reality would demand their due from Augustine, even as he struggled to keep the promise of his leap of faith. Augustine found that he constantly had to reinvent what his conversion would mean for him as he continued to discover the potential of his adopted system and of himself as its point of articulation in the face of the Manichaean challenge. That further story requires separate consideration.[10]

NOTES

INTRODUCTION

1. BeDuhn 2000.

2. Some limited sources on this living face of Manichaeism do exist, and have recently been added to by new finds from a fourth-century Manichaean community in Kellis, in the Dakhlah Oasis of Egypt. See esp. Gardner, Alcock, Funk 1999; Gardner 1996, 2007.

3. O'Meara 1954, 64.

4. Chadwick 1990, 222.

5. Coyle 2003, 22.

6. van Oort 1993, 276–77.

7. Fredriksen 1986, 24.

8. Fredriksen 1986, 34.

9. Collinge 1983, 70.

10. See, e.g., *Ep* 143.2; *SermDolb* 10.15.

11. *Augustinian Studies* 32 (2001) 204.

12. For a convenient collection of Skinner's programmatic essays and critical responses to them, see Tully 1988.

13. Gilson 1929, 310–11, cited affirmatively by Madec 1996, 69–70, and Harrison 2006, 18.

14. See Beit-Hallahmi and Argyle 1997; Hefner 1993a, b; Loveland 2003; Sherkat and Wilson 1995; Sherkat and Ellison 1999.

15. Foucault 1988, 18.

16. Butler 1997, 16.

17. Butler 1997, 14–15; cf. 21.

18. Butler 1997, 14.

19. Butler 1997, 19.

20. Mead 1934, 140.

21. Mead 1934, 142. He continues, "I know of no other form of behavior than the linguistic in which the individual is an object to himself, and, so far as I can see, the individual is not a self in the reflexive sense unless he is an object to himself. It is this fact that

gives a critical importance to communication, since this is a type of behavior in which the individual does so respond to himself."

22. Mead 1934, 178.

23. Mead 1934, 283.

24. Austin 1975.

25. Frankfurt 1988, 176.

26. Frankfurt 1988, 59–60.

27. Frankfurt 1988, 16–17.

28. Frankfurt 1988, 170.

29. Frankfurt 1988, 170.

30. Frankfurt 1988, 175–76.

31. Foucault 1986, 42.

32. Coyle 1999, 40.

33. More 1907/8, 609.

CHAPTER 1. BECOMING MANICHAEAN

1. In Africa itself, the councils of 393, 397, and 402 C.E. were crucial for defining and establishing a "Catholic Church" there. An official creed (the "Nicene" creed—actually the creed of Constantinople) and canon were put forward at Hippo in 393. That council's declarations were ratified at the council held at Carthage in 397 by representatives of churches of Africa Proconsularis and Byzacene, but not by the Numidians, who were experiencing a leadership crisis in the aftermath of the death of the primate Megalius. Only in 402, with the primacy issue settled, did the Numidian churches formally adopt the decisions of 397.

2. On the colonial character of Catholic Christianity in Africa, see Brisson 1958; Markus 1972; Markus 1970, 110.

3. While infant baptism was long established in North Africa, many made Monnica's choice to keep her sons unbaptized until the temptations of adolescence had passed. Should we consider her attitude evidence that she came from a rigorist background, perhaps even Donatist, but had been forced by marriage to a nonbeliever to associate herself with a more liberal, non-Donatist community?

4. See Ramirez 1981, who stresses the need to apply the standards of Augustine's own time.

5. See Brown's recent suggestion that the incident referred to here should be understood in the context of Augustine's recollections in one of the recently discovered "Dolbeau Sermons" (P. Brown 2000, 456–57): "When I went to vigils as a student in this city, I spent the night rubbing up beside women, along with other boys anxious to make an impression on the girls, and where, who knows, the opportunity might present itself to have a love-affair with them" (*SermDolb* 2.5).

6. Calculating back from the end of this relationship, then, he would have become involved with her in his first or second year in Carthage.

7. See *Acad* 1.1.4; 3.4.7; 3.14.31; *Sol* 1.10.17; *Conf* 3.4.7; 8.7.17. It should be noted that many of these passages refer to his rereading of the *Hortensius* in 386.

8. The divinity of the soul is often repeated in Cicero's works; see *Fin.* 2.40; *Off.* 3.44; *Tusc.* 1.65, 5.38, 5.70. Augustine's statement that reading Cicero turned his prayers to God may reflect the effects of Cicero's critique of providence, temporarily swaying Augustine from his evident predilection for providential and fate-bound constructs of the cosmos, such as astrology, towards a more indeterminate, open-ended cosmos such as Manichaeism taught.

9. The soul returns to heaven when it overcomes fallacious argument, apprehends truth, and in this way triumphs over the passions (Frag. 97 Müller; *Trin* 14.19.26). The person searching for truth is happy, even before arriving at it (Frag. 101 Müller; *Acad* 1.3.7).

10. The exact canon of the Bible was still in flux. Only at the regional council of Hippo in 393 did the coalescing North African Catholic Church adopt a scriptural canon.

11. This is the best explanation of the absence in the *Conf* of any account of a deconversion, however temporary, from the faith of his youth, noted by Ferrari 1995, 109–10, with a different interpretation.

12. Note again his remark in *Conf* 3.4.7 that it was reading the *Hortensius* that "turned my prayers to you yourself, Lord"—by implication they had not been so turned previously.

13. Ferrari 1973, 263.

14. Kirwan 1989, 60.

15. Bonner 1963, 60. Elsewhere he says, "The Manichaean faith . . . must be reckoned among the strangest and most bizarre of the many strange and bizarre fantasies which the human mind has conceived" (1963, 157). Yet Bonner goes on to attempt a sympathetic summary of the religion, and writes that, "A faith which proclaimed the existence of evil in the world but which offered the hope of liberation to myriads of men and women, which inculcated a moral discipline and respect for life often sadly lacking in those who denounced and persecuted it, and which could inspire its children to face torture and martyrdom uncomplaining, deserves better at the hands of the Christian theologian or Church historian than it sometimes receives" (1963, 158).

16. Bertrand 1914, 102.

17. Stock 1996, 47.

18. O'Donnell 1992, vol. 2, 185. Cf. W. O'Brien 1974, 441: "The gravest problem for one who wishes to recreate the horizon of myth"—i.e., the Manichaean period—"in Augustine's life is that it is this stage of his life about which Augustine is most critical when he is writing the *Confessions*, so that while it is fairly simple to mark out the Manichaean years as a distinct horizon, it is almost impossible from the *Confessions* to recover a sense of how life would appear to one living within this horizon before he became critical of it. It is not difficult to account for the vehemence of Augustine's criticism in terms of Augustine's later concern to put to rest certain charges coming from his enemies that his teaching was essentially Manichaean . . . but that is little consolation to one who wishes to discover what in the Manichaean teaching could so attract Augustine during his twenties."

19. Stroumsa 1986, 308.

20. The Manichaean Coptic *Psalm-Book*, 34, lists the names of early missionaries to Egypt: Salmaios, Pappos, Ozeos, and Addas. For other references to Salmaios, see the Manichaean Coptic *Homilies*, 86ff.; for Pappos, see Alexander of Lycopolis 2.4.17; for Addas, the most famous western Manichaean missionary of them all, see the summary of information in Lieu 1992, 90–92.

21. Manichaeism is first reported as present in Rome in a rescript of bishop Miltiades, dating between 311 and 314 (Coyle 1978, 29 n128). On the origins of African Manichaeism, see Decret 1978, 161–77; for the extent of its success there, Decret 1978, 191–203. P. Brown 1969 is still indispensable for its insights into the conditions of the initial Manichaean expansion into the Roman Empire, as well as into the ultimate failure of the Manichaean mission there; see more generally Lieu 1992, Stoop 1909, Cumont 1910.

22. Also called *diaconi* in closer correspondence to their original Syriac and Iranian titles, *Ep* 236.2.

23. Decret 1978, vol. 2, 153 n215, persuasively argues that the title *doctor* did not correspond to a formal hierarchical position, but was rather a label of respect for a renowned teacher of whatever rank. Thus Faustus is called both "doctor" and "bishop," while Felix is both "doctor" (*Retr* 2.34.1) and simply an "elect" (Possidius, *Vita* 16.4).

24. See Bruce 1983 for a defense of the date. Barnes 1976a, b and Thomas 1976 have argued for a date of 302, which requires an emendation of the text of the rescript. The proposed later date is based primarily upon arguments for when Diocletian would have been in Egypt, from which the rescript was addressed, as well as concerns to connect the rescript with other internal problems and programs of the Roman state. Yet the only reference in the rescript itself to such larger issues is a reference to Persia as a political enemy—a reference better situated during the Persian War of 297/298 than in 302, when the two states were at peace on terms favorable to Rome.

25. See van der Lof 1974.

26. See Ries 1981. Decret 1978, 171, associates the reference to *otia* specifically with the refusal of pacifist Manichaeans to participate in the militarism of Diocletian's regime at a time of supposed national emergency, and goes on to suggest, 172–73, that other sorts of Roman Christians had by this time gone sufficiently mainstream in their values to accommodate the state and serve in the army. Hence Manichaeism represented a new, vigorous introduction of the social radicalism previously characteristic of a broader swath of the Christian movement.

27. Text in P. Krüger and T. Mommsen, *Collectio librorum Juris antejustiniani*, vol. 3 (Berlin, Weidman, 1890), 187; for analysis see Seston 1940.

28. See Decret 1978, 188–203. It appears that references to small numbers usually intend the Elect alone: see, e.g., Ephrem, Against Mani, xcvii.

29. Decret 1978, 208.

30. See Decret 1978, 209–10.

31. Burrus 1995, 70.

32. On the preeminence of Manichaeism as the major external rival of the emergent

Nicene Christian community, see the analysis of its rhetorical distinction from all other heresies in Adkin 1993.

33. He then supplies a narrative of solving these problems in ways that destroyed the Manichaean advantage (in an order reverse of that in which he introduced them: the immorality of the biblical heroes, *Conf* 5.14.24; 6.4.6; anthropomorphism, *Conf* 7.1.1–7.2.3; evil, *Conf* 7.12.18).

34. On the refreshing alternative this offered to the stern unquestioning faith typically expected in North Africa at the time, see P. Brown 2000, 31–32.

35. See Alfaric 1918, 76–77; Bardy 1948, 27; Boyer 1953, 47; Du Roy 1966, 32; Feldmann 1975, 369–75. "Augustine is so insistent about this feature in the dialogues written shortly after his conversion, that one might almost be tempted to think it was the only reason for Manichaeism's appeal to him. . . . Augustine repeatedly credits the Manichees with encouraging him to reject the authoritarianism of 'infantile' blind faith, and 'rise up' to stand on his own two feet as an adult rational being, capable of thinking things out for himself" (O'Connell 1993c, 229).

36. Quoted by Augustine, *Trin* 14.19.26.

37. The classic treatment of Cicero's importance in the life and thought of Augustine is Testard 1958. See now also Rist 1994.

38. See van Oort 1995, 60 and the texts cited in nn17–20. Mani's favored epithet for God was "God of Truth," and Augustine recalls this identification of Truth as God's name in *Conf* 3.6.10. Long after he ceased to be a Manichaean, he retained this identification at the center of his thinking (see, e.g., *Conf* 10.24.35, where God is found to be *ipsam ueritatem*).

39. The long-standing question of how much access Augustine, as a Manichaean Auditor, would have had to the sacred texts of the sect, has recently been revisited by Coyle 2001 and 2003, who highlights Augustine's references to *hearing* rather than reading texts, and van Oort 2008, who makes a convincing counter-argument for Augustine having fairly open access to Manichaean literature. New evidence from a Manichaean community in Kellis, Egypt, supports van Oort's position by documenting Auditors actively copying Manichaean texts. While Coyle goes too far, therefore, in confining Augustine to largely oral instruction in the faith, his larger point is well substantiated: Augustine learned more about Manichaeism *after* his apostasy, and gained possession of Manichaean texts he had apparently not read while he was a member of the sect, whether from their lack of availability or his own lack of attention.

40. Bammel 1993, 8.

41. The Manichaeans were employing a polemical trope about the Christian resort to blind faith that had a long history in pagan philosophical critiques of Christianity, by such figures as Celsus (Origen, *C. Celsum* 3.75), Galen (*De pulsuum differentiis* 2.4), and Porphyry (*apud* Eusebius, *Praep. Evang.* 1.1).

42. On Augustine's surprising frankness about the superstitious character of the African Christianity of his youth, see Alfaric 1918, 70 n7; Courcelle 1968, 60–78; Solignac 1962, 127–28 n1; TeSelle 1970, 26–27.

43. Menasce 1956, 79. See also Decret 1978, 242–46; Chadwick 1990, 209; Mourant

1966, 72. Ferrari has gone so far as to offer the hypothesis that the spectacular appearance of Halley's comet in spring 374 prompted Augustine's conversion to Manichaeism (1977a; 1984, 34–44). But besides depending on giving some passages a specific interpretation that they will not bear, the hypothesis involves a miscalculation of when Augustine became a Manichaean, which he states as in his nineteenth year, that is, in the year between his eighteenth and nineteenth birthdays, which is the year *before* Halley's comet appeared. Ferrari is aware of the dating problem, and prefers to reinterpret what Augustine meant by his nineteenth year.

44. For examples of the characteristic Manichaean use of inductive reasoning, see Alexander of Lycopolis 18.25.1ff. ("Just as we see that, when the soul is separated from the body, the body itself perishes, so also, when the power had departed from matter, that which remains—i.e., matter—will fall apart and vanish"); Augustine, *JohTrac* 1.14; and *Fort* 20 ("Because it is a fact that we do sin against our wills . . . for this reason, we seek out a knowledge of the reason of things"). Starnes 1990, 173, makes a similar point about the inductive method with regard to the apparent logical gaps in the Manichaean account of the initial conflict between good and evil: since it is evident that we are in the midst of a conflict of good and evil, there must have been a situation that induced it, however difficult that is to reconcile with the inviolability of God.

45. TeSelle 1970, 27–28, identifies Ciceronian parallels to the Manichaean stance on leading people to knowledge through free inquiry rather than simply dictating truth to them on authority, even if the free inquiry is intended to arrive at these very truths.

46. O'Connell 1993c, 228.

47. E.g., *LA* 1.2.4, where the naturalness of evil behavior, compared to the self-discipline and education necessary to inculcate good behavior, is identified as one of the pieces of evidence that Augustine found persuasive.

48. E.g., P. Brown 2000, 35; cf. Outler 1955, 66, n.8: "The chief attraction of Manicheism lay in the fact that it appeared to offer a straightforward, apparently profound and rational solution to the problem of evil, both in nature and in human experience." See *MM* 2.2; *LA* 1.2.4, 1.2.10; *Conf* 3.7.12.

49. O'Meara astutely notes that the problem of evil and the spiritual nature of God were for Augustine "two of the greatest intellectual difficulties of his life. They were difficulties brought to his notice by the Manichees" (O'Meara 1954, 81–82).

50. See *Conf* 3.7.12; 6.3.4; 6.4.5; 6.11.18; *ME* 10.17.

51. Teske 1991a, 12. The same held true in the eastern half of the empire. When bishop Theophilus of Alexandria criticized an anthropomorphic conception of God in his festal letter of 399, he ignited a storm of protest that caused him not only to retract his position, but even to launch a campaign to purge the Egyptian church of anti-anthropomorphite Origenists (Clark 1990, 146–49).

52. Feldmann has taken this claim at face value, and made it the centerpiece of his analysis of Augustine's first conversion; see Feldmann 1975, 1980, and 1994.

53. "You maintain that Christ, who says, 'I am the truth,' feigned his incarnation, his death on the cross, the wounds of his passion, the marks shown after his resurrec-

tion" (*Faust.* 5.5). The Manichaean, Augustine tells us, "denies that Jesus was born of the seed of David, that he was made of a woman . . . he denies his death, his burial, and his resurrection. He holds that Christ had not a mortal body, and therefore could not really die; and that the marks of his wounds which he showed to his disciples . . . were not real" (*Faust.* 11.3). On the denial of the virgin birth, see *DEP* 2.2.3, and Evodius, *De fide* 22. The Manichaeans cited John 2:4 ("Woman, what have I to do with you?") and Matthew 12:48 ("Who is my mother?") against the idea that Jesus was born of Mary; see *Fid* 4.9. On Augustine's rejection of this docetic Christology, see also *AC* 18.20.

54. Menasce 1956, 87–88, has even suggested that Augustine's later interest in the mystical body of Christ reflects the lasting attraction of Manichaean Christology, which identified Christ with an extended presence permeating creation.

55. O'Connell 1996, 47.

56. By the time he quit the company of the Manichaeans, Augustine was fully familiar with their position that the text of the New Testament had been corrupted; but there is no evidence that he had given any thought at all to such arcane issues before joining them, or that such concern formed part of the Manichaean appeal for him. Such an idea presupposes a background of deep engagement with Christianity that Augustine entirely lacked. Courcelle 1968, 60–64, basing himself on remarks Augustine makes in *Serm* 51, goes so far as to call the discordance between the Matthean and Lucan genealogies Augustine's "principal difficulty" with the Bible in his youth. But while, as Courcelle demonstrates, some of the language used in *Serm* 51 echoes *Conf* 3.5.9, the specific issue of the gospel genealogies is an addition to Augustine's memory prompted by his recent encounter with Faustus's *Capitula*, and *Serm* 51 belongs to the same period as the more formal responses to Faustus on the latter's charges against the gospels, namely, *Faust* and *CE* (as rightly noted by O'Donnell 1992, vol. 2, 171–72). In fact, on more than one occasion Augustine says that he and his friends never found particularly persuasive the Manichaean claim that the New Testament text in wide circulation was corrupted.

57. Bonner 1963, 61; Mourant 1966, 72 concurs.

58. Chadwick 1990, 205–207; cf. Bonner 1977, 7. But for an attempt to balance the novelty of monastic asceticism against the background of broader voluntary celibacy in African Christianity, see Folliet 1961.

59. P. Brown, 176, citing *Conf* 5.10.18 and 4.3.4.

60. Rather typical of Augustinian scholarship to date is the uncautious remark of Starnes 1990, 201 n25, that Augustine's remarks on this subject offer "a very clear statement of the Manichaean position." A notable exception is Chadwick 1990, 210–11.

61. Menasce 1956, 91–93.

62. O'Brien 1974, 442. He further comments, "although in my attempt to understand the attraction of the Manichaean teachings I have resorted to an approach which discriminates cosmological and psychological levels of interpretation, to get a sense of the full force of the teaching it is necessary to react wholly to the teachings whose central images are perfectly able to keep together what I have taken apart" (442–43).

63. Decret has argued that all references in Augustine to the "small number" of Man-

ichaeans refer specifically to the Elect (1978, 188–91; 1991, 108–9). See *Adim* 15.2 and *MM* 15.36 for the equation of "Manichaean" with the "Elect"; in contrast, see *Faust* 30.6 for a reference to a large number of Auditors.

64. Alexander of Lycopolis 5.8.12–16 reports the appeal of Manichaeism to some of his "fellow philosophers."

65. Leo Ferrari plausibly suggests reminiscences of the appeal for Augustine of a secret society in his reflections in *JohTrac* 97.2 (Ferrari 1984, 27–28; see also Ferrari 1995,119–20). But it is a mistake to interpret Augustine's remark that he was expecting further initiation into secret mysteries (*Conf* 5.3.3) as an indication that there actually were such inner secrets in Manichaeism. On this subject, see Du Roy 1966, 32; Vannier 1990, 422.

66. This is correctly stressed by Stock 1996, 47–49.

67. Chadwick 1990, 218; Bonner 1963, 59, 62.

68. Coyle 1978, 85. That Augustine's attraction to Manichaeism may have been largely a matter of a youthful enthusiasm for a powerfully poetic world view that gradually yielded ground to more searching intellectual scrutiny (reflected also in Peter Brown's apt and insightful comparison of Augustine's little circle of Manichaeans to a group of intellectual communist "fellow travelers" in England or America in the middle of the twentieth century), puts one in mind of Clemenceau's famous dictum, "Not to be a socialist at twenty is proof of want of heart; to be one at thirty is proof of want of head."

69. Ferrari 1984, 12.

70. The Donatist Petilian claimed to have the word of a former Manichaean that they did practice baptism (*CLP* 3.17.20), eliciting Augustine's reply explicitly denying any such practice among them (cf. *DEP* 2.2.3), a fact confirmed by primary Manichaean sources critical of baptism; see Puech 1972, 598–99.

71. See *MM* 10–20.

72. O'Meara 1954, 49.

73. Evidence that the passage is not just the naked conscience of Augustine pouring itself out onto the page appears in its subtle structural aspects, elicited from the text in various ways by Ferrari 1970, 237ff.; 1979; and Shanzer 1996. Ferrari refers to the "dramatic genius" of Augustine at work here, and points to the structural parallelism in the *Confessions* between the pear tree and (1) the choice of trees from which to pluck fruit in the Garden of Eden, (2) the two kinds of fruit-bearing trees in Matthew 7.17–20, and (3) the fig tree under which Augustine decides to become a Catholic (*Conf* 8.12.28). Thus, a subtle connection is drawn between this event in Augustine's life and (1) original sin, (2) the problem of the choice between good and evil, and (3) Augustine's own choice of Catholicism over Manichaeism. As the "Tree of Life" on which Christ was hung corrects the original sin involving the Tree of Knowledge in Eden, so the fig tree under which Augustine weeps himself into a state of submission to God's will in the garden of Milan corrects the sign of original sin in his mindless assault on the pear tree (Ferrari 1970, 240).

74. Ferrari 1970, 237. Likewise, Johannes van Oort suggests, without further elaboration, that "a Manichaean background seems to be important" to understanding Augustine's handling of the Pear Incident in the *Confessions* (van Oort 1995, 66–67).

75. Ferrari 1970, 236–37.

76. E.g., *CMC* 6.7–8.14, 10.1–11; cf. *Faust* 6.4–8.

77. Shanzer 1996, 49, sees in the mention of pears in this passage simply an example of a proverbially cheap and common fruit.

78. "That he did not need what he stole is important to the problematic of sin" in what immediately follows "and the rest of the book" (O'Donnell 1992, vol. 2, 126).

79. "It is not that Augustine regarded robbing the pear-tree as the worst sin of his life but that he was appalled, on reflection, by the apparent lack of motive for the deed" (Bonner 1963, 54). As part of Augustine's reinterpretation of the incident, he resorts to the possible motive of a feeling of power (over the fruit, over the victim) that poorly imitates God's omnipotence, probably intended as an allusion to Adam and Eve's sinful aspiration to "be as God." This second explanation Augustine gives is linked to his thinking, emphasized particularly in *Conf*, that finds fault with all self-determination and pride, which is viewed as a kind of theft of God's glory. The roots of Augustine's emphasis on pride in Plotinus's concept of *tolma* (see esp. *Ennead* 5.1.1; 3.7.11) has been thoroughly explored by others. In Augustine, it assumes the character of an audacious imitation of God, and a desire to be God-like in one's freedom of action (see *ME* 12.20; *GCM* 2.5.6; *LA* 3.25.6; *Mus* 6.13.40).

80. Mann 1979 discerns that the passage is dominated by Augustine's struggle to solve the puzzle of the seeming gratuitousness of the incident, to the point of not even mentioning the secondary explanation Augustine finally offers. As a consequence of this latter oversight, Mann mistakenly concludes that Augustine means to affirm the apparent causelessness of evil as an anti-Manichaean argument, rather than recognizing that Augustine is struggling with a Manichaean argument critiquing the standard rationalization of evil by subjective perception of a good.

81. "An important rhetorical feature of the story of the pear theft lies in its demonstration that even the relatively minor events of human lives can become meaningful, if not happy or beautiful, when interpreted in terms of a larger framework of understanding" (Dixon 1999, 75).

82. That this initial analysis of the theft as apparently motiveless is Manichaean in inspiration has been recognized by Asher 1998, 238 and, following him, Kotzé 2004, 42.

CHAPTER 2. INHABITATION

1. I am making use of the very apt concept of Pierre Bourdieu, adjusting it to the more deliberative and planned environment of a religious system such as Manichaeism. Bourdieu's work (e.g., Bourdieu 1977) has emphasized the self-forming processes that evolve in general society without being planned or directed from any center, and are taken up unreflectively by individuals through socialization. The particular circumstances of a religion's deliberate program of self-formation creates more self-reflective conditions for those in the position of converts, who by definition are dealing with the juxtaposition of and transition between rival fields of *habitus* development.

2. See Butler 1997, 13–14.

3. Asad 1993, 63.

4. Butler 1997, 3.

5. Butler 1999, 125.

6. A good example of such a cell is attested in the abjuration statement of a Manichaean Auditor Felix, which describes his service to the Elect Eucharistus in a unit at Caesarea in Numidia that included also the fellow Auditors Maria and Lampadia (on which, see Decret 1978, 204–205). Another such cell has been reconstructed at Kellis in Egypt around the Elect Lysimachos (see Gardner, Alcock, and Funk 1999). Neither Diocletian's edict of 297 nor Valentinian I's of 372 mentions buildings to be confiscated. The latter refers instead to *domus et habitacula*, the private houses and apartments where Manichaean meetings took place.

7. See *Conf* 3.12.21; *Haer* 46.

8. As appears to be the case with Mourant 1966, 71 n18. Mourant nonetheless regards Augustine's Manichaean convictions as very strong, 78 and 78 n49, and states that, "We should be cautious in any minimizing of Augustine's Manichaeism," 82 n62.

9. The assumption that an Auditor was automatically expected to progress to the rank of an Elect leads Bertrand to idle speculation on why the Manichaean leadership might have delayed Augustine's initiation "into their secret doctrines" for so long (Bertrand 1914, 124).

10. Augustine himself explains this to Petilian, *CLP* 3.17.20: "the name of catechumen is not bestowed among them upon persons to denote that they are at some future time to be baptized, but that this name is given to such as are also called Hearers, on the supposition that they cannot observe what are considered the higher and greater commandments, which are observed by those whom they think right to distinguish and honor by the name of Elect." On the integral role of the Auditor to the Manichaean religious system, see BeDuhn 2000.

11. See *Keph 88*, 220.22–221.5.

12. E.g., *UC* 1.2; *Conf* 5.10.18. On whether as "progress" Augustine might have considered becoming an Elect, see O'Donnell 1992, vol. 2, 304.

13. Whether there were any such esoteric teachings reserved to the Elect has beens a debated question in contemporary scholarship. At least one contemporaneous Manichaean claimed that there were. Secundinus dismissed Augustine's anti-Manichaean writings by arguing that Augustine had never learned the *arcana* of the faith. Is this no more than a polemical ploy?

14. Starnes 1990, 90–92.

15. See Jerome, *Epistle* 22.13; 48.

16. Cf. Alexander of Lycopolis 4.7.19–21; Amphilocus of Iconium, *Exerc.* 19 and 28. On a meat test used to ferret out Manichaeans within the Nicene congregation in Alexandria under bishop Timothy contemporary with Augustine's own Manichaean period, see Stroumsa 1986, 312–314.

17. That is, whom one considers innocent, regardless of the law. See BeDuhn 2009a.

18. See *MM* 18.65; Alexander of Lycopolis 4.7.21ff.

19. The Manichaeans "take wives, which the law declares is for the procreation of children; but from this erroneous fear of polluting the substance of the deity, their intercourse with their wives is not of a lawful character; and the production of children, which is the proper end of marriage, they seek to avoid" (*Faust* 15.7), which in the later Augustine's eyes makes their marriages the equivalent of adultery.

20. Augustine reports, "they believe that the divine limbs of their God are subjected to restraint and contamination in these very carnal limbs of theirs. For they say that flesh is unclean; and it follows that God, in the part which is detained by the flesh, is made unclean: for they declare that he must be cleansed, and that till this is done, as far as it can be done, he undergoes all the passions to which flesh is subject, not only in suffering pain and distress, but also in sensual gratification. For it is for his sake, they say, that they abstain from sexual intercourse, that he may not be bound more closely in the bondage of the flesh, nor suffer more defilement" (*Faust* 6.3). In a typical extrapolation from actual Manichaean teaching to what he regards as necessary implications, Augustine says that the Manichaeans are taught to regard their parents as enemies, "because their union brought you into the bonds of flesh, and laid impure fetters even on your God."

21. Under Roman law, a marriage was a contractual arrangement between two families, establishing certain rights of inheritance and certain duties of dependency in the relationship between the two families and their properties, especially as they concerned any offspring of the couple. There was no religious ritual of marriage, although certain traditional celebrations could occur. Rather, a contract was made and the couple moved in together. This kind of formal marriage accounted for less than half the couples in the Roman Empire. For a good summary of the legal and social aspects of Augustine's concubinage, see Power 1992, esp. 50–51.

22. O'Connell rightly settles on this terminology (1996, 16). The technical term "morganatic marriage" could also be applied to Augustine's situation, provided we assume that there was a distinction between him and the woman in class status, barring them from entering into formal marriage. But such legal impediments were actually more rare than commonly assumed, and contra Ramirez 1981, 68–76, we have no reason to think Augustine's social status was high enough to invoke such legal restrictions. See Power 1992, 51. Augustine's own references to differences in "rank and fortune" (*BC* 5.5) refer not to class by birth, but to achieved status and envisioned prospects such as he had as rhetor of Milan in 384–386.

23. As Augustine himself states, *Serm* 224.3; *BC* 5.5). Jerome actually counseled such arrangements to leave a young man's options open for future celibacy and church service (*Epistula* 69.3.6; 4.2; 5.6–7), as eventually happened in Augustine's case—a position barely distinguishable from that of the Manichaeans. See Power 1992, 55 and n.74.

24. "Given by God"—a name generic enough to carry no specific religious identification, and perhaps even conveying a certain fatalistic acceptance of an unintended pregnancy in culturally provided terms. It was a Latinization of the indigenous—and pagan—name Iatanbaal; see Frend 1952, 79; P. Brown 2000, 52. The latter reports that it is well attested in Christian cemetery inscriptions from Africa.

25. Based on *Conf* 9.6.14, Adeodatus was nearly (*ferme*) in his fifteenth year when he was baptized in April 387. This information puts his birth in the summer of 373, Augustine's nineteenth year and the same year he became a Manichaean Auditor. His birth is commonly put one or even two years earlier in the secondary literature. But Mayer 1986, 37 has the correct date. So the child may have been born after Augustine's conversion, although conceived prior to it. There is no evidence that the Manichaeans encouraged abortion.

26. Manichaeans, he reports, "pour out their God by a shameful slip." A rhetorical— if not psychological—connection between this characterization and Augustine's repeated references in *Conf* to "pouring out" himself during his Manichaean period bears consideration, even though the latter passages have broader connotations informed by Neoplatonic treatment of the soul's engagement with material reality generally.

27. E.g., P. Brown 2000, 51–52, 80; Børresen 1994, 139; O'Donnell 1992, vol. 2, 359.

28. Chadwick 1990, 219; see also Power 1992, 53.

29. Power 1992, 52.

30. Suggested by P. Brown 2000, 80; Power 1992, 50–53.

31. Noted by Ramirez 1081, 75–76.

32. Starnes 1990, 91, 107 n10; see Courcelle 1968, 71 n2.

33. As suggested by Ramirez 1981, 70–71.

34. Decret 1978, 171, suggests that Diocletian's reference to the *otiosus* of the Manichaean Elect concerns specifically their adherence to pacifism, which the emperor regarded as a threat to the military resolve of the empire in the face of its Persian enemies. Ephrem states that those of "the school of Mani do not flee before a robber, and do not take refuge in citadels or (behind) walls" (*Second Discourse*, xlvii).

35. See Ephrem, *Fourth Discourse*, lxxxvi.

36. Cf. Ephrem, *Second Discourse*, xxx–xxxi.

37. Decret, picking up clues from Augustine, has speculated on the connections between the nonviolent ethic of Manichaeism and its relative popularity among people employed in trade rather than agriculture (Decret 1978, 208–9).

38. On Augustine's ultimate view against empathy with animal life and its consequences for western cultural attitudes toward the environment, see Miles 1995.

39. Foucault 1985, 26.

40. Foucault 1985, 26.

41. Foucault 1985, 27.

42. Foucault 1986, 62.

43. Foucault 1985, 27.

44. Foucault 1985, 28.

45. Foucault 1985, 28.

46. Butler 1997, 22.

47. Cary 2000.

48. Stendahl 1963.

49. Fort 3; *Faust* 14.11, 20.5.

50. Cf. *MM* 8.13; *GCM* 2.25.38; *EnPs* 25; *Ep* 236; Ephrem, *Fifth Discourse*, xciv.

51. Libanius, *Epistle* 1253, in defense of the Manichaeans against state persecution, characterizes them as harmless sun-worshipers.

52. Augustine provides the detail, "You call the sun a ship" (cf. Ephrem, *Fifth Discourse*, cxvi) and "you maintain that he is triangular, that is, that his light shines on the earth through a triangular window in heaven. Hence it is that you bend and bow your heads to the sun, while you worship not this visible sun, but some imaginary ship which you suppose to be shining through a triangular opening" (*Faust* 20.6).

53. "Sun and moon they honor most of all, not as gods, but as the means by which it is possible to attain to God" (5.7.27–8.1).

54. "They say, 'the moon receives the light which is refined, and during fifteen days draws it up and goes on emptying it out for another fifteen days" (*Second Discourse*, xxxvi). "They say that the sun receives the light from the moon" (*Second Discourse*, xxxviii). "They greatly magnify and call it 'the ship of light which,' as they say, 'bears away the burden of their refinings to the house of life'" (*Fifth Discourse*, cxvi).

55. Sachau 1887, vol. 2, 169 (quoted by al-Biruni).

56. "Free us by your skill, for we suffer here oppression, and torture, and pollution, only that you may mourn unmolested in your kingdom" (*Faust* 20.17).

57. Wheelock 1982, 65.

58. See BeDuhn 2008, 2009c.

59. Augustine refers to the "custom of making your disciples bring you food, that your teeth and stomach may be the means of relieving Christ, who is bound up in it. . . . You declare that Christ is liberated in this way . . ." (*Faust* 2.5). Novices of the Elect order consumed any food remaining at the end of the ritual (*MM* 16.52), thus avoiding throwing it away or handing it over to those who by eating it would reinvest the divine elements in the cycle of imprisoned rebirth.

60. "There are some people who think that alms should only be given to the just, while we ought to give nothing of the kind to sinners. The ones who take the lead in this error are the sacrilegious Manichaeans, who believe that pieces of God are mixed up and bundled together, and thus imprisoned, in every kind of food; and so they reckon we must spare these from being polluted by sinners and tied up in even more unpleasant knots" (*Serm* 164A.1).

61. Although here he is adapting this language to a different use, as part of a clever deployment of Manichaean rhetoric connected to the sacred meal throughout his narrative.

62. Cf. *Keph* 81; Ephrem, *Second Discourse*, xlii. The bodies of the Elect literally functioned as "workshops" or "laboratories," refining the divine elements from their mixture with evil substance (*Faust* 6.4, 15.7). The later Augustine delighted in ridiculing these ideas by his often repeated image of the Elect belching God back to heaven (e.g., *Faust* 5.10; the joke appears not to have been original with him: cf. Ephrem, *Second Discourse*, xlii–xliii), found amusement in the physiological details involved in Manichaean explanation of the processes involved (e.g., *Faust* 6.8), and happily associated the Manichaean focus on the ritual meal with Paul's criticism of those who make a god of their belly (*Faust* 6.5; cf. 20.13).

63. Yet, he tells us, "I had no relish for it, because the taste it left in my mouth was not the taste of truth . . . And it did not nourish me, but starved me all the more" (*Conf* 3.6.10).

64. See *Ep* 236: *auditores ante electos genua figunt ut eis manus supplicibus imponatur non a solis presbyteris vel episcopis aut diaconis sed a quibuslibet electis.*

65. While generally acknowledging the moral character of Manichaean conduct, Ephrem, *Hymn. c. haer.* 2.2–5, likewise criticizes the ease with which Manichaeans bestowed absolution (*šubqana* in the Syriac language Ephrem shared with Mani), compared to the position held by most western Christians that sin can be forgiven only once, through the waters of baptism; any sin committed after that requires a program of penance. The lighter Manichaean system of confession and absolution made serious inroads into later Catholic practice in the West, and seems to have become standard practice in the Nestorian Christian Church of the East as well (on the latter, see BeDuhn 2004).

66. For the most recent analysis of the sources on this ceremony, see Wurst 1995.

67. The social and psychological benefits of group membership extended well beyond Augustine's own circle of Carthaginian Manichaeans. When he was forced to flee Africa for Rome, his own life was preserved through a serious illness when he was taken in by his fellow Manichaeans there, despite being a total stranger to them. No doubt a personal commendation from the African Manichaean bishop Faustus, conveyed by the nameless traveling companion who accompanied Augustine on this journey, helped him gain their trust in a time of persecution. These same Roman compatriots went on to help him get set up in teaching, and then to arrange an important position for him close to the imperial court. Recent documentary finds at Kellis in Egypt attest similar local and long-distance bonds uniting Manichaeans into tight-knit communities of faith.

68. The phrasing is a clear allusion to the distinctive high quality of Manichaean books remarked upon by Augustine elsewhere.

69. See O'Meara 1954, 89–91.

70. He had two possible motives for being so frank about this positive experience at the time of writing the *Conf.* By it, he could partially excuse his long membership in the sect by the blandishments of such a group of friends. At the same time, he could appeal to this very circle of former companions to recognize that what was good in their time together was their togetherness, not its Manichaean context.

71. Mead 1964, 140.

72. See *Conf* 4.3.6, 7.2.3, 7.6.8. Although he was in Milan with Augustine in the crucial conversion period of 386, he was not baptized with him at Easter 387, but returned to Africa. He spent the next few years on his estate outside of Carthage, apparently bedridden much of the time. Augustine says Nebridius became a Catholic during this time (*Conf* 9.3.6), but his letters to Augustine reflect continued secular intellectual interests devoid of practically any reference to the cultic and devotional sphere.

73. P. Brown 2000, 43–44.

74. As P. Brown emphasizes, 2000, 44.

75. Vincentius was an adherent of the Rogatist sect of the Donatist Church, locked in

debate with Augustine over attempts to force Donatist union with the Catholic Church, when he exchanged letters with Augustine that included positive reminiscences of the latter's character during their school days together in Carthage, when Augustine had been a practicing Manichaean (*Ep* 93.51).

76. Frankfurt explains that a statement such as "A wants to X" "does not, by itself, indicate the relative strength of A's desire to X. It does not make clear whether this desire is at all likely to play a decisive role in what A actually does or tries to do. For it may correctly be said that A wants to X even when his desire to X is only one among his desires and when it is far from being paramount among them. . . . But the notion of the will, as I am employing it, is not coextensive with the notion of first-order desires. . . . Rather, it is the notion of an *effective* desire—one that moves (or will or would move) a person all the way to action. Thus the notion of the will is not coextensive with the notion of what an agent intends to do. For even though someone may have a settled intention to do X, he may nonetheless do something else instead of doing X because, despite his intention, his desire to do X proves to be weaker or less effective than some conflicting desire" (Frankfurt 1988, 13–14). Even a second-order desire, such as the one that moved Augustine to submit himself for formation by the Manichaean ethos, only indicates his will when it means that "A wants the desire to X to be the desire that moves him effectively to act. It is not merely that he wants the desire to X to be among the desires by which, to one degree or another, he is moved or inclined to act. He wants this desire to be effective—that is, to provide the motive in what he actually does" (15).

77. Frankfurt 1988, 174.

78. Frankfurt 1988, 164–165.

79. See Butler 1997, 13–14, 22.

80. Nietzsche 1967, 58.

81. Nietzsche 1967, 58.

82. Nietzsche 1967, 58.

83. Foucault 1979, 203.

84. See Foucault 1979, 30.

85. Butler 1997, 76; for her full discussion, see 71–78.

86. *Conf* 4.2.2–3.

87. *Conf* 4.3.4–4.16.31.

88. Starnes 1990, 92.

89. In the *Conf*, Augustine's effort to depict himself as a frivolous young cad is part of a demonstration that Manichaeism does not work, that it fails to motivate people to live moral lives. It was irrelevant to this purpose to dwell on the details of his Manichaean practices to which he alludes elsewhere.

CHAPTER 3. INDOCTRINATION

1. Vannier 1990, 421: "Les contraintes de la secte constituent une étape transitoire dans la recherche d'une explication rationelle du monde."

2. On some of the traits that may have distinguished the local North African Manichaeism from forms of the religion in other parts of the world, see Decret 1978, 191–92, 205–10.

3. This idea has a long history, going back to the polemical letter of Secundinus to Augustine (*Ep Sec* 3). One of its more recent advocates is Decret 1970, 10 and 28.

4. So, e.g., van Oort 2008.

5. Coyle 2001, 45; 2003, 10ff. He notes, 2001, 49–50, that Augustine reports postconversion circumstances for acquiring each of the Manichaean texts he quotes in his later writings.

6. An exception is Coyle 2001, 47, remarking of Augustine that, "he does not seem to have always understood even what he knew."

7. Thomas O'Laughlin observes that Augustine's adherence to Manichaeism, rather than simply continuing his studies of the sciences and liberal arts in a secular context, "indicates his desire to find all his answers in such a single combined teaching" that encompassed physics, metaphysics, and moral teachings (O'Laughlin 1992, 102). His later adoption of Nicene Christianity amounts to a second attempt at finding such a master discourse to which he can relate and even credit all of his other interests.

8. The complete version of this saying is found in the Sogdian text Ch 5554 (Sundermann 1985, lines 124–135); cf. *Keph* 154.

9. *et adtente audiui et temere credidi et instanter, quibus potui, persuasi et aduersus alios pertinaciter animoseque defendi.*

10. See Lim 1992, 253, noting such questions as "whence is evil?" (*Conf* 3.7.12), "how does the soul err, if it is made by God?" (*Conf* 4.15.26), and "whence is both sin and evil—if from humans, whence humans, if from angels, whence angels?" (*DA* 10).

11. "To your little ones, faithful Christians . . . I babbled away in my petulant fashion, asking, 'If God made the soul, why does it fall into error?'" (*Conf* 4.15.26).

12. "I derided your holy servants and prophets [and] laughed at them" (*Conf* 3.10.18).

13. West 1933, 51, 58.

14. See, e.g., Plutarch, *Isis and Osiris* 48: "Plato generally tries to hide his doctrine. It is for this reason that he often calls the principle of good 'unchanged being' and that of evil 'changeable being.' Nevertheless in his book *Laws* which he composed at an advanced age he expressly states that the world is not directed by one soul alone; there are perhaps a great number of souls, but at least two, one of which produces good and the other, opposed to this one, is the cause of evil." Aristotle shared Plutarch's understanding of Plato's position (*Metaphysics* 1.6.988a.7–16; see Plato's *Laws* 10.896; *Epinomis* 989d–e). Titus of Bostra noted such parallels to the Manichaean position, 1.6.

15. But Titus of Bostra 4.19 attributes it to the Iranian heritage of Mani.

16. See Plutarch, *De an. procr.* 1014B; Plotinus, *En.* 1.8.5, 1.8.11, 2.4.16, 2.4.25, Porphyry, *Sent.* 30.2.

17. Recognized at the time by Titus of Bostra, 1.29 and 1.32.

18. See *Timaeus* 30a.

19. See Troje 1948. Plato's concept of disorderly motion as the essential characteristic

of matter, its "soul," was maintained by such Middle Platonists as Albinus, Atticus (*apud* Proclus, *In Tim.* I, 391, 10; 381, 27D), Numenius (fr. 52 des Places), and Plutarch (*De Isid.* 369E-371E, *De an. procr.* 1015C). Both Alexander of Lycopolis and Augustine carry out intra-Platonic debates on the back of the Manichaeans, siding with those who, following Aristotle, consider *hylē* a passive substrate of material differentiated only by the infusion of eternal forms. "Not knowing what *hylē* or the subject-matter of things is, you make it the race of darkness, in which you place not only innumerable bodily forms of five different kinds, but also a formative mind. Such, indeed, is your ignorance or insanity, that you call this mind *hylē*, and make it give forms instead of taking them" (*Faust* 20.14).

20. See *MM* 3.5–5.7, 8.11; *CEF* 25.27, 35.39; *GL* 8.14.31; *NB* 4–9; cf. Ephrem, *Fourth Discourse*, lxxxiv.

21. O'Donnell 1992, vol. 2, 186.

22. Torchia 1999, 140–41.

23. This language of a "light air and light earth" and a "dark air and dark earth" can be confirmed from a number of other sources, e.g., Ephrem, *Third Discourse*, lviii; *Fifth Discourse*, xcvi-xcvii.

24. Cf. *CEF* 15.19–24.26; *Conf* 5.10.20; Titus of Bostra 1.9, 1.17. The Manichaeans, he reports, "tell of a land of light cut asunder on one side, as by a narrow wedge, by the land of the race of darkness" (*Faust* 4.2; cf. Titus 1.11; Ephrem, *Third Discourse*, lviii-lix).

25. Stroumsa and Stroumsa 1988, 40.

26. Of the Manichaean account of the realm of light, Augustine recalls, "Do you not remember your love-song, where you describe the chief ruler in perennial majesty, crowned with flowers? . . . a real king, bearing a sceptre and crowned with flowers. . . . The song goes on to tell of twelve seasons clothed in flowers, and filled with song, throwing their flowers at their father's feet. These are twelve great gods of yours, three in each of the four regions surrounding the first deity. . . . Besides, there are countless principalities, and hosts of gods, and troops of angels, which you say were not created by God, but produced from his substance. . . . Sing on then . . . you are invited to fabulous dwellings of angels in a happy clime, and to fragrant fields where nectar flows forever from trees and hills, in seas and rivers" (*Faust* 15.5–6; cf. *CEF* 13.16). Yet elsewhere he reports Manichaean objections to anthropomorphism, and relates that "Among you there is no one who will picture God in a human form" (*ME* 10.17). Of descriptions of the realm of darkness, he reports that it is "a nation of darkness, and in that nation they think there are bodies and forms and souls in those bodies" (*GCM* 1.4.7). Five "caves" constitute the dark region, each the source of one of five elements: darkness, water, wind, fire, and smoke (*MM* 9; *CEF* 18.20, 28.31; *Conf* 3.6.11; *Faust* 2.3). Each element produces a characteristic kind of creature: serpents from darkness, swimming creatures from water, flying creatures from winds, quadrupeds from fire, and bipeds from smoke (*MM* 9.14, 16–17; *CEF* 28.31). "They tell us, indeed, of the first bodies of these principles of darkness being generated like worms from trees of darkness; and the trees, they say, are produced from the five elements" (*Faust* 6.8). These creaturely forms are not animal life as we know it on earth, but the demonic "forms" which animal life in this world materializes (a distinction ignored for polemical purposes by Augustine in *MM* 9.16–17).

27. Indeed, Augustine read about precisely such a fall scenario in the *Hortensius* (fragment 97), where Cicero refers to the philosophical view that our souls have been joined to bodies as to a prison, to atone for some sins (*scelera*) committed in a higher existence, before our birth into this world.

28. See *MM* 9.17; *VR* 9.16; *AC* 4; *Cont* 5; Titus of Bostra 1.17; Alexander of Lycopolis 3.5.15ff.; Ephrem, *Second Discourse*, xxix, xlix; *Third Discourse*, lviii–lix; *Fourth Discourse*, lxxviii, lxxxiii.

29. "God, however, though being determined to punish it, could find no evil by means of which this punishment could have been administered. For there was no evil in God's house. So he sent a certain power which we call soul towards matter, which was to mingle with it throughout" (Alexander of Lycopolis 3.5.19ff.). Likewise, Ephrem says that according to the Manichaeans the course of action of the inhabitants of the realm of light was dictated in part by "the lack of walls, of which they had none" (*Second Discourse*, xlvii).

30. God's action was preemptive because he possessed foresight, an attribute the force of evil lacked. Augustine repeats from "the books of the Manichaeans" that "God took precautions against an invasion by his enemies" (*MM* 12.25), and that "he foresaw this from eternity" (*Faust* 16.28).

31. After his apostasy, while staying in Carthage after his return to Africa as a Catholic, he apparently heard for the first time the key detail of the myth that differentiated the vulnerability of God himself from that of the other inhabitants of the realm of light, such that "the kingdom of God had some territory which could be invaded by a hostile race, but . . . God himself could not be violated in any way" (*MM* 12.26).

32. Alexander of Lycopolis reports that the Manichaeans taught that the divine power "streamed into" matter (17.25.1–2), and that, true to their materialist understanding of the divine nature, it was divided into pieces in this process (20.28.1ff.).

33. See Proclus's reports of the views of Plutarch and Atticus, *In Tim.* I, 276, 30–277, 7; I, 381, 26–382, 12. Plotinus retained the idea that the soul may have entered into contact with matter to bring order to it, in tension with his more usual view of the soul's fall through a perverse ambition (*tolma*); see *En.* 4.3.17, 4.8.3. Similarly, the Pythagorean Numenius (fr. 11 des Places) describes the formation of the world in the following terms: "The first god, existing in his own place, is simple and, consorting as he does with himself alone, can never be divisible. The second and third gods, however, are in fact one; but in the process of coming into contact with matter, which is the Dyad, he (i.e., the second/third god) gives unity to it, but is himself divided by it, since matter has a character prone to desire and is in flux."

34. Cf. Ephrem, *Fourth Discourse*, lxxix: "He says the Primal Man cast his five bright ones into the mouth of the sons of darkness, in order that, as a hunter, he might catch them with his net."

35. "They say the essence of all the souls is one" (Ephrem, *Fifth Discourse*, cviii); "all the souls are from one nature, and their nature is pure and beautiful" (Ephrem, *Fifth Discourse*, cxi).

36. The Manichaeans "say that earth, and wood, and stones have sense, and that their

life is more intelligent than animal life" (*Faust* 15.4; cf. *MM* 17; *GLimp* 5.24), because the latter display a greater admixture of evil in their disorderly and sometimes violent behavior, governed by evil instincts and irrational fear (*MM* 17.59).

37. Cf. Ephrem, *Third Discourse*, lxix; *Fourth Discourse*, lxxxv.

38. E.g., brightness of color, pleasantness of odor, sweetness of taste, *MM* 16.39; cf. Ephrem, *Second Discourse*, xliii–xliv.

39. Augustine notes this distinctive theory of "recycling" in *GL* 7.11.17.

40. See *MM* 9.17–18, 15.36; *VR* 9.16; *AC* 4; Titus of Bostra 1.17; Alexander of Lycapolis 3.6.6ff.

41. See, e.g., Ephrem, *Second Discourse*, xxxiii–xxxvi; *Against Mani*, cviii.

42. See *Faust* 15.5–6; 20.9–11; 32.19.

43. The divine agents were thought to unfold from the one God as events dictated, "projected for our salvation from the mass of [God's] transplendent body" (*Conf* 5.10.20). Although Augustine concedes that the Manichaeans "hold all your gods to be of one substance" (*Faust* 20.10), he nonetheless considers them polytheists because they assign each of these beings to distinct "powers, functions, and employments." "One does battle with the race of darkness; another constructs the world from the part that is captured; another, standing above, has the world in his hand; another holds him up from below; another turns the wheels of the fire and winds and waters beneath; another, in his circuit of the heavens, gathers with his beams the members of your God from cesspools" (*Faust* 20.10).

44. The forces of light adapt their tactics to deal effectively with the nature of evil and further the purpose of liberation. For example, the division of life into sexes originates with evil, a reflection of its disunity (*Cont* 10); but good beings can reflect this gendered duality back to evil tactically in order to bring it into subjugation through its own disordered passions (*Faust* 15.7; cf. 20.6). Augustine regarded such myths of divine "seduction" as the basis for suspicions about Manichaean sexual conduct (*Faust* 20.8), but he appears not to have known these mythological details while a Manichaean himself, and only to have learned of them in the opening years of the fifth century (*Fel* 2.7, 2.22; *NB* 44; *Faust* 6.8, 22.98), since the scenario goes unmentioned in earlier writings where it would have been relevant and useful (e.g., *MM*, *Fort*). In another favorite episode among polemicists, the forces of light kinetically process the demonic thieves of light on the rotating sphere of the sky, causing them to yield up living substance, "miscarriages" that give rise to animal life on earth (*MM* 9.14, 18; 17.60–61; cf. *Faust* 6.8, 15.6, 20.10).

45. Nils Pedersen makes note of the relatively demythologized Manichaeism confronted by both Alexander of Lycopolis and Titus of Bostra (Pedersen 2004, 187ff.).

46. See Tardieu 1979, 1981; Decret 1980.

47. See Decret 1978, 89–90.

48. Maher 1945, 316–17.

49. Cf. *Faust* 20.10: "your fabulous descriptions . . . you neither explain nor represent in a visible form."

50. See Vannier 1990, 422; Du Roy 1966, 32; O'Meara 1954, 192 n53.

51. Cf. Hippolytus, *Ref. haer.* 1.2; Iamblichus, *Vita Pyth.* 81 and 87–89.

52. Cf. Alexander of Lycopolis, 10.16. In bringing up this mythic literalism when he does in his later polemic, Augustine's intention appears to be to forestall any belated demythologizing efforts on the part of his Manichaean opponents.

53. See *MM* 19.73; *Faust* 21.14; Titus of Bostra 1.38, 3.5, *Keph* 55, *Keph* 56.

54. Cf. 19.29; Ephrem, *Fourth Discourse*, lxxxv; *Fifth Discourse*, cii; *Keph 38*. Ephrem, *Second Discourse*, xxxi, says: "Darkness contrived to frame that body to be a prison-house for the soul that it might not go forth thence."

55. Cf. Ephrem, *First Discourse*, passim.

56. Ephrem reports that the Manichaeans taught that "the evil mixed in us injures us" (*Fifth Discourse*, ci) and that because the body disturbed the soul, it forgot its true identity and original home (*Fifth Discourse*, cvii, cix). Alexander of Lycopolis states that Manichaeans attribute changes of character and vices in the soul to matter (7.12.1f.), and that they regard passions such as *hēdonē* and *epithumia* the epitome of evil (15.22.5–7).

57. See Ephrem, *First Discourse*, passim; *Fifth Discourse*, cxii, cxviii.

58. These observations on the inherent sinfulness of the behavior even of an infant have been read in light of Augustine's later view of original sin, in particular as it emerged in connection with arguments with the Pelagians over infant baptism. But the *Confessions* were written more than a decade before that issue came to the forefront of Augustine's concern. Although they serve a function within Augustine's developing thinking on human sinfulness at the time of the *Confessions*, that does not account for the vividness of the recollection of observations made more than twenty years earlier. His close scrutiny of his child's behavior most likely reflects an active interest at the time in what it might indicate about human nature according to Manichaean teachings.

59. Does Augustine genuinely not have a position on the preexistence of the human soul, or is he rhetorically taking an agnostic position on the question in order to score a point with his Manichaean readers that such a question falls beyond what can be known through directly observed evidence, and therefore should not be grounds for ruling out non-Manichaean alternatives?

60. See Titus of Bostra 1.2; Ephrem, *First Discourse*, xx.

61. See *Keph 38*, 95.17–96.6.

62. E.g., Seneca's discussion of the determination of one's inborn nature by the specific mixture of elements that constitute the person (*De Ira* 20.2). On the fatalistic ethos of antiquity, see Amand 1973.

63. Augustine says that he held this opinion during his time at Rome, when he "began to hold in a more loose and careless manner those very tenets with which, if I came upon nothing better, I had resolved to be content" (*Conf* 5.10.18). He may be acknowledging, therefore, some recognition that he held views slightly askew of Manichaean teaching on the subject, and had missed the confessional intent of the Manichaean ethos regardless of how poorly that intent was served, in his opinion, by Manichaean ideology.

64. We cannot completely rule out the possibility that what appears to be given as personal recollection may be colored by polemical clichés Augustine had picked up from other critics of Manichaeism. Several fourth-century Christian writers before him had sought to

depict Manichaean ethical teachings as self-excusing and lax. Priscillian of Avila, for example, in his *Tractate on Genesis* 5.63.17–23, criticizes the Manichaean attribution of the human body to the devil, by which, he suggests, they seek to avoid responsibility for sin, "supposing that their corporeal sin is no concern to the divine disposition" (Burrus 1995, 72).

65. See Decret 1978, 241–42 on Augustine's misrepresentation.

66. See, e.g., Secundinus's use of Mt 18.7/Lk 17.1 in *Ep Sec* 1: . . . *malo, non quod nihil est, aut quod factione passioneque mortalium gignitur, sed quod paratum est ut veniat. Vae autem illi qui se eidem praebuerit occasionem.*

67. In hindsight, he characterized himself in his younger days as "a proud, contentious, young man" (*UC* 1.2).

68. Likewise, Alexander of Lycopolis notes, and objects to, the Manichaean doctrine of grace (16.23–24).

69. So Mani, in one of his letters, prays, "May grace and salvation be granted to you by our God, who is in truth true God, and may he himself illuminate your mind and reveal his justice to you, since you are the fruit of the divine root" (*Menoch* 172).

70. On the Manichaean docetic Christology, see *Serm* 2.2.2, 92.3.3, 183.1.1; *Conf* 5.10.20; *Faust* 3.1, 5.2–3, 11.3, 20.11, 23.1–2, 26.1, 28.1, 29.2, 32.17; *Ep* 236.2; *Haer* 46; also *Acta Archelai* 5, 55, and 59.

71. The Manichaean, Augustine relates, "holds that Christ did not have a mortal body, and therefore could not really die; and that the marks of his wounds which he showed to his disciples . . . were not real" (*Faust* 11.3). Cf. *Faust* 26.1–2; 29.1; *Serm* 116.4.4.

72. See the Manichaean interpretation of John 1 reported by Augustine in *JohTrac* 1.16.

73. See *Keph 98*, 249.16–21.

74. The Manichaeans believed that the book of Genesis contains a distorted version of this encounter, and they "found fault with the prohibition in paradise, and have praised the serpent for opening Adam's eyes" (*Faust* 1.3). In direct contrast to the Christian idea of Adam's fall, the Manichaeans taught that Adam had been awakened to truth by Christ. Both Augustine (*GCM* 2.26.39; *Faust* 15.9; cf. 22.49) and Titus of Bostra (3.7) claim that they actually identified the serpent in Eden with Christ, although Pedersen has expressed reservations about the claim as an oversimplification (Pedersen 2004, 84 and n72).

75. Mani explained some of the differences between religions by the specific locations and languages to which apostles were sent (*Keph 143*).

76. E.g., Lao Tzu in China, and even Hermes Trismegistus and Plato in the Roman world. Ephrem reports Manichaean recognition of Hermes Trismegistus and Plato as "heralds of that good one in the world" (*Against Mani*, xcviii–xcix; on Plato, cf. Severus of Antioch, *Hom. Cath.* 123). Faustus affirms the possibility of finding traces of truth in the Sibylline, Hermetic, and Orphic books, at least as a starting point for bringing people to the truth of Manichaeism (*Faust* 13.1). Alexander of Lycopolis, 5.8.5ff. also reports Manichaean use of pagan mythology (specifically, the myth of the Titanomachy, which was well known throughout the Near Eastern homeland of Mani) in proselytization efforts among pagans.

77. Cf. *Keph 56*, 142.12–32.

78. On this vulnerable metabolism of the human body, see BeDuhn 2001. On astrological influences as one of these sources of evil, see Schipper 2001.

79. Augustine says he never read in Manichaean books nor heard Manichaeans speak of ghosts or the shades of the dead surviving. "In fact, you generally oppose such ideas: for you tell us that the souls of the dead, if they are wicked, or not purified, are made to pass through various changes, or suffer punishment still more severe; while the good souls are placed in ships, and sail through heaven to that imaginary region of light which they died fighting for. According to you, then, no souls remain near the burying-place of the body" (*Faust* 20.21). Manichaeans rejected the physical resurrection of the body as antithetical to the return of the liberated soul to the realm of light (*Faust* 4.2). They are "accustomed to argue . . . against our faith in the doctrine of the resurrection of the body" by quoting the saying, "Flesh and blood shall not inherit the kingdom of God" (*Faust* 16.29).

80. See *GL* 7.11.17. Rebirth of the soul in trees is a possible fate threatened of those who commit violations of Manichaean ethical precepts (*MM* 17.55). Augustine maintains that the Manichaeans believed that souls in such a state lack the capacity to understand religious teaching or make moral progress, even though they can hear voices, understand language, perceive motion, and even in some sense know human intention (*MM* 17.56; cf. *GLimp* 5.24). His characterization appears to reflect the material incorporated into the narrative of Mani's life preserved in the *Cologne Mani Codex*.

81. The Manichaean view on this subject is akin to notions found in the likewise materialist understanding of human souls in Stoicism. Stoics spoke in terms of the degree of tension a soul has determining its cohesiveness. They likewise associated the more cohesive soul or part of soul with *nous*, and took the position that more rational souls with greater tension—namely, those of the wise—survive longer after death, whereas less cohesive souls dissolve after a short time (see Annas 1992, 68).

82. It is instructive that Augustine relates this episode out of sequence, turning back to it after relating his conversation on astrology with Vindicianus that probably took place some five years later (*Conf* 4.3.5). Vindicianus was probably proconsul in 380–381, and this would have been the time of Augustine's triumph in the rhetorical competition before him (Barnes 1985, 151–53). Augustine does not mean to provide a chronological account of developments while he was a Manichaean. Instead, he sifts through those years for weaknesses in his experience of the Manichaean system as a solution to his issues.

83. Burkitt 1925, 39–40.

84. In its lack of promise of a personal immortality, Manichaeism fit in well with the Stoic outlook widely disseminated as the popular philosophy of the time, as well as with the Platonic idea of separate individuality as a defective existence. The general Christian position on the immortality of the individual soul stands apart from these other strands of late antique thought on this subject.

85. In my opinion the reading of this passage offered by Starnes 1990, 95–96, runs into difficulties out of reliance on weak secondary sources on the Manichaean understanding of self and death. Augustine laments not the loss of the "concrete sensible" form of his friend

that includes evil as well as good components, but the dissolution of the soul that was the entirety of his friend as far as Augustine and the Manichaeans were concerned. Augustine quite clearly speaks of the love of one soul for another. He is troubled, therefore, by a sense of loss over what the Manichaean viewed as a temporary identity of soul stuff passing on to new combinations, rather than by finding himself loving things about his friend that Manichaeism would regard as evil.

86. The fact that the "God" Augustine told himself to trust is characterized as a fantasy reinforces that it was the particular God of the Manichaeans, connected to that religion's tenets about what God did or could do with respect to the death of his friend.

87. Here again, Starnes goes astray. Augustine's catalogue of the pleasures of life that had lost their appeal (*Conf* 4.7.12) is a purely Classical trope for describing the loss of a loved one, and not a critique of a Manichaeism for which "the absolute good was in the sensible" (Starnes 1990, 97). If there is subtle criticism of Manichaeism in this passage, it is simply that the religion had not led Augustine, as it should have, to transcend such everyday pleasures as "plays," "sumptuous banquets," and "the pleasure of the bedroom and the bed."

88. See Sundermann 2007.

89. See, e.g. Ovid, *Trist.* 4.4.72; Horace, *Carm.* 1.3.5–8.

90. For a careful consideration of the two possible eschatological outcomes of Manichaean salvation history, see Sala 2007.

91. See *Faust* 5.4, 11.3, 13.18; cf. Titus of Bostra 1.17, 1.39–41. Augustine confronts the Manichaeans with their belief that the "vulnerable Jesus" would not be entirely liberated in the end. "For you hold that some tiny particles of no value still remain in the excrement, to be mixed up and compounded again and again in various material forms, and to be released and purified at any rate by the fire in which the world will be burned up if not before. Nay, even then, you say, Christ is not entirely liberated; but some extreme particles of his good and divine nature, which have been so defiled that they cannot be cleansed, are condemned to stay forever in the horrid mass of darkness" (*Faust* 2.5). "The end of the whole argument is to bring the soul to believe that the reason for its misery in this world is that it is the means of preventing God from being deprived of his kingdom, and that God's substance and nature is so exposed to change, corruption, injury, and contamination, that part of it is incurably defiled, and is consigned by himself to eternal punishment in the mass of darkness, though when it was in harmless union with himself, and guilty of no crime, he knowingly sent it where it was to suffer defilement" (*Faust* 28.5).

92. Cf. *Faust* 26.6; CD 11.22; Ephrem, *Second Discourse*, xxix–xxx; *Third Discourse*, lxxi–lxxiii; *Fourth Discourse*, lxxiv–lxxv. "For part of your God was sent to suffer hopeless contamination, that there might be a covering for the mass in which the enemy is to be buried forever alive" (*Faust* 21.16).

93. A useful detail for associating the Manichaeans with the Stoics.

94. "You attempt, indeed, to vindicate the goodness of God, by asserting that *hyle* when shut up is prevented from doing any more injury to itself" (*Faust* 21.16).

95. Cf. *Faust* 22.22: "For this will be the accusation against those who will be con-

demned forever to the mass of darkness, that they suffered themselves to lose their original brightness, and became the enemies of sacred light"; 22.98: "The Manichaean says that this part, after mixture and combination with evil during the course of ages, has not been obedient." Mani appears to have written that the condemned portion of light is so alienated from its own identity that it actually "loves" the darkness (see Ephrem, *Fourth Discourse*, lxxx).

96. On the cultural expectation of secret doctrines given to initiates in the philosophical and mystery schools of the age, see O'Meara 192 n53.

97. See *Kephalaion* 9, and its ritual exposition by Puech 1972, 620–25.

98. See Ferrari 1984, 13; Ratzinger 1967.

99. See Du Roy 1966, 43; Vannier 1990, 422.

100. "So while holding that [the Manichaeans] had on balance the best position, he continued to study the non-Manichee explanations of the cosmos and its operation as well" (O'Laughlin 1992, 103). O'Laughlin emphasizes that Augustine's interest in astrology predated his commitment to Manichaeism and persisted beyond that commitment (1992, 106).

101. See *Keph* 69; *Hom* 30.3. On Manichaean astrological teachings, and their relation to other views of the time, see F. S. Jones 1997; Panaino 1997. For the grounds of Manichaean reservations about astrology, see also Sachau 1910, vol. 1, 381.

102. Augustine refers to those who "count the stars . . . measure the constellations in the sky and track down the paths of the stars" as "philosophers" (*Conf* 5.3.3).

103. See *Ep* 55.4.6–7.

104. See *Conf* 5.3.6; *GL* 1.19.39; *Trin* 3.2.7, 3.9.19; *Serm* 68.1.2; *SermMai* 126.4–5; *Ep* 199.10.34; *GPO* 2.23.7. After demonstrating that Augustine was an active practitioner of astrology, and highlighting some of the key differences between this ordinary popular astrology and the astrological views of the Manichaeans, Thomas O'Laughlin remarks, "His use of ordinary astrology is significant: it implies that not only had he difficulties over aspects of Manichee teaching while he was with them, but that he also engaged in activities which were tantamount to a denial of Mani" (O'Laughlin 1992, 118).

105. O'Laughlin 1992, 116–18.

106. See *Cont* 5.14: *et alii quidem qui sua consueverunt excusare peccata, fato se ad peccandum queruntur impelli, tanquam hoc decreverint sidera et coelum prius talia decernendo peccaverit . . . haec manichaeorum est immundissima insania.*

107. As argued by Svoboda 1933, 16. See especially Augustine's apparent reference to a dialogue setting for his deliberations in *Conf* 4.13.20. If Svoboda is correct, then Augustine maintained a consistent fondness for this genre across the divide of his conversion from Manichaeism to Nicene Christianity. Kato 1965, 238, suggests that it may have been a dialogue with himself, as the *Soliloquies* would later be.

108. Lee 1999, 23. On the Manichaean underpinnings of the work, see Alfaric 1918, 222–25; Boyer 1953, 42; Testard 1958, vol. 1, 55; Kato 1965; Starnes 1990, 102–106, 110–11 n80; van Oort 1995, 67. O'Meara regards the work as "a public expression of his Manichaean faith" (O'Meara 1954, 97). P. Brown comments: "When Augustine wrote a treatise of aes-

thetics at the age of 26, he will reflect, in an acceptable, classical, form this exotic and potent [Manichaean] myth" (P. Brown 2000, 41). On the debt to Cicero, and through Cicero to other metaphysical resources, see Testard 1958, vol. 1, 49–66; affirmed by Bonner 1963, 65.

109. In hindsight, Augustine reduces the book to a shallow bid for the advancement of his rhetorical career, dedicating it to a fellow rhetor from Africa who had made it big in Rome. Augustine surely means his brief account of it in the *Confessions* to serve as another indication that Manichaeism failed to direct his desires to more spiritual goals. Starnes's remark that the confusion of the quest for wisdom with the world's approbation "was inevitable for a Manichee" (1990, 102) is simply a continuation of Augustine's own polemic, albeit a misreading even of that polemic. Augustine's critique of Manichaeism is consistently that it failed to make him a better person, not that it actively sought to make him a worse person.

110. Augustine gives the impression that he does not have the work in front of him as he summarizes it in the *Confessions*, which if true means that his recollection of its content could have been colored by his later philosophical readings and commitments. John O'Meara thinks it likely that the work is being recalled through the lens of Plotinus's *On Beauty* (*Ennead* 1.6), which had since come to determine Augustine's thoughts on beauty, and identifies as well the influence of Platonism, Stoicism, and Pythagoreanism in the *Confessions* account of the work (O'Meara 1954, 98).

111. Lee 1999, passim. Neither does Augustine show any knowledge of Plato's disquisition on beauty, the *Symposium*.

112. On the Pythagorean underpinning of *The Beautiful*, see Solignac 1958; Svoboda 1933, 15; Kato 1965.

113. On the sort of Pythagorean texts that might have been available to Augustine, see Thesleff 1961 and 1965.

114. Calcidius, in his *Commentary on the Timaeus*, 295, reports of Numenius, "He says that Pythagoras calls the Godhead the monad, matter the dyad," and that other interpreters of Pythagoras are wrong when they suggest that the dyad was produced by the monad. The nondualistic view would suggest that "God would be changed into matter . . . . Even to people of mediocre education this is obviously impossible" (van Winden 1965, 103). Numenius thus represents the dualistic wing of Pythagoreanism, and displays many other ideas that suit Manichaeism, including the distinction of the Father from the creative agency (Des Places fr. 11, 21), apportioning the duties of the Demiurge to more than one creative agency (fr. 11), and the existence of two souls (fr. 44, 52).

115. Kato 1965, 236, building on Solignac 1958, 129 n44 and 133, cites Porphyry, *Life of Pythagoras*, 38; Ps.-Plutarch, *On the Life and Poetry of Homer*, 245; the *Theologumena arithmetikes* 100.6.4f.; and Nicomachus of Gerasa, *Arithmetical Introduction*, 2.17, 18.1, 18.4, 19.1, 20.2. For the latter, see TeSelle 1970, 30, who notes that the work had been translated into Latin by Apuleius. TeSelle points to the argument of Solignac that this work stands behind the commentary on Scipio's Dream by Favonius, a pupil of Augustine (see Solignac 1958, and 1962, 670–73). Andresen 1968 argues for Numenius and Calcidius as sources of Augustine's eclectic philosophical views with distinctly Pythagorean elements.

116. See Solignac 1958.

117. TeSelle 1970, 30.

118. On Cicero as a possible inspiration for Augustine's use of the concept of *aptum*, suggested by Testard 1958, 61 n1 and Kato 1965, 234, see *De finibus* 5.17, 5.23 and *De oratione* 3.20.

119. Cf. the related ideas in *Conf* 2.5.10. Starnes fundamentally misunderstands Augustine's construct when he claims that he equated the suitable with evil, and sought to explain the attractiveness of evil (Starnes 1990, 103). The suitable is not the evil dyad, but a secondary beauty retaining sufficient coherence to reflect its roots in the pure principle of beauty even though riven by the disintegrating dyadic force.

120. We may detect another echo of these ideas worked out in *The Beautiful* in *MM* 6.8, a section of the work dating to circa 388 C.E.: "Truly, conformity and harmony are the working of unity, by which things that are composite exist insofar as they exist; for simple things exist by themselves, since they are one. But things that are not simple imitate unity by the harmony of their parts; and they exist to the extent that they attain it. Wherefore, orderly arrangement brings about being, and disorderly arrangement non-being, which is also called perversion or corruption." The synthesis with Augustine's new Neoplatonism is well underway, but does not completely obscure his earlier ruminations.

121. A surprising late reminiscence of his early thinking. Cf. Augustine's comments, *MM* 4.6—perhaps only slightly overlaid with Neoplatonic ideas—that all mutable created things are good inasmuch as they participate in the immutable supreme good.

122. Although preserved in a considerably later Iranian text, M9.I, the parallel statement derives from one of Mani's writings, presumably available to Augustine: "the wise . . . are capable of recognizing the unbounded and timeless and unmixed goodness of paradise in the bounded and temporal and mixed goodness of the material world; and in the same way, the incalculable and unbounded evil of hell is known to exist through the numerable and bounded evil that is seen in the material world."

123. According to Lee, "In composing *De pulchro et apto*, Augustine took an inductive approach in a three-stage investigation: observation, abstraction, and contemplation" (Lee 1999, 24), and this method derives from Manichaeism (25). Despite Augustine's supposed conversion to the deductive approach employed by Neoplatonism, Lee maintains, "this method of inquiry continues to be employed after Augustine's conversion until the writing of *De uera religione* (390)" (23, n36).

124. It had been translated into Latin by Marius Victorinus (Cassiodorus, *Institutiones* 2.18), and apparently was the latest thing among intellectual circles in Carthage (Marrou 1938, 34). In the previous century, this work had been adopted as foundational by both the Platonic and Pythagorean traditions. For its Platonic appropriation, see Porphyry, *Isagoge* and *On Aristotle's Categories*; for its appropriation into the Pythagorean canon, see Ps.-Archytas, *Peri tōn katholou logōn* (see Thesleff, 1965, 21–32).

125. Aristotle asserts that "Primary substances . . . underlie all other things," and "All things whatsoever, save what we call primary substances, are predicates of primary substances or present in such as their subjects. And were there no primary substance, nought

else could so much as exist" (*Categories* 5.2b). Declaring that "substance can have no degrees" (*Categories* 5.4a), Aristotle rejects the idea of things being more or less existent (an idea which Augustine would adopt as a Neoplatonist and employ as a fundamental axiom throughout his later work); difference derives from variation in qualities, which admit of degrees and contraries, whereas substance does not (*Categories* 8.10b). Comparison and contrast can only occur on a shared substantial basis; and Aristotle identifies good and evil as *genera* of substance with subordinate species and individuals (*Categories* 11.13b–14a).

126. *Conf* 4.16.29.

127. Kato 1965, 230–31.

128. Frankfurt 1988, 165.

129. West 1933, 54.

130. See *Conf* 4.1.1. Augustine gives us two time references for his Manichaean period. He says he was a Manichaean for nine years, and that this was "from my nineteenth to my twenty-eighth year." The nine-year reference is found already in his earliest post-Manichaean writings ("a full nine years," *MM* 19.68; "nine years," *ME* 18.34, *CEF* 10.11; "about nine years," *UC* 1.2, *Conf* 3.11.20, 5.6.10, cf. *Conf* 4.1.1), and so had become a personal trope by the time he writes the *Conf.* To harmonize the two periods, we must assume that he became a Manichaean some months into his nineteenth year (November 372–November 373). Nonetheless, the calculation brings his time as a Manichaean up short of his departure from Africa by several months, and disregards completely his continued Manichaean activities in Rome for more than another year.

131. Although there had been some erosion of privileges for the pagans, and of rights for the Jews, conditions were just beginning to tighten up for the Manichaeans in the first, largely symbolic edict revoking toleration under Valentinian I (2 March 372), apparently directed to Rome alone.

132. Vindicianus was a doctor by profession, former court physician to Valentinian I, and so a "scientific" man, as Augustine aspired to be.

CHAPTER 4. FAUSTUS

1. For the title, see *Faust* 11.1; 23.1; 33.9. It means "Chapters," or "Topics," the Latin equivalent of the Greek *Kephalaia* used of an important foundation text of the Manichaeans. Faustus's composition is a sort of polemical and apologetic miscellany built around a few core themes. Monceaux has made the plausible suggestion, based on the wording of Faustus's prologue, that the full title was *Capitula de Christiana fide et verite* (Monceaux 1924, 16–17). Since it seems to reflect on his own persecution, it was probably written after his trial in 386, either during his exile or shortly after his release (Monceaux 1924, 14–16).

2. *Faust* immediately follows the *Conf* in Augustine's review of his works in the *Retr*, and Augustine mentions discussing Faustus in the *Conf* in the opening sentence of *Faust*. The two works were not composed concurrently, however, as has sometimes been suggested. It is evident that the portrait Augustine gives of Faustus in the *Conf* is made without

knowledge of Faustus's composition to which he responds in *Faust* (Monceaux 1924, 10; Decret 1970, 61). It appears that after the *Conf* was read by others who noted its discussion of Faustus, they brought the *Capitula* to Augustine's notice, and he set to work to refute it. Thus the date *post quem* for *Faust* would be around 401, the current consensus date for the completion of *Conf.* A date *ante quem* is provided by references to *Faust* in *CE* and in *Ep* 82, both dated to circa 405 (Decret 1970, 63 n7), as well as by an allusion to Jewish Christians as "Symmachians or Nazarenes" in *Cresc* 1.31.36 (also circa 405) that apparently derives from a remark by Faustus recorded in *Faust* 19.4.

3. P. Brown 2000, 43–44; see, e.g., *Faust* 18.2, 18.5, 20.4, 20.13.

4. *Pace* Decret 1970, 57–58; 1978, 362.

5. Augustine's limitation of Faustus's prior reading to "some of the orations of Cicero" and "one or two volumes of Seneca" (*Conf* 5.6.11) is clearly meant as a rhetorical minimization of his learning, and cannot be taken literally. Faustus undoubtedly had read more widely in Cicero, as we shall see. O'Donnell suggests Seneca's *De superstitione* as a work likely familiar to Faustus and possibly reflected in his criticisms of Christianity (O'Donnell 1992, vol.2, 301).

6. Faustus would have been answerable in the Manichaean church hierarchy to a regional "teacher." From the recent documentary finds from Kellis in Egypt, we know that such a Manichaean "teacher" was resident there (perhaps in Alexandria) in the 360s (Gardner, Alcock, and Funk 1999, 75–76), and it would probably be to this individual that Faustus would report. One of the Kellis letters states that literacy in Latin was an expectation of the teacher's entourage, no doubt for the purpose of communication with the Manichaeans under his jurisdiction in the western regions of the empire.

7. Augustine possibly exaggerates when he states that he awaited Faustus's return for the entire nine years of his membership in the Manichaean community prior to Faustus's arrival in 382. He may not have been in a position to meet such a high dignitary of the faith in his initial years as a Manichaean. That Faustus spent some of the time in Rome is suggested in Augustine's remark that he was well known to the Manichaeans there (*Faust* 5.7), which led Courcelle 1968, 76, mistakenly to identify Faustus as the bishop of Rome, a mistake repeated by Starnes 1990, 119, among others. Decret initially followed this opinion (Decret 1970, 58), but later corrected himself (Decret 1994, 12–13). The same mistake apparently stands behind O'Meara's speculation that Faustus came to Carthage from Rome to escape the new anti-Manichaean legislation (O'Meara 1954, 103); but Rome was a safe haven for Manichaeans where the laws went unenforced. All of these scholars overlook information Augustine provides that (1) Faustus was expected for some time in Carthage, and once he came remained there for four years, until his arrest; and (2) Augustine identifies another man as the Manichaean bishop in Rome (*MM* 20.74) at the same time as Faustus was still at liberty in Carthage.

8. E.g., *UC* 1.2: "they said we were terrorized by superstition and that we were commanded to have faith before rational understanding, but that they urged no one to believe until the truth was fully discussed and proved." This passage amounts to a précis of several key passages in Cicero's *Academica* (e.g., *Acad. pr.* 2.3.9), in light of which many of the

terms Augustine employs take on a technical value within the Academic system. Yet we can never be certain what period of his time among the Manichaeans such generic characterizations reflect; they could just as well sum up his later discussions with Faustus.

9. The "rude"—i.e., minimally educated—Manichaean bishop of Rome offers an interesting comparative example. Lacking Faustus's polish and charm, and displaying a somewhat dour character, he still earned Augustine's grudging respect as a zealous ascetic (*MM* 20.74).

10. There is more than meets the eye in Augustine's invocation of the wisdom of Socrates in praise of Faustus's intellectual modesty. It is meant to signal Faustus's adherence to Academic skepticism, for which Socrates was the ultimate model; see Cicero *Acad. post.* 1.4.16.

11. Monceaux 1924, 39, suggests this passage may have been the opening section of Faustus's book after its prologue.

12. van Oort 1995, 62–63.

13. See, e.g., *Faust* 5.7; cf. Decret 1970, 55: "Si, dans les Confessions, Augustin faisait prevue d'une sympathie condescendante envers le brave home de Milev, plus tard, quand il aura lu les *Capitula*, le jugement sera taut autre."

14. "Or, d'un ouvrage à l'autre, l'évêque manichéen change complètement de physionomie. Dans les *Confessions*, ce n'est qu'un bel espirt, orateur aimable sans doute, mais superficiel: un phraseur à l'esprit vide, à l'éloquence creuse. Dans le *Contra Faustum*, malgré toutes les réserves et les critiques, ce bel esprit devient un érudit, exégète avisé, vigoureux polémiste: un adversaire avec qui l'on doit compter. Des deux séries de textes se dégagent des conclusions divergentes, qui correspondent évidemment à des impressions très différentes produites sur l'auteur par le célèbre Manichéen" (Monceaux 1924, 9; cf. Decret 1970, 55, 62).

15. Monceaux considers the opposing interlocutor a literary fiction (Monceaux 1924, 27). But the questions and arguments seem far too specific and in some cases eccentric to be mere foils for Faustus's exposition, and there are a number of indications that Faustus is replying to a specific tract written against the Manichaeans (possibly the *Acta Archelai* or Titus of Bostra, both of whom raise many of the objections Faustus cites), or even perhaps to charges leveled in the process of his trial before the Proconsul Messianus (see, e.g., *Faust* 16.1–5). Whoever the interlocutor is, it is not Augustine (this old red herring has been repeated as recently as Teske 2007, 9); Faustus replies to none of Augustine's early criticisms of Manichaeism. For this reason, it should probably be dated prior to 390.

16. The one discrepancy we should expect and take into consideration is an absence of appeals to Mani's writings in the *Capitula*, as in his public talks and disputations involving the general public. The latter would not recognize Mani's status and so would not be persuaded by appeals to his authority. Faustus was perfectly willing to cite the authority of pagan and Christian sacred texts to members of those communities, but generally appealed to observation and reason accessible to all.

17. Adimantus appropriated Marcion's work, the *Antitheses*, updating it to reflect the larger New Testament canon accepted by the now predominant form of Christianity, but

maintaining Marcion's original thesis that the teachings of Christ and Paul were incompatible with the Jewish religious tradition. See BeDuhn 2007.

18. The prominence of the term *dogma* in Manichaean literature to characterize opposing positions (*CMC* 11.3, 39.20, 44.5, 65.2, 68.9, 73.10, 85.23, 86.8, 87.2, 87.11, 90.23, 101.22, 102.6, 102.12, 102.21, 104.14, 109.3, 109.12, 114.14, 116.9; *Hom* 8.4, 25.33, 26.17, 29.2, 36.27, 37.25, 53.27, 60.23, 72.14, 72.18, 73.12, 74.31, 79.9, 83.22, 84.9, 84.28, 87.13, 92.21; *Keph* 7.3, 12, 17.16, 17.27, 19.22, 27.15ff., 30.1, 33, 44.25–30, 49.4ff., 117.29, 184.16, 187.2, 288–289; *PsBk* 4.30, 15.7, 25.9f., 26.16f., 42.24f., 86.3–14, 93.12f.) suggests that Adimantus had familiarized himself with the philosophical divide between the skeptical and dogmatic approaches, and adopted skeptical rhetoric—if not actually skeptical positions—for polemical purposes.

19. Monceaux 1924, 20–21, Bruckner 1901, and Rougier 1958 contend that much of Faustus's biblical exegesis is his own, and that his criticisms of the Old Testament in particular mark a significant advance over the work of his predecessors. Faustus claims to have made an initial study of the Old Testament prior to adopting Manichaeism, an episode strikingly similar to one Augustine reports of himself in the *Conf.* But we are in a poor position to distinguish Faustus's own research from material he would have had available from previous digests of proof texts within the Manichaean tradition.

20. Bruckner 1901.

21. See Decret 1970, 67–69.

22. John Mourant's effort to demonstrate a natural affinity between Manichaeism and skepticism (Mourant 1966), while picking up on some valid connections, underestimates the idiosyncratic character of Faustus's adoption of the full Academic program.

23. See Stroumsa 1988, esp. 76.

24. Cf. *Faust* 18.2: "Christ says that a man when circumcised becomes twofold a child of hell (Mt. 23:15). It is plain also that Christ neither observed the Sabbath himself, nor commanded it to be observed. And regarding foods, he says expressly that man is not defiled by anything that goes into his mouth, but rather by the things which come out of it (Mt. 15:11). Regarding sacrifices, too, he often says that God desires mercy, and not sacrifice (Mt. 9:13)."

25. Faustus is quite prepared to concede that all of the patriarchs may be saved, just as the thief on the cross beside Jesus was saved. But this must be understood as an act of mercy by God. He emphasizes that the thieves and publicans and prostitutes and adulterers whom Christ forgave and redeemed were in each case told to sin no more. So Christ's compassion for them was not approval of their behavior, but a generous act toward those who did not deserve it. For divine mercy is stronger than sin (*Faust* 33.1). "Even though they may have been restored to light and liberty by Christ, that has nothing to do with the hateful character of their lives. We hate and eschew not their persons, but their characters; not as they are now, when they are purified, but as they were, when impure" (*Faust* 33.3).

26. On this subject, see BeDuhn 2000.

27. See the subscription of the Manichaean Felix to the agreement made at the end of the first day of debate with Augustine, reported in *Fel* 1.20: *Felix christianus cultor legis Manichaei.*

28. Hence, *pace* Stroumsa 1988, 75, this *imitatio Christi* is not "purely metaphorical."

The human soul can aspire to be what the docetic Christ was/is, even though Christ was without a physical body, because both possess the same essential good nature—Christ's unencumbered by embodiment, and ours striving to be as unencumbered as possible in this world, and perfectly conformed to Christ's liberty in the next world.

29. It is in this context that Faustus speaks of "the deserter accuses the soldier," that is, the Christians who no longer maintain the radical ethic of Christ turn on the Manichaeans who do. This generic remark is not a reference to a particular person who had deserted Manichaeism for the Christian opposition and to whom Faustus now responds (*pace* Decret 1970, 61).

30. In examining these definitions, Faustus is apparently participating in a discussion of great interest in Africa in the closing decade of the fourth century (De Veer 1968, 759–64).

31. Cf. Seneca, Frag. 123: "God is not worshipped with sacrifice and much blood, but rather with a pure mind, and with a good and honest intent."

32. Titus of Bostra 1.11 asserts the other side of Faustus's distinction, contending that the consensus of Christians, Jews, and pagans alike is that the universe is governed by a single (or, in the pagan case, at least harmonious) will. Could Faustus have been responding to Titus?

33. For the basis of this characterization in the practices of fourth century African Christianity, see Frend 1952, ch.8.

34. Cf. *Keph* 136: "Concerning the birth of the two men, the new man and the old man, how they are born. Once again the Apostle spoke: 'There are two births, which are not alike one another. The first birth is that of the flesh. The second is the birth of the spirit.'" See, e.g., Rom 6–7; 1 Cor 15; 2 Cor 4; Eph 3–4; Col 3.

35. Faustus appears to be picking up an argument made by Mani in his *Letter to Menoch* (*IulImp* 3.187.5–6): "If natural sin does not exist, why are infants baptized, who by themselves, it is agreed, have done no evil? . . . If every evil is actual, before someone does evil why does he receive the purification of water, when he has done by himself no evil? Or if he has not yet done (any) and must be purified, it is clear that they demonstrate the sprouting of the evil shoot naturally."

36. Jean de Menasce has identified a dissatisfaction over lack of moral progress—a doctrine at the real heart of Manichaeism—as the underlying impetus for Augustine's eventual departure from the faith (Menasce 1956, 80). His unhappiness with his own inability to emulate the purity of the Elect, Menasce opines, caused him to dwell more and more on the problem of moral responsibility (Menasce 1956, 80–81). Against this background of serious dissatisfaction, his doubts about Manichaean astronomy took on much greater importance than they otherwise would have. But how much of this dissatisfaction with moral progress is an anachronistic construct of the later Augustine of the *Confessions*?

37. On this issue, see Ferrari 1973, who suggests that Augustine's recognition that the astronomers had an account of celestial motion superior to that of the Manichaeans could have been heightened by two partial eclipses of the sun visible in Carthage in 378 and 381. His observance of such events is necessarily presupposed in his remark in *Conf* 5.3.4 about

successful prediction. An even more spectacular near-total eclipse occurred in April 386 that was visible in Milan.

38. O'Laughlin 1992, 106.

39. O'Laughlin 1992, 108.

40. O'Laughlin 1992, 114–15.

41. Menasce 1956, 81–82.

42. Decret 1978, 244ff., interprets Faustus's refusal to address Augustine's questions as a matter of safeguarding the sect's esoteric gnosis from an upstart Auditor who showed he was not ready for it. Thus he sees Faustus's position as strategic rather than programmatic. But the gaps and misunderstandings in Augustine's knowledge of Manichaeism to which Decret points are not substantial enough to support the model of guarded esoteric teachings, and can be attributed instead to Augustine's own inattention, his cultural conditioning, and perhaps some choices of emphasis in the local Manichaean community.

43. See, e.g., *Acad. pr.* 2.11.34; cf. *Tusc. disp.* 3.1.2; *Fin.* 5.21.59.

44. O'Donnell 1992, vol. 2, 303.

45. "Augustine's judgement *at the time* was that Faustus was not clever enough to answer his questions. Augustine now sees this was the wrong grounds on which to judge, for lack of cleverness is no sin; it was Faustus' Manichean error that put him wrong. His justice to Faustus here lies in seeing this" (O'Donnell 1992, vol. 2, 302, referring to *Conf* 5.7.12).

46. See van Oort 1995, 60–61.

47. He acknowledges that Academic skepticism no longer survived as a distinct philosophical school, *Acad* 3.18.41.

48. "Immediately after his conversion and for sometime thereafter, sanctity of life remained an Augustinian criterion for trust in authority" (Van Fleteren 1973, 36).

49. See Wurst 2000, 653; Coyle 2009.

50. Monceaux 1924, 3.

CHAPTER 5. EXILE

1. "This is how people in Africa would have remembered Augustine's relations with Faustus: Faustus arrives with Augustine in the lead among those praising him, later in friendly literary relations with him (5.7.13, 'coepi cum eo... agere vitam'). There is no visible break with Manicheism before Augustine left Africa, rather the opposite" (O'Donnell 1992, vol. 2, 300).

2. O'Meara 1954, 104.

3. See Frend 1954.

4. See BeDuhn 2009a.

5. The Theodosian Code (*Cod. Theod.*) is a digest of imperial edicts from the fourth and early fifth centuries compiled under the emperor Theodosius II.

6. As argued by Gottlieb 1973, 60, and supported with additional arguments by Williams 1995, 157–61.

7. Although, arguably, the first provision of *Cod. Theod.* 16.5.5 could be read as a prohibition of any public enunciation of Manichaeism: "If any profane man by his punishable teachings should weaken the concept of God, he shall have the right to know such noxious doctrines only for himself but shall not reveal them to others to their hurt."

8. Eutropius, as PPO Illyrici, was nominally under Gratian's authority, but apparently taking orders from Theodosius in Constantinople at this time. The edict cites as its precedent the earlier law of an imperial predecessor, that is, Valentinian I's anti-Manichaean edict of 2 March 372 (*Cod. Theod.* 16.5.3).

9. These conditions may also explain the unusual inclusion of rural settlements (*conventicula oppidorum*) in the expulsion orders. Typically laws against undesirables went no further than throwing them out of the cities. As evidence of Manichaeans in Illyria, a tombstone of a female Electa from Salona was published a century ago (Cumont 1908b).

10. Lieu 1992, 137 (translation slightly modified).

11. The only antecedents of this issue in the law involved Christian apostasy to Judaism under Constantius, e.g., *Cod. Theod.* 16.8.7.

12. Africa fell under the jurisdiction of the PPO Italiae et Illyrici, and laws issued to them were published for enforcement in Africa (an example close in time to this one being *Cod. Theod.* 11.16.13, issued to Hypatius's predecessor Syagrius after the close of the sailing season in 382 and published in Carthage after the reopening of the sea lanes, on 13 April 383).

13. Barnes 1985, 151–53; A. Jones 1971, 420.

14. Barnes 1985, 151–53; A. Jones 1971, 22.

15. Decret 1978, 214, believes that it is to the effects of the edict of 381 that Augustine alludes in *MM* 19.69. While it is possible that Gratian issued a duplicate version of this law for the western empire, until that is proven, Gratian's acts of 378 and 379 must remain the most likely sources of the restrictions in Carthage.

16. Eusignius was proconsul of Africa in 383–384 (Barnes 1985, 151–53). *Cod. Theod.* 1.3.1 (16 June 383) and 12.1.95 (26 February 383) were both issued to him in this capacity, the latter probably as a *mandata* prior to him officially taking office. He was later part of the court of Valentinian II, and PPO Italiae et Illyrici in 386–387.

17. *CLP* 3.16.19.

18. *CLP* 3.25.30. See BeDuhn 2009a and Chapter 7 below.

19. "The charge that he was fleeing from persecution of the Manichees in Africa cannot be substantiated, nor is it likely; for he could have met with persecution in Rome too" (O'Meara 1954, 104). But O'Meara himself quotes *Conf* 5.19 on the many Manichaeans secretly harbored in Rome (114).

20. Decret 1994, 16, cites the arrival of a Manichaean bishop, and the monastic experiment undertaken within the Roman Manichaean community at this time (both reported by Augustine, *MM* 20.74), as indicative of the security the Manichaeans enjoyed in Rome under Symmachus.

21. In *Acad* 2.2.3, he praises Romanianus for his patronage throughout his life, "even when, in your absence and without your knowledge, I sailed away, although you were

somewhat hurt with me for not telling you, as had been my wont," and speaks in this context of "your children deserted by their teacher."

22. See BeDuhn 2009a.

23. It has been conjectured that Augustine's host was Constantius, the wealthy Manichaean Auditor who subsequently sponsored a monastic experiment among the Elect of Rome. But the identification arises mostly by default, since Constantius is the only member of the sizable Roman Manichaean community we know anything about.

24. Bertrand 1914, 141.

25. O'Donnell 1992, vol. 2, 313.

26. Bertrand 1914, 134–35, 153.

27. Sherkat 1991; Sherkat and Wilson 1995, 1000; Loveland 2003, 154.

28. O'Laughlin 1992, 118.

29. *UC* 8.20.

30. See Ferrari 1975, 213–14.

31. In the apt words of Gerald Bonner, "no man was less temperamentally suited to a condition of deliberate doubt than he" (Bonner 1993, 110).

32. *Pace* Testard 1958, vol. 1, 83 n4, followed by TeSelle 1970, 31.

33. Quinn 1988, 165.

34. Barker 1998, 80.

35. Barker 1998, 80.

36. Barker 1998, 81.

37. Decret assumes that the person to whom Augustine reported the incident—to whom he refers simply as the "bishop"—was not Faustus, but another man serving as the local bishop of Carthage (Decret 1978, vol. 2, 152 n213). But Faustus was the Manichaean bishop of the whole of Africa; and his return was awaited at Carthage by his own parishioners. Augustine avoids mentioning Faustus by name in his early writings.

38. Besides the reference to the presence of the bishop, the late date for the incident would correlate well with the fact that the woman complained to Augustine, who would be a relatively senior Auditor after nine years in the sect.

39. This very issue is treated in the Manichaean text *Kephalaion* 88, where the Auditor is counseled to overlook lapses in the Elect, given the ongoing struggle with evil even the latter endure as long as they are in the body. It is interesting to contrast Augustine's great caution about casting aspersions based on mere rumor and innuendo when an analogous situation arose between a Catholic monk and priest in Hippo while he was bishop (*Ep* 77 and 78).

40. Augustine's first-hand knowledge of the content of the man's pleas as he was beaten suggests that he was in on the arranged beating, even if his Manichaean scruples may have held him back from throwing any punches himself.

41. Typically of this early work, Augustine avoids naming names.

42. Bertrand 1914, 157.

43. *Conf* 7.1.2.

44. Polanyi 1964, 42–45.

45. Cf. Cicero, *Acad. pr.* 2.3.7–9, part of Augustine's reading at this time.

46. On the prominence of Stoic ideas in Augustine's thinking at this time, see Baguette 1970, Verbeke 1958.

47. *Conf* 5.13.23. In the aftermath of the death of Gratian, an effort was made to build a complete court around his surviving brother Valentinian II at Milan, as counterbalance to the usurper Maximus's court at Trier. McLynn observes that the request for a *rhetoricae magister* was part of the development of Milan into a bona fide imperial city at precisely this time (1994, 169–70). That the request was made to Symmachus may suggest a conscious effort to choose someone aligned with the religiously liberal court against the power of Ambrose in the city.

CHAPTER 6. THE APOSTATE

1. On Milanese Catholicism as "un catholicisme nouveau" and "neo-catholicisme," see Masai 1961, 14 and 26, respectively.

2. Courcelle 1968, 106–38, 336–44; Madec 1974, 60–71; P. Brown 2000, 119; Masai 1961, 14–15, 26. McLynn suggests that in incorporating Neoplatonic material Ambrose was responding to the newly heightened intellectual climate that developed in Milan as a full court was built around Valentinian II in 383–385, of which the appointment of Augustine was a part (McLynn 1994, 241–42).

3. "Decisions are made on the basis of not only what is desired but what is known about alternatives. The impetus for change is new information about competing products. Once seduced into trying a cultural product, people may find they prefer it" (Sherkat and Wilson 1995, 998).

4. Courcelle 1963, 31, remarks that Augustine was converted in "un milieu chrétien imprégné de néoplatonisme." Madec 1987b and 1989 cautions about exaggerating the thoroughness of this melange. Christian appropriation of Platonism was selective, and we should be cautious about exaggerating the degree to which Augustine came into contact with anything like a systematic synthesis of Neoplatonism and Christianity. Ambrose drew not only directly upon Plotinus, but also on earlier and contemporary Christian writings that had already appropriated Middle Platonic and Neoplatonic rhetoric and imagery in a variety of ways. Ambrose made use of material from the Greek East in the Origenist tradition, as well as of such Latin synthesizers as Marius Victorinus. Therefore, Augustine encountered a set of experiments in reading materials from the two traditions in light of each other.

5. See Bertrand 1914, 164; P. Brown 2000, 71; Dixon 1999, 104. Although McLynn regards this interpretation as "unduly cynical," 1994, 240 n76, he considers it the likely appearance of things to "uncharitable onlookers," 2003, 258.

6. Note that Augustine's circuitous narrative in the *Confessions* scatters references to the same period across several books of the work.

7. We know precious little of this parade of court functionaries and wealthy aristocrats

whose names season Augustine's earliest letters and literary efforts: Zenobius, Hermogenianus, Manlius Theodorus. The later Augustine continues to value the texts they eagerly shared back in Milan while wishing to distance himself from individuals who had not followed exactly the same path he had chosen. TeSelle 1970, 32–33, emphasizes the degree to which this intellectual elite crossed religious boundaries.

8. Purportedly every Sunday (*Conf* 6.3.4).

9. When his mother arrived, she asked Augustine to inquire with the bishop whether she should continue to fast on Sunday, as was the custom in Africa, or conform to the practice of not fasting observed in Milan. Ambrose offered no reason for the Milanese practice, but simply cited custom, and advised conformity to such local custom (*Ep* 36.14.32; *Ep* 54.2.3; *Conf* 6.2.2). See Courcelle 1963, 19–21; Courcelle 1968, 88–92.

10. On his distaste for Isaiah reflecting his longstanding attitude toward the Old Testament characteristic of his Manichaean period, see Ferrari 1990a.

11. In 389 he would write to Siricius, bishop of Rome, reporting that he had acted to drive the Manichaeans from Milan in accordance with the emperor Theodosius's edict of that year, even though responsibility for acting on the edict more properly rested on the civic authorities (Ambrose, *Epistle* 44/42.13). In the same letter he rather outlandishly equates the followers of Jovinian with the Manichaeans. The two groups had little more in common than that they were opponents of Ambrose, and the Jovinianists in fact took the lead in condemning Manichaeism and in charging that those Christians (such as Ambrose or Jerome) who placed too much emphasis on ascetic values were dangerously close to being Manichaeans themselves.

12. Nor does he ever seem to have thought much of the polemicist Philaster of Brescia, whom he also reports seeing in Milan in the company of Ambrose (*Ep* 222).

13. In the characterization of R. A. Markus, "in the Milan of Ambrose, he encountered a cosmopolitan church, wielding wide influence over emperors and officials, occupying a place of leadership in society, confident of its power to absorb, mould, and transform it" (Markus 1970, 105). See Bertrand 1914, 165–69, on the ways Ambrose probably impressed Augustine as a powerful and imposing figure, from whom any kind gesture was treasured.

14. Sherkat 1991; Loveland 2003, 148, 154.

15. "A change in social position resulting from social mobility often leads people to change their preferences as they become exposed to new cultural goods or subject to new consumption norms" (Sherkat and Wilson 1995, 994). "[S]tudies of religious mobility have emphasized that individuals are disposed to bring their socioeconomic and religious statuses into line" (Sandomirsky and Wilson 1990, 1212). "[R]eligious preferences . . . are formed and sustained by the social relationships people maintain or discard" (Loveland 2003, 154).

16. Sandomirsky and Wilson 1990, 1215. "[C]onnections to people outside of the religious group can impose costs that . . . hinder commitment, especially when religious choices are considered deviant" (Sherkat and Ellison 1999, 381–382).

17. "[R]eligious choices are structured . . . through group norms that grant incentives for making particular choices and sanctions against making others" (Sherkat and Wilson

1995, 999). "Religious groups frequently serve as conduits for a variety of secular privi-leges . . . , and social ties to coreligionists provide solidary incentives for participation in religious organizations." (Sherkat and Ellison 1999, 381).

18. "Switching" is the term typically used in the study of religion for moving from one religious community to another without any deep conviction, but for various extrinsic reasons, such as marriage or career advancement.

19. Ebaugh 1988, 36.

20. More 1907/8, 614.

21. O'Connell 1980, 183.

22. Augustine makes no explicit citation from a work of Ambrose prior to circa 418, and may have had copies of few of his writings prior to that time. He alludes to having read in Milan various tracts of Ambrose circulating at the time, such as his exposition of Isaiah (lost except for Augustine's extracts). Of the works Ambrose had published prior to Augustine's arrival in the city, Augustine makes explicit reference only to the *De poenitentia*. The latter seems to be Ambrose's standard address to catechumens, which is one scripted lecture we know for certain Augustine attended. He would also have heard something like Ambrose's preserved baptismal lecture, *De Mysteriis*. If not these exact texts, Augustine would have heard something very much like them in the spring of 387, that is, *after* his "conversion." Yet we can assume that similar ideas peppered Ambrose's regular sermons which Augustine heard earlier.

23. "This darkness, this non-being that wraps us round, Plotinus had assured him—and the Manichee message was essentially the same—is the 'alien,' a diminishing addition which is, in the last analysis, unconnected with our real identity" (O'Connell 1963a, 37).

24. Cary 2000, 63.

25. Cary 2000, 86.

26. His later claim that Neoplatonism affirmed with Christianity that "the human soul, even though it bears testimony about the light, is not itself the light" (*Conf* 7.9.13, alluding to Jn 1:8), relies on a convenient rhetorical glossing of the different conceptions of the soul entailed in the two systems.

27. See *En.* 4.8, 4.3.13, and Bréhier 1928, 47–69. For the internal diversity of Platonism on this subject, see Dillon 1980, who elsewhere notes the debate over Plato's characteriza-tion of the human condition in this world as *en tini phrourai*, either "in a kind of prison" or "in a kind of guard-post" (Dillon 1995).

28. For the idea of a primordial collective fall, see *Paradiso* 2.11; for the fall as an indi-vidual's moral decay into materiality, see *Isaac* 7.60.

29. See Plotinus, *En* 4.8.4, 5.1.1, 5.8.4. O'Connell 1968, 173–82, has effectively demon-strated Augustine's appropriation of this Plotinian characterization of the fall as a miscon-ceived striving to be one's own in such places as *GCM* 2.15.22, 2.16.24.

30. Ambrose creatively found a deeper meaning to the seemingly innocuous com-mand, "Arise, let us go from here" in John 14:31, "teaching that each one should arise from the earth, raise up his soul that lies upon the ground, lift it to the things that are above" (*Bono mort* 5.16).

31. "The soul is bound to the body in so far as she is directed towards the feelings which proceed from the body. She is loosed therefrom in so far as she is impassible to corporeal promptings" (Porphyry, *Sententia* 7).

32. Cf. *Isaac* 6.52–54, *Bono mort* 5.16.

33. "Voluntary actions are only free to the extent that they suppose a choice of motives which do not belong to the body; they then constitute authentically free inclinations" (Leroux 1996, 305, citing *Ennead* 4.7.7). See Gerson 1994, 161.

34. "The bad soul is full of bad desires . . . , but the soul in such a state is not free" (Leroux 1996, 301).

35. See Plotinus, *En* 1.6.3, 5.8.11, 6.9.7.

36. Middle Platonic dualism and emanationism still pervade Plotinus's thought, despite his efforts in the direction of monism and omnipresence. See Armstrong 1967, 256–57.

37. Plato reinforced this quasi-animistic view of matter with several statements in support of an active, blind force standing behind the world's evil—an actual evil soul. E.g., *Laws*, book 10; *Epinomis* 989d–e: "the tendency and the movement towards good comes form the good soul, and on the contrary, the movement towards evil comes from the bad soul." Aristotle himself understood Plato to be a dualist (*Metaphysics* 1.6.988a, 7–16).

38. Plotinus does attempt to overlay a monistic scheme on this fundamentally dualist characterization, drawing on monistic antecedents in Pythagoreanism itself. Just as some Pythagoreans explained the unlimited dyad as an emanation from the monad, so Plotinus describes the unlimited as a kind of creative excess of the One, extending beyond the reach of the One's limiting order.

39. Plotinus, *En* 2.4.16. See Gerson 1994, 110, who notes Plotinus's divergence from Aristotle on this point: "Matter or privation or unlimitedness name an indestructible and irremovable feature of sensibles."

40. This account differs considerably in its emphases from Plotinus's better-known attribution of the fall to *tolma* and the exercise of the soul's free will (*En* 5.1.1).

41. See the remarks of Thonnard 1952, 128 and 537–39 n44, and of Bezançon 1965, 136.

42. See Cary 1994, 69–70.

43. "When I wished to think of my God, I could think of him only as a corporeal mass, because it seemed to me that anything else would not even exist. This was the principal and almost only cause of my inescapable error."

44. "I did not know how to think of a mind except as some sort of subtle body."

45. "I did not know that evil is nothing but the removal of good until finally no good remains. How could I see this when with the sight of my eyes I saw no more than material things and with the sight of my mind no more than their images?"

46. If he did not derive the idea directly from Aristotle (or a philosophical digest that included this element of Aristotle), bypassing Plotinus on this topic, which is a distinct possibility.

47. "Let us not search outside of ourselves or attribute to others the causes of that

of which we ourselves are sole masters," he adds. "Let us, rather, recognize these causes as belonging to us alone" (*Hex.* 1.8.31). Cf. *Conf* 5.10.18, 7.3.5, 8.10.22.

48. He goes on to refer explicitly to the Manichaean identification of the creator god of the Genesis narrative with evil. In *Cain et Abel* 1.1.4, he suggests that the struggle between Jacob and Esau in the womb of their mother Rebecca (Genesis 25) "interpreted spiritually" refers to the common generation of good and evil from the same source in the human soul.

49. "The soul, then, is the user, the body that which is being used, and thus the one is in command, the other in service; the one is what we are, the other what belongs to us" (*Bono mort* 7.27). The soul therefore "leads the body in its service where it will, fashions out of it the form it has chosen, and makes the virtues it has willed resound in it" (*Bono mort* 6.25; cf. *Hex* 6.6.39).

50. Cf. *Hex* 1.8.31: "We ought to attribute to ourselves the choice of an evil which we are unable to do without consent of the will rather than ascribe the same to others. In the courts of the world guilt so is imputed and punishment meted out, not to those compelled to crime by necessity, but to those who have acted voluntarily. . . . Wrong does not exist except when the mind and conscience are implicated and bound up in the guilt."

51. In *Iul* 1.9.44 Augustine says he learned the *privantur boni* solution to the problem of evil from Ambrose. It usually has been considered that in his conflict with Petilian Augustine wished to lay claim to Ambrose, so his remarks about what he learned from him are suspect. O'Donnell says that there are some doubts that Augustine really learned this solution in Milan at all (1992, Vol. 2, 448–49).

52. Plotinus, *Enneads* 1.6, 1.8, 3.2–3, 4.3, and 5.1 appear on the lists of most Augustinian scholars, with Cary offering a considerably expanded inventory (Cary 2000, 158 n11), and O'Meara arguing for the addition of the principal works of Porphyry (O'Meara, 1951a, 160 n.102, 161 n.103, with the text notes referenced there). The basic Platonic scheme of the fall and ascent of the soul that Augustine adopted at this time is outlined succinctly by Porphyry, *De abst.* 1.29–31. Since Augustine could read only Latin, we must contend with how (lost) Latin translations of Greek philosophical texts (in the case of Plotinus, in quite difficult and obscure Greek at that) might now mask exact matches of Augustine's statements to their sources. Based on what has survived of Marius Victorinus's translation of Porphyry's *Isagoge*, it appears that he translated freely, even paraphrastically (Alfaric 1918, 518–19). The passage of Plotinus preserved in Augustine's *Sent* 17 shows the quality of translation with which Augustine worked.

53. Decret 1994, 18, reasons that, since Augustine appears to have met the Manichaean bishop involved in the experiment personally, and since the anxious Constantius seems to have recruited him to it immediately upon his arrival in Rome, the events Augustine described must have unfolded in 384–385. We have no information on how long the community in Constantius's home persisted before the project was abandoned.

54. Courcelle has drawn attention to the close correspondence between Constantius's experiment in Rome and the contemporaneous plans among Augustine and his friends in Milan under the sponsorship of Romanianus (Courcelle 1968, 179, 228; cf. Decret 1994, 18–19).

55. Decret 1994, 16–17, speculates on the possible influence of Christian monastic experiments on the Manichaean community in Rome.

56. For the identification of the Auditor involved as Constantius, see *Faust* 5.5. On the fad of setting up religious communities in the homes of aristocrats, see Krautheimer 1983, 96–100. Decret emphasizes the novelty of the monastic experiment and the debt it owed to the wider Christian monastic movement (Decret 1994, 12–22).

57. Decret 1994, 20–22, borrowing a suggestion from Peter Brown regarding divisions within the Manichaean community, considers the possibility that Augustine's description of Constantius as *vehementer omnes ad omnia cogeret* indicates a type of Manichaean "fundamentalist."

58. Courcelle rightly notes that there were many sources of inspiration for such a community, including both Cicero and the legend of Pythagoras (Courcelle 1963, 21–26). Constantius's experiment offers an indication of how much such inspirations had infiltrated Manichaean circles, alongside their evident role in developments among non-Manichaean Christians.

59. Augustine refers to several bishops approached by the Auditor; they were not necessarily all resident in Rome, where we would expect only a single bishop in the normal Manichaean organizational structure. Decret 1994, 12–13, suggests that Augustine's remarks point to the possibility that Rome had become a refuge for several Manichaean bishops at the time.

60. Similarities to Catholic monastic experiments abound in this account, including a wealthy layperson converting personal property into a monastic institution and serving as the community's governing authority or preceptor, and the adoption of a charter or rule.

61. "La fondation entreprise par Constantius est entièrement originale dans le manichéisme d'Occident" (Decret 1994, 15). On Manichaean contact with the Catholic monastic movement in Egypt, see Stroumsa 1983a; Koenen 1983.

62. Menasce concludes, "ni la déconvenue de la rencontre avec Faustus, ni le scandale conventuel n'ont eu de poids dans la décision que devait prendre Augustin de quitter le manichéisme pour redevenir catholique. Mais ce dont le premier de ces épisodes nous instruit c'est qu'Augustin n'a pas été retenu dans le manichéisme uniquement pour des raisons de connaissance rationelle; nous verrons qu'il a pu, qu'il a dû y trouver une spiritualité pleine de chaleur; mais nous verrons aussi que seul le primat, à ses yeux, de la question de vérité explique son définitif abandon" (Menasce 1956, 82–83).

63. Implicitly, he must have still maintained cordial relations with Manichaeans to be informed of this insider story. It bears noting that the failure of the Manichaean monastic experiment coincided with the notorious scandal in the ascetic movement within the Nicene community of Rome, when, after the death of a young woman from the aristocracy from excessive fasting, the people gathered at her funeral began looking for monks, including Jerome, to drown in the Tiber. Augustine, who could scarcely not have heard about the incident, never mentions it, for obvious reasons.

64. Augustine strongly hints in *ME* and *MM* that such is the case, even though he would later concede the existence of rigorist Manichaean Elect who maintained the disciplines to the letter. In his much briefer account of the Roman experiment in *Faust* 5.5,

he reports that, "Constantius, who is still alive, and is now our brother in Catholic Christianity, once gathered many of your sect into his house at Rome, to keep these precepts of Manichaeus, which you think so much of, though they are very silly and childish. The precepts proved too much for your weakness, and the gathering was entirely broken up. *Those who persevered separated from your communion, and are called Mattari, because they sleep on mats.*" Anti-Manichaean laws of the period also bear witness to the influence of the monastic movement on Manichaean practices, esp. in the eastern part of the empire (unless this is a matter of confusion between Manichaeans and other groups in the ascetic movement); see *Cod. Theod.* 16.5.9.

65. On the date of Messianus's consulship, see Decret 1978, vol. 1, 216, and vol. 2, 164 n34, who notes that Augustine specifies the time of action taken against Manichaeans in Africa as after the consulship of Bauto, which extended through the year 385. Augustine notes that the date on the official *gesta* of the anti-Manichaean hearings named the consuls subsequent to Bauto's term (*Manicheos autem Messianus proconsul audierit post consulatum Bautonis, sicut dies gestorum ab eodem Petiliano insertus ostendit, CLP* 3.25.30), placing the proceedings in the early months of 386.

66. *Faust* 5.8.

67. *CLP* 3.16.19: *ignotorum mihi et notorum gesta recitet damnatorum et, quod ibi amicus quondam meus magis ad defensionem suam me nominauit absentem.*

68. *in calumniam praeiudicanti criminis nescio quo nouo et suo iure conuertat* (*CLP* 3.16.19).

69. His Donatist opponent Petilian claimed of Augustine, the latter reports, that "the *sententia* of the proconsul Messianus hit me so hard that I fled Africa" (*Messiani proconsularis sententia me fuisse percussum, ut ex Africa fugerem, CLP* 3.25.30).

70. Maximus claimed in a letter to bishop Siricius of Rome that in executing Priscillian and some of his associates he had suppressed a Manichaean cell (*Collectio Avellana* 40). On the case of Priscillian, see Burrus 1995.

CHAPTER 7. CONVERSION

1. See Nock 1933. On Augustine's own acceptance of such a model at the time of his baptism, and his gradual surrender of such a picture, see P. Brown 2000, 171–72. Van Fleteren also highlights Augustine's own assumption as found in the twelve or thirteen conversions related of himself and others in the *Confessions* that conversions were sudden, dramatic, and complete (Van Fleteren 1990b, esp. 69–70).

2. The dating of Romanianus's embassy to the summer of 386 appears to be indicated by Augustine's remarks in *Acad* 2.2.4 and 2.3.8.

3. Ferrari 1990a, 743; cf. Decret 1978, 215–17.

4. See Chapter 6, n.6.

5. Both conditions are classic markers of the conversion scenario confirmed in numerous studies; see Beit-Hallahmi and Argyle 1997, 114–38 and the literature cited there.

6. See Power 1992, 56–57. Note his later characterization of the dismissal of his previous partner and intention to marry a more well-connected woman as adultery, *BC* 5.5.

7. On *Conf* 6.11.18 as a précis of his indecision about the direction his life and thought should take, see the analyses of Boyer 1953, 107, and Courcelle 1963, 17–19.

8. This is the first, "pre-conversion" proposal for such a communal project that Augustine would realize "post-conversion" in Cassiciacum, Thagaste, and eventually Hippo (see Courcelle 1968, 179). The fact that it was first conceived with the Manichaeans Romanianus, Alypius, and Nebridius suggests that it might have owed some inspiration to the very monastic experiment in the home of the Manichaean Auditor Constantius at Rome known to Augustine, word of whose failure came to him later in Milan (Alfaric 1918, 364; Decret 1994, 18–19). Yet well established models of intellectual retirement in Greek and Roman literature culture certainly also contributed to the idea; see Trout 1988.

9. See Ferrari 1982 on the dramatic rise in references to Paul's conversion scene in Augustine's writings around the time he was composing the *Confessions*, and the subsequent drop-off of such references. Ferrari concludes, plausibly, that Augustine was looking for biblical precedents for a literarily crafted conversion account. Ferrari demonstrates the same peak of interest by Augustine in the story of the Prodigal Son at the time in Ferrari 1977b, to the evidence of which now should be added the reference in *SermDolb* 10, dated to 397.

10. See especially Courcelle 1968, 188–202; Buchheit 1968, 257–71; Ferrari 1989; Ferrari 1992; Heidl 2003, 47–61. Augustine's despair under the fig tree, for example, has been shown to reflect the biblical episode of Nathaniel in John, which Ambrose similarly appropriated autobiographically in *Virgin* 1.1.4 in a way that already introduced the theme of frustration with delay and unproductivity. Ferrari has drawn attention to a rehearsal of the combination of key motifs of conversion employed in the *Conf* (including the association of Nathaniel's fig tree with the cursed fig tree of Mt 21:19–22, and the story of Saul on the road to Damascus) in Sermon 89, dating to the time of the composition of the *Conf* (Ferrari 1982, 167–18; 1992, 101). For the Manichaean resonances of the scene, see the idea of getting entangled in the spiritual roots of a fig tree that one has planted (*Acta Archelai* 10.4; Epiphanius, *Panarion* 46,9,1).

11. The one told by Simplician concerning the philosopher Marius Victorinus (*Conf* 8.2.3–5), the other by a government agent named Ponticianus, prompted by seeing Augustine's copy of Paul's Letters, about the role of a chance hearing of scripture in the conversion of Anthony of Egypt, and the effect of Anthony's story on two men (much like Alypius and Augustine) connected to the court at Trier (*Conf* 8.6.13–15).

12. For Augustine's disapproval of *sortes biblicae* and attribution of its outcomes to mere chance, see *Ep* 55.37 and, remarkably, *Conf* 4.3.5–6.

13. Leo Ferrari has argued that the biblical passage supposedly opened to that day, Romans 13.13–14, plays no significant role in Augustine's thought, and is only cited by him once in his formal writings outside the *Conf* between 386 and 401. The single citation, in his exegetical treatise on Romans, occurs in a colorless manner that does not suggest any significance to his own life (Ferrari 1980). Yet Ferrari overlooks that this very passage is one

of the first quotations from Paul found in Augustine's letters, appearing in a letter to Aurelius, bishop of Carthage, circa 393, where it is used as a kind of negative formula for the Christian life (*Ep* 22.2). Even before then, it appears prominently in the moral comparison of Christian and Manichaean values in *MM* 14.31–32, written between 388 and 390.

14. See Van Fleteren 1990b, 70.

15. Matter 1990, 25. Cf. Buchheit 1968; Ferrari 1978a, 13–14.

16. Cf. *Sol* 1.10.17: "I commanded myself not to desire . . . a wife."

17. Frankfurt 1988, 53–54.

18. On gazing like a lover on the face of *philosophia*, see Cicero, *Tusc. disp.* 5.2.5–6; *Fin.* 1.14.46; Seneca, *Ep.* 115.3–7. For the conceit of the soul being held back from flight by its vices as if tangled in a thicket, see Cicero, *Hortensius* fr. 24; *Tusc. disp.* 2.13. Cf. Courcelle 1970; Wilson 1990, 264–65.

19. See Ferrari 1984, 60–63.

20. O'Connell 1993c, 223.

21. On the identification of Cornelius, the recipient of this letter, with Romanianus on the basis of an inscription from Thagaste, see Gabillon 1978.

22. Gourdon 1900, 46.

23. Fredriksen 1986, 20.

24. O'Donnell 1985, 92. He continues, "The first works after the crucial events (mainly the Cassiciacum dialogues) do not support the narrative of the *Confessions* in abundant detail. If the garden scene of Book 8 was so crucial to his whole life, why does no trace of it appear in any of the early works, some written as soon as three months after the event?" O'Donnell resorts to the explanation of genre: the Cassiciacum dialogues were not devotional, but philosophical works, and therefore should not be expected to contain the very personal aspects of Augustine's thinking at the time (O'Donnell 1985, 93).

25. Both the phrase and the concept were coined by Fredriksen 1986.

26. A point made by Séjourné 1951, 354 n1, against the suggestion of Boyer 1953, 17–18, similar to O'Donnell's just mentioned, that Augustine's desire to compose in a Classical mode led him to suppress his religious identity. Based on the fact that Augustine makes open references to Christianity in his works of the time, "c'est apparemment que 'la déception platonicienne' n'est pas encore très vive."

27. Alfaric intended the book to be the first in a multivolume study of Augustine's intellectual development, but no more volumes appeared.

28. Alfaric 1918, viii. Alfaric has slightly overstated the case, since Augustine alludes to "the mysteries into which we are being initiated," that is, the catechetical instruction he received prior to baptism, in *Ord* 2.9.27. Yet that allusion only confirms that there was nothing about the genre or nature of the writings Augustine produced at the time that excluded discussion of his religious commitments. One notes with Alfaric that no further mention occurs in the texts Augustine continued to produce both during his preparation for baptism, nor in its immediate aftermath.

29. O'Connell remarks, "Few propositions are better calculated to raise the hackles of dedicated Augustine scholars than the suggestion that the convert of Milan . . . was

articulating so thoroughly a Neo-Platonic form of Christianity as I claim. No sooner is the suggestion made than the ghost of that *enfant terrible*, Prosper Alfaric, is immediately invoked. The mere intimation that one or other view of Augustine represents a 'return to Alfaric' is calculated to cut short all further discussion of the matter" (O'Connell 1968, 203). While acknowledging the work's shortcomings, O'Connell speaks of it as a milestone. "If nothing else, it left us with a tangled skein of problems scholars have been unraveling ever since. And one has the uneasy feeling that the closer the scholar surveys the evidence, the more qualifications he inserts into his rejection of Alfaric's position, the less confidently he reaches for thoser explosive adjectives which abounded in the earlier reactions to the work" (O'Connell 1968, 203).

30. Alfaric 1918, 515.

31. Roland Teske observes, "Augustine's enthusiasm for what he learned in the libri Platonicorum is largely due to their supplying him with the concept of an incorporeal and timeless God— a concept that the whole Western Church lacked, apart from a handful of Neoplatonists in Milan, prior to Augustine" (Teske 1991a, 49 n7).

32. Alfaric 1918, 517–18. See the review of Augustine's early philosophical influences in TeSelle 1970, 43–55.

33. Alfaric 1918, 519.

34. Including (1) an identification of God with being rather than beyond being, (2) a modification of Plotinus's hierarchical three hypostases in the direction of a neo-Nicene equal Trinity, (3) a view of the soul and world as created rather than emanated entities, (4) an interposition of a judging deity into the idea of the fall of souls into embodiment, and (5) a refusal to include animals and plants in the same category of ensouled beings with humans (Alfaric 1918, 519–22). Not all of these modifications were in place immediately, however. Some Augustine would have learned from Christian Platonists around him in Milan; some he may have developed himself as he became more acquainted with Nicene Christian positions and their advantages for drawing a sharper distinction from Manichaean views.

35. Alfaric 1918, 522.

36. O'Daly notes that Augustine makes little use of specifically Neoplatonic critiques of skepticism in *The Academics*, probably because he does not yet know them (O'Daly 2001, 159).

37. See Cary 1994, 78, for a nicely balanced statement of Augustine's growing facility with both systems in the years following his conversion.

38. Alfaric 1918, ii–iii, 526–27.

39. See *Ep* 143.2; *Retr* Prologue.3; *SermDolb* 10.15.

40. Markus 1989, esp. 41–42. Like Alfaric, Markus sees the impact of Paul in the mid-390s as the fundamental Christianizing and biblicizing of Augustine (Markus 1989, 18–23).

41. Courcelle 1968.

42. Courcelle's well-supported argument on this point raises the question why Augustine so carefully distinguishes in the *Confessions* that which was thoroughly intermixed in his experience. The answer lies, I think, in the particular intention and audience he had in

mind, for which he thought crediting Platonism as a solution apart from its Christian appropriation would gain an entry to the attention of his potential Manichaean readers.

43. Courcelle's view has been adopted, for instance, by Solignac, 1962, 529–36, and Mandouze 1968, 459–60.

44. A point well made by Madec 1987b, particularly with respect to Ambrose.

45. O'Connell 1968, esp. 204.

46. O'Donnell 1992, vol. 1, xxvi.

47. O'Donnell 1992, vol. 1, xxviii. See Cicero, *Natura deorum* 2.8: *religio id est cultus deorum.*

48. Fredriksen 1986.

49. O'Connell fails to grasp how Fredriksen's treatment circumvents the old dichotomy of truth/lie, as he shows by his references to the conscious mind's supposed "lies" and "deceptions" in his review of her construct (O'Connell 1996, 263–64).

50. E.g., LeBlond 1950; Séjourné 1951, esp. 251–54; Mallard 1980, esp. 81–85; Van Fleteren 1990b, 65.

51. Hefner 1993a, 18.

52. Hefner 1993a, 18.

53. Van Fleteren 1990b, 65. Mallard 1980, esp. 81–85, highlights the mistake of taking the "that" question (*that* Augustine was a Catholic) as sufficient without investigating the "how" question (*how* he was a Catholic, in what manner and to what degree).

54. Bonner 1963, 86. This apologetic characterization dates back to Thomas Aquinas, who maintained, "Augustine knew the doctrines of the Platonists well; whenever he discovered in their teaching something which was consistent with Christian faith, he adopted it; and those things which he found to be inconsistent with faith, he amended" (*Summa Theologiae* 1 Q. 84 a. 5., *Resp.*).

55. Alfaric 1918, 399.

56. See the insightful remarks of P. Brown 2000, 96–97.

57. Comments O'Meara, "that is, the teaching of the Platonist books" (O'Meara 1951a, 177–78 n24; cf. TeSelle 1970, 36).

58. Possidius says that Augustine heard Ambrose answer in his sermons "certain questions regarding God's Law . . . in a manner contradicting that error," that is, Manichaeism (Possidius, *Vita* 1.4).

59. Trout 1988, 135.

60. Trout 1988, 137.

61. Peter Brown suggests that Simplician had sized Augustine up to be a person of the same stamp as Victorinus when he repeated the story to him (2000, 95).

62. See *QA* 7.12.

63. See Van Fleteren 1973, 49.

64. O'Connell 1984b, 6.

65. O'Connell 1968, 264.

66. Hefner 1993b, 120–21.

67. Butler 1997, 2–4.

68. Butler 1997, 93.

69. See Butler 1997, 88.

70. See Butler 1997, 99.

CHAPTER 8. RATIONALIZING FAITH

1. This is a Neoplatonic construct; cf. Plotinus, *En.* 5.9.6; 5.2.2; 5.5.3. See also *BV* 4.34.

2. He later chose to participate in the very public annual baptism at Easter time, rather than to accept private baptism, which was a readily available option.

3. The amnesty declared, in part: *et unde publica terrenorum principum uota per indulgentiam solent relaxare damnatos. denique non multo post inde omnes eadem solemni sorte dimissi sunt.* The relevance of this amnesty to the fate of the Manichaeans condemned by Messianus was first noted by Monceaux 1924, 3; see also Decret 1978, 217.

4. The autumn vacation extended from 23 August to 15 October (*Cod. Theod.* 2.8.19).

5. Ferrari 1990a, 744.

6. Foley 1999 argues that Augustine's Cassiciacum trilogy of dialogues is permeated with Cicero, and conceived as a kind of replacement corpus for a set of Cicero's classics. Just as *Acad* is a response to Cicero's *Academica*, so *BV* parallels *De finibus* and its sequel *Tusculanae disputationes*, and *Ord* corresponds to the trilogy *De natura deorum, De divinatione*, and *De fato*. Foley points to the use of cover letters, certain types of setting, and long concluding speeches in Augustine's dialogues as characteristically Ciceronian in inspiration.

7. Courcelle 1968, 58 and the works cited there, n4.

8. While usually referred to in secondary literature as *Against the Academics*, Augustine himself varied in his references to it between *De academicos* and *Contra academicos*, and expressed uncertainty over whether the work's outcome was an interpretation or refutation of Academic Skepticism (*Ep* 1; *Retr* 1.1).

9. In a cover letter for the finished work, he reports that in working through the composition of *Acad* he had "broken a most hateful bond whereby I was held back from philosophy's breast by a despair for truth" (*Ep* 1.3). In *Ench* 7.20, written in the 420s, he talks of writing *Acad* "at the beginning of my conversion to prevent the contrary arguments of those who were voicing their objections at the very threshold, as it were, from being an obstacle to us. Unquestionably there was need to remove the despair of finding truth." Finally, in *Retr* 1.1.1, he describes the position of the Academics as "troubling" him, and *Acad* as an effort to resolve his opinion about their views.

10. Augustine reports that he composed *BV* in early November 386, and the first book of *Acad* some time shortly before (*Retr* 1.2.1). He drafted the other two books of *Acad* and the two books of *Ord* at some unspecified later time, and the occasional anachronistic allusion points to early 387; e.g., *Ord* 2.9.27: "All this is being delivered to us so distinctly and steadily by the sacred rites *into which we are now being initiated*" (*quibus initiamur*). Augustine did not even submit his name as a candidate for initiation until January 387,

and the initiation process took place over the Lent season in the spring of that year. Since he states that he composed the second and third volumes of *Acad* after *Ord* (*Retr* 1.3.1), by implication these, too, date to spring 387. Yet Augustine gives the impression in *Retr* 1.5.1 that all these works were completed before his return to Milan.

11. *BV* to the well-connected Milanese Christian intellectual Manlius Theodorus; *Ord* to another prominent figure, Zenobius, later *magister memoriae* of the imperial court (see *Ep* 2 and 117); *Acad* dedicated to his long-time patron, the Manichaean Romanianus, but sent as well to one Hermogenianus (*Ep* 1).

12. The notion that these are actual transcripts of discussions, rather than fictitious dialogues composed in the style of Cicero and Plato, however much inspired by actual discussions, is one of those surprisingly naive notions endemic to Augustinian studies. For an argument that the entire Cassiciacum trilogy is consciously composed on Ciceronian models, see Foley 1999. For the general issue, see O'Meara 1951b, and for *Acad* specifically, O'Meara 1951a, 23–32. The degree to which the contents of the participants' statements can be shown to derive from Cicero's *Academica* is surely decisive in confirming O'Meara's position.

13. On Augustine emulating the *otium liberale* of the aristocratic philosopher, see Marrou 1958, 161–86; Holte 1962, 73–190, 303–27.

14. Trout 1988, 136.

15. Van Fleteren 1973, 51.

16. Cf. Plotinus, *En.* 5.8.10, 5.8.13, 6.9.11.

17. Coyle 1978, 85.

18. O'Connell 1996, 103.

19. O'Connell 1968, 223ff., makes the strongest case for Plotinus, who at various places speaks of the gap between abandoning the senses and making progress in the intellect as filled by "belief." *En.* 5.8 seems convincingly to stand behind Augustine's anti-skeptical premise that one could not even believe in one's own existence if there was not some confidence in the existence of one's mind, and Plotinus characterizes this confidence as belief (5.8.11.33–40). The beginner "must give himself to a kind of entry as does the one who learns by belief" (5.8.11.13–17)—how much might Augustine have misread this loose analogy as a literal declaration of the need for faith? O'Connell himself misses the point that Plotinus is making an analogy here (O'Connell 1968, 224), and that what the beginner does is give himself to the meditative, visionary, direct experience as a student gives himself to the authority of a master. But Augustine could have made the same oversight in his reading.

20. Van Fleteren 1973, 56.

21. Pacioni 1999, 493; see Porphyry, *Life of Pythagoras* 37; Iamblichus, *Vita Pyth.* 82ff.

22. Sedley 1989.

23. Augustine possibly found inspiration for—or confirmation of—his insight into the priority of authority over reason in the practical procedure of the Christian mysteries. In the initiation process of baptism, one went through the ritual by direction, without understanding the meaning of the acts and with an explanation of their symbolic meaning

given only afterward; see Ambrose, *De Mysteriis* 1.2. This accords with Augustine's enunciated view of baptism as an act designed to prepare the mind for the work of understanding to come.

24. For the first criterion, see *Faust* 32.20; *CEF* 14.17. For the second criterion, see *Faust* 5.1–3, 6.1, 10.1, 19.4–6, 32.3–4; *Conf* 5.5.9. Cf. Augustine's later discussion of human authority in *Ep* 147.4.

25. *ME* and *MM*, composed over the next couple of years.

26. On these criteria, see Collinge 1983, 65.

27. Cf. *De fide rerum* 7.10.

28. See Markus 1970, 147 ff.; Van Fleteren 1973, 38 and n32.

29. On the matter of conduct, however, Augustine was never very persuasive in trying to argue for Nicene moral superiority, and with the benefit of a decade of more exposure to actual Nicene Christian communities he was forced to concede many of the damning observations of Christian conduct made by Faustus in his *Capitula*. The argument therefore rings true only of his own personal experience, not as an objective comparison of one community as a whole to the other.

30. Augustine highlights from the story of Victorinus's conversion the detail that when forced to choose between his public career and his Christian faith in the time of Julian, Victorinus chose the latter, retiring into the very *otio* for which Augustine ached (*Conf* 8.5.10).

31. Augustine states, regarding the information Ponticianus had supplied about Antony of Egypt and the growing monastic movement, "We had known nothing of all this" (*Conf* 8.6.15).

32. O'Meara 1951a, 18. Similarly, Bernard Diggs understands *Acad* as "an attempt to prove and to understand what has already been believed . . . Augustine seeks by his argument not to confirm his belief that truth can be found, but in combatting the sceptics to attain an understanding of it." He adds that, "to interpret Augustine's 'beliefs' as hypotheses to be confirmed would be to misconceive his whole position" (Diggs 1949, 92).

33. Mosher 1981, 103.

34. See Neiman 1982, 271.

35. Mosher 1981, 101.

36. The arguments of Mourant 1966 and Neiman 1982 for a natural affinity between Academic Skepticism and Manichaeism are based on taking Faustus as a typical, rather than exceptional, representative of Manichaeism.

37. *Conf* 8.8.19.

38. For example, metaphors or allegories or myths or representations of deity may not be literal communications of truth, but have truth value.

39. Cf. *Faust* 21.16, 22.22.

40. Cf. *De praedestinatione sanctorum* 2.5: "To believe is nothing other than to think with assent (Quanquam et ipsum credere, nihil aliud est, quam cum assensione cogitare)."

41. See Van Fleteren 1973, esp. 56–58.

42. As we will see, he achieves this narrative affect by transposing all of the rational-

ization process that followed his conversion, in the years 387 to 397, back into the pre-conversion part of the story.

43. See Van Fleteren 1990b, 70.

44. See LeBlond's characterization of Augustine's conversion as "la soumission à l'Eglise, et à Dieu, dont elle est la mandataire, sans connaissance bien distincte de ce que cette soumission impose" (LeBlond 1950, 110).

45. On the latter, see *De Mysteriis* 9.55.

46. See Mourant 1971.

47. See Teske 1999.

48. Hefner 1993b, 120.

CHAPTER 9. A NEW MAN?

1. Hefner 1993a, 17.

2. Foucault 1986, 42.

3. Hefner 1993b, 120.

4. Swann 1983; Mauss 1998, 55.

5. Bakhtin 1990, passim.

6. See Foote 1951.

7. In *CLP* 3.25.30, Augustine says that he returned to Africa after the death of Maximus, which occurred on 27 August 388.

8. He seems to have completed what is now book 1 and part of book 2 while in Rome, finishing books 2 and 3 only after becoming a priest at Hippo in 391: *Quorum secundum et tertium in Africa iam Hippone Regio presbyter ordinatus, sicut tunc potui, terminaui* (*Retr* 1.8.1). Some commentators have suggested a compositional seam around *LA* 2.16.43 (Du Roy 1966, 237–38; supported by TeSelle 1970, 135). Note the quote of Wisdom 6:17, characteristic of the early Augustine, at 2.16.41. Augustine circulated the work in its shorter, earlier form among his friends, including Romanianus (implied in *Ep* 31.7), and was able to send the complete three-book edition to Paulinus of Nola in 396 (*Ep* 31.7).

9. J. Kevin Coyle has effectively demonstrated that, contrary to Augustine's recollection in *Retr*, he appears to have finished only the first thirty chapters of *ME* as a complete and separate work while in Rome, adding the last five chapters and a prologue a year or two later in Africa when he decided to link the work to *MM* (Coyle 1978, 66ff.) Coyle's conclusion resolves a dating issue raised previously by Thimme 1908, 8–9, and noted thereafter by Alfaric 1918, 90 n4, and Mayer 1974, 280–85, involving three internal pieces of evidence: (1) *ME* 1.1 refers to "other books" that defend against Manichaean attacks on the Bible, which are most likely to be the two books of *GCM*, written in Thagaste in 389; (2) *ME* 33.70 and *MM* 20.74 refer to Rome in a manner suggesting that Augustine is not there as he writes (*Romae etiam plura cognoui*, and *Romae autem me absente quid gestum sit, totum longum est explicare . . . et ego quidem postea Romae cum essem, omnia uera me audisse firmaui*); (3) *MM* 12.26 refers to having been recently in Carthage (*Illud uero nondum dictum erat, quod nuper*

apud Carthaginem audiui). Coyle points to a change from one biblical text base to another in the scriptural citations of the work as marking a clear break in its composition.

10. Later joined with *The Morals of the Manichaeans* (*De moribus Manichaeorum*), whose own internal evidence suggests that Augustine prepared its first half (chapters 1–9) in Rome as notes on Manichaean positions relevant to his analysis of theodicy in *LA*. Perhaps wishing to keep the latter study general and constructive, and not frame it as a specifically anti-Manichaean polemic, he may have kept more explicit discussion of Manichaean views aside, gradually building them into a separate work.

11. Arguing for an anti-Manichaean purpose for *Acad*: Mourant 1966, Mosher 1981, Neiman 1982; for *Ord*: O'Connell 1970, 50; 1978, 14.

12. O'Connell 1968, 16.

13. Frag. 57–62 Grilli.

14. Frag. 77–85 Grilli.

15. Frag. 88–92 Grilli.

16. Frag. 110 Grilli.

17. Frag. 112–114 Grilli.

18. Frag. 106–109 Grilli.

19. On African Manichaeism as a Christ-centered discourse, see *Faust* 13.1.

20. On the Incarnation as an uncomprehended *symbolus*, see *QA* 33.76; cf. Mallard 1980, 80–98, esp. 92.

21. See *Conf* 3.6.10; *CEF* 7.8; *Faust* 20.2, and the many hymnic examples in the Coptic *PsBk*.

22. Particularly his construct of the Trinity as *principium, intellectus,* and *ratio* (*Ord* 2.5.16, 2.9.26) which, besides its obvious Neoplatonic antecedents, disperses roles to Father, Son, and Spirit in close accord with a Manichaean model found in Faustus (*Faust* 20.2), according to which Jesus is the supramundane *nous*, while the Holy Spirit permeates the cosmos as an ordering principle in service of liberational processes.

23. Lee 1999, 29.

24. In the *Conf*, Augustine rather disingenuously claims that what he learned from Ambrose exonerated Christians en masse from charges of anthropomorphism. "I rejoiced to find that your one and only Church . . . that Church within which I had been signed with Christ's name in my infancy, did not entertain infantile nonsense or include in her sound teaching any belief that would seem to confine you . . . in any place however vast and spacious, in any place that would hem you in on every side after the manner of human bodies" (*Conf* 6.4.5). In fact, no such thing had been shown, nor could be shown, to Augustine, because he was in Italy at the time rather than Africa, and this spiritualizing interpretation of the meaning of scriptures did not have the same currency in the latter place as in the former.

25. Burns 1990, 374–77, draws this same connection between Augustine's "Photinian" view of Christ and a post-apostasy readjustment of the higher Christology he would have held as a Manichaean, making a comparison between Augustine's characterization of his view and that he attributes to Porphyry in *CD* 19.23. Burns is reluctant to extend this

transitional period into the Cassiciacum compositions, however, where he claims to detect "a proper understanding of Catholic faith in the incarnation of the word" (378). But "understanding" is precisely the wrong characterization of the way the incarnation turns up in these earliest works. Augustine indeed refers to Christ's incarnation, but has formulated no clear and consistent interpretation of it. He appears to offer a participationist view of Jesus as most purely and directly in contact with the divine *nous*, and this lingers on in his later references to Jesus as "the Lord's man."

26. On some of the issues surrounding the Christological uncertainties of Augustine and his associates, see Madec 1970.

27. See Du Roy 1966, 97 n1; Sage 1967, 215; Folliet 1987, 211; Cary 2000, 112.

28. As noted by Geerlings 1972, and *pace* Harrison 2006, 260–68, who cites Augustine's references to the incarnation as if they include or otherwise imply a recognition of the soteriological role of Jesus' death. See *DQ* 25, in which Augustine states that the cross was a tangible lesson to the believer not to fear death, and *DQ* 43, in which he says, "the Son of God came to show men a pattern for living." But this emphasis is not entirely attributable to a Manichean reflex. Augustine was converted in an environment still dominated by an Athanasian emphasis on the incarnation of Christ rather than his crucifixion as the essential act of reconciliation of humanity to God. The shift of emphasis to the cross was a product of the close attention to Paul prompted by the Manichaeans in the latter half of the fourth century, in which Augustine himself would play no small part.

29. E.g., 1Cor 1:24 (*Acad* 2.1.1; *BV* 4.34; *QA* 33.76); Jn 14:6 (*BV* 4.34).

30. In *Acad* 2.2.5, he refers to an earlier unsuccessful engagement with Paul, presumably during his Manichaean years. Pauline allusions in his works prior to *ME* include Rm 11:36 (*QA* 34.77) and Col 2:8 (*Ord* 1.11.32); otherwise, he appears most familiar with John: Jn 6:38 (*Ord* 1.10.28); Jn 14:6 (*BV* 4.34; *ME* 13.22; cf. *Fort* 3); Jn 17:3 (*LA* 2.2.6); Jn 18:36 (*Ord* 1.11.32).

31. He states his intention to cite only passages that he knows the Manichaeans accept (or, perhaps more realistically, those of which he knows of no Manichaean objection). His accuracy in this respect can be confirmed for most of the verses he uses, e.g., Mt 6:24 (*PsBk* 97.30), 11:27 (*PsBk* 122.11), 15:11 (*Faust* 16.6, 18.2); 1Cor 15:49 (*PsBk* 150.29), 2Cor 4:16 (*PsBk* 155.8); Gal 1:10 (*PsBk* 40.18–19); Eph 3:16 (*Faust* 24.1); 1Tim 6:10 (*Fort* 21); Tit 1:15 (*Faust* 31.1).

32. As noted by P. Brown 2000, 104.

33. O'Connell 1996, 262 and 307 n6; 1968, 237.

34. Ferrari 1980, 1987, 1991.

35. Bammel 1993.

36. They preferred a gospel harmony, either Tatian's *Diatessaron* or a related text, although in North Africa at least they were willing to adapt to the separate gospels for the sake of discussions with Christians.

37. O'Donnell 1992, vol. 2, 353, commenting on *Conf* 6.5.7.

38. Eccl 1:2 in *QA* 33.76; Eccl 7:26 in *LA* 2.8.24; Wisdom 8:1 in *LA* 2.11.30; Wisdom 6:17 in *LA* 2.16.41; Wisdom 7:27 in *LA* 2.17.45.

39. Ps 79:8 in *Ord* 1.8.23; Ps 50:12 in *QA* 33.75; Ps 101:27–28 [102.26–27] in *LA* 2.17.45; Ps 13:1 in *LA* 2.18.47.

40. This claim about his thinking as a Manichaean seems directly to contradict his usual assertion that Manichaeism is deterministic, and denies the ability to act by one's own will alone. This is one of several pieces of evidence that Augustine was aware of greater nuance in Manichaean ethical teachings than he normally acknowledges.

41. P. Brown 2000, 73, citing Ambrose, *In Ps.* 61.21.

42. Coyle 1978, 239–40.

43. Mourant 1966, 78–79.

44. He may have been persuaded in this regard by the sermons or writings of Ambrose, who insisted, "The enemy is right inside you, the cause of your erring is there, inside I say, shut up in ourselves alone" (Ambrose, *Hex* 1.8.31).

45. Alfaric 1918, 525–26. Augustine would later attack Porphyry and Iamblichus for ascribing efficacy to ritual action.

46. The latter title incorporated the study of *astrologia* as the highest form of order in the sensible universe. Augustine had completed only the treatises on grammar and music when he abandoned the project around the time of his ordination to the priesthood (*Retr* 1.6).

47. On this project, see Marrou 1958, 161–327.

48. Hadot's argument in favor of Porphyry as a source (I. Hadot 1984) has not won wide acceptance.

49. Pacioni 1999. Augustine refers to Varro in *Ord* 2.12.35 and 2.20.54

50. Pacioni 1999, 492.

51. Dyroff 1930, 37ff., supported by Cipriani 1996, 396ff., argues for Varro as the intermediary of such Pythagorean antecedents.

52. Dyroff 1930 and Cipriani 1997 have previously proposed this Pythagorean background to Augustine's project.

53. O'Connell 1996, 103.

54. He defined the human being as "a rational soul using a mortal and earthly body" (*ME* 27.52), with the soul "suited to rule the body" (*QA* 13.22) due to its superior ontological status. Cf. *Ep* 3.40.

55. Cary 1994, 72. He goes on to speculate that Augustine's quixotic efforts to prove the immortality of the soul—a proposition no one in Augustine's environment actively questioned—involve an attempt to find an alternative to Manichaean (and Stoic) models of the soul's immortality that relied upon an identity of substance between the soul and God.

56. Commenting on this passage in *Retr* 1.1.3, he says it would have been "safer" to say *go* rather than *return*, given his ongoing uncertainty over the validity of the idea of the soul's preexistence (and the resistance to that idea in certain Christian circles). Yet even here, at the end of his life, he goes on to cite scriptural and ecclesiastical authorities in favor of a preexistent, heavenly background for the soul.

57. He refers to "knowledge of God or of the soul, either of the soul within us or of the

ubiquitous soul (*anima usquequaque*)" (*Ord* 2.11.30; cf. *IA* 15.24; *QA* 32.69; *GLimp.* 4.17). He continued to consider the idea of a world-soul possible in *CE* 1.23.35 and *Retr* 1.11.4. See Teske 1983; Bourke 1954.

58. "For if I should tell you that there is only one soul, you will be at sea because of the fact that in one it is happy, in another unhappy; and one and the same thing cannot be both happy and unhappy at the same time. If I should say that it is one and many at the same time, you will smile. . . . But if I say simply that it is many, I shall have to laugh at myself." (*QA* 32.69).

59. See, e.g., Seneca, *Epistle* 65.16.

60. O'Connell 1978a, cites this passage, 60–61, and draws comparisons to Manichaean views, 63–64.

61. See, e.g., *QA* 15.25–26; *IA* 10.17.

62. See Stroumsa 1988, 78.

63. He acknowledges having trouble grasping what this teaching means in a way compatible with his assumptions about the soul's character and destiny (*QA* 33.76)

64. Augustine's adherence to the Neoplatonic idea of ascent of the soul, with no place for bodily resurrection, has been extensively demonstrated in the work of Robert O'Connell; see a summary and assessment of this issue in Rombs 2006. In *IA* 3.3, Augustine outlines the interdependence of the idea of the soul's liberation from the bodily and material and that of its ultimate static perfection, since there can be no motion in the absence of material substance.

65. Augustine reveals his synchronic conception of the "two worlds" and of the possible passage of the soul from the one to the other most clearly in *Ord* 1.11.32. In *Retr* 1.3.2, he would correct this view with the orthodox teaching of the eschatological future kingdom; but at the time he had not yet understood the diachronic structure of the non-Manichaean Christian view of salvation.

66. References to "disputation" in Augustine's early writings consistently signal a jab at Manichaean discursive technique.

67. We see the same critique of ethics without progress in reason in an earlier passage of the same work, *Ord* 2.9.26.

68. "Nothing which comes into being can be equal to that which brings it into being. . . . Therefore, when God made man, although he made him very good, nevertheless he did not make him what he himself is" (*DQ* 2).

69. Cf. *Conf* 7.11.17. With phrasing drawn largely from the Psalms and the book of Wisdom, Augustine's primary biblical reading in his Italian days, this passage has a good chance of reflecting part of his meditation on this subject at the time.

70. Clearly enunciated in the opening prayer of *Sol* 1.1.2, whose construction from a variety of literary "souvenirs" and anti-Manichaean design is noted by Doignon 1987 ("O God, creator of the universe, . . . by whom all things come into existence which by themselves would not exist; who permits not to perish even that which destroys itself; who out of nothing did create this world which the eyes of all perceive to be most beautiful; who does no evil so that existence is good because it is thy work, who shows that evil is

nothing to the few who take refuge in the truth; by whom the universe even with its sinister aspects is perfect; by whom there is no absolute disharmony because bad and good together harmonize," etc.).

71. Macdonald 2001, 73.

72. *Acad* 1.1.1.

73. Cf. Cicero, *Tusc. disp.* 5.9.25.

74. To the obvious Manichaean objection that, if God loves order (as both Manichaeans and Augustine believe), then including evil in order suggests that God loves evil (*Ord* 1.7.17), Augustine replies that God loves the ordering of things, not the things in themselves. God does not love evil, and that unloved characteristic of evil is precisely its order, the mark of its place in the overall order (*Ord* 1.7.18). Therefore, "the fact that evil had a beginning, is surely not brought about by the order of God; but when it had become a fact, it was included in God's order" (*Ord* 2.7.23). Yet Manichaeans could express themselves in strikingly similar terms, as Augustine well knew (*MM* 12.25).

75. James 1987, 85–86.

76. James 1987, 86.

77. James 1987, 87.

78. James himself works with a simpler model of inner psychological needs seeking to bring perception of the exterior world into line with those needs, 87.

79. Cf. *Conf.* 7.13.19: "For you [i.e., God] evil has no being at all, and this is true not of yourself only but of everything you have created, since apart from you there is nothing that could burst in and disrupt the order you have imposed on it. In some parts of it certain things are regarded as evil because they do not suit certain others; but these same things do fit in elsewhere, and they are good there, and good in themselves." The argument appears to derive from Plotinus, *En.* 1.8.4: "It is the irrational part of the soul which is receptive of evil, that is, of unmeasuredness and excess and defect, from which comes unrestrained wickedness and cowardice and all the rest of the soul's evil, involuntary affections which produce false opinions, making it think that the things which it shuns and seeks after are evil and good respectively."

80. See TeSelle 1970, 140.

81. See Armstrong 1954, 277–78.

82. Du Roy 1966, 186–96. Porphyry's commentary on Aristotle's *Categories*, for instance, put forward the proposition that only *nothing*, nonbeing in a literal sense, could be the opposite of Being, correcting Plotinus's tendency to use "nonbeing" of an existent evil.

83. The point of Plotinus's distinction is that the intelligible and the material are two totally different *kinds* of being, such that the qualities of stable, permanent identity we associate with being belong only to the intelligible, while the unstable, changing character of phenomena—*becoming* rather than *being*—belongs to the material. The nonbeingness of matter, therefore, means not a lack of its existence, but a lack of any inherent self-defining characteristics—any form—by which it could be usefully described as something.

84. O'Connell 1996, 108. Whether Augustine relied on prior harmonizations of Ploti-

nus and Aristotle in the "books of the Platonists" he read, or arrived at his position out of his own interest in avoiding dualism by attributing the creation of matter to a good God, is a subject for further research.

85. Rist 1994, 106 n46; Bonner 1963, 201–24. On the larger problem of convertibility of privation of being and matter, see Inge 1968, vol. 1, 128–50; D. O'Brien 1996, esp. 178–81.

86. While Plotinus finds Aristotle's description of matter-in-itself as utterly deprived of form useful for making an equation of matter and evil, he expressly rejects treating "evil" as no more than another term for something comparatively less good. Plotinus reserves the tag "evil" only for an "absolute lack." "What falls in some degree short of the good is not evil; considered in its own kind it might even be perfect. But where there is utter dearth, there we have essential evil, void of all share in good; this is the case with matter" (*En.* 1.8.5).

87. On the ubiquity of this position on the nonexistence of evil as an ontological principle among fourth-century anti-Manichaean writers, see Klein 1991, 118–25.

88. Cf. *Sol* 1.1.2; *MM* 2.2–7.8, 8.11; *VR* 20.39, 23.44; *DQ* 6; *CEF* 40.46; *Cont* 8.21; *Conf* 7.12.18, 7.16.22; *NB* 4; *Ench* 12–14.

89. Macdonald 2001, 83–84.

90. Du Roy 1966, 184 n4.

91. Babcock 1993b, 240–41.

92. Babcock 1993b, 241.

93. Dillon 1996.

94. See, e.g., Ambrose, *Iacob* 1.1.1, 1.1.4; *Hex* 1.8.31. The only qualification of this staunch free will position comes when Ambrose cautiously, and apparently reluctantly, offers an exegesis of Romans 6–8 in *Iacob* 1.3.12–6.23. Ambrose famously resisted the repeated requests of his associate Simplician to give more attention to exegeting Paul, insisting that he was not up to the task, "since his depth of meaning is understood only with difficulty" (Ambrose, *Ep.* 54/37; cf. *Ep.* 69/75: "nothing is more difficult than treating properly the Apostle's meaning"). In his treatment of Romans 6–8, Ambrose closely repeats Paul's language of servitude and the penalty deriving from Adam's sin, along with Christ's redemption of humans from sin, without integrating it with his broader discussion of moral responsibility. But he makes it clear that Paul's language of disability means only that we need God's aid to support our will to be good; he has no notion that the will to be good itself must be initiated in us by God.

95. E.g., Basil of Caesarea, *Quod Deus non est auctor malorum* (PG 31, 329–54); *Hexaemeron* 2.4–5; Serapion of Thmuis, *Against the Manichaeans* 5; Epiphanius of Salamis, *Panarion* 66.15.3ff. See Stroumsa and Stroumsa 1988, 48; Klein 1991, 113–18; Lamberigts 2001, 115; Pedersen 2004, 144–45.

96. Cf. *LA* 1.11.21–22. Augustine's recollection closely parallels Ambrose, *Iacob* 1.3.10: "It is not that we can attribute our trouble to anything but our own will. No one is held to guilt unless he has gone astray by his own will. Actions which are imposed on those who resist contain no fault; the malevolence of sin follows only upon actions perpetrated voluntarily, and this fault we would divert to others."

97. The first nine chapters of *MM* appear to be constituted of specifically anti-Manichaean notes on the problem of evil closely related to the concerns of *LA*, and possibly set aside in order to give the latter work a less polemical focus. Later, however, Augustine openly admitted its anti-Manichaean subtext: "The disputation was undertaken on account of those who deny that evil derives its origin from the free choice of the will and who contend accordingly that God the creator of all things is to be blamed. In this way, following their impious error—for they are Manichaeans—they seek to introduce an evil nature, unchangeable and coeternal with God" (*Retr.* 1.8.2; cf. O'Connell 1973, 8). The shift of theme between the first nine chapters of *MM* and the later ones closely parallels that identified in *ME* by J. Kevin Coyle as indicating a compositional theme, and the same biblical base text that Coyle links to the African portion of the *ME* appears only after chapter nine of *MM*.

98. He strives valiantly and fruitlessly to reconstrue Manichaean definitions of evil through a Neoplatonic lens that would render them all into aspects of nonbeing: *MM* 6.8, 8.11.

99. For example, the beating he received in school (*Conf* 1.9.14).

100. Augustine recognized that his position would not be acceptable to Manichaeans: *MM* 2.4, 3.5.

101. Matthews 1980, 57.

102. Babcock 1988, 34.

103. The Stoics maintained a unitary understanding of the human mind/soul. "As a consequence, it becomes impossible that one part of the mind fights against or enslaves or decides against other parts of the mind" (Bobzien 1998, 286–87).

104. BeDuhn 2001.

105. On the place of astrology in Manichaean concepts of human vulnerability to the environment, see Schipper 2001, BeDuhn 2001. The view of the body's own functions being in part determined by the influences of the stars was already found in later Stoic thought and in Bardaisan.

106. Alexander of Lycopolis correctly discerns that the place of randomness in the Manichaean account of evil matter makes any advancement or improvement of human character rather more accidental than determined (Alexander of Lycopolis 16.23.15–19).

107. Bobzien 1998, 411–12.

108. "Apparently Augustine is quite willing to guarantee the invulnerability of beatitude by defining power exclusively in normative terms. . . . These affections have no power to disrupt beatitude, because they have no right or authority to do so. The norm, 'Order must subordinate disorder,' serves as well for the principle of power" (Wetzel 1992, 76).

109. Augustine employs the Plotinian *audacia* for this concept in his Italian works (e.g., *ME* 12.20), substituting the more Christianized term *superbia* in the later works of his African period (Torchia 1987).

110. See Bammel 1989. On the work's unrestrained use of Plotinus, see Pepin 1964.

111. See Cary 1994, 76–77.

112. Teske 1991a, 117 n103; cf. *GCM* 2.14.21: "Even now nothing else happens in each of us when one falls into sin than occurred then" in the Garden of Eden.

113. Babcock 1993a, 227.

114. Babcock 1993a, 227.

115. Cf. Augustine's attempt to write over this statement in *Retr* 1.9.2.

116. *MM* 5.7.

117. Wetzel 1992, 78.

118. It is equally essential to Augustine's unqualified affirmation of the Classical forensic model that no collective or "original" sin be involved. One does not punish the descendant for the crime of the ancestor. Nor can the child of a criminal necessarily be a criminal by inherited nature, since that would mean that one did not freely choose to act as one did, and so could not be held liable. Therefore, "sins harm only the nature of him who commits them" (*GCM* 2.29.43).

119. Augustine attempts to correct the broadness of this statement in *Retr* 1.12.5, taking a convoluted position that effectively negates the Classical forensic principles that guide his earlier work.

120. See Aristotle, *Nicomachean Ethics* 3.7.1135a23, for the definition of free will as an absence of constraint and presence of knowledge.

121. See Gerson 1994, 162.

122. See Rist 1967, 130–38; Leroux 1996, 310–11, Dillon 1996, 330.

123. Even though Evodius, ostensibly the conversation partner underlying the dialogue, had himself never been a Manichaean.

124. Wetzel thinks this answer runs afoul of the Classical exoneration of someone acting from ignorance, constrained by bad information about what constitutes a genuine good (Wetzel 1992, 78–79).

125. Cf. the same conclusion reached via an elaboration of the ontological version of the argument, *LA* 2.18.48.

126. Babcock 1988, 35–36. Note cautious allusions to the fall scenario in *LA* 1.11.23, 1.12.24, 1.13.28.

CONCLUSION

1. See Sandomirsky and Wilson 1990.

2. Polanyi 1964, 26, 34–35; 1958, 266.

3. Kuhn 1970, 129.

4. Kuhn 1970, 78.

5. Fish 1980.

6. Manichaeism had helped him "become more upright" in his thinking and escape the "superstition" of the sort of African Christianity he had experienced as a child (*BV* 1.4). See O'Connell 1986 for this—in my opinion correct—reading of this passage. First to recognize that Augustine uses "superstition" here to refer to the Christianity of his youth was Alfaric, 70 n7. Among those concurring are TeSelle 1970, Van Fleteren 1973, O'Donnell 1992, vol. 2, 175–76.

7. Hefner 1993a, 17.

8. To take a suitably prominent example, Goulven Madec criticizes Alfaric's minimization of Augustine's Catholicism in the 380s for "le préjugé du plein doctrinal," the assumption that the writings of a particular period express the doctrinal *plenum*, the complete sum of Augustine's thinking at the time (Madec 1989).

9. Butler 1997, 20–21.

10. For which see BeDuhn 2011.

BIBLIOGRAPHY

PRIMARY: AUGUSTINE

AC: *De agone christiano.* (*The Christian Combat*)
Text: CSEL 41.
English Translation: R. P. Russell, *The Christian Combat*, Fathers of the Church 2.
New York: Catholic University of America Press, 1947.
Acad: *Contra Academicos.* (*Against the Academics*)
Text: CCL 29.
English Translation: John J. O'Meara, *St. Augustine, Against the Academics*, Ancient
Christian Writers 12. New York: Newman, 1951.
Adim: *Contra Adimantum Manichei discipulum.* (*Against Adimantus*)
Text: CSEL 25.1
English Translation: Roland Teske, *The Manichean Debate*, Works of Saint Augustine,
I/19. Hyde Park, N.Y.: New City Press, 2006, 176–223.
BC: *De bono coniugali.* (*The Good of Marriage*)
Text: CSEL 41.
English Translation: Roy J. Deferrari, *Saint Augustine, Treatises on Marriage and Other
Subjects*, Fathers of the Church 27. Washington, D.C.: Catholic University of America
Press, 1955, 9–51.
BV: *De beata vita.* (*The Good Life*)
Text: CCL 29.
English translation: Ludwig Schopp, *Writings of Saint Augustine*, Vol. 1, Fathers of the
Church 1. New York: Catholic University of America Press, 1948.
CALP: *Contra adversarium legis et prophetarum.* (*Against the Adversaries of the Law and
Prophets*)
Text: CCL 49.
English Translation: Roland Teske, *Arianism and Other Heresies*, Works of Saint Au-
gustine I/18. Hyde Park, N.Y.: New City Press, 1995.
CD: *De civitate Dei.* (*The City of God*)
Text: CCL 47–48.

English Translation: Henry Bettenson, *Augustine: City of God*. New York: Penguin, 1972.

CE: *De consensu euangelistarum*. (*The Agreement of the Evangelists*)
Text: CSEL 43.
English Translation: Philip Schaff, *Nicene and Post-Nicene Fathers*, First Series 6. Grand Rapids, Mich.: Eerdmans, 1997.

CEF: *Contra epistulam Manichaei quam vocant fundamenti*. (*Against the Fundamental Epistle*)
Text: CSEL 25.
English Translation: Roland Teske, *The Manichean Debate*, Works of Saint Augustine, I/19. Hyde Park, N.Y.: New City Press, 2006, 234–67.

CLP: *Contra litteras Petiliani*. (*Against the Letters of Petilian*)
Text: CSEL 52.
English Translation: Philip Schaff, *Nicene and Post-Nicene Fathers*, First Series 4. Grand Rapids, Mich.: Eerdmans, 1997.

Conf: *Confessiones*. (*Confessions*)
Text: CCL 27.
English Translation: Maria Boulding, *The Confessions*, Works of Saint Augustine I/1. Hyde Park, N.Y.: New City Press, 1997.

Cont: *De continentia*. (*Continence*)
Text: CSEL 41.
English Translation: M. F. McDonald, "Continence," in Roy J. Deferrari, *Saint Augustine, Treatises on Various Subjects*, Fathers of the Church 16. New York: Catholic University of America Press, 1952, 189–231.

CR: *De catechizandis rudibus*. (*Catechizing the Uncultured*)
Text: CCL 46.
English Translation: *The First Catechetical Instruction*, Ancient Christian Writers 2. New York: Newman, 1946.

Cresc: *Ad Cresconium grammaticum partis Donati*. (*To Cresconius*)
Text: CSEL 52.
French Translation: G. Finaert, *Traités Anti-Donatistes*, Volume IV: *Contra Cresconium Libri IV, De Unico Baptismo*. Paris: Desclée de Brouwer, 1968.

DA: *De duabus animabus*. (*The Two Souls*)
Text: CSEL 25.
English Translation: Roland Teske, *The Manichean Debate*, Works of Saint Augustine I/19. Hyde Park, N.Y.: New City Press, 2006, 117–34.

DC: *De doctrina Christiana*. (*Christian Doctrine*)
Text: CCL 32.
English Translation: R. P. H. Green, *Augustine. De Doctrina Christiana*. Oxford: Clarendon Press, 1995.

DEP: *Contra duas epistulas Pelagianorum*. (*Against Two Letters of the Pelagians*)
Text: CSEL 60.

English Translation: Roland Teske, *Answer to the Pelagians, II*, Works of Saint Augustine I/24. Hyde Park, N.Y.: New City Press, 1998, 116–219.

DP: *De dono perseverantiae.* (*The Gift of Perseverance*)
Text: PL 45
Translation: J. A. Mourant and W. J. Collinge, *Four Anti-Pelagian Writings*, Fathers of the Church 86. Washington, D.C.: Catholic University of America Press, 1992.

DQ: *De diversis quaestionibus octoginta tribus.* (*Eighty-Three Diverse Questions*)
Text: CCL 43a.
English Translation: Boniface Ramsey, *Responses to Miscellaneous Questions*, Works of Saint Augustine I/12. Hyde Park, N.Y.: New City Press, 2008, 31–157.

EnPs: *Enarrationes in Psalmos.* (*Explanations of the Psalms*)
Text: CCL 38–40.
English Translation: Maria Boulding, *Expositions of the Psalms*, Works of Saint Augustine III/14–17. Hyde Park, N.Y.: New City Press, 2000– .

Ep: *Epistulae.* (*Letters*)
Text: CSEL 34, 44.
English Translation: Roland Teske, *Letters 1–99*, Works of Saint Augustine II/1. Hyde Park, N.Y.: New City Press, 2001; Roland Teske, *Letters 100–155*, Works of Saint Augustine, II.2. Hyde Park, N.Y.: New City Press, 2003.

Faust: *Contra Faustum Manicheum.* (*Against Faustus*)
Text: CSEL 25.1.
English Translation: Roland Teske, *Answer to Faustus a Manichean*, I.20. Hyde Park, N.Y.: New City Press, 2007.

Fel: *Acta contra Felicem.* (*Against Felix*)
Text: CSEL 25.2.
English Translation: Roland Teske, *The Manichean Debate*, Works of Saint Augustine I/19. Hyde Park, N.Y.: New City Press, 2006, 280–316.

Fid: *De fide et symbolo.* (*Faith and the Creed*)
Text: CSEL 41.
English Translations: J. H. S. Burleigh, *Augustine: Earlier Writings*. Philadelphia: Westminster, 1953, 349–69; R. P. Russell, *Faith and the Creed*, Fathers of the Church 27. New York: Catholic University of America Press, 1955, 311–45.

Fort: *Acta contra Fortunatum Manicheum.* (*Against Fortunatus*)
Text: CSEL 25.1.
English Translation: Roland Teske, *The Manichean Debate*, Works of Saint Augustine, I/19. Hyde Park, N.Y.: New City Press, 2006, 145–62.

GCM: *De Genesi contra manichaeos.* (*Genesis Against the Manichaeans*)
Text: CSEL 91.
English translation: Roland J. Teske, *Saint Augustine On Genesis: Two Books on Genesis against the Manichees and On the Literal Interpretation of Genesis: An Unfinished Book*, Fathers of the Church 84. Washington, D.C.: Catholic University of America Press, 1991.

GL: *De Genesi ad litteram.* (*Genesis Literally*)
Text: CSEL 28.1
English Translation: John Hammond Taylor, *The Literal Meaning of Genesis*, Ancient Christian Writers 41–42. New York: Newman, 1982.
GLimp: *De Genesi ad litteram imperfectus liber.* (*Genesis Literally Unfinished*)
Text: CSEL 28.1.
English translation: Roland J. Teske, *Saint Augustine On Genesis: Two Books on Genesis Against the Manichees and On the Literal Interpretation of Genesis: An Unfinished Book*, Fathers of the Church 84. Washington, D.C.: Catholic University of America Press, 1991.
GPO: *De gratia Christi et peccato originale.* (*The Grace of Christ and Original Sin*)
Text: CSEL 42.
English translation: Roland Teske, *Answer to the Pelagians I*, Works of Saint Augustine I/23. Hyde Park, N.Y.: New City Press, 1997, 391–448.
Haer: *De haeresibus.* (*Heresies*)
Text: CCL 46.
English Translation: Roland Teske, *Arianism and Other Heresies*, Works of Saint Augustine I/18. Hyde Park, N.Y.: New City Press, 1995.
IA: *De immortalitate animae.* (*The Immortality of the Soul*)
Text: CSEL 89.
English translation: Ludwig Schopp, *Writings of Saint Augustine*, Vol. 2, Fathers of the Church 2. New York: Catholic University of America Press, 1947.
Iul: *Contra Iulianum.* (*Against Julian*)
Text: PL 44.
English Translation: Roland Teske, *Answer to the Pelagians II*, Works of Saint Augustine I/24. Hyde Park, N.Y.: New City Press, 1998, 268–536.
Iulimp: *Contra Iulianum opus imperfectum.* (*Against Julian Unfinished*)
Text: PL 45.
English Translation: Roland Teske, *Answer to the Pelagians III*, Works of Saint Augustine I/25. Hyde Park, N.Y.: New City Press, 1999.
JohTrac: *In Johannis evangelium tractatus.* (*Treatise on John*)
Text: CCL 36.
English Translation: John W. Rettig, *Tractates on the Gospel of John*, Fathers of the Church 78–. Washington, D.C.: Catholic University of America Press, 1988–.
LA: *De libero arbitrio.* (*Free Choice*)
Text: CCL 29.
English Translation: J. H. S. Burleigh, *Augustine: Earlier Writings*. Philadelphia: Westminster, 1953, 106–217.
Mag: *De magistro.* (*The Teacher*)
Text: CCL 29.
English Translations: J. H. S. Burleigh, *Augustine: Earlier Writings*. Philadelphia: Westminster, 1953, 69–101.

ME: *De moribus ecclesiae catholicae.* (*The Morals of the Catholic Church*)
Text: CSEL 90.
English Translations: Donald A. and Idella J. Gallagher, *The Catholic and Manichaean Ways of Life*, Fathers of the Church, 56. Washington, D.C.: Catholic University of America Press, 1965; Roland Teske, *The Manichean Debate*, Works of Saint Augustine, I/19. Hyde Park, N.Y.: New City Press, 2006, 31–68.

Mend: *De mendacio.* (*Lying*)
Text: CSEL 41.
English Translation: M. S. Muldowney, "Lying," in Roy Deferrari, *Saint Augustine, Treatises on Various Subjects*, Fathers of the Church 16 (New York: Catholic University of America Press, 1952, 45–110.

MM: *De moribus Manichaeorum.* (*The Morals of the Manichaeans*)
Text: CSEL 90.
English Translations: Donald A. and Idella J. Gallagher, *The Catholic and Manichaean Ways of Life*, Fathers of the Church, 56. Washington, D.C.: Catholic University of America Press, 1965; Roland Teske, *The Manichean Debate*, Works of Saint Augustine, I/19. Hyde Park, N.Y.: New City Press, 2006, 69–103.

Mus: *De musica.* (*Music*)
Text: PL 32.
English Translation: Ludwig Schopp, *Writings of Saint Augustine*, Vol. 2, Fathers of the Church 2. New York: Catholic University of America Press, 1947.

NB: *De natura boni.* (*The Nature of Good*)
Text: CSEL 25.2.
English Translation: J. H. S. Burleigh, *Augustine: Earlier Writings*. Philadelphia: Westminster, 1953.

Nupt: *De nuptiis et conscupiscentia.* (*Marriage and Lust*)
Text: CSEL 42.
English Translation : Roland Teske, *Answer to the Pelagians II*, Works of Saint Augustine I/24. Hyde Park : New City Press, 1998, 28–96.

Ord: *De ordine.* (*Order*)
Text: CCL 29.
English Translation: Robert P. Russell, in *Divine Providence and the Problem of Evil.* New York: Cosmopolitan Science and Art Service, 1942; reprinted in *Writings of Saint Augustine*, Vol. 1, ed. Ludwig Schopp, Fathers of the Church 1. New York: Catholic University of America Press, 1948.

QA: *De quantitate animae.* (*Quantifying Soul*)
Text: F. E. Tourscher, *The Measure of the Soul*. Philadelphia: Reilly, 1933.
English Translations: F. E. Tourscher, *The Measure of the Soul*. Philadelphia: Reilly, 1933; J. J. McMahon, in Ludwig Schopp, *Writings of Saint Augustine*, Vol. 2, Fathers of the Church 2. New York: Catholic University of America Press, 1947, 51–149; Joseph M. Colleran, *St. Augustine: The Greatness of the Soul, The Teacher*, Ancient Christian Writers 9. New York: Newman, 1950.

Retr: *Retractationes.* (*Revisions*)

    Text: CCL 57.

    English Translation: M. I. Bogan, *Saint Augustine, The Retractations*, Fathers of the Church 60. Washington, D.C.: Catholic University of America Press, 1968.

Sec: *Contra Secundinum Manicheum.* (*Against Secundinus*)

    Text: CSEL 25.

    English Translation: Roland Teske, *The Manichean Debate*, Works of Saint Augustine, I/19. Hyde Park, N.Y.: New City Press, 2006, 363–90.

Sent: *Liber XXI Sententiarum.* (*Twenty-One Passages*)

    Text & French Translation: F. Dolbeau, Le Liber XXI Sententiarum (CPL 373): Edition d'un texte de travail. *RA* 30 (1997): 113–65.

Serm: *Sermones.* (*Sermons*)

    Text: CCL 41.

    English Translation: Edmund Hill, *Sermons*, Works of Saint Augustine III/1–10. Hyde Park, N.Y.: New City Press, 1990–1997.

SermDolb: *Sermones Dolbeau.* (*Dolbeau Sermons*)

    Text: F. Dolbeau, *Vingt-six sermons au peuple d'Afrique*. Paris: Études Augustiniennes, 1996.

    English Translation: Edmund Hill, *Newly Discovered Sermons*, Works of Saint Augustine III/11. Hyde Park, N.Y.: New City Press, 1997.

SermDom: *De sermone Domini in monte.* (*The Lord's Sermon on the Mount*)

    Text: CCL 35.

    English Translation: Jon Jepson, *St. Augustine, The Lord's Sermon on the Mount*, Ancient Christian Writers 5. New York: Newman, 1948.

SermMai: *Sermones A. Mai.* (*Mai Sermons*)

    Text: *Miscellanea Agostiniana*, Vol. 1. Rome: Tipografia Poliglotta Vaticana, 1930, 285–386.

    English Translation:

Simpl: *Ad Simplicianum.* (*To Simplician*)

    Text: CCL 44.

    English Translation: J. H. S. Burleigh, *Augustine: Earlier Writings*. Philadelphia: Westminster, 1953, 376–406.

Sol: *Soliloquia.* (*Soliloquies*)

    Text: CSEL 89.

    English Translation: J. H. S. Burleigh, *Augustine: Earlier Writings*. Philadelphia: Westminster, 1953, 23–63.

UC: *De utilitate credendi.* (*The Usefulness of Belief*)

    Text: CSEL 25.1.

    English Translation: J. H. S. Burleigh, *Augustine: Earlier Writings*. Philadelphia: Westminster, 1953, 287–323.

VR: *De uera religione.* (*True Religion*)

    Text: CCL 32.

English Translation: J. H. S. Burleigh, *Augustine: Earlier Writings*. Philadelphia: Westminster, 1953, 225–83.

PRIMARY: MANICHAEAN

CMC: *Cologne Mani Codex*
Text: L. Koenen and C. Römer, *Der Kölner Mani*-Kodex. Opladen: Westdeutscher Verlag, 1988.
EpSec: *Epistle of Secundinus*
Text: CSEL 25
English Translation: Roland Teske, *The Manichaean Debate*, Works of Saint Augustine, I/19. Hyde Park, N.Y.: New City Press, 2006.
Hom: *Homilies*
Text & German Translation: H. J. Polotsky, *Manichäische Homilien*. Stuttgart: Kohlhammer, 1934.
Text & English Translation: Nils-Arne Pedersen, *Manichaean Homilies*, Corpus Fontium Manichaeorum, Series Coptica 2. Turnhout: Brepols, 2006.
Keph: *Kephalaia*
Text & German Translation: H. J. Polotsky and A. Böhlig, *Kephalaia I, Erster Hälfte (Lieferung 1–10)*. Stuttgart: Kohlhammer, 1940; A. Böhlig, *Kephalaia I, Zweite Hälfte (Lieferung 11/12)*. Stuttgart: Kohlhammer, 1966; W.-P. Funk, *Kephalaia I, Zweite Hälfte (Lieferung 13/14)*. Stuttgart: Kohlhammer, 1999; W.-P. Funk, *Kephalaia I, Zweite Hälfte (Lieferung 15/16)*. Stuttgart: Kohlhammer, 2000.
English Translation: Iain Gardner, *The Kephalaia of the Teacher*, Nag Hammadi and Manichaean Studies 37. Leiden: Brill 1995.
Men: *Epistle to Menoch*
Text & English Translation: G. Harrison and J. BeDuhn, "The Authenticity and Doctrine of (Ps?) Mani's *Letter to Menoch*," in P. Mirecki and J. BeDuhn, *The Light and the Darkness: Studies in Manichaeism and Its World*, Nag Hammadi and Manichaean Studies 50. Leiden: Brill, 2001, 128–72.
PsBk: *Psalm Book*
Text & English Translation: C. R. C. Allberry, *A Manichaean Psalm-Book, Part II*. Stuttgart: Kohlhammer, 1938.
TebCod: *Tebessa Codex*
Text & English Translation: J. BeDuhn and G. Harrison, "The Tebessa Codex: A Manichaean Treatise on Biblical Exegesis and Church Order," in P. Mirecki and J. BeDuhn, *Emerging from Darkness: Studies in the Recovery of Manichaean Sources*, Nag Hammadi and Manichaean Studies 43. Leiden: Brill, 1997, 33–87.

PRIMARY: OTHER

Acta Archelai:

C. H. Beeson, *Hegemonius, Acta Archelai*, GCS 16. Leipzig, 1906.

Mark Vermes, *Hegemonius, Acta Archelai (The Acts of Archelaus)*. Turnhout: Brepols, 2001.

Alexander of Aphrodisias:

R. W. Sharples, *Alexander of Aphrodisias on Fate*. London: Duckworth, 1983.

Alexander of Lycopolis:

Augustus Brinkmann, *Alexandri Lycopolitani. Contra Manichaei Opiniones Disputatio.* Stuttgart: Teubner, 1989.

P. W. van der Horst and J. Mansfeld, *An Alexandrian Platonist against Dualism: Alexander of Lycopolis' Treatise 'Critique of the Doctrines of Manichaeus'*. Leiden: Brill, 1974.

Ambrose of Milan:

H. de Romestin et al., *Some of the Principal Works of St. Ambrose*, Nicene and Post-Nicene Fathers, Second Series 10. Peabody: Hendrickson, 1994.

John J. Savage, *Saint Ambrose: Hexameron, Paradise, and Cain in Abel*, Fathers of the Church 42. New York: Fathers of the Church, Inc., 1961.

Roy J. Deferrari, *Saint Ambrose: Theological and Dogmatic Works*, Fathers of the Church 44. Washington, D.C.: Catholic University of America Press, 1963.

Michael P. McHugh, *Saint Ambrose: Seven Exegetical Works*, Fathers of the Church 65. Washington, D.C.: Catholic University of America Press, 1972.

Aristotle:

Harold P. Cooke, *Aristotle, Categories*, Cambridge, Mass.: Harvard University Press, 1938.

Ephrem Syrus:

C. W. Mitchell, *S. Ephraim's Prose Refutations of Mani, Marcion, and Bardaisan*, London: Williams and Norgate, 1912–1921.

Epiphanius of Salamis:

Frank Williams, *The Panarion of Epiphanius of Salamis*, Leiden: Brill, 1987.

Iamblichus:

Gillian Clark, *Iamblichus: On the Pythagorean Life*, Liverpool: Liverpool University Press, 1989.

Jerome:

C. C. Mierow and T. C. Lawler, *Jerome, Epistles 1–22*, Ancient Christian Writers 33, Philadelphia: Westminster, 1963.

W. H. Fremantle, *The Principal Works of St. Jerome*, Nicene and Post-Nicene Father, Second Series, Vol. 6, Peabody: Hendrickson, 1994.

Leo:

H. G. Schipper and J. van Oort, *St. Leo the Great, Sermons and Letters against the Manichaeans*, Turnhout: Brepols, 2000.

Nemesius of Emesa:
William Telfer, *Cyril of Jerusalme and Nemesius of Emesa*, Library of Christian Classics 4, Philadelphia: Westminster, 1955.
Plotinus:
A. H. Armstrong, *Plotinus*. Cambridge, Mass.: Harvard University Press, 1966–1988.
Porphyry:
Life of Pythagoras
Moses Hadas and Morton Smith, *Heroes and Gods: Spiritual Biographies of Antiquity*, London: Routledge and Kegan Paul, 1965.
Possidius:
John E. Rotelle, *The Life of Saint Augustine*, Villanova, Pa.: Augustinian Press, 1988.
Serapion of Thmuis:
Robert Pierce Casey, *Serapion of Thmuis, Against the Manichees*, Cambridge, Mass.: Harvard University Press, 1931.
Severus of Antioch:
M.-A. Kugener and F. Cumont, *Recherches sur le manichéisme II: Extrait de la CXXIIIᵉ homélie de Sévère d'Antioche*, Bruxelles: H. Lamertin, 1912.
Titus of Bostra:
P. A. de Lagarde, *Titus Bostrenus syriace et graece*, Wiesbaden: Harrassowitz, 1967.

SECONDARY

Adkin, Neil
　1992　"Filthy Manichees." *Arctos* 26: 5–18.
　1993　Heretics and Manichees. *Orpheus* (n.s.) 14: 135–40.
Alfaric, Prosper
　1918　*L'évolution intellectuelle de s. Augustin*, vol. 1: *Du manichéisme au néo-platonisme*. Paris: E. Nourry.
Amand, David
　1973　*Fatalisme et liberté dans l'antiquité grecque*. Amsterdam: Adolf M. Hakkert.
Andresen, Carl
　1968　Gedanken zum philosophischen Bildungshorizont Augustins vor und in Cassiciacum: Contra academ. II 6, 14f.; III 17–19, 37–42. *Augustinus* 13: 77–98.
Annas, Julia
　1992　*Hellenistic Philosophy of Mind*. Berkeley: University of California Press.
Armstrong, Hilary
　1954　Spiritual or Intelligible Matter in Plotinus and St. Augustine. *Augustinus Magister I: Congrès International Augustinien, 1954*, ed. Fulbert Cayré. Paris: Études augustiniennes, 277–83.

1967 Plotinus. *The Cambridge History of Later Greek and Early Mediaeval Philosophy.* Cambridge: Cambridge University Press.

Asad, Talal

1993 *Genealogies of Religion: Discipline and Reasons of Power in Christianity and Islam.* Baltimore: Johns Hopkins University Press.

Asher, Lyell

1998 The Dangerous Fruit of Augustine's *Confessions. Journal of the American Academy of Religion* 66: 227–55.

Austin, J. L.

1975 *How to do Things with Words*, 2nd ed. Cambridge, Mass.: Harvard University Press.

Babcock, William S.

1988 Augustine on Sin and Moral Agency. *Journal of Religious Ethics* 16: 28–55.

1993a Sin, Penalty, and the Responsibility of the Soul: A Problem in Augustine's *De Libero Arbitrio III. Studia Patristica* 27: 225–30.

1993b Sin and Punishment: The Early Augustine on Evil. *Collectanea Augustiniana: Augustine, Presbyter Factus Sum*, ed. J. Lienhard et al. New York: Peter Lang. 235–48.

Baguette, C.

1970 Une période stoïcienne dans l'évolution de la pensée de saint Augustin. *REA* 16: 47–77.

Bakhtin, Mikhail

1990 *Art and Answerability.* Austin: University of Texas Press.

Bammel, Caroline P.

1989 Adam in Origen. *The Making of Orthodoxy: Essays in Honour of Henry Chadwick*, ed. R. Williams. Cambridge: Cambridge University Press, 62–93. Reprinted in Bammel 1995.

1993 Pauline Exegesis, Manichaeism and Philosophy in the Early Augustine. *Christian Faith and Greek Philosophy in Late Antiquity: Essays in Tribute to George Christopher Stead*, ed. L. R. Wickham and C. P. Bammel. Leiden: Brill, 1–25.

1995 *Tradition and Exegesis in Early Christian Writers.* Aldershot: Variorum.

Bardy, Gustave

1948 *Saint Augustin. L'homme et l'œuvre*, 7th ed. Paris: Desclée de Brouwer.

Barker, Eileen

1998 Standing at the Cross-Roads: The Politics of Marginality in "Subversive Organizations." *The Politics of Religious Apostasy*, ed. D. G. Bromley. Westport, Conn.: Praeger, 75–93.

Barnes, Timothy D.

1976a Imperial Campaigns. *Phoenix* 30: 174–93.

1976b Sossianus Hierocles and the Antecedents of the "Great Persecution." *Harvard Studies in Classical Philology* 80: 239–52.

1985   Proconsuls of Africa, 337–392. *Phoenix* 39: 144–53, 273–74.

Beduhn, Jason D.

2000   *The Manichaean Body: In Discipline and Ritual.* Baltimore: Johns Hopkins University Press.

2001   The Metabolism of Salvation: Manichaean Concepts of Human Physiology. *The Light and the Darkness: Studies in Manichaeism and Its World,* ed. P. A. Mirecki and J. D. Beduhn. Leiden: Brill. 5–37.

2004   The Near Eastern Connections of Manichaean Confessionary Practice. *ARAM* 16: 161–77.

2007   Biblical Antitheses, Adda, and the Acts of Archelaus. In *Frontiers of Faith: The Christian Encounter with Manichaeism in the Acts of Archelaus,* ed. J. Beduhn and P. Mirecki. Leiden: E. J. Brill. 131–47.

2008   The Domestic Setting of Manichaean Religious Practice in the Roman Empire. *Archiv für Religionsgeschichte* 10: 247–59.

2009a   Augustine Accused: Megalius, Manichaeism, and the Inception of the *Confessions. JECS* 17: 85–124.

2009b   A Religion of Deeds: Scepticism in the Doctrinally Liberal Manichaeism of Faustus and Augustine. *New Light on Manichaeism: Papers from the Sixth International Congress on Manichaeism,* ed. J. D. Beduhn. Leiden: Brill. 1–28.

2009c   Digesting the Sacrifices: Ritual Internalization in Jewish, Hindu, and Manichaean Traditions. In *Essays in Honor of Patrick Olivelle,* ed. Steven Lindquist. Firenze: Firenze University Press (in press).

2011   *Augustine's Manichaean Dilemma, 2: Making a "Catholic" Self, 389–401 C.E.* Philadelphia: University of Pennsylvania Press.

Beit-Hallahmi, Benjamin and Michael Argyle

1997   *The Psychology of Religious Behavior, Belief and Experience.* London: Routledge.

Bertrand, Louis

1914   *Saint Augustin,* trans. Vincent O'Sullivan. London: Constable.

Bezançon, Jean-Noël

1965   Le mal et l'existence temporelle chez Plotin et saint Augustin. *RA* 3: 133–60.

Bobzien, Susanne

1998   *Determinism and Freedom in Stoic Philosophy.* Oxford: Clarendon.

Boissier, Gaston

1888   La Conversion de saint Augustin. *Revue des deux mondes* 85: 43–69.

Bonner, Gerald

1963   *St. Augustine of Hippo: Life and Controversies.* Philadelphia: Westminster.

1977   Vera Lux Illa Est Quae Illuminat: The Christian Humanism of Augustine. *Reform and Renewal in the Church,* ed. Derek Baker. Oxford: Oxford University Press, 1–22.

1993   Augustine's "Conversion": Historical Fact or Literary Device? *Augustinus* 37: 103–19.

Børresen, Kari Elisabeth

1994   Patristic "Feminism": The Case of Augustine. *AS* 25: 139–52.

Bourdieu, Pierre

1977   *Outline of a Theory of Practice.* Cambridge: Cambridge University Press.

Bourke, Vernon J.

1954   St. Augustine and the Cosmic Soul. *Giornale de Metafisica* 9: 413–40.

1990   The Body-Soul Relation in the Early Augustine. *Collectanea Augustiniana. Augustine: "Second Founder of the Faith"*, ed. J. C. Schnaubelt and F. Van Fleteren. New York: Peter Lang, 435–50.

Boyer, Ch.

1953   *Christianisme et néo-platonisme dans la formation de saint Augustin*, 2nd ed. Rome: Officium Libri Catholici.

Bréhier, Émile

1928   *La philosophie de Plotin.* Paris: Boivin.

Brisson, J. P.

1958   *Autonomisme et Christianisme dans l'Afrique romaine.* Paris: Boccard.

Brown, Peter R. L.

1969   The Diffusion of Manichaeism in the Roman Empire. *Journal of Roman Studies* 59: 92–103. Reprinted in P. Brown, *Religion and Society in the Age of Saint Augustine.* London: Faber and Faber. 1972, 94–118.

2000   *Augustine of Hippo*, Rev. ed. Berkeley: University of California Press.

Brown, Robert

1978   The First Evil Will must be incomprehensible: A Critique of Augustine. *JAAR* 46: 315–39.

Bruce, Lorne D.

1983   Diocletian, the Proconsul Iulianus, and the Manichaeans. *Studies in Latin Literature and Roman History, III*, ed. Carl Derooux. Bruxelles: Latomus, Revue d'études latines, 336–47.

Bruckner, Albert Emil

1901   *Faustus von Mileve. Ein Beitrag zur Geschichte des abendländischen Manichäismus.* Basel: Friedrich Reinhardt.

Bruning, Bernard

1990   De l'Astrologie à la Grâce. *Collectanea Augustiniana: Mélanges T. J. Van Bavel*, ed. B. Bruning, M. Lamberigts, J. van Houtem. Leuven: Leuven University Press, 575–643.

Buchheit, Vinzenz

1968   Augustinus unter dem Feigenbaum, *Vigiliae Christianae* 22: 257–71.

Burkitt, F. C.

1925   *The Religion of the Manichees.* Cambridge: Cambridge University Press.

Burns, J. Patout
    1990   Ambrose Preaching to Augustine: The Shaping of Faith. *Collectanea Augus-*
            tiniana. Augustine: "Second Founder of the Faith", ed. J. C. Schnaubelt and F.
            Van Fleteren. New York: Peter Lang, 373–86.
Burrus, Virginia
    1995   *The Making of a Heretic: Gender, Authority, and the Priscillianist Controversy.*
            Berkeley: University of California Press.
Bushman, Rita Marie
    1952   St. Augustine's Metaphysics and Stoic Doctrine. *New Scholasticism* 26:
            283–304.
Butler, Judith
    1997   *The Psychic Life of Power: Theories in Subjection.* Stanford, Calif.: Stanford
            University Press.
    1999   Performativity's Social Magic. *Bourdieu. A Critical Reader*, ed. Richard Shus-
            terman. Oxford: Blackwell, 113–28.
Cary, Phillip
    1994   God in the Soul: Or, the Residue of Augustine's Manichaean Optimism.
            University of Dayton Review, Summer: 69–82.
    2000   *Augustine's Invention of the Inner Self: The Legacy of a Christian Platonist.* Ox-
            ford: Oxford University Press.
Chadwick, Henry
    1990   The Attractions of Mani. *Pléroma. Salus carnis. Homenaje a Antonio Orbe*, ed.
            E. Romero-Pose et al. Santiago de Compostela, 203–22.
    1994   On Re-Reading the *Confessions. Saint Augustine the Bishop: A Book of Essays*,
            ed. F. LeMoine and C. Kleinhenz. New York: Garland, 139–60.
Cipriani, N.
    1996   L'influsso di Varrone sul pensiero antropologico e morale nei primi scritti di
            S. Agostino. *Studia Ephemerides Augustinianum* 53: 369–400.
    1997   Il rifiuto del pessimismo Porfiriano nei primi scritti di S. Agostino. *Augustini-*
            anum 37: 113–46.
Clark, Elizabeth A.
    1990   New Perspectives on the Origenist Controversy: Human Embodiment and
            Ascetic Strategies. *Church History* 59: 145–62.
Collinge, William
    1982   Augustine and Theological Falsification. *AS* 13: 43–53.
    1983   The Role of Christian Community Life in Augustine's Apologetics. *AS* 14:
            63–73.
Courcelle, Pierre
    1954   Saint Augustin manichéen à Milan. *Orpheus* 1: 81–85.
    1963   *Les Confessions de saint Augustin dans la tradition littéraire.* Paris: Études
            augustiniennes.

1968   *Recherches sur les Confessions de saint Augustin*, 2nd ed. Paris. Boccard.

1970   Le personnage de Philosophie dans la litterature latine. *Journal des savants*: 209–52.

Coyle, J. Kevin

1978   *Augustine's* De moribus ecclesiae catholicae: *A Study of the work, Its Composition and Its Sources.* Fribourg: Fribourg University Press.

1999   Anti-Manichean Works. *Augustine Through the Ages: An Encyclopedia*, ed. Allan D. Fitzgerald. Grand Rapids, Mich.: Eerdmans, 39–41.

2001   What Did Augustine Know About Manichaeism When He Wrote His Two Treatises *De moribus? Augustine and Manichaeism in the Latin West: Proceedings of the Fribourg-Utrecht Symposium of the International Association of Manichaean Studies (IAMS)*, ed. J. van Oort, O. Wermelinger, and G. Wurst. Leiden: Brill. 43–56.

2003   Saint Augustine's Manichaean Legacy (The 2002 St. Augustine Lecture). *AS* 34: 1–22.

2009   Characteristics of Manichaeism in Roman Africa. *New Light on Manichaeism: Papers from the Sixth International Congress on Manichaeism*, ed. Jason BeDuhn. Leiden: Brill. 101–14.

Cress, Donald A.

1976   Hierius and St. Augustine's Account of the Lost 'De Pulchro et Apto': Confessions IV, 13–15. *AS* 7: 153–63.

1989   Augustine's Privation Account of Evil: A Defense. *AS* 20: 109–28.

Cumont, Franz

1908a   *Recherches sur le Manichéisme, I. La cosmogonie manichéenne d'après Théodore bar Khôni.* Bruxelles: H. Lamertin.

1908b   Une inscription manichéenne de Salone. *Revue d'histoire ecclésiastique* 9:19–20.

1910   La propagation du manichéisme dans l'empire romain. *Revue d'histoire et de littérature religieuses* n.s. 1: 31–43.

Decret, François

1970   *Aspects du manichéisme dans l' afrique romaine. Les controverses de Fortunatus, Faustus et Felix avec saint Augustin.* Paris : Études augustiniennes.

1978   *L'Afrique manichéenne (IVᵉ–Vᵉ siècles): Étude historique et doctrinale.* Paris: Études augustiniennes.

1980   Encore le manichéisme. *REA* 26: 306–12.

1991   De Moribus ecclesiae catholicae et de moribus Manichaeorum, livre II: De moribus Manichaeorum. *De moribus ecclesiae Catholicae et de moribus Manichaeorum, De quantitate animae di Agostino d'Ippona*, Lectio Augustini 7, ed. J. K. Coyle et al. Palermo: Edizioni Augustinus. 59–119.

1994   Le Manichéisme présentait en Afrique et à Rome des particularismes régionaux distinctifs? *Augustinianum* 34: 5–40.

Diggs, Bernard J.
1949   St. Augustine against the Academicians. *Traditio* 7: 73–93.

Dillon, John M.
1980   The Descent of the Soul in Middle Platonic and Gnostic Theory. *The Rediscovery of Gnosticism*, ed. Bentley Layton. Leiden: Brill. Vol. 1, 357–64.
1995   Rejecting the Body, Refining the Body: Some Remarks on the Development of Platonist Asceticism. *Asceticism*, ed. V. L. Wimbush and R. Valantasis. New York: Oxford University Press, 80–87.
1996   An ethic for the late antique sage. *The Cambridge Companion to Plotinus*, ed. Lloyd P. Gerson. Cambridge: Cambridge University Press, 315–35.

Dixon, Sandra Lee
1999   *Augustine: The Scattered and Gathered Self.* St. Louis: Chalice.

Doignon, Jean
1987   La prière liminaire des *Soliloquia* dans la ligne philosophique des Dialogues de Cassiciacum. *Augustiniana Traiectina*, ed. J. den Boeft and J. van Oort. Paris: Études augustiniennes, 85–105.

Du Roy, Olivier
1966   *L'intelligence de la foi en la Trinité selon saint Augustin: Genèse de sa théologie trinitaire jusqu'en 391.* Paris: Études augustiniennes.

Dyroff, A.
1930   Über Form und Begriffsgehalt der augustineschen Schrift *De Ordine. Aurelius Augustinus*, ed. M. Grabmann and J. Mausbach. Köln: J. P. Bachem, 15–62.

Ebaugh, Helen Rose
1988   *Becoming an Ex.* Chicago: University of Chicago Press.

Feldmann, Erich
1975   *Der Einfluß des Hortensius und des Manichäismus auf das Denken des jungen Augustinus von 373.* Diss. Münster.
1980   Christus-Frömmigkeit der Mani-Jünger: Der suchende Student Augustinus in ihrem "Netz"? *Pietas: Festschrift für Bernhard Kötting*, ed. E. Dassmann and K. S. Frank. Münster: Aschendorff, 198–216.
1989   Unverschämt genug vermaß er sich, astronomische Anschauungen zu lehren: Augustins Polemik gegen Mani in *conf.* 5,3ff. *Signum Pietatis. Festgabe für Cornelius Petrus Mayer OSA zum 60. Geburtstag*, ed. Adolar Zumkeller. Würzburg: Augustinus-Verlag, 105–20.
1994   Confessiones. *Augustinus-Lexikon*, vol. 1, ed. C. Mayer et al. Basel: Schwabe, 1134–93.

Ferrari, Leo Charles
1970   The Pear-Theft in Augustine's "Confessions." *REA* 16: 233–42.
1973   Astronomy and Augustine's Break with the Manichees. *REA* 19: 263–76.
1975   Augustine's "Nine Years" as a Manichee. *Augustiniana* 25: 210–16.

1977a   Halley's Comet of 374 AD. New Light upon Augustine's Conversion to Man-
         ichaeism. *Augustiniana* 27: 139–50.

1977b   The Prodigal Son in St Augustine's *Confessions*. RA 12: 105–18.

1978a   The "Food of Truth" in Augustine's Confessions. AS 9: 1–14

1978b   The Peculiar Appendage of Augustine's Ennaratio in Psalmum LXI. *Augus-
         tiniana* 28: 18–33.

1979   The Arboreal Polarisation in Augustine's *Confessions*. REA 25: 35–46.

1980   Paul at the Conversion of Augustine (*Conf.* VIII,12,29–30). AS 11: 5–20.

1982   Saint Augustine on the Road to Damascus. *AS* 13: 151–70.

1984   *The Conversions of Saint Augustine* (The Saint Augustine Lecture, 1982). Vil-
         lanova, Pa.: Villanova University Press.

1987   An Analysis of Augustine's Conversional Reading (*Conf.* 8.12,29). AS 18:
         30–51.

1989   Saint Augustine's Conversion Scene: The End of the Modern Debate. *Studia
         Patristica* 235–50.

1990a   Isaiah and the Early Augustine. *Collectanea Augustiniana. Mélanges T. J. van
         Bavel*, ed. B. Bruning, M. Lamberigts, and J. Van Houtem. Leuven: Leuven
         University Press, 739–56.

1990b   Truth and Augustine's Conversion Scene. *Collectanea Augustiniana. Augus-
         tine: "Second Founder of the Faith"*, ed. J. C. Schnaubelt and F. Van Fleteren.
         New York: Peter Lang, 9–28.

1991   Augustine's "Discovery" of Paul (Confessions 7.21.27). *AS* 22: 37–61.

1992   Beyond Augustine's Conversion Scene. *Augustine: From Rhetor to Theologian*,
         ed. Joanne McWilliam. Waterloo: Wilfrid Laurier University Press, 97–107.

1995   Young Augustine: Both Catholic and Manichee. *AS* 26: 109–28.

Fish, Stanley

1980   *Is There a Text in This Class? The Authority of Interpretive Communities*. Cam-
         bridge, Mass.: Harvard University Press.

Foley, Michael P.

1999   Cicero, Augustine, and the Philosophical Roots of the Cassiciacum Di-
         laogues. *REA* 45: 51–77.

Folliet, G.

1961   Aux origines de l'ascéticisme et du cénobitisme africain. *Studia Anselmia* 46:
         25–44.

1987   La Correspondance entre Augustin et Nébridius. *L'Opera Letteraria di Agos-
         tino tra Cassiciacum e Milano*, ed. G. Reale et al. Palermo: Edizioni Augusti-
         nus, 191–215.

Foote, Nelson

1951   Identification as the Basis for a Theory of Motivation. *American Sociological
         Review* 16: 14–21.

Foucault, Michel

1979   *Discipline and Punish*. New York: Random House.

1985   *The Use of Pleasure. The History of Sexulaity*, Volume 2. New York: Random
        House
1986   *The Care of the Self. The History of Sexuality*, Volume 3. New York: Random
        House.
1988   Truth, Power, Self: An Interview with Michel Foucault October 25, 1982.
        Technologies of the Self, ed. M. Foucault et al. Amherst: University of Mas-
        sachusetts Press, 1988.
1997   *Ethics: Subjectivity and Truth. Essential Works of Foucault 1954–1984*, Volume
        1, ed. Paul Rabinow. London: Penguin.
Frankfurt, Harry G.
1988   *The Importance of What We Care About: Philosophical Essays.* Cambridge:
        Cambridge University Press.
Fredriksen, Paula
1986   Paul and Augustine: Conversion Narratives, Orthodox Traditions, and the
        Retrospective Self. *Journal of Theological Studies* n.s. 37: 3–34.
Frend, William Hugh Clifford
1952   *The Donatist Church. A Movement of Protest in Roman North Africa.* Oxford:
        Clarendon Press.
1954   Manichaeism in the Struggle between Saint Augustine and Petilian of Con-
        stantine. *Augustinus Magister* (Congrès International Augustinien, Paris,
        21.–24. Septembre 1954), Vol. 2. Paris: Études augustiniennes, 859–66.
Gabillon, A.
1978   Romanian alias Cornelius. *REA* 24: 58–70.
Gardner, Iain
1996   *Kellis Literary Texts*, Volume 1. Oxford: Oxbow.
2007   *Kellis Literary Texts*, Volume 2. Oxford: Oxbow.
Gardner, Iain, Anthony Alcock, and Wolf-Peter Funk
1999   *Coptic Documentary Texts from Kellis*, Volume 1. Oxford: Oxbow.
Geerlings, Wilhelm
1971   Zur Frage des Nachwirkens des Manichäismus in der Theologie Augustins.
        Zeitschrift für katholische Theologie 93: 45–60.
1972   Der manichäische "Jesus Patibilus" in der Theologie Augustinus. *Theologische
        Quartalschrift* 152: 124–13.
Gerson, Lloyd P.
1994   *Plotinus.* London: Routledge.
Gilson, Etienne
1929   *Introduction a l'étude de saint Augustin.* Paris: Vrin.
Gottlieb, Gunther
1973   *Ambrosius von Mailand und Kaisar Gratian.* Göttingen: Vandenhoeck and
        Ruprecht.
Gourdon, Louis
1900   *Essai sur la conversion de saint Augustin.* Cahors: A. Coueslant.

Hadot, I.
1984   *Arts liberaux et Philosophie dans la pensée antique.* Paris: Études augustiniennes.
Harrison, Carol
2006   *Rethinking Augustine's Early Theology: An Argument for Continuity.* Oxford: Oxford University Press.
Hefner, Robert W.
1993a   World Building and the Rationality of Conversion. *Conversion to Christianity: Historical and Anthropological Perspectives on a Great Transformation,* ed. Robert W. Hefner. Berkeley: University of California Press, 3–44.
1993b   Of Faith and Commitment: Christian Conversion in Muslim Java. *Conversion to Christianity: Historical and Anthropological Perspectives on a Great Transformation,* ed. Robert W. Hefner. Berkeley: University of California Press, 99–125.
Heidl, György
2003   *Origen's Influence on the Young Augustine.* Piscataway, N.J.: Gorgias Press.
Holte, Ragnar
1962   *Béatitude et sagesse: saint Augustin et le problème de la fin de l'homme dans la philosophie ancienne.* Paris: Études augustiniennes.
Inge, W. R.
1968   *The Philosophy of Plotinus,* 3rd ed. New York: Greenwood Press.
James, William
1987   *Writings 1902–1910.* New York: Library Classics of the United States.
Jones, A. H. M
1971   *Prosopography of the Later Roman Empire,* Vol. 1. Cambridge: Cambridge University Press.
Jones, F. S.
1997   The Astrological Trajectory in Ancient Syriac-Speaking Christianity (Elchasai, Bardaisan, and Mani). *Atti del Terzo Congresso Internazionale di Studi 'Manichaismo e Oriente Cristiano Antico,* ed. L. Cirillo and A. van Tongerloo. Louvain/Napoli: Brepols, 183–200.
Kato, Takeshi
1965   Melodia interior. Sur le traité *De pulchro et apto. REA* 11: 229–39.
Kirwan, Christopher
1989   *Augustine.* London: Routledge.
Klein, Wolfgang Wassilios
1991   *Die Argumentation in den Griechisch-Christlichen Antimanichaica.* Wiesbaden: Harrassowitz.
Koenen, Ludwig
1983   Manichäische Mission und Klöster in Ägypten. *Das römisch-byzantinische Ägypten.* Mainz : P. von Zabern, 93–108.
Kotzé, Annemaré
2004   *Augustine's Confessions: Communicative Purpose and Audience.* Leiden: Brill.

Krautheimer, Richard
  1983   *Three Christian Capitals: Topography and Politics.* Berkeley: University of California Press.
Kuhn, Thomas
  1970   *The Structure of Scientific Revolutions,* 2nd ed. Chicago: University of Chicago Press.
Lamberigts, Mathijs
  2001   Was Augustine a Manichaean? The Assessment of Julian of Aeclanum. *Augustine and Manichaeism in the Latin West: Proceedings of the Fribourg-Utrecht Symposium of the International Association of Manichaean Studies (IAMS),* ed. J. van Oort, O. Wermelinger, and G. Wurst. Leiden: Brill, 113–36.
Le Blond, J.-M.
  1950   *Les conversions de saint Augustin.* Paris: Aubier.
Lee, Kam-lun Edwin
  1999   *Augustine, Manichaeism, and the Good.* New York: Peter Lang.
Leroux, Georges
  1996   Human freedom in the thought of Plotinus. *The Cambridge Companion to Plotinus,* ed. L. P. Gerson. Cambridge: Cambridge University Press, 292–314.
Lieu, Samuel N. C.
  1992   *Manichaeism in the Later Roman Empire and Medieval China,* 2nd ed. Tübingen: Mohr/Siebeck.
Lim, Richard
  1992   Manichaeans and Public Disputation in Late Antiquity. *RA* 26: 233–72.
Lof, L. J. van der
  1974   Mani and the Danger from Persia in the Roman Empire. *Augustiniana* 24: 75–84.
Loveland, Matthew T.
  2003   Religious Switching: Preference Development, Maintenance, and Change. *Journal for the Scientific Study of Religion* 42: 147–57.
Macdonald, Scott
  2001   The divine nature. *The Cambridge Companion to Augustine,* ed. E. Stump and N. Kretzmann. Cambridge: Cambridge University Press, 71–90.
Madec, Goulven
  1986   L'historicité des *Dialogues* de Cassiciacum. *REA* 32: 207–31.
  1987a   La conversion d'Augustin: intériorité et communauté. *Lumen Vitae* 42: 184–94
  1987b   Le milieu milanais, philosophie et christianisme. *Bulletin de littérature ecclésiastique* 88: 194–205.
  1989   Le néoplatonisme dans la conversion d'Augustin. *Internationales Symposion über den Stand der Augustinus-Forschung,* ed. C. Mayer and K. H. Chelius. Würzburg: Augustinus-Verlag, 9–25.

1996   *Introduction aux Revisions et à la lecture des oeuvres de saint Augustin.* Paris: Études augustiniennes.

Maher, John P.

1944   St. Augustine's Defense of the Hexaemeron Against the Manicheans, parts 1 & 2. *Catholic Biblical Quarterly* 6: 289–98, 456–75.

1945   St. Augustine's Defense of the Hexaemeron Against the Manicheans, parts 3, 4, 5, and 6. *Catholic Biblical Quarterly* 7: 76–90, 206–22, 306–25.

Mallard, William

1980   The Incarnation in Augustine's Conversion. *RA* 15: 80–98.

Mandouze, André

1968   *Saint Augustin: L'aventure de la raison et de la grace.* Paris: Études augustiniennes.

Mann, William

1979   The Theft of the Pears. *Apeiron* 12: 51–58.

Markus, R. A.

1970   *Saeculum: History and Society in the Theology of St. Augustine.* Cambridge: Cambridge University Press.

1972   Christianity and Dissent in Roman North Africa: Changing Perspectives in Recent Work. *Schism, Heresy and Religious Protest. Papers read at the 10th Summer Meeting and the 11th Winter Meeting of the Ecclesiastical History Society,* ed. Derek Baker. Cambridge: Cambridge University Press, 21–36.

1989   *Conversion and Disenchantment in Augustine's Spiritual Career.* Villanova: Villanova University Press.

Marrou, H.-I.

1958   *S. Augustin et la fin de la culture antique.* Paris: Boccard.

Masai, L.

1961   Les conversions de saint Augustin et les débuts du spiritualisme en occident. *Le moyen âge* 67: 1–40.

Matter, E. Ann

1990   Conversion(s) in the Confessiones. *Collectanea Augustiniana. Augustine: "Second Founder of the Faith,* ed. J. C. Schnaubelt and F. Van Fleteren. New York: Peter Lang, 21–28.

Matthews, Alfred Warren

1980   *The Development of St. Augustine from Neoplatonism to Christianity* 386–391 A.D. Washington, D.C.: Catholic University of America Press.

Matthews, Gareth

1972   Augustine on Speaking from Memory. *Augustine. A Collection of Critical Essays,* ed. R. A. Markus. Garden City, N.Y.: Anchor, 168–75.

Mauss, Armand

1998   Apostasy and the Management of Spoiled Identity. *The Politics of Religious Apostasy: The Role of Apostates in the Transformation of Religious Movements,* ed. David G. Bromley. Westport, Conn.: Praeger, 51–73.

Mayer, Cornelius P.

1974   Die antimanichäische Schriften Augustinus. *Augustinianum* 14: 277–313.

1986   Augustins Bekehrung im Lichte seiner "Bekenntnisse": Ein Exempel der kirchlichen Gnadenlehre. *AS* 17: 31–45.

McLynn, Neil B.

1994   *Ambrose of Milan: Church and Court in a Christian Capital.* Berkeley: University of California Press.

2003   Seeing and Believing: Aspects of Conversion from Antoninus Pius to Louis the Pious. *Conversion in Late Antiquity and the Early Middle Ages: Seeing and Believing,* ed. K. Mills and A. Grafton. Rochester: University of Rochester Press, 224–70.

McWilliam, Joanne

1990   The Cassiciacum Autobiography. *Studia Patristica* 18: 14–43.

Mead, George Herbert

1934   *Mind, Self, and Society.* Chicago: University of Chicago Press.

1964   *Selected Writings.* Chicago: University of Chicago Press.Menasce, Pierre Jean de

1956   Augustin manichéen. *Freundesgabe für Ernst Robert Curtius zum 14. April 1956,* ed. M. Rychner and W. Boehlich. Bern: Francke Verlag, 79–93.

Miles, Margaret

1995   "Jesus patibilis": Nature and Responsibility in Augustine's Debate with the Manichaeans. *Faithful Imaginings: Essays in Honor of Richard R. Niebuhr,* ed. S. H. Lee, W. Proudfoot, and A. Blackwell. Atlanta: Scholars Press, 3–18.

Monceaux, Paul

1924   *Le Manichéen Faustus de Milev: Restitution de ses Capitula* (Extrait des memoires de l'academie des inscriptions et des belles lettres, 43). Paris: Imprimerie Nationale.

More, Paul E.

1907/8   The Dualism of Saint Augustine. *Hibbert Journal* 6: 606–22.

Mosher, David L.

1981   The Argument of St. Augustine's *Contra Academicos. AS* 12: 89–113.

Mourant, John A.

1966   Augustine and the Academics. *RA* 4: 67–96.

1971   Remarks on the *De Immortalitate Animae. AS* 2: 213–17.

Nédoncelle, Maurice

1962   L'abandon de Mani par Augustin, ou la logique de l'optimisme. *RA* 2: 17–32.

Neiman, Alven Michael

1982   The Arguments of Augustine's Contra Academicos. *Modern Schoolman* 59: 255–279.

Nietzsche, Friedrich

1967   *On the Genealogy of Morals,* trans. Walter Kaufmann. New York: Random House.

Nock, A. D.
    1933   *Conversion: The Old and the New in Religion from Alexander the Great to Augustine of Hippo.* Oxford: Clarendon Press.
O'Brien, Denis
    1996   Plotinus on matter and evil. *The Cambridge Companion to Plotinus*, ed. Lloyd P. Gerson. Cambridge: Cambridge University Press, 171–95.
O'Brien, William
    1974   Toward Understanding Original Sin in Augustine's "Confessions." *Thought* 49: 436–46.
O'Connell, Robert J.
    1963a   Ennead VI,4 and 5 in the Works of St. Augustine. *REA* 9: 1–39.
    1963b   The Plotinian Fall of the Soul in St. Augustine. *Traditio* 19: 1–35.
    1968   *St. Augustine's Early Theory of Man, A. D. 386–391.* Cambridge, Mass.: Harvard University Press.
    1970   *De Libero Arbitrio* I: Stoicism Revisited. *AS* 1: 49–68.
    1973   Augustine's Rejection of the Fall of the Soul. *AS* 4: 1–32.
    1978a   *Art and the Christian Intelligence in St. Augustine.* Cambridge, Mass.: Harvard University Press.
    1978b   The Human Being as "Fallen Soul" in St. Augustine's *De Trinitate. Mediaevalia* 4: 33–58.
    1980   Pre-Existence in the Early Augustine. *REA* 26: 176–88.
    1984a   St. Augustine's Criticism of Origen in the *Ad Orosium. REA* 30: 84–99.
    1984b   *Saint Augustine's Platonism*, The Saint Augustine Lecture 1981. Villanova, Pa.: Villanova University Press.
    1986   On Augustine's "First Conversion" Factus Erectior (De Beata Vita 4). *AS* 17: 15–29.
    1993   Augustinism: Locating the Center. *Collectanea Augustiniana. Augustine, Presbyter Factus Sum*, ed. J. Lienhard et al. New York: Peter Lang, 209–33.
    1994   The Visage of Philosophy at Cassiciacum. *AS* 25: 65–76.
    1996   *Images of Conversion in St. Augustine's Confessions.* New York: Fordham University Press.
O'Daly, Gerard J. P.
    1991   Hierarchies in Augustine's Thought. *From Augustine to Eriugena. Essays on Neoplatonism and Christianity in Honor of John O'Meara*, ed. F. X. Martin and J. A. Richmond. Washington, D.C.: Catholic University of America Press, 143–54.
    2001   The response to skepticism and the mechanisms of cognition. *The Cambridge Companion to Augustine*, ed. E. Stump and N. Kretzmann. Cambridge: Cambridge University Press, 159–70.
O'Donnell, James J.
    1985   *Augustine.* New York: Twayne.
    1992   *Confessions.* Oxford: Clarendon Press.

O'Laughlin, Thomas

1992   The *Libri Philosophorum* and Augustine's Conversions. *The Relationship be-tween Neoplatonism and Christianity*, ed. T. Finan and V. Twomey. Dublin: Four Courts, 101–25.

O'Meara, John J.

1951a   *St. Augustine, Against the Academics*. New York: Newman Press.

1951b   The Historicity of the Early Dialogues of Saint Augustine. *Vigiliae Christianae* 5: 150–78.

1951c   St. Augustine's View of Authority and Reason in A. D. 386. *Irish Theological Quarterly* 18: 338–46.

1954   *The Young Augustine: An Introduction to the* Confessions *of St. Augustine*. London: Longman.

Oort, Johannes van

1993   Augustinus en het manicheïsme, *Nederlands Theologisch Tijdschrift* 47: 276–91.

1995   Augustine's Critique of Manichaeism: The Case of *Confessions* III 6,10 and Its Implications. *Aspects of Religious Contact and Conflict in the Ancient World*, ed. Pieter W. van der Horst. Utrecht: Faculteit der Godgeleerdheid, Universiteit Utrecht, 57–68.

2008   The Young Augustine's Knowledge of Manichaeism: An Analysis of the *Confessiones* and Some Other Relevant Texts. *Vigiliae Christianae* 62: 441–66.

Outler, Albert C.

1955   *Confessions and Enchiridion*. Philadelphia. Westminster.

Pacioni, Virgilio

1999   Liberal Arts. *Augustine Through the Ages: An Encyclopedia*, ed. Allan D. Fitzgerald. Grand Rapids, Mich.: Eerdmans, 42–44.

Panaino, A.

1997   Visione della volte celeste e astrologia nel Manicheismo. *Atti del Terzo Congresso Internazionale di Studi Manichaismo e Oriente Cristiano Antico*, ed. L. Cirillo and A. van Tongerloo. Louvain/Napoli: Brepols, 249–95.

Pedersen, Nils Arne

2004   *Demonstrative Proof in Defence of God: A Study of Titus of Bostra's* Contra manichaeos*: The Works Sources, Aims and Relation to Its Contemporary Theology*. Leiden: Brill.

Pépin, J.

1964   Une nouvelle source de saint Augustin: Le Zètèma de Porphyre sur l'union de l'âme et du corps. *REA* 86: 53–107.

Polanyi, Michael

1958   *Personal Knowledge*. London: Routledge and Kegan Paul.

1964   *Science, Faith and Society*, 2nd ed. Chicago: University of Chicago Press.

Power, Kim

1992   Sed unam tamen: Augustine and His Concubine. *AS* 23: 49–76.

Puech, Henri-Charles
    1968   The Concept of Redemption in Manichaeism. *The Mystic Vision: Papers from the Eranos Yearbooks*, ed. Joseph Campbell. Princeton, N.J.: Princeton University Press, 247–314.
    1972   Le manichéisme. *Histoire des religions*, II, ed. H.-C. Puech. Paris: Gallimard, 523–645.
Quinn, John M.
    1988   Anti-Manichaean and Other Moral Precisions in Confessions 3.7.12–9.17. *AS* 19: 165–94.
Ramirez, J. Roland E.
    1981   Demythologizing Augustine as Great Sinner. *AS* 12: 61–88.
Ratzinger, J.
    1967   Rezension von A. Adam, *Dogmengeschichte. Jährbücher für Antike und Christentum* 10: 222.
Ries, Julien
    1981   Sotériologie manichéenne et paganisme romain. *La soteriologia dei Culti Orientali nell'Impero Romano*, ed. U. Bianchi and M. J. Vermaseren. Leiden: Brill, 762–77.
Rist, John M.
    1967   *Plotinus: The Road to Reality.* Cambridge: Cambridge University Press.
    1994   *Augustine: Ancient Thought Baptized.* Cambridge: Cambridge University Press.
Rombs, Ronnie J.
    2006   *Saint Augustine and the Fall of the Soul: Beyond O'Connell and His Critics.* Washington, D.C.: Catholic University of America Press.
Rougier, P.
    1958   La critique biblique dans l'antiquité: Marcion et Fauste de Milève. *Cahiers du Cercle Ernest Renan* 18: 1–16.
Sachau, E.
    1887   *Al-Biruni's India.* London: Kegan Paul, Trench, Trübner.
Sage, Athanase
    1965   La volonté salvifique universelle de Dieu dans la pensée de saint Augustin. *RA* 3: 107–31.
    1967   Péché originel. Naissance d'un dogme. *REA* 13: 211–48.
    1969   Le péché originel dans la pensée de saint Augustin, de 412 à 430. *REA* 15: 75–112.
Sala, Tudor
    2007   Narrative Options in Manichaean Eschatology. *Frontiers of Faith: The Christian Encounter with Manichaeism in the Acts of Archelaus*, ed. J. BeDuhn and P. Mirecki. Leiden: Brill, 49–66.
Sandomirsky, S. and J. Wilson
    1990   Processes of Disaffiliation: Religious Mobility Among Men and Women. *Social Forces* 68: 1211–29.

Schipper, H. G.
    2001   Melothesia: A Chapter of Manichaean Astrology in the West. *Augustine and Manichaeism in the Latin West: Proceedings of the Fribourg-Utrecht Symposium of the International Association of Manichaean Studies (IAMS)*, ed. J. van Oort, O. Wermelinger, and G. Wurst. Leiden: Brill, 195–204.

Sedley, David
    1989   Philosophical Allegiance in the Greco-Roman World. *Philosophia Togata: Essays on Philosophy and Roman Society*, ed. M. Griffin and J. Barnes. Oxford: Clarendon Press, 97–119.

Séjourné, Paul
    1951   Les conversions de saint Augustin d'après le *De Libero Arbitrio*, L. I. *Revue des sciences religieuses* 25: 243–64, 333–63.

Shanzer, Danuta
    1996   Pears before Swine: Augustine, *Confessions* 2.4.9. *REA* 42: 45–55.

Sherkat, Darren E.
    1991   Leaving the Faith: Testing Sociological Theories of Religious Switching Using Survival Models. *Social Science Research* 20: 171–87.

Sherkat, Darren and Christopher Ellison
    1999   Recent Developments and Current Controversies in the Sociology of Religion. *Annual Review of Sociology* 25: 363–94.

Sherkat, Darren and John Wilson
    1995   Preferences, Constraints, and Choices in Religious Markets: An Examination of Religious Switching and Apostasy. *Social Forces* 73: 993–1026.

Solignac, Aimé
    1958   Doxographies et manuels dans la formation philosophique de saint Augustin. RA 1: 113–48
    1962   *Les Confessions, Livres I–VIII*. Paris: Desclée de Brouwer.

Starnes, Colin
    1990:   *Augustine's Conversion: A Guide to the Argument of Confessions I–IX*. Waterloo: Wilfrid Laurier Press.

Stendahl, Krister
    1963   The Apostle Paul and the Introspective Conscience of the West. *Harvard Theological Review* 56: 199–215.

Stock, Brian
    1996   *Augustine the Reader: Meditation, Self-Knowledge, and the Ethics of Interpretation*. Cambridge, Mass.: Harvard University Press.

Stoop, E. de
    1909   *Essai sur la diffusion du manichéisme dans l'empire romain*. Ghent: E. van Goethem.

Stroumsa, Gedaliahu G.
    1983a   Monachisme et Marranisme chez les Manichéens d'Egypte. *Numen* 29: 184–201.

1983b   The Incorporeality of God. *Religion* 13: 345–58.
1986   The Manichaean Challenge to Egyptian Christianity. *The Roots of Egyptian Christianity*, ed. B. A. Pearson and J. E. Goehring. Philadelphia: Fortress, 307–19.
1988   The Words and the Works: Religious Knowledge and Salvation in Augustine and Faustus of Milevis. *Cultural Traditions and Worlds of Knowledge*, ed. S. N. Eisenstadt and I. Friedrich-Silber. Greenwich, Conn.: Jai Press, 73–84.

Stroumsa, Gedaliahu and Sarah Stroumsa
1988   Aspects of Anti-Manichaean Polemic in Late Antiquity and Under Early Islam. *Harvard Theological Review* 81: 37–58.

Sundermann, Werner
1985   Ein manichäisch-soghdisches Parabelbuch. Berlin: Akademie Verlag.
2007   God and His Adversary in Manichaeism: The Case of the "Enthymesis of Death" and the "Enthymesis of Life." *Religious Texts in Iranian Languages*, ed. F. Vahman and C. V. Pedersen. Copenhagen: Kongelige Danske Videnskabernes Selskab, 137–49.

Svoboda, Karl
1933   *L'esthétique de Saint Augustin et ses sources.* Brno: Spisy Filosofické Fakulty Maraykovy University v Brno.

Swann, W. B.
1983   Self Verification: Bringing Social Reality into Harmony with the Self. *Psychological Perspectives on the Self*, ed. J. Suls and A. G. Greenwald. Hillsdale, N.J.: Erlbaum, 33–66.

Tardieu, Michel
1979   Vues nouvelles sur le manichéisme africain? *REA* 25: 249–55.
1981   *Le Manichéisme.* Paris: Presses Universitaires de France.

TeSelle, Eugene
1970   *Augustine the Theologian.* New York: Herder and Herder.

Teske, Roland J.
1983   The World-Soul and Time in St. Augustine. *AS* 14: 75–92.
1991a   *Saint Augustine On Genesis: Two Books on Genesis Against the Manichees and On the Literal Interpretation of Genesis: An Unfinished Book.* Washington, D.C.: Catholic University of America Press.
1991b   St. Augustine's View of the Original Human Condition in *De Genesi Contra Manichaeos. AS* 22: 141–55.
1999   De Immortalitate Animae. *Augustine Through the Ages*, ed. Allan Fitzgerald. Grand Rapids, Mich.: Eerdmans, 443–44.
2007   *Answer to Faustus a Manichean.* Hyde Park, N.Y.: New City Press.

Testard, M.
1958   *S. Augustin et Cicéron.* Paris: Études augustiniennes.

Thesleff, Holger
1961   *An Introduction to the Pythagorean Writings of the Hellenistic Period.* Åbo: Åbo Akademi.

1965   *The Pythagorean Texts of the Hellenistic Period.* Åbo: Åbo Akademi.

Thimme, W.

1908   *Augustins geistige Entwicklung in den ersten Jahren nach seiner "Bekehrung,"* *386–391.* Berlin: Trowitzsch und Sohn.

Thomas, J. D.

1976   The date of the revolt of L. Domitius Domitianus. *Zeitschrift für Papyrologie und Epigraphik* 22: 253–79.

Thonnard, F. J.

1952   *Dialogues philosophiques III. De l'âme à Dieu: De magistro, De libero arbitrio.* Paris: Desclée de Brouwer.

Torchia, N. Joseph

1987   St. Augustine's Treatment of *superbia* and Its Plotinian Affinities. *AS* 18: 66–80.

1999   *Creatio ex nihilo and the Theology of St. Augustine: The Anti-Manichaean Polemic and Beyond.* New York: Peter Lang.

Troje, L.

1948   Zum Begriff ΑΤΑΚΤΟΣ ΚΙΝΗΣΙΣ bei Platon und Mani. *Museum Helveti-cum* 5: 96–115.

Trout, Dennis E.

1988   Augustine at Cassiciacum: *Otium honestum* and the Social Dimensions of Conversion. *Virgiliae Christianae* 42: 132–46.

Tully, James

1988   *Meaning and Context: Quentin Skinner and His Critics.* Princeton, N.J.: Princeton University Press.

Van Fleteren, Frederick

1973   Authority and Reason, Faith and Understanding in the Thought of St. Au-gustine. *AS* 4: 33–71.

1978   The Cassiciacum Dialogues and Augustine's Ascents at Milan. *Mediaevalia* 4: 59–82.

1990a   A Reply to Robert O'Connell. *AS* 21: 127–37.

1990b   St. Augustine's Theory of Conversion. *Collectanea Augustiniana. Augustine: "Second Founder of the Faith",* ed. J. C. Schnaubelt and F. Van Fleteren. New York: Peter Lang, 65–80.

Van der Lof, L. J.

1974   Mani as the Danger from Persia in the Roman Empire. *Augustiniana* 24: 74–84.

Vannier, M. A.

1990   Manichéisme et pensée augustinienne de la création. *Collectanea Augustini-ana. Augustine: "Second Founder of the Faith",* ed. J. C. Schnaubelt and F. Van Fleteren. New York: Peter Lang, 421–31.

Verbeke, Gérard

1958   Augustin et le stoïcisme. *RA* 1: 67–89.

West, Rebecca

    1933   *St. Augustine.* Edinburgh: Peter Davies.

Wetzel, James

    1992   *Augustine and the Limits of Virtue.* Cambridge: Cambridge University Press.

Wheelock, Wade

    1982   The Problem of Ritual Language: From Information to Situation. *Journal of the American Academy of Religion* 50: 49–71.

Williams, Daniel

    1995   *Ambrose of Milan and the End of the Nicean-Arian Conflicts.* Oxford: Clarendon.

Wilson, Anna M.

    1990   Reason and Revelation in the Conversion Accounts of the Cappadocians and Augustine. *Collectanea Augustiniana. Mélanges T. J. van Bavel,* ed. B. Bruning, M. Lamberigts, and J. Van Houtem. Leuven: Leuven University Press, 259–78.

Winden, J. C. M. van

    1965   *Calcidius on Matter: His Doctrine and Sources.* Leiden: Brill.

Wurst, Gregor

    1995   *Das Bemafest der ägyptischen Manichäer.* Altenberge: Oros Verlag.

    2001   Bemerkungen zu Struktur und *genus litterarium der Capitula* des Faustus von Mileve. *Augustine and Manichaeism in the Latin West,* ed. J. van Oort, O. Wermelinger, and G. Wurst. Leiden: Brill, 307–24.

INDEX

GENERAL INDEX

(Entries refer only to substantive quotation or
discussion)

ACKNOWLEDGMENTS

Augustine's Manichaean Dilemma, 1: Conversion and Apostasy, 373–388 C.E. is the first in a planned trilogy examining the contact between Augustine of Hippo and the Manichaeans of North Africa, and the degree to which he was shaped as a historical individual and as a theologian by this contact. The inspiration for the project came from two meetings with Peter Brown in 1993 and 1994, when he was a guest of the Religious Studies program at Indiana University, where I was completing my Ph.D. with a dissertation on Manichaeism. He urged me to follow up this work with a reexamination of Augustine's debt to Manichaeism, and has continued to encourage me on this path in the years since. For his support and patience, I dedicate this first volume to him.

Of the many others who have offered assistance and encouragement along the way, I can only single out a few: Elizabeth Clark, J. Kevin Coyle, David Brakke, Michael Williams, and Larry Clark. I would also like to extend my appreciation to the anonymous readers of the manuscript in two distinct iterations for their many helpful suggestions, as well as to the *Divinations* series editorial board—Daniel Boyarin, Virginia Burrus, and Derek Krueger—for their close attention and interest in the project. I have been delighted to bring this project to the University of Pennsylvania Press, and benefit from the energetic and supportive editorial oversight of Jerry Singerman and Alison Anderson.

This project was supported at a critical juncture by a John Simon Guggenheim Foundation fellowship in 2004–2005, and before that by two Northern Arizona University Organized Research grants. Its successful completion would not have been possible without the untiring efforts of the team working in the Document Delivery Service at the Cline Library of Northern Arizona University, and the ILLiad network through which they acquired the enormous amount of material I asked of them.

Finally I wish to express my appreciation and wonder at the patience of my beloved wife, Zsuzsanna Gulácsi, who has lived with Augustine in the house far longer than even the best of guests would be welcome. For hearing out the many reformulations of my ideas, likewise, I am grateful to her.